# Biodiversity and the
# Precautionary Principle

# Biodiversity and the Precautionary Principle

## Risk and Uncertainty in Conservation and Sustainable Use

Edited by Rosie Cooney and Barney Dickson

London • Sterling, VA

First published by Earthscan in the UK and USA in 2005

★ ★ ★ This book has been with produced with the financial assistance of the
★　　★ European Union under the Action 'The Precautionary Principle Project:
★　　★ Sustainable Development, Natural Resource Management and Biodiversity
★ ★ ★ Conservation', and the UK Department for Environment, Food and Rural
Affairs. The contents can under no circumstances be regarded as reflecting the position of either institution.

ISBN-10:  1-84407-277-0 paperback
          1-84407-276-2 hardback

ISBN-13:  978-1-84407-277-4 paperback
          978-1-84407-276-7 hardback

Typesetting by MapSet Ltd, Gateshead, UK
Printed and bound in the UK by Bath Press
Cover design by Susanne Harris

For a full list of publications please contact:

Earthscan
8–12 Camden High Street
London, NW1 0JH, UK
Tel:  +44 (0)20 7387 8558
Fax: +44 (0)20 7387 8998
Email:  earthinfo@earthscan.co.uk
Web:  www.earthscan.co.uk

22883 Quicksilver Drive, Sterling, VA 20166-2012, USA

Earthscan is an imprint of James and James (Science Publishers) Ltd and publishes in association with the International Institute for Environment and Development.

A catalogue record for this book is available from the British Library.

Library of Congress Cataloging-in-Publication Data:

Biodiversity and the precautionary principle : risk and uncertainty in conservation and sustainable use / edited by Rosie Cooney and Barney Dickson.
  p. cm.
ISBN 1-84407-276-2 (hardback) — ISBN 1-84407-277-0 (paperback)  1. Biological diversity conservation—Government policy. 2. Precautionary principle.  I. Cooney, Rosie. II. Dickson, Barney.
QH75.B5318 2005
333.95'16—dc22

                                                                    2005021489

Printed on elemental chlorine-free paper

# Foreword

When it first appeared, the precautionary principle or approach represented an important advance in environmental policy, law and implementation. It recognized that decisions that raise environmental threats must be predicated on something more than an administrative (or even a legislative) determination that such risks are 'acceptable' in light of relevant objectives. Rather, precaution imposes a further requirement on such decisions – the requirement to give the environment the benefit of any doubts about such risk. Specifically, the precautionary principle calls on decision-makers to ensure that where there is a lack of full scientific certainty regarding a risk, that lack of certainty is not used as a basis for failure to protect against that risk.

Yet despite the importance of this ground-breaking policy development, application of the precautionary principle around the world remains a controversial and sometimes confusing process – one that remains a central element of many international instruments and processes, and a primary concern for many countries and organizations around the world. One difficult area in which this controversy has arisen is biodiversity conservation and sustainable use decision-making and management. Here the dynamics of applying the precautionary principle can be very different to its use in more familiar industrial contexts, such as pollution or climate change. For instance, the principle may be invoked to address uncertainties of a very different nature, such as uncertainties regarding whether utilization levels are sustainable.

This book represents one significant component of a major collaboration to examine and address the precautionary principle in the context of its application to biodiversity conservation and natural resource management (NRM). Among the multitude of books and articles addressing the legal implications and applications of the precautionary principle, this collection represents one of the first efforts to focus on the practical role and impact of the principle in biodiversity and NRM decisions. As such, it does not seek to provide a comprehensive analysis of the principle in this context but an initiation of and stimulus to broader and very necessary study. It presents a range of examinations and analyses of the precautionary principle in theory and practice, contributed by 34 authors from 12 countries, in areas including fisheries, invasive alien species, utilization and trade of wildlife, protected area management and forestry. These examples provide a range of perspectives on the impacts of application of the principle within widely varying socio-cultural situations and governance systems. They yield a wealth of insights that inform the Guidelines for Best Practice included as an Appendix.

The collaboration that gave rise to this publication provides an indication of both the importance and complexity of efforts to address the practical implementation of the precautionary principle. In at least one sense, this collaboration began at the First IUCN World Conservation Congress in 1996, where a coalition of IUCN member organizations and governments success-fully proposed a resolution calling on IUCN to examine and advise on the application of the precautionary principle in the context of conservation and sustainable use. This work was taken forward initially by the efforts of the Africa Resources Trust and the Percy FitzPatrick Institute, which convened a 1997 workshop in Cape Town, addressing the application of the precaution-ary principle in relation to wildlife conservation in southern Africa. This initial effort was followed up by an international workshop in 2000 sponsored by Africa Resources Trust, TRAFFIC, IUCN Species Programme's Wildlife Trade Programme, the IUCN Environmental Law Centre in Cambridge and the Lauterpacht Research Centre for International Law (also in Cambridge). Beginning in 2002, a more intensive effort was commenced, under which the IUCN Species Programme, the IUCN Environmental Law Centre, the IUCN Regional Office for Southern Africa, TRAFFIC, Fauna & Flora International and ResourceAfrica (previously Africa Resources Trust) developed the Precautionary Principle Project, supported primarily by IUCN and the European Commission (DG Development).

This three year project has included regional workshops undertaken in Africa, Asia and Latin America in 2004 and early 2005; discussions at major international policy forums, including the IUCN Vth World Parks Congress and the Third IUCN World Conservation Congress; and an international workshop held at White Oak Conference Center in July 2005. It has produced, and is producing, a variety of analytical works, including this book and its Guidelines for Best Practice, designed to increase understanding of and improve the effectiveness of implementation of the precautionary principle as a tool for achieving and supporting biodiversity conservation and sustainable use objectives.

The authors whose work appears in this book were selected on the basis of an international call for proposals for case studies addressing the applica-tion of the precautionary principle in biodiversity and NRM decision-making and management. Over 75 proposals were submitted. The ultimate selection was based on the desire that this publication reflect a range of different perspectives and experiences, involving input from many regions, and address-ing a range of sectors and biomes where the principle is relevant and applied.

We believe that this publication provides a useful and important insight into the multitude of views, issues, successes, challenges, and controversies that have characterized the first decades of the precautionary principle's life. We hope and expect that this work will provide a strong foundation on which to build greater collective understanding of how the principle can become an even more effective tool in biodiversity conservation and natural resource management.

Jon Hutton (ResourceAfrica)
Jane Smart (IUCN Species Programme)
Alejandro Iza (IUCN Environmental Law Centre)
James Murombedzi (IUCN Regional Office for Southern Africa)
Steve Broad (TRAFFIC)
Barney Dickson (Fauna & Flora International)
*Cambridge, 2005*

# Contents

## INTRODUCTION

## SECTION ONE: THE PRECAUTIONARY PRINCIPLE IN INTERNATIONAL REGIMES AND POLICY PROCESSES

## SECTION TWO: NATIONAL EXPERIENCE IN APPLYING THE PRECAUTIONARY PRINCIPLE

## SECTION THREE: MAKING DECISIONS ABOUT UNCERTAIN THREATS: PRECAUTION, PROHIBITIONS AND ADAPTIVE MANAGEMENT

# SECTION FOUR: THE PRECAUTIONARY PRINCIPLE AND LOCAL LIVELIHOODS

# SECTION FIVE: ANALYTICAL PERSPECTIVES ON PRECAUTION

# CONCLUSION

# List of Figures, Tables and Boxes

## FIGURES

## TABLES

# BOXES

# List of Acronyms and Abbreviations

| | |
|---|---|
| AAT | Administrative Appeals Tribunal, Australia |
| ACCOBAMS | Agreement on Conservation of Cetaceans of the Black Sea, Mediterranean Sea and Contiguous Atlantic Area, 1996 |
| ADB | Asian Development Bank |
| AFMA | Australian Fisheries Management Authority |
| AFZ | Australian Fishing Zone |
| AIDA | Interamerican Association for Environmental Defense |
| AIR | All India Reporter |
| APN | Administration of National Parks, Argentina |
| AQIS | Australian Quarantine and Inspection Service |
| ATFS | American Tree Farm System |
| BA | Biosecurity Australia |
| BRS | Bureau of Rural Sciences, Australia |
| CAMP | Collection Area Management Plan |
| C&I | criteria and indicators |
| CBA | cost–benefit analysis |
| CBD | Convention on Biological Diversity |
| CBFMP | Community-based Forest Management Programme, Philippines, 1996 |
| CCAMLR | Commission for the Conservation of Antarctic Marine Living Resources |
| CCC | Caribbean Conservation Corporation |
| CCSBT | Commission for the Conservation of Southern Bluefin Tuna |
| CEA | cost-effectiveness analysis |
| CEAA | Canadian Environmental Assessment Act, 2003 |
| CEDARENA | Environmental and Natural Resources Law Center, San Jose, Costa Rica |
| CFP | Federal Fisheries Council, Argentina |
| CITES | Convention on International Trade in Endangered Species of Wild Fauna and Flora, 1973 |
| CMS | Convention on Migratory Species, 1982 |
| COFEMA | Environmental Federal Council, Argentina |
| COP | Conference of the Parties |
| CPEU | Centre for People's Empowerment in the Uplands, Philippines |
| CRC | Cooperative Research Centre for Plant-based Management of Dryland Salinity, Australia |

| | |
|---|---|
| CSA | Canadian Standards Association |
| CSIRO | Commonwealth Scientific and Industrial Research Organisation |
| DA | decision analysis |
| DAFF | Department of Agriculture, Fisheries and Forestry, Australia |
| DANR | Department of Agriculture and Natural Resources, Philippines |
| DEH | Department of the Environment and Heritage, Australia |
| DENR | Department of Environment and Natural Resources, Philippines |
| DNR | Department of Natural Resources, Philippines |
| EC | European Commission |
| EIA | environmental impact assessment |
| EIB | European Investment Bank |
| EIS | environmental impact statement |
| EIT | Economies in Transition |
| EPBC | Environment Protection and Biodiversity Conservation Act, Australia, 1999 |
| ERA | ecological risk assessment |
| ESA | Endangered Species Act, US, 1973 |
| ESD | Ecologically Sustainable Development, Australia, 1992 |
| EU | European Union |
| FAA | Fisheries Administration Act, Australia, 1991 |
| FAO | Food and Agriculture Organization of the United Nations |
| FCM | Fisheries Conservation and Management Act, Malawi, 1997 |
| FD | Forest Department, Uganda |
| FMA | Fisheries Management Act, Australia, 1991 |
| FMU | forest management unit |
| FRDC | Fisheries Research and Development Corporation |
| FSC | Forest Stewardship Council |
| GAO | General Accounting Office, US |
| GEL | General Environmental Law, Argentina, 2002 |
| GMO | genetically modified organism |
| HCVF | high conservation value forest |
| IA | impact assessment |
| IAIA | International Association for Impact Assessment |
| ICCAT | International Commission for the Conservation of Atlantic Tunas |
| ICES | International Council for Exploration of the Sea |
| ICRW | International Convention for the Regulation of Whaling, 1946 |
| IEE | initial environmental examination |
| IFF | International Forum on Forests |
| IGAE | Intergovernmental Agreement on the Environment, Australia, 1992 |
| INCOPESCA | Costa Rican Fisheries Authority |

| | |
|---|---|
| INIDEP | National Institute of Fishing Research and Development, Argentina |
| IOTC | Indian Ocean Tuna Commission |
| IPF | International Panel on Forests |
| IPCC | Intergovernmental Panel on Climate Change |
| IPOA | International Plan of Action |
| IPRA | Indigenous People's Rights Act, Philippines, 1997 |
| ISF | Integrated Social Forestry, Philippines |
| ITLOS | International Tribunal for the Law of the Sea |
| IUCN | World Conservation Union |
| IUU | illegal, unreported and unregulated |
| IWC | International Whaling Commission |
| LGERA | Local Government and Environment Reports of Australia |
| LMNP | Lake Mburo National Park, Uganda |
| MAC | Management Advisory Committee |
| MFP | minor forest produce |
| MVP | minimum viable population |
| NASCO | North Atlantic Salmon Conservation Organization |
| NBS | National Biodiversity Strategy |
| NCCW | National Council for Conservation of Wildlife |
| NDF | non-detriment finding |
| NEAA | Newfoundland Environmental Assessment Act, Canada, 2000 |
| NEP | National Environmental Policy, India |
| NEPA | National Environmental Policy Act, US, 1969 |
| NGIA | Nursery and Garden Industry Australia |
| NGO | non-governmental organization |
| NIPAS | National Integrated Protected Areas System, Philippines, 1992 |
| NPOA | national plan of action |
| NRC | National Research Council, US |
| NRM | natural resource management |
| NTFP | non-timber forest product |
| NWFP | North West Frontier Province, Pakistan |
| NZCPS | New Zealand Coastal Policy Statement, 1994 |
| OCS | Offshore Constitutional Settlement, Australia |
| OECD | Organisation for Economic Co-operation and Development |
| PA | protected area |
| PAMB | Protected Area Management Board, Philippines |
| PANP | Prince Albert National Park, Canada |
| PDO | Pacific Decadal Oscillation |
| PPLS | Peñablanca Protected Landscape and Seascape, Philippines |
| PRETOMA | Sea Turtle Restoration Programme |
| PROFOR | Program on Forests |
| RBA | risk–benefit analysis |
| REECS | Resources, Environment and Economics Center for Studies, Inc., Manila, Philippines |

| | |
|---|---|
| RFA | Regional Forest Agreement |
| RFMO | regional fisheries management organization |
| RMA | Resource Management Act, New Zealand, 1991 |
| SAC | Special Area of Conservation |
| SADC | Southern African Development Community |
| SAGPyA | Secretariat of Agriculture, Livestock, Fisheries and Food, Argentina |
| SAyDS | Secretariat of Environment and Sustainable Development, Argentina |
| SBT | southern bluefin tuna |
| SC | Scientific Committee |
| SEA | strategic environmental assessment |
| SFI | Sustainable Forestry Initiative |
| SFM | sustainable forest management |
| SMS | safe minimum standard |
| SPA | Special Protection Area |
| SPS | sanitary and phytosanitary |
| TAC | total allowable catch |
| TCP | Torghar Conservation Programme, Pakistan |
| TEK | traditional ecological knowledge |
| TLA | Timber License Agreements |
| TNP | Tortuguero National Park, Costa Rica |
| UK | United Kingdom |
| UN | United Nations |
| UNCED | United Nations Conference on Environment and Development, 1992 |
| UNCLOS | United Nations Convention on the Law of the Sea, 1982 |
| UNFCCC | United Nations Framework Convention on Climate Change, 1992 |
| UNFF | United Nations Forum on Forests |
| UNFSA | United Nations Fish Stocks Agreement, 1995 |
| USFWS | US Fish and Wildlife Service |
| VBNC | Voisey's Bay Nickel Company Ltd |
| WBCA | Wild Bird Conservation Act, US, 1992 |
| WLPA | Wildlife (Protection) Act, India, 1972 |
| WRA | weed risk assessment |
| WSPA | World Society for the Protection of Animals |
| WTO | World Trade Organization |
| WTO SPS | World Trade Organization Agreement on the Application of Sanitary and Phytosanitary Standards |
| WWF | World Wide Fund for Nature |

# List of Inter-Governmental Agreements and Declarations

African Convention for the Conservation of Nature and Natural Resources (Revised) (2003, not yet in force), available at www.africa-union.org/Official_documents/Treaties_%20Conventions_%20Protocols/offTreaties_Conventions_&_Protocols.htm

African-European Waterbird Agreement (1995, entered into force 1999), available at www.cms.int/species/aewa/aew_text.htm

Agreement on the Conservation of Albatrosses and Petrels (2001, entered into force 2004), available at www.acap.aq

Agreement on the Conservation of Cetaceans of the Black Sea, Mediterranean Sea and Contiguous Atlantic Area (1996, entered into force 2001), available at www.accobams.org

Agreement on the Conservation of Populations of European Bats (1991, entered into force 1994), available at www.eurobats.org/documents/agreement_text.htm

Cartagena Protocol on Biosafety (2000), available at www.biodiv.org/biosafety/protocol.asp

Convention for the Conservation of Biological Diversity and Protection of Priority Protected Areas in Central America (1992), available at www.iucn.org/places/orma/pdfs/bioeng.pdf

Convention for the Conservation of Salmon in the North Atlantic Ocean (1982, entered into force 1983), available at www.nasco.int

Convention for the Prevention of Marine Pollution by Dumping from Ships and Aircraft (the Oslo Convention); (1972, entered into force 1974), available at http://sedac.ciesin.org/entri/texts/marine.pollution.dumping.ships.aircraft.1972.html

Convention for the Prevention of Marine Pollution from Land-Based Sources (the Paris Convention); (1974, entered into force 1978), available at http://sedac.ciesin.columbia.edu/entri/texts/marine.pollution.land.based.sources.1974.html

Convention for the Protection of the Marine Environment of the North-East Atlantic (the OSPAR Convention); (1992, entered into force 1998), available at www.ospar.org/eng/html/welcome.html

Convention on Biological Diversity (1992), available at www.biodiv.org

Convention on Nature Protection and Wildlife Preservation in the Western Hemisphere (1940, entered into force 1942). available at www.fws.gov/international/whp/whpconv.html

Convention on the Conservation and Management of Highly Migratory Fish Stocks in the West and Central Pacific Ocean (2000, entered into force 2004), available at http://sedac.ciesin.org/entri/texts/fish.west.cent.pac.2000.html

Convention on the Conservation of Migratory Species of Wild Animals (the Bonn Convention); (1979, entered into force 1983), available at www.cms.int

Convention on International Trade in Endangered Species of Wild Fauna and Flora (1973, entered into force 1975), available at www.cites.org

Convention on Wetlands of International Importance especially as Waterfowl Habitat (the Ramsar Convention); (1971, entered into force 1975), available at www.ramsar.org

InterAmerican Convention for the Protection and Conservation of Sea Turtles (1996, entered into force 2001), available at www.seaturtle.org/iac/

International Convention for the Conservation of Atlantic Tunas (1966, entered into force 1969), available at www.iccat.es

International Convention for the Regulation of Whaling (1946, entered into force 1948), available at www.iwcoffice.org/commission/convention.htm

Rio Declaration on Environment and Development (1992), available at www.unep.org/resources/gov/keydocuments.asp

United Nations Agreement for the Implementation of the Provisions of the United Nations Convention on the Law of the Sea of 10 December 1982 relating to the Conservation and Management of Straddling Fish Stocks and Highly Migratory Fish Stocks (the Fish Stocks Agreement or Straddling Stocks Agreement); (1996, entered into force 2001), available at www.un.org/Depts/los/convention_agreements/convention_overview_fish_stocks.htm

United Nations Convention on the Law of the Sea of 10 December 1982 (1982, entered into force 1994), available at www.un.org/Depts/los/index.htm

United Nations Framework Convention on Climate Change (1992), available at www.unfccc.int

# List of Contributors

Paul W. Adams — College of Forestry, Oregon State University, Corvallis, Oregon, US

Steinar Andresen — Department of Political Science, University of Oslo, Blindern, Norway

Tonie O. Balangue — Resources, Environment and Economics Center for Studies, Inc. (REECS)/Resources and Environmental Economics Foundation of the Philippines (REAP), Quezon City, Manila, The Philippines

Peter J. Balint — Department of Public and International Affairs, George Mason University, Fairfax, Virginia, US

Abwoli Banana — Faculty of Forestry and Nature Conservation, Makerere University, Kampala, Uganda

Rolando Castro — The Environmental and Natural Resources Law Center (Centro de Derecho Ambiental y de los Recursos Natural (CEDARENA)), San José, Costa Rica

Nupur Chowdhury — The Energy and Resources Institute (TERI), New Delhi, India

Rosie Cooney — The Precautionary Principle Project – a partnership of World Conservation Union (IUCN), Fauna & Flora International, ResourceAfrica and TRAFFIC, c/o Fauna & Flora International, Cambridge, UK

Maria Eugenia Di Paola — Environment and Natural Resources Foundation (Fundación Ambiente y Recursos Naturales (FARN)), Buenos Aires, Argentina

Barney Dickson — Fauna & Flora International, Cambridge, UK

Lucy Emerton — Ecosystems and Livelihoods Group Asia (Environmental Economics, Biodiversity & Species, Marine & Coastal), IUCN, Colombo, Sri Lanka

Maryanne Grieg-Gran — International Institute for Environment and Development (IIED), London, UK

Mikkel Kallesoe — Ecosystems and Livelihoods Group Asia (Environmental Economics, Biodiversity & Species, Marine & Coastal), IUCN, Colombo, Sri Lanka

Nanki Kaur — The Energy and Resources Institute (TERI), New Delhi, India

| | |
|---|---|
| M. A. Khalid | The Energy and Resources Institute (TERI), New Delhi, India |
| Nigel Leader-Williams | Durrell Institute of Conservation and Ecology, University of Kent, Canterbury, UK |
| Tim Low | Invasive Species Council, Australia |
| Natalia Machain | Environment and Natural Resources Foundation (Fundación Ambiente y Recursos Naturales (FARN)), Buenos Aires, Argentina |
| Stephen P. Mealey | Boone and Crockett Club, Leaburg, Oregon, US |
| Brendan Moyle | Department of Commerce, Massey University, Auckland, New Zealand |
| Adrian Newton | School of Conservation Sciences, University of Bournemouth, Poole, UK |
| Sara Oldfield | Chair of IUCN/SSC Global Trees Specialist Group, Fauna & Flora International, Cambridge, UK |
| Jorge Rabinovich | Center for the Study of Parasites and Vectors (CEPAVE), National University of La Plata, Argentina |
| Kristin Rosendal | Fridtjof Nansen Institute, Lysaker, Norway |
| Alison Rosser | IUCN Wildlife Trade Programme, Cambridge, UK |
| Harold J. Salwasser | College of Forestry, Oregon State University, Corvallis, Oregon, US |
| Glenn Sant | TRAFFIC Oceania, Sydney, Australia |
| Chandra S. Silori | Resources and Environment Institute (TERI), New Delhi, India |
| Ronald E. Stewart | Department of Environmental Science and Policy, George Mason University, Fairfax, Virginia, US |
| Naseer Tareen | IUCN Sustainable Use Specialist Group, Quetta, Pakistan |
| Jack Ward Thomas | College of Forestry and Conservation, University Of Montana, Missoula, US |
| Jo Treweek | Environmental Consultant, UK |
| Graham Tucker | Ecological Solutions, Huntingdon, UK |
| Lars Walløe | Department of Physiology, University of Oslo, Norway |

# Preface

Over recent years the precautionary principle has become both popular and controversial. While, at least at international level, it was first explicitly applied to issues of marine pollution in Europe, it has since been applied in the context of a broad range of environmental issues, including biodiversity conservation and natural resource management. It has been endorsed in a wide variety of international environmental agreements and is increasingly incorporated into national environmental law and policy across the world. While there have been many recent examinations of the precautionary principle, this book, and the project from which it has emerged (see Foreword), is distinctive in several ways.

The first is its subject matter. The precautionary principle has been most comprehensively discussed and elaborated with respect to industrial or 'brown' issues – issues of pollution, food safety and toxic chemicals. This book deals with its application to the conservation of biodiversity and management of biological resources. The subjects that arise in connection with this application are, to some extent, different from those that arise in relation to brown issues. The nature and extent of uncertainty, the stakeholders involved, the institutional and scientific context, and the established procedures and mechanisms for dealing with risk and uncertainty, can all be widely divergent from brown scenarios. Further, the background to many biodiversity problems is causally complex, making the choice of the most precautionary remedy far from straightforward. We must state at the outset that we have not included discussion of genetically modified organisms within this volume. This is not only because this topic is extensively discussed elsewhere, but because the issues that shape that debate, including political and economic tensions, are not necessarily easily transferable to other biodiversity and resource management contexts.

The second distinction of this book is that it seeks to highlight voices and perspectives from developing countries. The international policy debate about the precautionary principle has been largely a Northern debate, often a Europe versus the US debate, and typically an environmental versus corporate debate. However, the vast majority of the world's biodiversity is in the developing world. This means that sustainable development, local livelihoods and poverty alleviation are critical issues in the context of biodiversity conservation in general and application of the precautionary principle in particular.

The book begins with an initial chapter setting the scene, introducing the principle, its various formulations and versions, and some of the questions and issues it raises. From there the book is divided into five main sections. Section

One examines the precautionary principle in a number of highly divergent international regimes and policy processes, where the acceptance, interpretation and implementation of the precautionary principle is shaped by the need to cooperate on issues of transboundary impact or common concern, by economic rivalries between states, by North–South tension, and by the different approaches and priorities adopted by different states and regions.

Section Two focuses on implementation of the principle (or lack thereof) at national level. An increasing array of countries explicitly incorporate the precautionary principle in national legislation or policy governing natural resource use and biodiversity conservation, but its impact on actual decision-making and management is far from clear. Common to all the chapters in this section is the presence of clear legal obligations for decision-makers to implement a precautionary approach: for fisheries, endangered species, invasive alien species or biodiversity in general.

Section Three examines how decision-makers should respond when faced by uncertainty, critically assessing responses based on prohibitions compared with alternative responses such as adaptive management. While these chapters address this issue from a number of different disciplinary, sectoral and national standpoints, common to all is the recognition that simply banning or prohibiting potentially threatening activities is not necessarily an appropriate or effective response and may raise as many problems as it solves.

Section Four focuses on livelihoods. Many rural people in developing countries are directly dependent, in different ways, on wild species and the broader natural environment in which those species live. So while all precautionary action is likely to have some impact on some livelihoods needs and dynamics, precautionary action that is undertaken in developing countries to protect biological resources can be expected to have a particularly significant impact on the lives of the rural poor, whether positive or negative.

Section Five moves beyond examination of specific cases, sectors or contexts to broad analytical perspectives on the precautionary principle and reflections on key issues to be taken into account when applying precaution.

Following this section, a concluding chapter by the editors draws together the key lessons and insights from these various studies and analyses for effective and equitable use of the precautionary principle in practice.

The purpose and objective of these studies was to inform the development of Guidelines for Applying the Precautionary Principle to Biodiversity Conservation and Natural Resource Management. These Guidelines, developed through an international consultative process, are presented in the Appendix.

Barney Dickson and Rosie Cooney
*Cambridge, September 2005*

# Introduction

1

# From Promise to Practicalities: The Precautionary Principle in Biodiversity Conservation and Sustainable Use

*Rosie Cooney*

Biodiversity underpins human life and well-being. It directly provides food, medicine, fuel and building materials; supports ecosystem services such as crop pollination, soil fertility, nutrient cycling and flood control; offers aesthetic, spiritual and recreational benefits; and more broadly contributes to human security, resilience, health, social relations and freedom of choices and action (Millennium Ecosystem Assessment, 2005a, b). Biodiversity and biological resources face serious threats. Over the past few hundred years human activities have increased species extinction rates to up to 1000 times the background rate (Millennium Ecosystem Assessment, 2005a) and around one in eight of the world's bird species, a quarter of its mammals and one in three amphibian species are threatened with extinction (Baillie et al, 2004). Around 60 per cent of the ecosystem services that support life on Earth are currently being degraded or used unsustainably (Millennium Ecosystem Assessment, 2005b).

Attempts to conserve biodiversity and manage wild resources must grapple with persistent and often intractable uncertainties and a high level of ignorance (Dovers and Handmer, 1995). Underlying biological and ecological knowledge is limited: it is not known, for instance, how many species currently exist to the nearest ten million (Stork, 1997; May, 2000). There are major gaps in understanding of both biology and threats: while vertebrates are relatively well documented, comparatively little is known about non-terrestrial systems (freshwater and marine), many species-rich habitats (such as tropical forest or the ocean depths) or species-rich groups such as invertebrates, plants and fungi (which together compose the overwhelming majority of species).

Understanding of the interactions between species in complex ecological systems is in its infancy (Redford and Feinsinger, 2001). There are insufficient data and no chance of experimentation to assess the long-term biodiversity impacts of major recent interventions and innovations such as widespread tropical deforestation, dramatically increased trade and transport between regions, and commercialization of many wild resources. More fundamentally, in a biological resource use scenario, understanding the *drivers* of threats and *why* some human uses or impacts become unsustainable requires consideration of an enormous variety of not just ecological but socio-economic and political factors interacting in a complex system not amenable to ready quantification or prediction (Holling, 2001; Zaccagnini et al, 2001).

Historically, human decision-making has done a demonstrably poor job of reacting to early warning signs of threats to the environment or human health (Harremoes et al, 2002). The presence of uncertainty about the existence, causation, likelihood or magnitude of a harm has often been used to justify postponing or delaying decisions to protect health or the environment, with frequently disastrous and sometimes irreversible results. In fisheries, for instance, uncertainty regarding stock status and the level of risk posed by fishing has consistently been used as a reason to avoid, defer or oppose strong limitations on harvest levels (Ludwig, 2001; MacGarvin, 2002). Overexploitation of fisheries can cause unexpected long-term effects, such as trophic cascades, that may mean stock depletion is effectively irreversible (see for example Frank et al, 2005).

In response to this dismal history the precautionary principle, or precautionary approach (see Box 1.1), has emerged as a broad and promising guide for law, policy, management and decision-making in cases of uncertainty. It shifts the balance in decision-making in favour of anticipating, monitoring, preventing and mitigating potential threats. While it is important in addressing threats both to the environment and to human health, this discussion and the chapters that follow are largely confined to the environmental arena.

This chapter seeks to provide background and context for the more specific explorations and examinations of the precautionary principle that follow. Here I introduce the precautionary principle in its various forms, highlight controversies around it, summarize its incorporation into international and national biodiversity and natural resource law and policy, and introduce some issues that, I suggest, need to be addressed in efforts to translate it into practice.

## WHAT IS THE PRECAUTIONARY PRINCIPLE?

As a broad and general principle, the precautionary principle is subject to many different formulations in different contexts (see below). However, all reflect the premise that complete certainty regarding an environmental harm should not be a prerequisite for taking action to avert it. The precautionary principle counters the presumption that activities should proceed until and unless there is clear evidence that they are harmful, and supports action to

## BOX 1.1 PRECAUTIONARY PRINCIPLE OR PRECAUTIONARY APPROACH?

There has been much debate over whether the terminology 'precautionary principle' or 'precautionary approach' are equivalent and/or should be used in particular contexts. In some quarters, the 'precautionary approach' is preferred, due to the perception that 'the precautionary principle' appears to mandate that risk-averse actions always be taken, while 'the precautionary approach' implies flexible operational measures that are context sensitive and allow for the balancing of various objectives, including economic ones. For instance, in fisheries, the term 'precautionary principle' is often viewed as a hard-line approach requiring complete prohibitions, leading to favouring of the 'precautionary approach' (Mace and Gabriel, 1999). However, given that the general definition of a legal principle implies flexible, context-specific guidance rather than mandating a particular outcome (as for a 'rule'; see Dworkin, 1976), this distinction does not appear a useful one. Some have a different concern – that recognizing precaution as a 'principle' of environmental law implies a general obligation to apply precaution in decision-making. Some prefer to view precaution as merely one particular policy/management 'approach' to dealing with uncertain risks, which may be chosen over alternative approaches according to circumstance. While it is undisputed that in specific contexts there are clear legal requirements or guidance in favour of precaution, this debate relates to an extensive (unresolved) question about whether precaution has become part of customary international law (see for example Cameron and Abouchar, 1996; Trouwborst, 2002; De Sadeleer, 2003). It may also reflect the difficulty of some regulatory systems, such as that of the US, in accommodating broad, generally applicable principles that allow wide discretion in decision-making (Wiener, 2003).

Different approaches to this terminology have emerged. The Government of Canada, in a discussion document, uses the term 'precautionary principle/ approach' and draws no distinction between them (Government of Canada, 2001). Australian fisheries policy specifies that the precautionary principle is implemented through the precautionary approach (Department of Environment and Heritage (Australia), 2001). US policy-makers tend to prefer the 'approach' while European Community institutions prefer 'principle' (Graham, 2004). A recent comprehensive legal treatment of the precautionary principle concludes that the distinction is 'an irrelevant debate, a semantic squabble between decision-makers' and that the terms can be used interchangeably (De Sadeleer, 2003). In general little is made of the distinction in this book.

anticipate and avert environmental harm in advance of, or without, a clear demonstration that such action is necessary. The most widely cited version is probably Principle 15 of the Rio Declaration on Environment and Development (1992):

> *In order to protect the environment the Precautionary Approach*
> *shall be widely applied by States according to their capabilities.*
> *Where there are threats of serious or irreversible damage, lack of*

> *full scientific certainty shall not be used as a reason for*
> *postponing cost-effective measures to prevent environmental*
> *degradation.* (Rio Declaration)

Beyond this basic characterization, however, defining the precautionary principle runs into complexities. It can be variously viewed as a broad ethical standpoint, a narrow legal doctrine, specific guidance for decision-making, or as a general tool for advocacy. There is no single definition, indeed, one author unearthed 19 definitions (Sandin, 1999), a number that has since no doubt expanded considerably. Furthermore, when it comes to the crucial issue of turning the abstract principle into practice there is considerable lack of clarity about what it actually means to apply the precautionary principle or take precautionary measures (Stone, 2001; Sandin, 2004).

Here I distinguish three general forms of the precautionary principle, of increasing stringency (adapted from the characterization of Wiener, 2002).

The first and least restrictive allows preventive measures to be taken in the face of scientific uncertainty, but does not call for or require them. For example, the Preamble of the 1992 Convention on Biological Diversity (CBD) states that:

> *where there is a threat of significant reduction or loss of biologi-*
> *cal diversity, lack of full scientific certainty should not be used as*
> *a reason for postponing measures to avoid or minimize such a*
> *threat.*

However, this form of the principle is limited in effect: while it provides an effective response to the argument that measures should not be taken unless there is scientific certainty of harm, it leaves open the possibility that some other factor, such as socio-economic cost, could be used as a reason to postpone such measures. In practice even those who are strong critics of the precautionary principle have little objection to this version (for example Sunstein, 2002).

In more stringent but still moderate versions of the principle, the presence of an uncertain threat is a basis for action – once there is a plausible basis for believing that a sufficiently serious threat exists, regulation is justified or compelled. For example, the UK Biodiversity Action Plan states:

> *In line with the precautionary principle, where interactions are*
> *complex and where the available evidence suggests that there is a*
> *significant chance of damage to our biodiversity heritage occur-*
> *ring, conservation measures are appropriate, even in the absence*
> *of conclusive scientific evidence that the damage will occur.*
> (Department of the Environment (UK), 1994, para 6.8)

It is important to note that there is a major difference between the previous and this version – here there is a positive basis for obligations to take precautionary measures.

In strong versions of the principle, the burden of proof (evidentiary presumption) is reversed so that actions or substances are considered 'guilty until proven innocent' rather than 'innocent until proven guilty'. So, for instance, the Earth Charter (2000)[1] states: '[W]hen knowledge is limited, apply a precautionary approach... Place the burden of proof on those who argue that an activity will not cause significant harm' (article 6). This version not only allows, justifies or requires action, but gives an idea of what action to take: prohibit the action unless shown to be safe (Nollkaemper, 1996). Typically reversal of the burden of proof is applied to restrict actions that by their nature or context appear likely to be harmful. For instance, many countries prohibit all harvest, 'take' or killing of endangered species, or of wild resources within strictly protected areas, unless it can be shown that this will not be harmful to the conservation of the species. At the extreme, precaution may involve bans and prohibitions on entire classes of potentially threatening activities or substances, without the option for proponents or others to demonstrate that they are harmless.

Most official versions of the precautionary principle include language that establishes a 'threshold' for application of the principle, which modifies its stringency and/or provides for some form of balancing of the environmental interest against other interests (such as economic cost or feasibility). For instance, the Rio Declaration limits the relevance of precaution to 'where there are threats of serious or irreversible harm' and 'cost-effective' actions are available, and provides that the precautionary approach should be applied by states 'according to their capabilities'. Some versions include consideration of 'reasonableness', with respect to either the evidence of possible threat (the threshold) or the measure taken. So, for instance, the European Commission has stated that the precautionary principle is relevant where 'preliminary objective scientific evaluation, indicates that there are reasonable grounds for concern' (European Commission, 2000). A US Presidential Council has stated that 'even in the face of scientific uncertainty, society should take reasonable actions to avert risks where the potential harm to human health or the environment is thought to be serious or irreparable' (President's Council on Sustainable Development, 1996). Some versions include the requirement for some form of proportionality between the measures taken and the potential risks. So, for instance, the 1973 Convention on International Trade in Endangered Species of Wild Fauna and Flora (CITES) criteria for listing species in Appendices I and II includes the text:

> *when considering proposals to amend Appendix I or II, the Parties shall, by virtue of the precautionary approach and in case of uncertainty... act in the best interest of the conservation of the species concerned and adopt measures that are proportionate to the anticipated risks to the species.* (CITES, Resolution Conf. 9.2.4 (Rev. CoP13))

Likewise, the Australian Inter-Governmental Agreement on the Environment (1992)[2] states:

> *In the application of the precautionary principle, public and private decisions should be guided by: (i) careful evaluation to avoid, wherever practicable, serious or irreversible damage to the environment; and (ii) an assessment of the risk-weighted options of the various options.*

## CONTROVERSY OVER THE PRECAUTIONARY PRINCIPLE

The precautionary principle, in all its various forms, has been controversial, sparking intense international debate. It has been described in highly divergent terms from 'profoundly revolutionary' (O'Riordan and Cameron, 1994) to 'common sense',[3] from the 'fundamental environmental principle' (Cameron and Abouchar, 1991) to the 'paralyzing principle' (Sunstein, 2002), and from a stimulus for innovation (Tickner and Geiser, 2004) to 'a tool for risk-averse neo-Luddites' (C. S. Prakash's comment printed on the cover of Goklany, 2001).

Critics have argued that the wide discretion the principle provides to decision-makers makes it susceptible to arbitrary, irrational or abusive application, including for purposes of trade-protectionism (Conko, 2003; Marchant and Mossman, 2004). Some argue that exercising precaution stifles innovation; that it can generate 'false positives' (i.e. regulate or ban activities that would not in fact be harmful); that it can be counter-productive (i.e. stop activities that would actually yield benefits); or that it can infringe on valid human rights and interests, including personal liberties, development and poverty alleviation (see for example Morris, 2000; Goklany, 2001; Sunstein, 2002; Wiener, 2002). Many of these concerns have been voiced in the context of biodiversity and natural resource management (NRM). Commentators and researchers have also voiced concerns that the principle could be applied in ways that impose Western views of nature on indigenous people (Colchester, 2003); that conflict with human rights, development priorities or livelihoods (Freese, 1996; Mohammed-Katerere, 2001; Risby, 2002; Colchester, 2003); lead to static and inflexible conservation policies that do not respond to on-the-ground realities (Walters et al, 2003); or be counter-productive through not recognizing the potential conservation benefits of activities that also pose some threats (Moyle, 2004). It should be noted, however, that the force of these criticisms depends much on which version of the precautionary principle is at issue and how it is applied.

Disputes about the precautionary principle are in reality often disputes about how competing interests should be balanced, against a background level of uncertainty or poor knowledge that precludes a clear technical resolution. Adopting a precautionary approach will typically, perhaps necessarily, involve restrictions on some activities, and often impose some form of social or

## BOX 1.2 THE PRECAUTIONARY PRINCIPLE AND ALIEN INVASIONS: TENSIONS BETWEEN TRADE AND ENVIRONMENT REGIMES

The movement of species into areas where they are not indigenous, and where they are not subject to natural predators, pathogens or other restraints, can lead to their dramatic expansion. This can wreak environmental and economic havoc driving native species extinct or into decline, altering the structure of ecological communities, and having major impacts on agriculture, forestry, fishing or shipping. Species can be introduced intentionally (for example for agriculture, horticulture or pets) or unintentionally (for example through 'hitch-hiking' with tourists, in ships' ballast, in agricultural produce or in wood packaging). Crucially, it is typically impossible to predict with any reliability whether a species will become invasive – by the time it has entered and spread, it may be too late to prevent damage. The Global Strategy on Invasive Species states 'Every alien species needs to be managed as if it is potentially invasive, until convincing evidence indicates that it presents no such threat' (McNeely et al, 2001). Several environmental agreements, including the CBD, call for the application of a precautionary approach to preventing the spread of invasives, including requiring risk analysis in advance of any intentional introduction (rather than only where there is some evidence of threat), and only permitting introduction of those species unlikely to threaten biological diversity (see CBD Decision VI/23 Principles 1, 10). The use of trade measures based on such precaution is, however, highly controversial. There has been much debate and controversy over whether this approach may be in conflict with the Sanitary and Phytosanitary Agreement (SPS Agreement 1994) of the World Trade Organization (WTO), which reflects a very different emphasis. The SPS Agreement is designed to ensure that measures taken for the stated reason of protecting human, animal or plant life or health from pests and disease are not a disguised restriction on international trade (measures against invasives are generally considered to fall under SPS provisions). It requires that any measure to restrict import must be based on 'sufficient scientific evidence' and risk assessments. Note the key difference, reflecting the differing priorities in the different agreements: the CBD principles require risk analysis before any species should be admitted, where the SPS requires risk assessment before any restriction can be imposed. Dispute resolution under this agreement suggests that these requirements are interpreted stringently and place tight constraints on the leeway for countries to apply a strong precautionary approach. However, the SPS does make limited recognition of scientific uncertainty, and allows members to take 'provisional measures' on condition that they seek further information and subject these measures to review in a reasonable period of time. It thus appears possible for countries to take a precautionary approach where every species is considered 'guilty until proven innocent', but this is likely to require considerable financial and technical resources in order to carry out extensive research and review to justify protective measures.

*Source:* Cooney (2004a)

economic costs on some groups. The stronger forms, at least, of the precautionary principle therefore weight the environmental interest above these other interests. As Wiener (2002) has pointed out 'Uncertainty is not the crucial issue. Trade-offs are the crucial issue'. Discussion of the precautionary principle in biodiversity conservation and NRM is made more complicated and heated by the fact that it taps into a number of ongoing debates about how (potentially) competing values should be weighed and balanced. For example, the precautionary principle is a major point of potential tension between the international trade regime, geared toward trade liberalization, and multilateral environmental agreements, aimed at environmental protection. This tension is well illustrated, for instance, with respect to invasive alien species (see Box 1.2). Likewise, precaution is a key issue in ongoing disputes and discussion around regulation of genetically modified organisms (GMOs), with the US and European Union taking notably different stances. As a very different example, involving a very different set of interests, precautionary conservation strategies that restrict the rights and access to biological resources of indigenous and local people tap into tensions and debates surrounding 'conservation versus development' or 'conservation versus poverty alleviation' (see for example Sanderson and Redford, 2003; Adams et al, 2004; Roe and Elliott, 2004; Mahsood, 2005).

## The Rise and Rise of the Precautionary Principle

Despite ongoing controversy, the precautionary principle has spread rapidly in multilateral and national environmental law (for recent reviews of its origin and spread see for example Freestone, 1999; Trouwborst, 2002; De Sadeleer, 2003; Douma, 2003). The principle is now incorporated into a very wide range of international hard and soft law instruments across many fields including climate change, biodiversity, wildlife trade, biosafety, marine fisheries, food standards, transport of hazardous waste, pollution control and chemicals regulation. While extensive analysis has focused on whether the precautionary principle has 'crystallized' into a principle of customary international law (see for example Trouwborst, 2002; De Sadeleer, 2003), it may conservatively be said that while it is not unequivocally accepted as having the status of customary international law (Marceau, 2002), it can probably be described as customary international law in some sectors (Gehring and Cordonier-Segger, 2002).

With respect to biodiversity conservation and management of biological resources, there is widespread (if uneven) recognition and incorporation of the precautionary principle in law and policy at international level (for a more comprehensive discussion see Cooney, 2004b). The principle is expressed in the Preamble of the CBD and has subsequently been extensively included in CBD decisions and related work on a wide range of issues, including marine and coastal biodiversity, invasive alien species and sustainable use of wild living resources. The precautionary approach is strongly affirmed in the CBD's Cartagena Protocol on Biosafety (2000), concerned with international trade in living genetically modified organisms. CITES has adopted a version of the principle to guide decisions on which species should be listed in the CITES Appendices and therefore subject to international trade controls. While other major global biodiversity agreements of broad scope such as the Ramsar Convention on Wetlands (1971) and the Convention on Migratory Species (CMS, 1982) do not include the precautionary principle in their Convention texts, it has been incorporated in various subsequent resolutions[4] and in agreements concluded under the auspices of the CMS.[5]

In the fisheries context, recent decades have seen the strong emergence in international, regional and national fisheries law and policy of a 'precautionary approach' to fisheries management (Garcia, 2000). For instance, the UN Fish Stocks Agreement[6] was the first global fisheries agreement requiring a precautionary approach, which is to be applied to fisheries conservation, management and exploitation measures. The precautionary approach is increasingly adopted by many regional fisheries agreements, such as the North Atlantic Salmon Conservation Organization (NASCO) and the International Commission for the Conservation of Atlantic Tunas (ICCAT). By contrast, recognition of the precautionary principle is extremely rare in the context of multilateral instruments relating to forests.

Many regional conservation and NRM instruments now invoke the precautionary principle. For instance, the newly amended (not yet in force) African Convention on the Conservation of Nature and Natural Resources (2004) contains a strong endorsement of the precautionary principle as part of its fundamental obligation. In the EU, the 1992 the Habitats Directive[7] does not explicitly incorporate the precautionary principle, but takes a clearly precautionary approach to protected sites: in the case of a project likely to have a significant effect on a protected site 'competent national authorities shall agree to the plan or project only after having ascertained that it will not adversely affect the integrity of the site concerned'.

At national level the precautionary principle is increasingly being explicitly incorporated in national law and policy related to biodiversity or natural resources (for instance in Australia, Costa Rica, Argentina, South Africa and Cameroon), sometimes within legislation implementing the CBD. Of course, countries not explicitly incorporating the precautionary principle into law or policy may nonetheless establish regulatory or management frameworks that embody strong precautionary elements. In many countries, including Australia and Costa Rica, the precautionary principle has been a key issue raised in legal disputes related to biodiversity. It is important to note, however, that in a large number of countries the principle remains unfamiliar and there is little practical experience with its application.

# FROM PRINCIPLE TO PRACTICE

As a general principle, the precautionary principle will require 'materialization' into specific regulatory frameworks, practices, decision-making processes, restrictions or rules in particular contexts. The principle can support a wide and context-specific range of operational measures to anticipate, avert or mitigate various sources of threat to biodiversity and the sustainability of biological resource management. Operational measures may range from strict prohibitions and bans on activities, to requiring demonstration of safety before allowing activities to proceed, to establishing monitoring or licensing frameworks, to imposing conditions and restrictions to mitigate possible risks, to leaving a 'margin of error' in harvesting levels, to adopting a management approach that addresses and responds dynamically to variable and uncertain threats.

Operationalizing the principle requires tackling a number of questions and challenges. How are different interests to be balanced? Whose views, priorities and opinions should be involved in decision-making? How can choices be made between different courses of action or conservation strategies that may each pose risks of different sorts and over different timescales (see Box 1.3)? What is the role of expert opinion and assessment when information is inadequate or incomplete? Who bears the burden of proof? Who pays the costs of applying precaution, and how can any distributional impacts be remedied?

A number of policy instruments and initiatives have sought to tackle some of these questions and provide guidance on applying the precautionary principle in various contexts. For instance, at a regulatory level, the European Commission *Communication on the Precautionary Principle* sets out that implementation of the principle in the EU should be guided by the principles of proportionality, non-discrimination, consistency, examination of the costs and benefits of action and inaction, and examination of scientific developments (European Commission, 2000). At an advocacy/research level, there have been important efforts in recent years to elaborate general guidance, procedures and checklists for applying a precautionary approach in the environmental/health context (for example Tickner and Raffensperger, 1999; Harremoes et al, 2002; Myers and Raffensperger, forthcoming). These initiatives have emphasized the importance of *process* in applying the precautionary principle, emphasizing elements such as assessment of alternative courses of action, broad stakeholder participation and transparency. Guidance on what precaution should look like in practice is also available in some specific resource management contexts. A particularly well-elaborated example is the Technical Guidelines on the Precautionary Approach in Fisheries developed by the UN Food and Agriculture Organization (FAO, 1995). The FAO guidance considers the meaning and implications of a precautionary approach, and sets out a very broad range of provisions for management, research and technology development, including with respect to management planning and design, monitoring, stock assessment methods, review and evaluation of new technologies, and cooperation and information systems.

---

## Box 1.3 Precaution and multiple risks: conservation of giant otters in Manu National Park

Debates about ecotourism based on viewing of giant river otters *Pteronura brasiliensis* in Peru illustrate the 'two-edged' nature of many conservation strategies and multiple threats that must be balanced when implementing a precautionary conservation approach. Giant otters are site-loyal, predictable and hyperactive animals highly attractive to tourists, and are probably the most easily managed and viewed large mammalian predator of the South American rainforest. In the 1980s a research team in Manu National Park, Peru, developed a method of close-range, predictable viewing of these charismatic carnivores. They used walkie-talkies to call one tourist canoe at a time to observe each otter group. Each tourist canoe had to watch from a spot chosen by the researcher. Until Brazilians developed a similarly compelling method in 1995, this method offered the world's first close-range, extended viewing of giant otters. From 1983 to 1988, tourism to Manu grew from 20 to 700 tourists per year, largely based on excellent otter viewing. In the early 1990s, however, this close-range otter tourism drew concern from another team of otter researchers, who feared that close-range viewing might disrupt otter reproduction. While evidence of impact was very limited, authorities responded by closing many of the best otter viewing lakes, making it much harder for tourists to view the Manu otters predictably and at close range. While these restrictions were based on valid conservation concerns, some argue that, paradoxically, these precautionary efforts have in fact been counter-productive to long-term conservation of the otters and their rainforest habitat. Tourist numbers to Manu have remained at about 2400 to 2800 tourists per year since 2000. By contrast, tourism to less restricted otter viewing areas in nearby Tambopata, Peru, has skyrocketed from less than 500 in 1996 to over 11,000 in 2005. The relative stagnation of the nascent tourism industry in Manu may contribute to a pervasive lack of political will to protect the region's biodiversity, particularly from the region's economically important, legal and illegal loggers and gold miners. Loggers and miners are major threats to the otters in the region, with loggers shooting otters and other sensitive wildlife, and miners spilling mercury into rivers, leading to highly toxic fish being eaten by southeast Peru's 200 giant otters and 80,000 people. This example highlights the complexity of determining how the precautionary principle should be applied in real-life conservation scenarios. Actions against one threat can handicap attempts to counter more serious threats, which suggests that threats cannot be assessed purely in biological terms, but require consideration of the broader socio-political context of conservation.

*Source:* Charles Munn, in correspondence with R. Cooney, 2005

---

However, while precautionary obligations proliferate in the biodiversity and NRM context, there remains very little shared understanding or practical guidance for its operational implementation. Such guidance is badly needed if the principle is to move beyond a controversial catchphrase, observed largely in the breach, to become a practical and effective principle to guide decision-making and management.

## NOTES

1    Earth Charter (undated) *The Earth Charter Handbook*, Earth Charter International Secretariat, San José, Costa Rica. Available at www.earthcharter.org
2    Australian Inter-Governmental Agreement on the Environment (1992) (article 3.5.1).
3    Justice Stein in the NSW Land and Environment Court decision of Leatch v. Shoalhaven City Council (1993) 81 LGERA 270.
4    These include, for example, the Ramsar Guidelines on Management Planning for Wetlands (Resolution VIII.14 Chapter VI) and the Resolution on Allocation and Management of Water (Resolution VIII.1 Article 10.1), and the CMS resolution on Wind Turbines and Migratory Species (Resolution 7.5).
5    These include the Agreement on Conservation of Cetaceans of the Black Sea, Mediterranean Sea and contiguous Atlantic Area (ACCOBAMS, 1996), the African-Eurasian Waterbird Agreement (1995), and the Agreement on the Conservation of Albatrosses and Petrels (2001).
6    Agreement for the Implementation of Provisions of the United Nations Convention on the Law of the Sea of 10 December 1982 Relating to the Conservation and Management of Straddling Fish Stocks and Highly Migratory Fish Stocks (1995).
7    EC Directive on the Conservation of Natural Habitats and of Wild Flora and Fauna (Directive 92/43).

## REFERENCES

Adams, W. M., Aveling, R., Brockington, D., Dickson, B., Elliott, J., Hutton, J., Roe, D., Vira, B. and Wolmer, W. (2004) 'Biodiversity conservation and the eradication of poverty', *Science*, vol 306, pp1146–49

Baillie, J. E. M., Hilton-Taylor, C. and Stuart, S. N. (eds) (2004) *2004 IUCN Red List of Threatened Species. A Global Species Assessment*. IUCN, Gland, Switzerland and Cambridge, UK.

Cameron, J. and Abouchar, J. (1991) 'The precautionary principle: a fundamental principle of law and policy for the protection of the global environment', *Boston College International and Comparative Law Review*, vol 14, no 1, pp1–27

Cameron, J. and Abouchar, J. (1996) 'The status of the precautionary principle in international law', in D. Freestone and E. Hey (eds), *The Precautionary Principle and International Law: The Challenge of Implementation*, Kluwer, The Hague, pp29–52

Colchester, M. (2003) 'Applying the precautionary principle: visions of nature and cultural diversity', presentation at 'The precautionary principle in parks management' side-event, IUCN Vth World Parks Congress, 8–17 September 2003, Durban, South Africa

Conko, G. (2003) 'Safety, risk and the precautionary principle: rethinking precautionary approaches to the regulation of transgenic plants', *Transgenic Research*, vol 12, no 6, pp639–47

Cooney, R. (2004a) *Precaution and invasive alien species: challenges at the interface of trade and environment regimes*. Paper given at 'Biodiversity loss and species extinctions: Managing risk in a changing world', World Conservation Forum, 18–20 November, Bangkok, Thailand. Available at www.iucn.org/congress/wcforum/forum_th_biodiversity-proceed.htm

Cooney, R. (2004b) *The Precautionary Principle in Biodiversity Conservation and Natural Resource Management: An Issues Paper for Policy-makers, Researchers and Practitioners*, IUCN Policy and Global Change Series, no 2, IUCN, Gland, Switzerland and Cambridge, UK

De Sadeleer, N. (2003) *Environmental Principles: From Political Slogans to Legal Rules*, Oxford University Press, Oxford

Department of Environment and Heritage (Australia) (2001) *Guidelines for the Ecologically Sustainable Management of Fisheries*, Department of the Environment and Heritage, Canberra, Australia. Available at www.deh.gov.au/coasts/fisheries/guidelines.html

Department of the Environment (UK) (1994) *Biodiversity: The UK Action Plan*, HMSO, London

Douma, W. T. (2003) *The Precautionary Principle: Its Application in International, European and Dutch Law*, Rijksuniversiteit, Groningen

Dovers, S. and Handmer, J. (1995) 'Ignorance, the precautionary principle, and sustainability', *Ambio*, vol 24, pp92–97

Dworkin, R. (1976) *Taking Rights Seriously*, Harvard University Press, Cambridge, MA

European Commission (2000) *Communication on the Precautionary Principle*, COM (2000) 1

FAO (1995) *Precautionary Approach to Fisheries*, FAO Fisheries Technical Paper 350/1, Food and Agriculture Organization, Rome

Frank, K., Petrie, B., Choi, J. and Leggett, W. (2005) 'Trophic cascades in a formerly cod-dominated ecosystem', *Science*, vol 308, pp1621–23

Freese, C. H. (1996) *The Commercial, Consumptive Use of Wild Speicies: Managing it for the Benefit of Biodiversity*, WWF-US and WWF-International, Washington, DC, and Gland

Freestone, D. (1999) 'International fisheries law since Rio: the continued rise of the precautionary principle', in A. Boyle and D. Freestone (eds) *International Law and Sustainable Development: Past Achievements and Future Challenges*, Oxford University Press, Oxford, pp135–64

Garcia, S. M. (2000) 'The precautionary approach to fisheries: progress review and main issues, 1995–2000', in J. Norton Moore and M. Nordquist (eds) *Current Maritime Issues and the Food and Agricultural Organization of the United Nations*, Martinus Nijhoff Publishers, The Hague, pp479–560

Gehring, M. W. and Cordonier-Segger, M. (2002) *Precaution in World Trade Law: The Precautionary Principle and its Implications for the World Trade Organization*, Center for International Sustainable Development Law, Montreal

Goklany, I. (2001) *The Precautionary Principle: A Critical Appraisal of Environmental Risk Assessment*, Cato Institute, Washington, DC

Government of Canada (2001) *A Canadian Perspective on the Precautionary Approach/Principle Discussion Document*, Environment Canada, Ottawa. Available at www.ec.gc.ca/econom/discussion_e.htm

Graham, J. (2004) *Risk and Precaution*, Event Transcript 04–24, AEI-Brookings Joint Center for Regulatory Affairs, Washington, DC. Available at www.aei-brookings.org/admin/authorpdfs/page.php?id=1064

Harremoes, P., Gee, D., MacGarvin, M., Stirling, A., Keys, J., Wynne, B. and Guedes Vas, S. (eds) (2002) *The Precautionary Principle in the 20th Century: Late Lessons from Early Warnings*, Earthscan, London

Holling, C. (2001) 'Understanding the complexity of economic, ecological, and social systems', *Ecosystems*, vol 4, pp390–405

Ludwig, D. (2001) 'Can we exploit sustainably?', in J. Reynolds, G. Mace, K. Redford and J. Robinson (eds) *Conservation of Exploited Species*, Cambridge University Press, Cambridge, pp 16–38

Mace, P. and Gabriel, W. (1999) 'Evolution, scope, and current applications of the precautionary approach in fisheries', proceedings, Fifth National Marine Fisheries Service National Stock Assessment Workshop, US, published as *National Oceanic and Atmospheric Administration Tech Memo* NMFS-F/SPO-40

MacGarvin, M. (2002) 'Fisheries: taking stock', in P. Harremoes, D. Gee, M. MacGarvin, A. Stirling, J. Keys, B. Wynne and S. Guedes Vas (eds) *Late Lessons from Early Warning: The Precautionary Principle in the Twentieth Century*, Earthscan, London, pp10–25

Mahsood, E. (2005) 'Protecting biodiversity "may clash with pursuit of MDGs"', *SciDevNet News*, no 19, May, Science and Development Network, http://www.scidev.net/News/index.cfm?fuseaction=readNews&itemid=2100&langu age=1

Marceau, G. (2002) 'The precautionary principle under WTO law', in UNEP/GEN *Precaution: From Rio to Johannesburg. Proceedings of a Geneva Environment Network Roundtable*, United Nations Environment Programme/Geneva Environment Network, Geneva, pp23–28

Marchant, G. and Mossman, K. (2004) *Arbitrary and Capricious? The Precautionary Principle in the European Courts*, American Enterprise Institute for Public Policy Research, Washington, DC

May, R. (2000) 'The dimensions of life on earth', in P. Raven (ed) *Nature and Human Society*, US NAS Press, Washington, DC, pp30–45

McNeely, J., Mooney, H., Neville, L., Schei, P. and Waage, J. (2001) *Global Strategy on Invasive Alien Species*, Global Invasive Species Programme, IUCN, Gland and Cambridge

Millennium Ecosystem Assessment (2005a) *Ecosystems and Human Well-Being: Biodiversity Synthesis*, World Resources Institute, Washington, DC

Millennium Ecosystem Assessment (2005b) *Millennium Ecosystem Assessment Synthesis Report*, pre-publication final draft approved by MA Board 23 March 2005, Millennium Ecosystem Assessment, Washington, DC

Mohammed-Katerere, J. (2001) 'The precautionary principle: implications for development and poverty alleviation in Southern Africa', *IUCN Environmental Law Programme Newsletter*, no 1, pp7–9

Morris, J. (2000) *Rethinking Risk and the Precautionary Principle*, Butterworth Heinemann, Oxford

Moyle, B. (2004) *Uncertainty, Complexity and the Precautionary Principle*, presentation to the Workshop on The Precautionary Principle in Natural Resource Management and Biodiversity Conservation, Manila, 21–23 June 2004, www.pprinciple.net

Myers, N. and Raffensperger, C. (eds) (forthcoming) *Precautionary Tools for Reshaping Environmental Policy*, MIT Press, Cambridge, MA

Nollkaemper, A. (1996) 'What you risk reveals what you value, and other dilemmas encountered in the legal assaults on risks', in D. Freestone and E. Hay (eds) *The*

*Precautionary Principle and International Law: The Challenge of Implementation*, Kluwer Law International, The Hague, pp73–94

O'Riordan, T. and Cameron, J. (eds) (1994) *Interpreting the Precautionary Principle*, Earthscan, London

President's Council on Sustainable Development (1996) *Sustainable America: A New Consensus*, President's Council on Sustainable Development, Washington, DC. Available at http://clinton2.nara.gov/PCSD/Publications/index.html

Redford, K. and Feinsinger, P. (2001) 'The half-empty forest: sustainable use and the ecology of interactions'. In J. Reynolds, G. Mace, K. Redford and J. Robinson (eds) *Conservation of Exploited Species*. Cambridge University Press, Cambridge, pp350–399

Risby, L. (2002) *Defining Landscapes, Power and Participation. An Examination of a National Park Planning Process for Queen Elizabeth National Park, Uganda*, PhD thesis, Cambridge University, Cambridge

Roe, D. and Elliott, J. (2004) 'Poverty reduction and biodiversity conservation: rebuilding the bridges', *Oryx*, vol 38, pp137–39

Sanderson, S. and Redford, K. (2003) 'Contested relationships between biodiversity conservation and poverty alleviation', *Oryx*, vol 37, pp389–90

Sandin, P. (1999) 'Dimensions of the precautionary principle', *Human and Ecological Risk Assessment*, vol 5, pp889–907

Sandin, P. (2004) 'The precautionary principle and the concept of precaution', *Environmental Values*, vol 13, pp461–75

Stone, C. (2001) 'Is there a precautionary principle?', *Environmental Law Reporter*, no 31, pp10790–99

Stork, N. (1997) 'Measuring global biodiversity and its decline', in M. Reaka-Kudla, D. Wilson and E. Wilson (eds) *Biodiversity II: Understanding and Protecting Our Biological Resources*, Joseph Henry Press, Washington, DC, pp41–68

Sunstein, C. (2002) 'The paralyzing principle', *Regulation*, Winter 2002–2003, pp32–37

Tickner, J. and Geiser, K. (2004) 'The precautionary principle stimulus for solutions- and alternatives-based environmental policy', *Environmental Impact Assessment Review*, vol 24, no 7–8, pp801–24

Tickner, J. and Raffensperger, C. (1999) *The Precautionary Principle in Action: A Handbook*, Science and Environmental Health Network, Windsor, ND. Available at www.sehn.org/rtfdocs/handbook-rtf.rtf

Trouwborst, A. (2002) *Evolution and Status of the Precautionary Principle in International Law*, Aspen Publishers, New York

Walters, L., Balint, P., Desai, A. and Stewart, R. (2003) *Risk and Uncertainty in Management of the Sierra Nevada National Forests*, report to USDA Forest Service, Pacific Southwest Region, George Mason University, Fairfax, Virginia

Wiener, J. B. (2002) 'Precaution in a multi-risk world', in D. Paustenbach (ed) *The Risk Assessment of Human and Environmental Health Hazards*, Wiley-Interscience, Hoboken, New Jersey, pp1509–31

Wiener, J. B. (2003) 'Whose precaution after all? A comment on the comparison and evolution of risk regulatory systems', *Duke Journal of Comparative and International Law*, vol 13, pp207–62

Zaccagnini, M., Cloquell, S., Fernandez, E., González, C., Lichtenstein, A. N., Panigati, J. L., Rabinovitch, J. and Tomasini, D. (2001) *Analytic Framework for Assessing Factors that Influence Sustainability of Uses of Wild Living Natural Resources*, IUCN Sustainable Use Specialist Group, Gland, Switzerland. Available at http://www.iucn.org/themes/ssc/susg/docs/analytic_framework_nov01.pdf

# The Precautionary Principle in International Regimes and Policy Processes

# 2

# Forest Policy, the Precautionary Principle and Sustainable Forest Management

*Adrian Newton and Sara Oldfield*

## INTRODUCTION

In recent decades, the precautionary principle has become increasingly accepted as a component of environmental management and associated policy, aiming to avoid environmental harm in the absence of scientific certainty about the potential impacts of human activities. Although the principle superficially appears sensible and rational, its application has proved to be highly controversial, leading to an active and ongoing debate (Sunstein, 2003).

This case study reviews the application of the precautionary principle in relation to the forest sector. We first examine the degree to which reference to the precautionary principle is made in existing international law or policy instruments relating to forests. We then describe recent developments in policy and practice relating to sustainable forest management, examine to what extent such developments are consistent with the precautionary principle, and explore whether the precautionary approach should be adopted as a tenet in forest management. Finally, we consider the application of the precautionary principle to tree species, with particular reference to the sustainable management of the commercially valuable and ecologically vulnerable species, mahogany (*Swietenia macrophylla*).

# TO WHAT EXTENT HAS THE PRECAUTIONARY PRINCIPLE BEEN APPLIED TO THE FOREST SECTOR?

Although the precautionary approach is explicitly referred to under Principle 15 of the Rio Declaration on Environment and Development proclaimed at the United Nations Conference on Environment and Development (UNCED) in 1992, as noted by Brunnée and Nollkaemper (1996) the Statement of Forest Principles[1] made at the event makes no reference to precaution. Neither is it featured in the International Tropical Timber Agreement, the Convention on Biological Diversity (CBD) Programme of Work on Forests (see Decisions IV/7, V/4, VI/9, VI/22), the Global Strategy for Plant Conservation (Decision VI/9), or the deliberations of the United Nations Forum on Forests (UNFF), the International Forum on Forests (IFF) or the International Panel on Forests (IPF) (see Cooney, 2004). We examined a wide range of documents and text on forests from the Global Environment Facility, the UN Framework Convention on Climate Change, the Montreal Process, the UN Food and Agriculture Organization (FAO) Committee on Forestry, the International Tropical Timber Organisation, the International Conference on the Contribution of Criteria and Indicators for Sustainable Forest Management: The Way Forward (CICI 2003), and the Johannesburg Plan of Implementation (para 45). None contained explicit reference to precaution, with the exception of a single reference made within an information note to the CBD on the status and trends of, and major threats to, forest biological diversity (UNEP/CBD/SBSTTA/7/INF/3), which highlights the 'value of following the precautionary principle when there is a reasonable doubt about the impacts of human activities on a forest ecosystem'. The World Bank's Revised Strategy and Operational Policy on Forests (World Bank, 2004) states that the 'fundamental guidance given to Bank staff and clients is that in assessing the significance of change they must take a precautionary approach'.

It is perhaps surprising that so few of these policy statements make any reference to the precautionary principle or approach. This can be attributed, at least in part, to the prevailing paradigm of state sovereignty over forest resources (Brunnée and Nollkaemper, 1996), illustrated by Principle 2 of the Rio Declaration, which notes that 'States have ... the sovereign right to exploit their own resources pursuant to their own environmental and development policies'. This paradigm has certainly dominated development of international forest policy over the past decade, and may account for the slow progress in the development of an international forest law as advocated by Brunnée and Nollkaemper (1996). However, discussions relating to international forest law are ongoing within UNFF; an Ad Hoc Expert Group met in September 2004 to discuss a legal framework on all types of forests for consideration at UNFF5. Interestingly, the report of this meeting (UNFF, 2005) made no reference to the precautionary principle, despite the fact that Brunnée and Nollkaemper (1996) considered that it should become part of any emerging international forest law.

At the national level, a number of countries have incorporated the precautionary principle within policies relating to forests, including Peru, Cameroon and Mozambique (Cooney, 2004). As noted by Cooney (2004), Australia has been pre-eminent in referring to precaution within environmental policies, and this includes those relating explicitly to forests. The 1995 National Forest Policy Statement states that, 'in keeping with the "precautionary principle" the State Governments will undertake continuing research and long term monitoring so that adverse impacts that may arise can be detected and redressed through revised codes of practice and management plans' (Commonwealth of Australia, 1995). In addition, the most comprehensive study of the Australian forest sector undertaken to date (Resource Assessment Commission, 1992) also indicated that it is 'important that the "precautionary principle" be followed when managing timber harvesting in multiple use native forests'. The Commonwealth government and some state governments have entered into a number of Regional Forest Agreements (RFAs) that provide a framework for forest management and the implementation of the National Forest Policy Statement. Some of these RFAs also make explicit reference to the precautionary principle; for example the RFA for the South West Forest Region of Western Australia states that 'planning and management of forests should be guided by the precautionary principle'.

We believe that the recent focus on sustainable forest management in international forums may be a key factor responsible for the lack of reference to the precautionary principle in international forest policy. It is significant that in the Australian policy statements cited above, the precautionary principle is referred to in the context of ecologically sustainable forest management. This implies an interpretation of the principle that potentially permits a degree of forest use. The definition and assessment of sustainable forest management (SFM) has dominated forest policy discussions at the international level since UNCED in 1992, and therefore any consideration of the relevance of the precautionary principle to forests should be placed in this context. Below, we provide a summary of these policy developments, and then explore the potential links between SFM and the precautionary principle.

## DEVELOPING CRITERIA, INDICATORS AND STANDARDS FOR SFM

The definition and assessment of SFM has been the focus of intense international discussion since the development of the Forest Principles and chapter 11 of Agenda 21, which called for the identification of criteria and indicators (C&I) for evaluating progress in national efforts towards the management, conservation and sustainable development of all types of forests. Criteria may be defined as the essential elements or major components that define SFM, whereas indicators are qualitative or quantitative parameters of a criterion that provide a basis for assessing the status of, and trends in, forests and forest management (UNFF, 2004). Nine regional or international criteria and indicator processes have been developed, involving the participation of 149 countries (UNFF, 2004). Countries are increasingly using C&I as a framework for formulating national forest policy and strategic planning, monitoring of SFM, and supporting stakeholder participation in forest planning and decision-making (UNFF, 2004).

Most processes have focused on developing C&I for application at the regional or national level. However, increasing attention is being paid to development of C&I at the level of the forest management unit (FMU), driven by the growth of interest in forest certification.

Forest certification is essentially a tool for promoting responsible forestry practices. It involves certification of forest management operations by an independent third party against a set of standards. Typically, forest products (generally timber but also non-timber forest products) from certified forests are labelled so that consumers can identify them as having been derived from well-managed sources. At least at a general level, the standards developed by certification bodies can be viewed as supporting SFM, although not all certifying organizations use this precise terminology.

## SFM AND THE PRECAUTIONARY PRINCIPLE

We will now consider the links between the precautionary principle and SFM. First, we examine whether precaution is explicitly mentioned by any of the C&I processes or by certification standards. With respect to the nine C&I processes mentioned above, we were unable to find any reference to the precautionary principle, with the exception of the African Timber Organization process, which states under sub-indicator 1.1.12.3: 'at the national level, decisions relating to forests of high conservation value are taken within the context of the precautionary principle' (ATO/ITTO, 2003). With respect to the four North American forest certification organizations (the Sustainable Forestry Initiative (SFI) Programme, American Tree Farm System (ATFS), Canadian Standards Association (CSA) Sustainable Forest Management Programme, and the Forest Stewardship Council (FSC)), only the FSC explicitly refers to the precautionary principle. Principle 9 of the FSC Principles and Criteria, which relates to the maintenance of 'high conservation value forests', states that 'decisions regarding high conservation value forests shall always be considered in the context of a precautionary approach', and that 'the management plan shall include and implement specific measures that ensure the maintenance and/or enhancement of the applicable conservation attributes consistent with the precautionary approach' (FSC, 2004, subparagraph 9.3).

The concept of 'high conservation value forest' as first defined by FSC is increasingly being used in conservation and natural resource planning and advocacy, and considered in government policies (Jennings et al, 2003). Identification of high conservation value forest, or HCVF, is seen as important in ensuring that rational management decisions are consistent with protection of a forest area's important environmental and social values. There is a growing realization that the management of HCVF for timber production may be very difficult to achieve in practice without a significant shift in how the forest is managed and in the actions of forest operators.

Our brief overview suggests that the precautionary principle is not explicitly considered either by most SFM C&I processes or by many forest certification bodies. However, could precaution be considered as an implicit part of SFM? In fact, the links between SFM and the precautionary principle have received very little attention either from policy-makers or researchers. The World Conservation Union (IUCN), the Program on Forests (PROFOR) and the World Bank (IUCN et al, 2004) provide a discussion paper on the relationship between ecosystem approaches and SFM, arising out of the fact that the CBD has emphasized the importance of the former as a 'strategy for the integrated management of land, water and living resources that promotes conservation and sustainable use in an equitable way'. According to the definition adopted by the CBD (Decision V/6), 'the ecosystem approach requires adaptive management to deal with the complex and dynamic nature of ecosystems and the absence of complete knowledge or understanding of their functioning... Management must be adaptive in order to be able to respond to such uncertainties'.

As pointed out by Cooney (2004), according to these definitions the ecosystem approach will usually involve precautionary management, but need not necessarily do so. IUCN, PROFOR and the World Bank (IUCN et al, 2004) also point out that the ecosystem approach draws heavily on the precautionary principle, and suggest that it represents a broadening of the concept of SFM as currently defined by C&I sets, giving greater emphasis to landscape functionality, integration of conservation and development, and limiting the damage that resource extraction can cause to natural resource systems. Other comparisons between SFM and the ecosystem approach similarly suggest that the scope of the latter is broader, with greater emphasis on cross-sectoral integration and the interaction between habitat types or ecosystems within a landscape (Ellenberg, 2003; Schlaepfer et al, 2004). In contrast, Wilkie et al (2003) suggest that ecosystem management and SFM express similar goals and could readily be integrated. However, the precautionary principle received little or no explicit consideration by any of these authors.

Such comparisons suggest that the concepts of the ecosystem approach and SFM are likely to become more closely integrated in future, something that the CBD has explicitly called for (Decision VI/12). This integration could potentially increase the role of the precautionary principle within SFM, for example by explicitly including references to the principle within sets of C&I or within forest certification standards.

However, we believe that the precautionary principle is already implicitly included within current definitions of SFM. This contention depends critically on how the precautionary principle is defined. Cooney (2004) provides a thorough account of different definitions of the principle, noting that it has been interpreted in various ways. As a minimum, Cooney (2004) suggests that 'the precautionary principle will require that scientific certainty of environmental harm is not required as a prerequisite for taking action to avert it'.

It is generally recognized that forest management operations (especially the harvesting of timber) can represent a threat to the environment, for example by loss of genetic resources or populations of the target species, negative impacts on associated species, and changes in ecological functioning of the forest. Commercial timber harvesting is commonly cited as a major threat to forest ecosystems (see for example the Ad Hoc Technical Expert Group on Forest Biological Diversity report (2001), UNEP/CBD/ SBSTTA/7/6).

The perceived harm from timber harvesting led to the call for SFM in the early 1990s. While the general principles of silviculture are well established, the environmental impacts of forestry operations are often uncertain. For example, the specific effects of harvesting a particular tree species on the populations of other organisms associated with that species are often very poorly understood. Given this, it could be argued that precautionary measures should be taken in such circumstances. The key issue, then, is whether SFM C&I or forest certification standards represent precautionary measures. Our belief is that when such indicators or standards are applied at the local scale and directly influence forest management decisions, then this is precisely what they represent. In other words, these indicators or standards actually provide a means of operationalizing the precautionary approach.

Our view is that SFM is based on the concept of using the precautionary principle as a guiding rule to safeguard the integrity of forest ecosystems when undertaking management activities (Wang, 2004). Is this contention borne out by current forest management practice? In the following section, we critically examine current approaches to forest management to identify whether or not they are consistent with the precautionary principle.

# ARE CURRENT APPROACHES TO SUSTAINABLE FOREST MANAGEMENT PRECAUTIONARY?

A large number of countries are now engaging in C&I processes aiming to support SFM (UNFF, 2004), and over 30 countries or initiatives are developing national standards and schemes for forest certification, many of which are based on C&I sets. However, the extent to which forest management actually complies with these standards is difficult to evaluate (Leslie, 2004). Based on a recent review by Rametsteiner and Simula (2003), it can be inferred that the development of C&I and forest standards has had a limited but generally positive impact on forest management to date, but that these impacts vary between geographic regions.

To what extent are these impacts consistent with the precautionary approach? This depends on the precise C&I and standards adopted. Holvoet and Muys (2004) provide a detailed comparison of forest standards developed to date, drawing on those generated by both certification bodies and C&I processes. Although the precautionary approach is not referred to explicitly in this analysis, the research provides a valuable synthesis with which to examine the extent to which precautionary approaches are currently incorporated within SFM standards.

In total, the reference standard presented by Holvoet and Muys (2004) covers seven principles, 47 criteria and 308 indicators. They include:

- assessment of whether policy and planning include all necessary elements for monitoring and evaluation of current management;
- existence of procedures for monitoring damage to forest resources caused by a comprehensive set of 16 different threats;
- assessment of whether adequate measures for the prevention of damage exist, considering individually a comprehensive set of 16 different threats;
- assessment of the area or percentage of forest cover with disturbed ecological processes, disturbed canopy, or any other form of ecosystem damage;
- existence of procedures in case of environmental disasters;
- monitoring of regeneration of each harvested wood forest product;
- existence of procedures for the determination of terrestrial biological diversity and its changes;
- existence and implementation of measures for the minimization of negative impacts of forest management on biological diversity;
- monitoring of the use of exotic tree species and their impacts on the environment;
- existence and implementation of regulations for the use of biocides and fertilizers;
- existence of measures for preserving or improving forest stability;
- existence and implementation of regulations to leave parts of the forest estate undisturbed;
- monitoring of the protected forest area and its changes;
- existence of measures to maintain soil fertility and site productivity; and
- monitoring of the effects of sustainable forest management on the water cycle.

We propose that these forest standards are consistent with the precautionary approach, and could directly support its implementation. According to Cooney (2004), precaution 'shifts the balance in decision making toward "prudent foresight", in favour of monitoring, preventing or mitigating uncertain potential threats' – issues that are explicitly incorporated in the 'reference standard' referred to above. Critically, there is no requirement for forest managers to demonstrate certainty of environmental harm arising out of forest management interventions as a prerequisite for taking action to avert it. The forest standard lists the precautionary measures that should be taken in forest management, even though the cause-and-effect relationships have not been fully established scientifically. Interestingly, there is one issue absent from deliberations relating to standards for SFM that is widespread in the discourse relating to the precautionary approach. This is the need to assess risks or uncertainties. In fact, risk assessment appears to play a relatively small role in forest management, but this does not undermine the commitment to precaution enshrined in the forest standards highlighted above.

It can therefore be argued that current approaches designed to support SFM are precautionary in nature, even if relatively few forests are currently being managed according to the specified standards. This raises a key issue: whether originating from involvement in a C&I process or in a certification initiative, engagement with SFM is currently voluntary and therefore constitutes an example of 'soft law' (Hickey, 2004). Is this enough to ensure that the precautionary principle is adopted in forest management? More fundamentally, should the role of the precautionary principle in forest management be strengthened, for example by its incorporation in 'hard law' relating to forests? These issues will be considered in the following section.

## SHOULD THE PRECAUTIONARY PRINCIPLE INFORM FOREST MANAGEMENT?

Few researchers have critically examined the practical application of the precautionary principle to forest management. This is perhaps ironic, given that the concept was first incorporated in national law (in Germany) as a result of concern about forest dieback resulting from aerial pollution (Myers, 2002). We are aware of only one example that has investigated this issue in detail. Walters et al (2003) describe an examination of decision-making relating to the management of Sierra Nevada national forests in a policy environment characterized by multiple and conflicting risks and uncertainties. These researchers addressed the uncertainties facing decision-makers in the region, differentiating between scientific uncertainties (arising out of inadequate scientific understanding of ecological systems), administrative or implementation uncertainty (referring to the dynamics of the political environment under which decisions are made), and the stochastic uncertainty of events that are largely unpredictable and uncontrollable, such as fires caused by lightning.

As a result of their research, Walters et al (2003) conclude that planning the management of the Sierra Nevada national forest is a 'wicked' problem because not only is scientific uncertainty high, but agreement on values held by different stakeholders is low, resulting in a need for significant dialogue among scientists, stakeholders and decision-makers. Wicked problems may be defined by the following characteristics (Allen and Gould, 1986):

- each stakeholder defines the problem differently, therefore there is no single correct formulation of the problem;
- outcomes are not scientifically predictable;
- the decision-maker cannot know when all feasible and desirable solutions have been explored;
- the resources of ecosystems and the capabilities of organizations combine with stakeholder demands in idiosyncratic ways, and therefore any solution is likely to be unique and one-off; and
- solutions are generally better or worse, rather than true or false.

It is likely that the management of many forest areas would fit the definition of a 'wicked' problem, particularly given the multiple uses and values of forest ecosystems and the conflicting demands of different stakeholders. The conclusions of Walters et al (2003) regarding the precautionary principle are therefore particularly noteworthy. They suggest that the principle does not provide a useful basis for decision-making in the context of wicked problems, which have multiple uncertainties affecting all decision options, including the status quo. In such cases, application of the precautionary principle may lead to contradictory recommendations when applied to separate components of the problem, leading to 'decision-making paralysis'. Because it is fundamentally risk averse, the precautionary principle can limit flexibility in policy choices and thus conflict with adaptive management. For example, uncertainty about possible adverse outcomes would lead to potentially risky treatments or management strategies being avoided, even though they may be preferable to the status quo according to some stakeholders.

To illustrate the difficulties that can occur when the precautionary principle is applied to wicked problems, Walters et al (2003) highlight the fact that fire management and old growth forest habitat protection are two key issues in this case study. Both are associated with risks and uncertainties. In some cases, a cautious approach designed to reduce risk of adverse outcomes in one of these two areas may increase risk in the other. This results in potential conflicts, for example between the fuel management strategy for the forest and protection of a key species, the California spotted owl. A cautious approach to management of forest habitat for this owl, for example, could directly lead to an increase in fire risk. The research also indicated that the precautionary approach could place constraints on the ability to trade off short-term losses for long-term gains. For example, if forest management and fuel treatment strategies were identified that were likely to cause modest losses in owl habitat over the short term but significant gains over the longer term, application of the precautionary principle would preclude or severely restrict implementation of such actions (Walters et al, 2003; Mealey et al, this volume).

Interestingly, surveys of stakeholder opinion indicated that stakeholders generally do not favour strict application of the precautionary principle, but prefer some form of adaptive management of the forests. Stakeholders generally appeared to be willing to accept some adverse outcomes resulting from management interventions in order to learn about the consequences of implementing such decisions. Overall, the research highlights that the precautionary approach limits options for adaptive management and thereby reduces the likelihood that overall management goals can be achieved (Walters et al, 2003). It should be noted, however, that Walters et al (2003) adopt a relatively strong definition of the precautionary principle, implying that if consequences of a proposed activity are uncertain and potentially harmful, the activity should not be undertaken until further research clarifies the risks. According to Cooney (2004), in some sectors (such as fisheries) the precautionary approach is not seen as strongly restrictive or prohibitive, but is seen as consistent with and contributing to adaptive management.

The idea that the precautionary principle leads to decision-making 'paralysis' is further explored by Sunstein (2003), who suggests that the main problem with the concept when defined 'strongly' is that it offers no guidance to decision-makers, forbidding all courses of action, including inaction. Examples where such paralysis appears to have occurred are available in the forest conservation literature, such as the case of Prince Albert National Park (PANP) in Saskatchewan (LeRoy, 2003). Such problems with the practical implementation of the precautionary principle raise questions regarding the usefulness of the concept for supporting forest management and conservation.

## THE PRECAUTIONARY PRINCIPLE AND THE MANAGEMENT OF MAHOGANY

We turn now to explore the implementation of the principle in the practical management of a high value timber species, mahogany. Management of forests can clearly be for a wide range of uses, and in the development of SFM the emphasis has generally been on the management of forests for the production of timber. Within this context the emphasis is on management at the ecosystem level rather than species level. Traditionally, however, foresters have been concerned with sustained yield using various techniques developed to promote regeneration at a species level. Where there is concern about the conservation status of a timber species this introduces a species conservation element into its management and implies the need for a precautionary approach to production. Furthermore, commercial timber species may be considered as keystone species. As noted in CBD information note UNEP/CBS/SBSTTA/7/INF/3:

> *Critical levels of biodiversity loss/change which can affect forest ecosystem functioning and, in turn, the goods and services provided by forests, are still hard to discern, and this needs to be a focus for future work. Keystone species or structures and functional groups need to be identified and validated in order to develop reliable indicators. While it is likely that some degree of biodiversity loss in some situations will have little or no long term effect on other goods and services, as long as the forest remains relatively intact, the linkages between biodiversity and ecosystem functions and the critical thresholds of impacts on biodiversity loss must be understood. This reinforces the value of following the precautionary principle when there is a reasonable doubt about the impacts of human activities on a forest ecosystem.*

Mahogany *Swietenia macrophylla* is a widespread species (see Box 2.1) that is commonly considered an ecological and economic keystone species of its tropical forest biome. Mahogany has declined in significant parts of its range as a result of forest clearance and logging. As a general objective, management of mahogany *Swietenia macrophylla* should reflect the need to make adequate

## Box 2.1 Biological, ecological and geographical characteristics of *Swietenia macrophylla*

*Swietenia macrophylla* is a large deciduous tree that frequently grows to over 30m and reaches a diameter at breast height of over 1.5m. Individual mahogany trees may live for several hundred years. The seeds are relatively heavy and generally do not disperse far. Seed viability is only retained for a few months, not long enough for the creation of a soil seed bank. Germination is thought to be stimulated by rainfall rather than availability of light. Despite the commercial importance of mahogany, detailed information on its distribution, abundance, ecology and management requirements is surprisingly limited. The species has a wide geographical and ecological range, growing naturally in a broad range of tropical dry and tropical wet forests on a large variety of soil types. It is distributed from Mexico southward into western South America and extending over a broad crescent area across southern Amazonia, covering 235 million ha of forest (CITES Proposal 12.50, 2002). Within this range, distribution data is variable in quality and quantity.

Within its natural range, stocking density (i.e. local abundance) of mahogany is extremely variable and its distribution is patchy. Mahogany is sparsely distributed in many forests but high population densities have been recorded in some areas. This clearly has implications for the impact of logging and the sustainability of mahogany extraction at a local scale. In addition, mahogany seedlings are relatively demanding of light. As a result, mahogany does not readily regenerate under a dense forest canopy, as may often be found in undisturbed moist tropical forests. In such cases, large-scale disturbance, such as that caused by fire, flooding or storms, may be required for substantial mahogany regeneration (Brown et al, 2003).

provision for conservation of the species and its genetic resources while at the same time maintaining supplies of timber and the income that this generates. Management also needs to meet international requirements as set out by CITES, which requires that the role of the species in its ecosystem be taken into account when determining exports to be sustainable. Arguably, management also needs to meet the expectations of environmentally conscious consumers in importing countries. The management needs for the species and its forest ecosystems therefore demonstrate a 'wicked problem' with all the characteristics defined by Allen and Gould (1986).

Baseline information for use in formulating policy prescriptions and the practical management of mahogany stocks is somewhat limited, making the application of the precautionary principle both relevant and challenging. Precautionary approaches can be applied to the management of the species in a variety of ways and at different levels from international policy deliberations to local site-level decisions. The importance of the precautionary principle in relation to the management of *Swietenia macrophylla* is pointed out by Barreto (2004), referring to the situation in the Brazilian Amazon. He reports that there is limited information on mahogany stocks, but there are concerns nevertheless because all mahogany forest in this region is economically accessible for harvesting. The forests also face pressures from occupation and destruction by fire, agriculture and mining. At the same time there is limited experience of effective management. He suggests that the practical application of the precautionary principle through management could include the creation of reserves and measures to ensure regeneration of the species at the local level.

As set out in this paper, SFM can be viewed as inherently precautionary, providing the means to operationalize the precautionary principle for forest management purposes. The majority of mahogany entering into international trade is, however, currently from unmanaged natural forests (Mayhew and Newton, 1998), and countries are faced with major challenges in improving the supply of sustainably managed mahogany. Although most mahogany-producing countries have laws and regulations in place to support sustainable forest management as well as specific regulations for mahogany, major problems remain in their practical implementation. Given the actual status of sustainable forest management on the ground, the creation of reserves or other forms of protected areas containing sufficient stocks of mahogany, as advocated by Barreto (2004) and also by Kometter et al (2004), is desirable as a precautionary measure until management of timber production is improved.

Where a forest site is independently certified as sustainably managed then the mahogany extracted from it can be considered to be sustainably sourced in a precautionary manner. Independent forest certification is starting to become significant as a proportion of mahogany production in certain countries, for example in Guatemala where mahogany is the second major timber species exported in terms of volume and value. However, less than 1 per cent of the range of mahogany is currently harvested according to FSC standards (Kometter et al, 2004).

# THE REQUIREMENTS OF CITES

Mahogany *Swietenia macrophylla* has been included in Appendix II of CITES since 2003. The primary aim of this convention is to protect listed species against overexploitation caused by international trade. Determining when international trade is likely to be non-detrimental to the survival of a species is essential to achieving the aims of the Convention. For species listed in Appendix II, export requires the prior granting of an export permit that can only be issued when, inter alia, a Scientific Authority of the State of export has advised that such export will not be detrimental to the survival of that species (Article IV 2(a)).

In some cases these 'non-detriment findings' (NDFs) are based on annual export quotas. The Scientific Authority is also required to monitor exports and advise on measures to limit exports in order to maintain a species throughout its range at a level consistent with its role in the ecosystems in which it occurs and well above the level at which that species might become eligible for inclusion in Appendix I. The Scientific Authority is thus required to ensure that an Appendix II species is managed in such a way as to allow exports on a sustainable basis that will not damage the conservation status of the species or its ecological functioning.

Since international agreement was reached to include *Swietenia macrophylla* in Appendix II of CITES, considerable attention has been given to the development of procedures for making NDFs for the species. This was considered at the Second meeting of the CITES Mahogany Working Group held in Belem in October 2003. A paper prepared for this meeting suggests that:

> NDFs *for* Swietenia macrophylla *should be based as far as possible on national forest policy and legislation in order to harmonize CITES and forestry requirements. Given the current status of natural forest management in the countries where* Swietenia macrophylla *occurs it would seem appropriate to make NDFs in a progressively refined way. In each country the NDF may initially be a pragmatic determination based on known mahogany stocks and levels of trade. As increased information becomes available and sustainable forest management policies, monitoring mechanisms and controls are institutionalized, more detailed NDFs could be made. It is recommended that three components should form the basis for developing NDFs for mahogany:*
> 1  *National or regional level stock assessment as a basis for determining overall quantities for export, for example through an annual export quota.*
> 2  *Requirements for management plans for forest management units from which mahogany is harvested for export. Management plans should demonstrate provisions for sustainable management of the forest unit and mahogany stocks as a prerequisite for determining that export will be non-detrimental.*
> 3  *Monitoring of mahogany harvesting in the forest management units and timber exports against the overall export quota.* (Oldfield and Newton, 2003)

The paper also suggests that for an NDF to be made at the local level, for example for a specific forest management unit (FMU), the criteria listed below should be considered:

- the existence of a management plan for the FMU that demonstrates a sustainable approach to harvesting, based on an adequate inventory of the resource and appropriate monitoring of harvesting impacts;
- the presence of adequate regeneration, either from natural sources, or using artificial means that have been demonstrated to be successful within the area in question;
- a policy of retaining sufficient seed trees to ensure adequate regeneration following harvesting;

- demonstration that legal rights to access and harvest the timber are established; and
- the adoption of harvesting and timber extraction approaches that minimize environmental damage (for example directional felling and extraction along well-constructed logging roads). (Oldfield and Newton, 2003)

Oldfield and Newton (2003) argue that fulfilment of these criteria should be accepted as implementing an implicitly precautionary approach. Information regarding some or all of these criteria may be collected as part of an assessment of SFM undertaken in support of one of the C&I processes, or as part of the process of certifying a timber source as sustainable. These processes themselves would indicate an inherently precautionary approach was being followed. The complementarity between forest certification and CITES implementation has been noted by WWF (2002). In a paper on the subject, the World Wide Fund for Nature (WWF) states, 'with respect to practical complementarity, timber extracted from an FSC certified forest should certainly qualify for a non-detriment finding, and national Management Authorities could automatically issue export permits to timber sourced from these forests'.

Given the imperative for current implementation of CITES provisions, the setting of export quotas based on the best available information may be seen as an immediate priority. In practical terms, 'cautious' or precautionary national quotas are those that are small in relation to the likely national population size, and are likely to pose little or no risk to the conservation status of the species concerned. Export quotas can be revised annually in response to any changes to the status of the resource or to additional information becoming available.

## CONCLUSIONS

Cooney (2004) suggests that little explicit reference to the precautionary principle is made within existing international law or policy instruments relating to forests. While this finding is generally supported by our own research, we suggest that the major focus of forest policy initiatives over the past 12 years – the development of C&I and standards for SFM – is entirely consistent with the precautionary approach. Furthermore, the development of these standards offers a tool for operationalizing the precautionary principle.

In practice C&I and standards for SFM are not yet operational in most tropical forest areas where arguably the challenges of SFM are the greatest. The use of CITES for certain tropical timbers has taken place in parallel with the development of C&I and standards for SFM. Mahogany *Swietenia macrophylla* is the most commercially important timber species currently listed by the Convention. CITES provisions require a determination that trade will not be detrimental (an NDF finding) prior to international trade in the species, which can logically be linked to C&I and standards for SFM.

Basic requirements for making CITES NDFs for mahogany can include the development of a quota based on national stock assessment, harvesting of timber in accordance with an agreed management plan, and exports of managed timber to the level of the agreed quota. Management plans should be designed to ensure sustainability of harvest at a local level. Where a forest management unit has been certified by an independent forest certification body this will demonstrate that an acceptable management plan is in place and can be considered fully in accordance with the precautionary principle.

If standards and C&I for SFM are seen as the main mechanism for incorporating the precautionary principle within the forest sector, then it is likely that this will rely on 'soft' rather than 'hard' law, except in the specific instances of species listed under CITES such as mahogany. Examples of such 'soft' law include third party certification, non-binding international treaties and industry-led initiatives (Hickey, 2004), which have characterized the recent history of policy development in the forest sector. However, as noted in this review, there it little evidence that such 'soft' law initiatives have had a positive impact on forest conservation and sustainable use to date. This supports the suggestion made by Cooney (2004) that the precautionary principle will have little impact on practice unless formulated as an obligation. As international forest law continues to develop, there may be scope to refer to the precautionary principle within it, as recommended by Brunnée and Nollkaemper (1996). This could potentially strengthen application of the principle, for example by incorporating it as an obligation in 'hard' law. A key question remains: is this desirable?

As indicated here, relatively strong definitions of the precautionary principle can hinder decision-making relating to forests. Such problems are widely recognized (Sunstein, 2003). However, even weak definitions of the principle may be difficult to implement in practice. Conko (2003) points out that delaying or avoiding the introduction of some new form of technology or management intervention, in accordance with the precautionary principle, will itself introduce risks – and may even increase the risk of harm in the long term. Such perspectives raise serious doubts about the value of the principle as a tool for informing decision-making. Rather, according to Conko (2003), the precautionary principle has, in practice, often been used to legitimize a bias against change.

Such 'misuse' of the principle is further considered by Cooney (2004), who highlights its use as a 'tool of convenience' to disguise ideological objections to utilization per se, rather than sustainability concerns. According to Cooney (2004), the potential for such misuse has 'contributed to corrosion of the legitimacy of the precautionary principle within certain constituencies'. Within the forest sector, similar potential for 'misuse' exists. It is significant to note that in relation to forests, explicit reference to the precautionary principle tends to be made primarily by organizations involved in advocacy for forest conservation. For example, in its campaign for the protection of 'ancient' forests (primary, old growth, natural forests), Greenpeace International (undated) invokes the precautionary principle in calling for regional moratoria on logging and other industrial-scale projects. These moratoria are proposed to provide a means of moving from uncontrolled development of forest regions into sustainable development, but clearly the overriding objective of this campaign is increased protection for 'ancient' forests. There are direct parallels in the explicit mention of precaution in the FSC principle relating to high conservation value forests. Yet do such interpretations of the principle genuinely constitute a form of misuse?

Generally users of the precautionary principle appear to interpret it to further their own aims. It is possible that the real value of the precautionary principle may lie in its use as a tool for advocacy – by offering an alternative to the 'sustainable use' paradigm that has become so prevalent but that is largely unproven in forest management. Although sustainable use through timber production has been widely promoted as a means to conserve forests, there are instances where no timber extraction is the preferred option, whether to conserve stocks of individual species such as mahogany or more typically to conserve representative, threatened or highly biodiverse forest ecosystem types.

Differing interpretations of how the precautionary principle should be implemented in practice cut to the heart of one of the main debates in conservation: protectionism versus sustainable use. Should the principle be seen as a fundamental tool for sustainable development? Or is it more useful as a tool to promote environmental protection? As Cooney (2004) rightly points out, implementation of the principle will inevitably involve political and value-based trade-offs between biodiversity/resource conservation interests and economic or livelihood interests. However, application of the principle by itself does not help in making these trade-offs. Its value in supporting decision-making is arguably limited. As noted by Sunstein (2003), the precautionary principle seems to offer guidance only because by invoking it, decision-makers ignore some risks and focus instead only on a subset of the hazards that are at stake. What decision-makers actually require are more accurate assessments of the risks associated with different actions, so that more informed judgements can be made.

## NOTE

1   Non-Legally Binding Authoritative Statement of Principles for a Global Consensus on the Management, Conservation and Sustainable Development of All Types of Forests (1992). Available at www.un.org/documents/ga/conf151/aconf1526-3annex3.htm

## REFERENCES

Allen, G. M. and Gould, E. Jr (1986) 'Complexity, wickedness, and public forests', *Journal of Forestry*, vol 84, no 4, pp20–23

ATO/ITTO (2003) *Principles, Criteria and Indicators for the Sustainable Management of African Natural Tropical Forests*, ITTO Policy Development Series, no 14, African

Timber Organization, Libreville, Gabon, and International Tropical Timber Organization, Yokohama, Japan

Barreto, P. (2004) 'Presentation given at the ITTO Workshop on capacity building for the implementation of CITES Appendix II listing of Mahogany (*Swietenia macrophylla*)', 17–21 May, Pucallpa, Peru

Brown, N., Jennings, S. and Clements, T. (2003) 'The ecology, silviculture and biogeography of mahogany (*Swietenia macrophylla*): a critical review of the evidence', *Perspectives in Plant Ecology, Evolution and Systematics*, vol 6, nos 1, 2, pp37–49

Brunnée, J. and Nollkaemper, A. (1996) 'Between the forests and the trees – an emerging international forest law', *Environmental Conservation*, vol 23, no 4, pp 307–14

Commonwealth of Australia (1995) 'National Forest Policy Statement: a new future for Australia's forests', Commonwealth of Australia, Canberra

Conko, G. (2003) 'Safety, risk and the precautionary principle: rethinking precautionary approaches to the regulation of transgenic plants', *Transgenic Research*, vol 12, no 6, pp639–47

Cooney, R. (2004) *The Precautionary Principle in Biodiversity Conservation and Natural Resource Management: An Issues Paper for Policy-makers, Researchers and Practitioners*, IUCN Policy and Global Change Series, no 2, IUCN, Gland, Switzerland and Cambridge, UK

Ellenberg, H. (2003). *Ecosystem Approach Versus Sustainable Forest Management – Attempt at a Comparison*, Federal Research Centre for Forestry and Forest Products, Hamburg

FSC (2004) *FSC Principles and Criteria for Forest Stewardship*, FSC reference code: FSC-STD-01-001 (April 2004), Forest Stewardship Council, A.C., Bonn

Greenpeace International (undated) *M for Moratoria*, Greenpeace International, Amsterdam, www.greenpeace.org/international en/

Hickey, G. M. (2004) 'Regulatory approaches to monitoring sustainable forest management', *International Forestry Review*, vol 6, no 2, pp89–98

Holvoet B. and Muys, B. (2004) 'Sustainable forest management worldwide: a comparative assessment of standards', *International Forestry Review*, vol 6, no 2, pp 99–122

IUCN, PROFOR and the World Bank (2004) 'Ecosystem approaches and sustainable forest management', a discussion paper for the UNFF Secretariat prepared by the Forest Conservation Programme of IUCN, Gland, Switzerland, the Program on Forests (PROFOR), Washington, DC and the World Bank, New York

Jennings, S., Nussbaum, R., Judd, N. and Evans, T. (2003) *The High Conservation Value Forest Toolkit*, Edition 1, Proforest, Oxford

Kometter, R. F., Martinez, M., Blundell, A. G., Gullison, R. E., Steininger, M. K. and Rice, R. E. (2004) 'Impacts of unsustainable mahogany logging in Bolivia and Peru', *Ecology and Society*, vol 9, no 1, p12, www.ecologyandsociety.org/vol9/iss1/art12

LeRoy, S. (2003) 'An SOS for Canada's Parks: solving the precautionary problems of national park management', *Fraser Forum*, July, pp30–32

Leslie, A. D. (2004) 'The impacts and mechanics of certification', *International Forestry Review*, vol 6, no 1, pp30–39

Mayhew, J. E., and Newton, A. C. (1998) *The Silviculture of Mahogany*, CABI Publications, Wallingford, UK

Myers, N. (2002) 'The precautionary principle puts values first', *Bulletin of Science, Technology & Society*, vol 22, no 3, June, pp210–19

National Forest Policy Statement (1995) *A New Focus For Australia's Forests.*, 2nd edition, Australian Government Department of Agriculture, Fisheries and Forestry, Canberra. Available at www.affa.gov.au/

Oldfield, S. F. and Newton, A. (2003) *Technical Paper on the Making of Non-detriment Findings for Trade in* Swietenia macrophylla *in Compliance with Article IV of CITES*, Unpublished report prepared on behalf of the IUCN/SSC Global Trees Specialist Group for the CITES Secretariat for presentation at the 2nd Mahogany Working Group meeting, Belem (Brazil), 6–8 October 2003

Rametsteiner, E. and Simula, M. (2003) 'Forest certification – an instrument to promote sustainable forest management?', *Journal of Environmental Management*, vol 67, no 1, pp87–98

Resource Assessment Commission (1992), *Forest and Timber Inquiry Final Report*, vol 1, AGPS, Canberra

Schlaepfer, R., Gorgerat, V. and Bütler, R. (2004) *A Comparative Analysis between Sustainable Forest Management (SFM) and the Ecosystem Approach (EA)*, Report for the Swiss Agency for Environment, Forests and Landscape, Swiss Forest Agency, Laboratory of Ecosystem Management, Swiss Federal Institute of Technology, Lausanne

Sunstein, C. R. (2003) *Beyond the Precautionary Principle*, Chicago Public Law and Legal Theory Working Paper, no 38, The Law School, University of Chicago, Chicago

UNFF (2004) *Criteria and Indicators of Sustainable Forest Management*, report of the Secretary-General, E/CN.18/2004/11, United Nations Economic and Social Council, New York. Available at www.un.org/esa/forests/documents-unff.html

UNFF (2005) Report of the Ad Hoc Expert Group on Consideration with a View of Recommending the Parameters of a Mandate for Developing a Legal Framework on all Types of Forests, E/CN.18/2005/2, United Nations Forum on Forests, New York. Available at www.un.org/esa/forests/documents-unff.html

Walters, L., Balint, P., Desai, A. and Stewart, R. (2003) *Risk and Uncertainty in Management of the Sierra Nevada National Forests*, report to USDA Forest Service, Pacific Southwest Region, George Mason University, Fairfax, Virginia

Wang, S. (2004) 'One hundred faces of sustainable forest management', *Forest Policy And Economics*, vol 6, nos 3–4, pp205–13

World Bank (2004*) Sustaining Forests: A Development Strategy*, World Bank, Washington, DC

Wilkie, M. L., Holmgren, P. and Castañeda, F. (2003) *Sustainable Forest Management and the Ecosystem Approach: Two Concepts, One Goal*, Forest Management Working Paper, no 25, Forest Resources Development Service, Forest Resources Division, FAO, Rome

WWF (2002) *CITES Appendix II Listing and FSC Certification: Complementary Strategies for Conservation and Sustainable Management of Timber Species?*, WWF Discussion Paper, WWF International Species Programme, Godalming, UK

# 3

# The Precautionary Principle: Knowledge Counts but Power Decides?

*Steinar Andresen, Lars Walløe and Kristin Rosendal*

## INTRODUCTION

The precautionary principle is held in high regard by the green community and was considered a major achievement when it was first adopted. Over the last two decades considerable time and energy have been spent on incorporating this principle into most major environmental and marine living resources agreements. The basic underpinning of the precautionary principle is that scientific uncertainty should not be a reason to postpone conservation or management measures in cases where environmental degradation or resource depletion are perceived.

Why was there a need to adopt this management approach? The main reason is that scientific consensus is difficult to achieve and scientific uncertainty and controversy have frequently been politically exploited by reluctant actors who have used them as an excuse to postpone or delay taking action in relation to perceived environmental threats (Andresen et al, 2000). Although today the principle has gained increasing support within many arenas dealing with the environment and biological resources, it is still contested by certain actors and in certain forums.

So far, most political and scholarly attention has been directed towards the significance of this principle being included in various international agreements. However important this may be, as the principle has been around for some time, the purpose of this paper is to discuss and shed light on the question of the *practical significance of the precautionary approach*. In the second section of this chapter we clarify this question by relating it to a discussion of the effectiveness of international regimes. The role of science is one key component in explaining regime effectiveness, and we discuss the significance of science and how this relates to the precautionary approach. Finally we introduce two distinct international relations perspectives with different assumptions about the significance of the precautionary principle. In section three we discuss the significance of this principle in some selected global and regional regimes. In the following section we take a closer look at a case where the precautionary approach has seemingly played a crucial role. We conclude by summing up and exploring how we can gain increased and more precise insight into the research question that lies at the heart of this paper.

## ANALYTICAL APPROACH

What do we mean by 'practical significance' of the precautionary approach? We look at this in relation to the question of the *effectiveness* of international environmental regimes (Miles et al, 2002; Underdal and Young, 2004). Effectiveness can be measured in a number of ways. For our current purposes, we will mention two indicators: output and outcome. Output deals with regulations and programmes that have been adopted; these are an indication of the stringency or the ambition of the regime in question. Outcome deals with possible behavioural consequences resulting from these rules – whether the target groups move in the 'right' direction. While the stringency of rules adopted can be fairly easily established, behavioural consequences are extremely hard to measure because of the high number of intervening variables that may also serve to explain changes in behaviour.[1] One useful approach to explain both of these factors is to consider whether the environmental problems being tackled are *malign* or *benign* problems; the more malign a problem, the lower the effectiveness of the regimes is likely to be – and vice versa. Whether problems are classified as malign or benign rests on their characterization along two dimensions, an intellectual dimension and a political dimension. A malign problem is characterized both by high scientific uncertainty and/or controversy, as well as deep-seated political conflicts. In contrast, a benign problem is characterized by a solid, consensual knowledge base as well as few political conflicts (Miles et al, 2002).

How does the precautionary approach fit into this perspective? Does the adoption of this principle contribute to increasing the effectiveness of the regimes in question, either by leading to stricter rules (output) or shifting behaviour in the 'right' direction? The latter question is the most important for determining the practical consequences of the precautionary approach. However, here we will not use this indicator systematically because the causal chain between this principle and behaviour is too long, complex and uncertain to analyse properly – at least within the scope of this chapter. To establish a causal link between the precautionary approach and the methodologically less demanding output indicator relating to rules and regulations is, as we shall see, also a tall order. Thus, the purpose of this chapter is rather modest and primarily aims to discuss and shed light on our research question, rather than to answer it conclusively.

From our perspective, the precautionary principle clearly belongs to the intellectual dimension of problems addressed by environmental regimes – responding to the state of the scientific knowledge of the problem at hand. While (to our knowledge) little is known about the practical significance of the precautionary approach in international environmental regimes, much more is known about the role of science. Therefore, in order to outline assumptions about the significance of the precautionary principle, we will first briefly account for what we know about the role and influence of science in selected regimes. To do this, we take as our point of departure one particular effort to answer this question, the work of Andresen et al (2000),[2] while at the same time recognizing that other contributions may have reached different conclusions.

In the first place, science is seen as a relevant supplier of knowledge in all the regimes studied. All have established scientific bodies as a part of their organizational set-up. Second, some type of collective action is usually taken in response to scientific advice. This can include adopting targets, rules and regulations. Third, maybe the most significant role played by science is as an 'early warning agent' or agenda setter in identifying problems. Fourth, in the face of consensual knowledge within the relevant scientific body, decision-makers rarely dispute such messages. True, uncertainties may be exploited politically, especially in the early phases, but if the scientific message holds, it is rarely explicitly disputed. Fifth, although scientists are listened to, decisions taken are based on multiple decision criteria of which science is hardly ever the most important. That is, decisions are, not surprisingly, typically driven by policy rather than science. The 'normal' pattern is that decision-makers stop far short (in terms of environmental protection) of scientific advice, but there are also incidents when they go further than recommended by the scientists. As a point of departure this indicates that under certain conditions decision-makers may be driven by true environmentally proactive mechanisms like the precautionary principle.

In short, scientists have a legitimate role to play within international environmental and resources regimes. However, their actual impact on decisions appears to be modest. This is particularly pronounced when there are strong political conflicts or strong conflicts over values and a weak or disputed knowledge base – what we have described as 'malign' problems. In such cases, the room for science is usually modest.

What do these 'lessons learned' on the significance of science in decision-making suggest about the impact of the precautionary principle? Our main assumption is that in most cases the significance of the precautionary principle will be weak. This is based on two observations. First, overall the significance of science, even when consensual, is quite weak as a decision premise. Second, when science is uncertain, as it is supposed to be when the precautionary principle is invoked, its significance is usually marginal. However, we expect the room for a precautionary approach to be larger, or at least appear to be larger, when it comes to politically 'benign' problems. This is especially the case when the solution to problems is relatively 'easy' on account of available technological cures or market incentives to act. In short, when the economic costs of actions are not prohibitive, rather, when there may be something to gain by action, a precautionary approach is more likely.

What insights can we gain into the likely practical significance of the precautionary principle from the study of international relations? There are different opinions in this discipline regarding the significance of *norms* like the precautionary principle. The dominant school in the study of international relations has traditionally been the *realist* and the neo-realist school of thought. These are systemic and state-centric perspectives that emphasize the necessity of focusing on narrow national interests. They are mostly preoccupied with security issues and tend to downplay the significance of 'softer' issues like trade and environment. Moreover, most relevant to our perspective, the role of ideas, values and norms is largely neglected (Morgenthau, 1956; Mearsheimer, 1995). Either they are seen as 'disturbing' to narrow national interests or they are seen as a convenient ideological wrapping for the underlying interests of the dominant states. Realists would consequently argue that if the precautionary principle is to have any significance, it would have to be in the interests of the dominant states to act accordingly. When applied to the context of this chapter, *realists predict that the precautionary principle in itself will have no effect. The principle has no intrinsic value and will have no consequences for the development of the regimes.* The realist perspective is still quite dominant in the study of international relations but its significance has become somewhat reduced since the end of the cold war.

The traditional contrasting school of thought is the liberal, 'institutionalist' approach. This approach stresses the significance of international institutions and regimes as vehicles for cooperation and thereby adopts a more optimistic world view (Keohane, 1984). Of greater interest to this chapter, however, is a more recent perspective, the *social constructivist* school of thought, which is gaining increasing prominence since the conclusion of super-power rivalry (Wendt, 1992; Ruggie, 1998). It is beyond the scope of this paper to go into this approach in any depth. Compared to realism, however, it is a more novel and exploratory approach with less empirical backing. Within the scope of our chapter it is, however, highly relevant in that it stresses the significance of knowledge, norms and principles. In keeping with the logic of *appropriateness* (in contrast to the logic of consequences), states and other actors might, for various reasons, want to do the 'right' things (March and Olson, 1989). This approach also stresses the significance of non-state actors as well as of the new transnational issues, where environment is one key area. To cut a long story short, in a social constructivist perspective *norms like the precautionary perspective have an intrinsic value and may also cause states and other relevant actors to act accordingly.*

Thus, we have two simple and competing assumptions as to the effect of the precautionary approach. Realists will hold that the precautionary approach is insignificant because norms do not matter unless the major states see it as in their interest to invoke it. The social constructivists will maintain that the precautionary principle may be of significance because norms do count and the logic of appropriateness does influence outcomes. Our examination of the role of science in international regimes, however, suggests that the realists may offer a truer picture than the social constructivists – the chances are slim for applying the precautionary principle when science is not consensual, unless problems are benign and relatively easy to solve.

In the next section we give a brief and simplified outline of the role of the precautionary principle within some global and regional regimes: biodiversity, climate change and the North Sea. Thereafter we look at one case in greater depth, that of the whaling regime, where the precautionary principle seems to play a very strong role.

## THE ROLE OF THE PRECAUTIONARY PRINCIPLE IN SELECTED REGIMES

### Biodiversity: no precaution globally but some progress domestically?

If we look at the 1992 Convention on Biological Diversity (CBD), the precautionary approach has been prominent in discussions and decision-making on a number of topics that as a whole make up the issue of biodiversity. Examples of this can be found in the negotiations on the Biosafety Protocol, as well as in discussions on invasive alien species by the parties at the sixth and seventh Conferences of the Parties. The Preamble to the Convention instructs its parties that 'where there is a threat of significant reduction or loss of biological diversity, lack of full scientific certainty should not be used as a reason for postponing measures to avoid or minimize such a threat'. However, in the actual national implementation phase, there is less evidence that the precautionary principle has had a wide application. The Millennium Ecosystem Assessment Report found little evidence of any progress towards the 2010 goal of halting the loss of biodiversity (UNEP, 2004). In essence, there is a high degree of scientific agreement that there is a problem, but a great deal of uncertainty as well as a high level of dispute regarding causes and broader impacts. This should be a prime example of where there is need for a precautionary approach.

Biodiversity is an incredibly complex subject, which incorporates a tremendous variety of issues. It is even more complex than most other regimes covered in this chapter because it includes all ecosystems, species and the genetic diversity within species worldwide. There is a high degree of scientific consensus with regard to the severity of biodiversity loss (Martens et al, 2003), and there is scientific agreement that the current rate of species extinction is about 100 times faster than the natural average rate would be without human intervention (Heywood, 1995). However, on a smaller scale there is generally a great deal of disagreement about the driving forces and causes of processes such as deforestation or the overexploitation of species.

Despite the severity of the problem, the fact that loss of biodiversity takes place in a gradual manner and hardly ever achieves shocking headlines reduces the chances of political action. Moreover, there is little or no room for market-driven mechanisms or quick technological solutions. Adding to the 'malignancy', it involves important sectors like agriculture, fisheries and forestry, and biotechnology, including pharmaceutical as well as chemical industries. Furthermore, while biodiversity is found primarily in the global South, many of the most significant beneficiaries from the utilization of Southern biological resources are found in developed countries. This issue therefore accentuates the North–South divide. In essence, policies to mitigate biodiversity loss will frequently place the main burden on parts of the South – and may have short-term adverse effects on some key sectors. Further exacerbating the problem is the fact that while the main bulk of terrestrial species' diversity is found in developing countries (UNEP, 1995), the main beneficiaries from the utilization of genetic resources are found in developed countries. These global challenges can probably only be solved over the very long term, if ever.

Are there any signs of precaution at the domestic level in small wealthy and 'green' countries that can certainly afford to deal with such problems, like Norway? An examination of Norway reveals that this does not appear to be the case. Norwegian biodiversity policies generally fall short *even* of the objective of adhering to scientific advice. This implies that there is not much chance of any precautionary approach. This is most apparent in the forest sector, where the main bulk of Norway's threatened species are found; however, to date, only one quarter of the scientifically recommended area has been protected (Rosendal, 2004). Most of the protected areas in Norway consist of non-productive mountain ecosystems (Ministry of Environment, 2000–01). Instead we see a practice of questioning and undermining the credibility of scientific advice, most notably from the forestry sector, leaving little or no room for precaution (Ministry of Environment, 2000–01). There are talks about the precautionary approach in the fisheries sector, but they appear to be in their infancy and restricted to input to international cooperation processes in this field (Ministry of Environment, 2000–01).

What about the performance of other Organisation for Economic Co-operation and Development (OECD) actors? We do not know if there are discussions in the European Union (EU) about precaution in the fisheries sector; however, we do know that there are no signs of it in practice as, overall, the state of EU fisheries is characterized by overexploitation and overcapacity. In other areas the situation appears to be slightly different. Compared to Norway, the EU, with its Habitat Directive, has adopted a more proactive policy (Reinvang, 2003). The Natura 2000 Plan of the Habitat Directive includes concrete demands for the protection of the habitats of threatened species. More than 15 per cent of EU territory is included in the Plan. Natura 2000, the EU's protected sites' network, has moved closer to completion following the adoption by the European Commission of a fifth regional sites list. The region covers one fifth of EU land area.

Does this mean that the EU demonstrates a more precautionary approach? While there are certainly differences in approaches to conservation, it is not necessarily straightforward to say the EU approach is more precautionary, as different strategies may have both conservation advantages and disadvantages. This difference can be illustrated using the example of the negotiations that took place to draw up the CBD. Several EU member countries preferred listings of habitats and threatened species, while the Nordic countries advocated applying environmental integration and sustainable use not just within the 'islands' of protected areas, but outside them too. Norway may have gone further in formulating goals for sector integration, but sector integration may end up costing much more and yielding less visible conservation results. The EU is the front runner when it comes to legal instruments that actually protect specific species and habitats (through the Habitat Directive), thereby achieving more visible results and realizing a higher score on measures of conservation success (Rosendal, 2004). However, this begs the troublesome question of whether this approach leads to the practice of reducing biodiversity conservation to small 'islands' of protected areas rather than to integration in all sectors. The EU approach is more simple and brings visible environmental triumphs for politicians, but there is worldwide scientific agreement that this will not be enough to halt the loss of biodiversity (UNEP, 2004).

In short, at the global level, true precaution seems like a distant dream because of the malignancy of the issue, while at a national level there does seems to be progress among some of the more wealthy countries.

## Climate change: political creativity and institutional energy, but not much precaution?

Various scientific actors, individuals and institutions played a key role as agenda setters by triggering political attention to *climate change* in the 1970s and 1980s (Andresen and Agrawala, 2002). This eventually led to the adoption of the UN Framework Convention on Climate Change (UNFCCC) (1992) and subsequently to the Kyoto Protocol (1997). The role of the Intergovernmental Panel on Climate Change (IPCC), which brings together hundreds of scientists, has been crucial to the subsequent scientific and political process (Skodvin, 2000). As early as 1990, in its first report, the IPCC maintained that gas emissions would have to be reduced by some 60 per cent if the climate was to be stabilized. However, although formal negotiations have continued for some 15 years now, global emissions continue to rise. Although this is the overall and rather bleak picture, it does not mean than nothing has happened in the scientific and political arenas.

Given that the scientific message was more uncertain and contested at the time of the adoption of the Convention, it may be argued that some notion of precaution probably underpinned its adoption, and it is explicitly stated that 'The Parties shall take precautionary measures to anticipate, prevent or minimize the causes of climate change and mitigate its advese effects' (Article 3.3). However, the Convention was weak because it did not include any binding emission targets. Thus, there were few or no political or economic costs associated with ratification of the treaty and, as a result, its effectiveness in terms of output was indeed very weak. The Kyoto Protocol, which was adopted five years later, did not come into force until 2005. This was also a weak document in terms of stringency and in the light of scientific warnings because it only called for a 5 per cent reduction in emissions in the North and contained no obligations for the South (Grubb et al, 1999). Why have we not seen stronger action?

If we go back to our initial reasoning, the answer is simple, climate change is an extremely malign political problem. If more ambitious climate measures are to be adopted, they will require a change in the affluent lifestyles in the North, and be an impediment to economic growth in the South. Political conflicts about this abound both within the North and the South as well as between them (Grubb et al, 1999). Moreover, although there is an emerging consensus that global warming is caused by human activities, scientific uncertainties still abound about regional impacts, the speed and strength of global warming, as well as its link to hurricanes and storms.

What role has the precautionary principle played within the wider debate on climate change? One of the first forums where it was hotly debated was at the so-called Bergen Conference in 1990. This was a regional preparatory conference for the 1992 Rio Conference where climate change was the key focus (Andresen and Wettestad, 1990). The debate followed a pattern that was to become familiar in subsequent years. The US played the role of laggard, rejecting the precautionary principle, while the EU and small Western countries were pushers, favouring a precautionary approach.

Whatever the opinions of the various actors on the need to include this principle, there has not been much precautionary action by any states – including the EU – in the subsequent period. That said, however, there are variations between them. In fact, it seems that attitudes towards the precautionary principle are reasonably well correlated with action. For example, the US is a laggard when it comes to climate measures and strongly rising emissions, while the EU has a far better track record. That said, the strength of the EU climate policy stems from considerably reduced emissions in both the UK and Germany. However, the reasons underlying most of the reduced emissions in both these cases are, ironically, unrelated to the climate regime[3] (Gupta and Grubb, 2000). In Norway, a strong believer in the precautionary principle, at least in official speeches, emissions continue to rise. Overall, the record of the parties is very poor when considered in relation to the harsh scientific message of what is necessary to solve this problem.

## The North Sea: some precaution, but poor implementation?

Some smaller and more benign regional regimes are more promising when it comes to the application of the precautionary principle. One example is the North Sea marine pollution regime. This regime has a long history and is composed of several parts. The Oslo Dumping Convention was established in 1972 and a separate Paris Convention for the Prevention of Marine Pollution from Land-based Sources was signed in 1974. Two separate commissions were established and in 1992 the two conventions were merged into one single legal instrument, the OSPAR Convention for the Protection of the Northeast Atlantic.[4] Since the mid-1980s there have been regular North Sea Ministerial Conferences and a number of relevant EU directives also cover the North Sea (Skjærseth, 2000).

The very fact that this regime was established is in itself an example of precaution – although the concept was not developed at the time. Events that triggered the creation of the regime included dramatic incidents like the Torrey Canyon disaster in 1967 and the Stella Maris incident in 1971.[5] These episodes caused immense public alarm and attracted media attention. ICES (the International Council for Exploration of the Sea) also issued warnings about the large amounts of waste being dumped in the North Sea, but overall knowledge of the environmental state of the North Sea at the time was very limited. In short, a combination of general scientific warnings and public and media attention was instrumental in the creation of the regime. In the 1970s and early 1980s, political action, such as the adoption of binding decisions, was very modest and knowledge about the state of the environment was still weak and uncertain (Wettestad, 2000).

The 1987 North Sea Ministerial Conference is seen by most observers as the turning point in the history of North Sea marine pollution. The Conference called for strong and quantified reductions in emissions – up to 50 per cent for many substances – within a set time limit (1995), and dumping was to be phased out. It has been argued that this was the first time a precautionary approach was agreed upon and adopted internationally (Freestrone and Iljstra, 1990). Subsequent North Sea Conferences, the OSPAR Commission (established under the OSPAR Convention) and EU directives have contributed to strengthening commitments and the goal is now to eliminate the dumping of hazardous waste by 2020. In short, at least in terms of output, this regime stands out as quite effective and ambitious.

This development, however, has *not* taken place as a result of new scientific evidence. Although this is one of the most studied ocean areas in the world, the Quality Status Reports that have been published have generally been characterized by uncertainty and a lack of alarming scientific indicators. '[T]he fact that decision makers are told that they have to accept uncertainty has contributed to strengthen the need for a precautionary approach' (Andresen, 2001). Why was this approach adopted and why at the North Sea Conference in 1987? What may be labelled 'contextual factors' seem to have been decisive. In 1984, during the first North Sea Conference, international environmental issues were not on political radar screens. This situation had changed dramatically by 1987. There were a number of 'external shocks' just before the Conference, for example, the discovery of the 'ozone hole', perceived *Waldsterben* ('forest die-off') in Germany, the Chernobyl accident, as well as the publication of the so-called Brundtland Report by the UN, to mention just a few. All these suddenly placed the environment very high on the international agenda and in the Western world there was a strong increase in the demand for green politics, which policy-makers were eager to provide to secure re-election (Andresen, 2001). This also helps to explain the adoption of fairly strong and precautionary measures in relation to ozone levels and acid rain during the latter half of the 1980s (Wettestad, 2000).

Much has been achieved within this multi-component regime; however, some of the political momentum seems to have been lost in relation to ocean pollution when compared to issues like climate change. There have been problems of implementation and the necessity of some of the more costly measures suggested has been questioned scientifically. Nevertheless, the case is interesting in that it sheds light on what may be important *preconditions* for a precautionary approach.

## THE RECENT HISTORY OF THE INTERNATIONAL WHALING COMMISSION (IWC): MISUSE OF THE PRECAUTIONARY PRINCIPLE?

### Overexploitation and early regulations

The decisions made by the International Whaling Commission (IWC) in the period from 1974 to the present day are a rare example of the active use of the precautionary principle. That said, we argue they essentially represent a misuse of the precautionary principle for political purposes.

The early history of commercial whaling, however, is an entirely different story. From the 16th century to the early 1960s, whaling took the form of continuous overexploitation of one whale stock after the other, starting with the black right whale in the North Atlantic and ending with the hunting down of humpback, blue and fin whales in the Southern Ocean in the first half of the 20th century. No attention was paid to the warnings from scientists and some governments more than a hundred years ago, who were already concerned about overexploitation (Hjort, 1902; Budker, 1958; Tønnessen and Johnsen, 1982). However, gradually regulatory measures were introduced, first for whaling operations from land stations and subsequently in national waters. Eventually the International Convention for the Regulation of Whaling (ICRW) was signed in 1946, and the first meeting of the IWC was held in London in May 1949.

The dual objectives of the Convention are 'to provide for the proper conservation of whale stocks and thus make possible the orderly development of the whaling industry'. The IWC may amend the Schedule of the ICRW (the section containing the regulatory measures) if the proposed amendment is 'based on scientific findings' and supported by a three-quarters majority. However, the original Schedule was not able to fulfil the dual purpose of the Convention, and proposals for reductions in total quotas as well as effective inspection schemes were undermined both in the Scientific Committee (SC)

(Schweder, 2000, 2001) and in the Commission. Thus overexploitation continued into the early 1960s, with annual takes of about 30,000 blue and fin whales, until the hunt was no longer profitable. Looked at in terms of our analytical perspective, the effectiveness of the IWC during this period was very low: little or no attention was paid to scientific advice and there is no evidence of a precautionary approach (Andresen, 2002).

However, alongside the commercial hunting of large whales, another whaling activity had been going on. As far back as we have knowledge, coastal people of many countries have harvested dolphins and small whales to use for food and other purposes. In some countries this coastal harvest has continued uninterrupted to the present day (Basberg et al, 1993). The IWC considered most of these whaling operations to be sustainable prior to the 1970s (IWC, 1975, 1977).

## The IWC is 'captured' by the anti-whaling movement: much precaution – no science?

In 1972 the UN organized the first World Conference on the Environment in Stockholm. The main environmental concerns at the time were air, river and sea pollution as a result of industry and agriculture. However, during the conference some industrialized countries proposed that there be a total ban on all whaling operations. The resolution was adopted. These countries had no impressive environmental record and had either quit their whaling operations or had no previous whaling history. In short they had nothing to lose from this proposal. There was speculation that this was just a way to win cheap 'green points' as the whale was on the verge of being adopted as a symbol by the emerging 'green' community (Andresen, 2002). However, the proposal was rejected at the next IWC meeting both by the SC and by the Commission (IWC, 1974, 1975). The IWC stated that all large-scale whaling operations had been phased out ten years earlier and that the remaining small-scale whaling activities were probably sustainable. But the US and some other industrialized countries refused to give up. In collaboration with some non-governmental organizations (NGOs) such as Greenpeace, they convinced a number of new countries with no history of whaling to join the IWC. The number of member countries increased from 15 in 1974 to 37 in 1982, and, with a sufficient majority in favour, a ban on all commercial whaling was then introduced in the Schedule. It became valid in 1986. The provision stated that it should 'be kept under review, based upon the best scientific advice, and by 1990 at the latest the Commission will undertake a comprehensive assessment of the effects of this decision on whale stocks and consider modification of this provision and the establishment of other catch limits' (§10(e) of the Schedule, as modified in 1982).

Some countries with small-scale whaling traditions (Iceland, Japan and Norway) that provided products for human consumption launched large-scale scientific research programmes to investigate the abundance, stock identity and other biological aspects of their relevant whale species and stocks. New substantial sets of results were presented to the SC every year. It was shown that there were large numbers of minke whales in the North Atlantic and in the Southern Ocean, large numbers of minke whales and Brydes whales in the Pacific, and that most stocks of depleted whales were rapidly increasing (IWC, 1993). The large majority of the SC accepted these new estimates. The SC itself developed a Revised Management Procedure that was tested for robustness in a large number of computer simulation trials (IWC, 1993). It was demonstrated that minke whaling and whaling for some other species of baleen whales could be carried out in a sustainable manner, even if all realistic levels of scientific uncertainty were taken into account. However, the majority of IWC member countries were not convinced, and the moratorium on commercial whaling was not lifted. As the scientific documentation was overwhelming, it is hard to escape the conclusion that the reason was that policy-makers in key countries had discovered that they got 'environmental credit' in their constituencies from being anti-whaling. They had nothing to lose economically and a lot to gain politically. Some countries like Australia and the United Kingdom were against whaling as a matter of principle – it was not the morally 'right' thing to do. Others, like the US, were in a different position. The US was (and is) conducting aboriginal whaling. Considering the text of the whaling Convention, with the exception of political expediency, their point of view seems difficult to defend and understand:

> '*These amendments to the Schedule (a) shall be such as are neces-sary to carry out the objectives and purposes of this Convention and to provide for the conservation, development, and optimum utilisation of the whale resources; (b) shall be based on scientific findings; (c)... ; and (d) shall take into consideration the inter-ests of consumers of whale products and the whaling industry*'.

In countering the arguments from the pro-whaling nations, their strategy was to exaggerate by an order of magnitude all scientific uncertainty (Schweder, 2000) and to invoke the precautionary principle to justify a continuation of the moratorium.

In our opinion, from 1982 to the present day it is hard to escape the conclusion that there has been a continuous abuse of the precautionary princi-ple, to some extent in the SC and especially in the Commission.[6] Any disagreement within the SC, however ill-founded from a scientific point of view, has been used by the Commission to ask for more and better research. Another area of misuse of the precautionary principle has been in the develop-ment of inspection and control regimes for possible future commercial whaling. It appears that anti-whaling countries are demanding more and more layers of control measures on top of each other, again invoking the precau-tionary principle. Once more, it is hard to escape the conclusion that this is a method – for political purposes – to try to make whaling so difficult and expen-sive that nobody will be tempted to try it.

What will be the long-term consequences of this use of the precautionary approach in the IWC? It is not likely to stop whaling of species that can be harvested sustainably in countries where people like whale meat or blubber (for example Japan and Norway). Rather, the misuse of the precautionary principle may in the long run destroy the IWC as an effective international conservation instrument for those whale species and stocks that really need help to survive.

## THE SIGNIFICANCE OF THE PRECAUTIONARY PRINCIPLE: CONCLUDING OBSERVATIONS

What conclusions can we draw from our brief survey of the role of the precautionary principle in various regimes? First, as we have looked at few cases, we cannot generalize about our findings, and as the treatment is superficial, our conclusions about the regimes surveyed are by no means robust. With that caveat, we find limited support for the social constructivist assumption that such principles have much significance on their own. The one regime where the precautionary approach is strongly invoked appears to be the international whaling regime. However, here our judgement is that it is applied because it is in the interest of the strong states, most notably the US, to do so. As such, this fits with the realist assumption. The same goes for the overall lack of precaution that can be observed in the global and politically malign regimes like climate change and biodiversity loss. That said, the use of the precautionary approach in the North Sea regime appears to lend more support to the social constructivist perspective. The causal mechanisms, however, are quite complex as the use of this approach is linked to contextual factors like external shocks and strong public demand for actions. When these factors are not present, the prospects for a precautionary approach become bleaker. This reminds us that usually both precaution and science are quite weak as decision premises. In most cases, however, consensual science has a stronger likelihood of being listened to and acted upon than uncertain science or precaution.

Within the international environmental community we believe that the precautionary principle is unconditionally seen as a 'good' approach. In our opinion the general idea behind the principle is good, but under certain circumstances we think it is problematic because it may weaken science as a decision premise. This is primarily illustrated by the whaling case where we suggest the precautionary principle is invoked to sidetrack science for political purposes. This does *not* mean that we think that science with a capital S is always the 'truth', it needs to be weighed against other premises. Still, if it is completely disregarded, management will be based only on luck or politics and this is not a strong basis for effective conservation.

Finally two comments, one on the future of the precautionary principle and one on future research. Is there any chance that the practices we have observed in the IWC will spread to other regimes? Yes, to some extent the same polarization and power politics witnessed in the IWC have spread to

CITES in relation to *some* highly visible species, often characterized as 'charismatic megafuana' like whales and elephants (Friedheim, 2001). Although this is only relevant to a small portion of the work of CITES, it illustrates that the problem should be taken seriously. The problem should not, however, be exaggerated because in most environmental regimes (such as climate change) the strong political and economic actors are not on the side of precaution. That is why we still need the precautionary principle. Finally, as to future research, in this chapter we have only scratched the surface. Much more detailed and in-depth case studies are needed to learn more about the long road from the adoption of a rather vague principle to its practical impact on behaviour.

## NOTES

1   Consider the strong reduction of $CO_2$ emissions from the Economies in Transition (EIT) countries from the early 1990s to the present. This is not due to the climate regime, but rather to economic recession that followed as a result of the transition to market economies.
2   The following is based on Andresen et al, 2000. The five regimes under study were the International Whaling Commission (IWC), the climate regime, the ozone regime, the North Sea pollution regime and the acid rain regime.
3   The fall in emissions in Germany has been due to the reunification of East and West Germany, while the reduction in UK emissions is mainly due to the 'dash for gas' over the last decade.
4   The Convention came into force in 1998.
5   For further elaboration, see Andresen, 2001.
6   A very small but vocal and influential minority in the SC, with close connections to the 'green' community, has ensured that no advice on stock abundance or stock identity has been provided unanimously from the SC to the Commission.

## REFERENCES

Andresen, S. (2001) 'The North Sea and beyond: lessons learned', in Valencia, M. (ed) *Maritime Regime Building*, Kluwer Law International, The Hague, pp51–64
Andresen, S. (2002) 'The International Whaling Commission (IWC): more failure than success?', in E. L. Miles, A. Underdal, S. Andresen, J. Wettestad and J. B. Skjaerseth (eds) *Environmental Regime Effectiveness: Confronting Theory with Evidence*, MIT Press, Cambridge, MA, pp379–405
Andresen, S. and Agrawala, S. (2002) 'Leaders, pushers and laggards in the making of the climate regime', *Global Environmental Change*, vol 12, pp41–51
Andresen, S., Skodvin, T., Underdal, A. and Wettestad, J. (2000) *Science and Politics in International Environmental Regimes*, Manchester University Press, Manchester
Andresen, S. and Wettestad, J. (1990) 'Climate failure at the Bergen Conference?', *International Challenges*, vol 10, no 2, pp17–24
Basberg, B. L., Ringstad, J. E. and Wexelsen, E. (1993) (eds) *Whaling and History: Perspectives on the Evolution of the Industry*, Sandefjordmuseene, Sandefjord

Budker, P. (1958) *Whales and Whaling*, Harrap, London

Freestone, D. and Iljstra, T. (1990) 'The North Sea: perspectives on regional environmental cooperation', special issue of *The International Journal of Coastal and Estuarine Law*, Graham & Trotman, London

Friedheim, R. (2001) (ed) *Towards a Sustainable Whaling Regime*, University of Washington Press, Seattle, WA

Grubb, M. Vroolijk, C. and Brack, D (1999) *The Kyoto Protocol: A Guide and Assessment*, Royal Institute of International Affairs, London

Gupta, J. and Grubb, M. (eds) (2000) *Climate Change and European Leadership*, Kluwer Academic Publishers, Dordrecht

Heywood, V. (ed.) (1995) *Global Biodiversity Assessment*. Cambridge University Press, Cambridge, UK

Hjort, J. (1902) *Fiskeri og hvalfangst i det nordlige Norge [Fisheries and Whaling in Northern Norway]*, John Griegs forlag, Bergen

IWC (1974) *Report of the International Whaling Commission*, 24, International Whaling Commission, Cambridge, UK

IWC (1975) *Report of the International Whaling Commission*, 25, International Whaling Commission, Cambridge, UK

IWC (1977) *Report of the International Whaling Commission*, 27, International Whaling Commission, Cambridge, UK

IWC (1993) *Report of the International Whaling Commission*, 43, International Whaling Commission, Cambridge, UK

Keohane, R. (1984) *After Hegemony*, Princeton University Press, New Jersey

March, J. G. and Olsen, J. P. (1989) *Rediscovering Institutions: The Organizational Basis of Politics*, The Free Press, New York

Martens, P., Rotmans, J. and de Groot, D. (2003) 'Biodiversity: luxury or necessity?', *Global Environmental Change*, vol 13, pp75–81

Mearsheimer, J. (1995) 'The false promise of international institutions', *International Security*, vol 19, no 3, pp5–49

Miles, E. L., Underdal, A., Andresen, S. Wettestad, J. and Skjaerseth, J. B. (2002) *Environmental Regime Effectiveness*, MIT Press, Cambridge, MA

Ministry of the Environment (2000–01) *Biological Diversity. Sector Responsibility and Coordination [Biologisk mangfold. Sektoransvar og samordning]*', Report No. 42 to the Storting, Ministry of the Environment, Oslo

Morgenthau, H. (1956) *Politics Among Nations*, Alfred A Knopf, New York

Reinvang, R. (2003) *Norway, EU, and Environmental Politics*, Report 1/03, Framtiden i Våre Hender [The Future in Our Hands], Oslo

Rosendal, K. (2004) 'Biodiversity: international bungee jump domestic bungle', in Birger Skjærseth, J. (ed) *International Regimes and Norway's Environmental Policy: Crossfire and Coherence*, Ashgate, Hampshire, pp161–194

Ruggie, J. G. (1998) 'What makes the world hang together? Neo-utilitarianism and the social constructivist challenge, *International Organization*, vol 52, no 4, pp855–885

Schweder, T. (2000) 'Distortion of uncertainty in science: Antarctic fin whales in the 1950s', *Journal of International Wildlife Law and Policy*, vol 3, pp73–92

Schweder, T. (2001) 'Protecting whales by distorting uncertainty: non-precautionary mismanagement?', *Fisheries Research*, vol 52, pp217–225

Skjærseth, J. B. (2000) *North Sea Cooperation: Linking International and Domestic Pollution Control*, Manchester University Press, Manchester

Skodvin, T. (2000) *Structure and Agent in the Scientific Diplomacy of Climate Change*, Kluwer Academic Publishers, Dordrecht

Tønnessen, J. and Johnsen, A. (1982) *The History of Modern Whaling*, University of California Press, Berkeley and Los Angeles

Underdal, A. and Young, O. (eds) (2004) *Regime Consequences: Methodological Challenges and Research Strategies*, Kluwer Academic Publishers, Dordrecht

UNEP (1995) *Global Biodiversity Assessment*, United Nations Environment Programme, Nairobi, Kenya

UNEP (2004) *Millennium Ecosystem Assessment*, review of the draft reports for UNEP/CBD/SBSTTA/10/6, 13 December 2004, tenth meeting, 7-11 February 2005, Convention on Biological Diversity Secretariat, Montreal, Canada

Wendt, A. (1992) 'Anarchy is what states make of it: the social construction of power politics', *International Organization*, vol 46, no 2, pp391–425

Wettestad, J. (2000) 'Dealing with land-based marine pollution in the north-east Atlantic: the Paris Convention and the North Sea', in S. Andresen, T. Skodvin, A. Underdal and J. Wettestad (eds) *Science and Politics in International Environmental Regimes*, Manchester University Press, Manchester, pp70–95

4

# The Precautionary Principle, Uncertainty and Trophy Hunting: A Review of the Torghar Population of Central Asian Markhor *Capra falconeri*

*Alison M. Rosser, Naseer Tareen and Nigel Leader-Williams*

## INTRODUCTION

The Convention on Biological Diversity (1992) seeks to promote conservation and sustainable use of biodiversity, and the equitable sharing of its benefits. The CBD recognizes that sustainable use can provide incentives to conserve biodiversity, particularly where the opportunity costs of different forms of land use determine decisions on whether or not to conserve biodiversity (Hutton and Leader-Williams, 2003). Incentive-driven conservation is based on the premise that rural people who derive benefits from biodiversity that exceed the costs of living with that biodiversity, are more likely to conserve than those who derive no benefits (Emerton, 2001). If appropriately regulated and managed, trophy (or sport) hunting has proved an important way to provide incentives for conservation, particularly in remote areas where game-viewing tourism is not an option, and where there is political instability (Leader-Williams and Hutton, 2005). However, many conservationists remain nervous of its widespread adoption because of the numerous examples of overuse arising from other forms of hunting (Caughley and Gunn, 1996; Milner-Gulland and Mace, 1998), while other groups oppose any forms of hunting or extractive use on welfare grounds (Hoyt, 1994).

When declining populations are faced with various threats in situations of uncertainty, the international community often turns to CITES (The Convention on International Trade in Endangered Species of Wild Fauna and Flora, 1973) to address one potential threat, international trade. However, in many situations where a ban on international trade is proposed through CITES, there is often little direct evidence that sanctioned trophy hunting by international sportsmen is the main driver of the decline. Instead, for many species it appears that factors such as unregulated illegal hunting and/or habitat loss are primarily responsible (Caughley et al, 1990; Milner-Gulland and Beddington, 1993). Indeed, where trophy hunting is properly managed and provides significant revenue, this form of use may provide incentives to better manage other drivers of decline, such as unregulated meat hunting or loss of habitat arising from conversion of land to other uses (Murphree, 1993; Bond, 1994, 2001; Leader-Williams and Hutton, 2005). Nevertheless, various anti-hunting, welfare or conservation groups may invoke the precautionary principle to argue against trophy hunting of individual animals (LACS, 2004; Species Survival Network, 2004), whatever the conservation benefits that trophy hunting may produce for the species.

This chapter reviews the uncertainties associated with seeking to reverse the decline of a mammalian sub-species, the straight-horned markhor in Pakistan, with particular reference to the Torghar population of markhor (Johnson, 1997; Ahmed et al, 2001; Shackleton, 2001; Frisina et al, 2002; Woodford et al, 2002; Bellon, in preparation). We examine the mechanisms in place to deal with uncertainty, including listing on CITES Appendix I and proposing and implementing a trophy-hunting regime through CITES-approved quotas. While documenting our review, we noted that none of the minuted decisions taken by CITES specifically invoked the precautionary principle or a precautionary approach. Indeed, we suggest that this is the norm for many decisions in natural resource management that implicitly adopt a precautionary approach toward uncertain threats. Furthermore, even those groups specifically citing the precautionary principle to support their opposition to trophy hunting and other forms of use only refer to the principle in a general way (see references cited above), without specifying the particular uncertainty that the principle is invoked to address. As a result, reviews of different natural resource management scenarios, such as this, must necessarily rely on retrospective inferences about the uncertainty taken into account in formal decision-making processes some years previously.

# INTERPRETATION OF THE PRECAUTIONARY APPROACH

## Formulations used in this review

While there have been many formulations of the precautionary principle or a precautionary approach (see Cooney, 2004), we make reference to two formulations: first, Principle 15 of the Rio Declaration on Environment and Development (1992) states that:

*In order to protect the environment the Precautionary Approach shall be widely applied by States according to their capabilities. Where there are threats of serious or irreversible damage, lack of full scientific certainty shall not be used as a reason for postponing cost-effective measures to prevent environmental degradation.*

Second, the formulation used in CITES Resolution Conf. 9.24 before its revision in 2004 declares that:

*Recognizing that by virtue of the precautionary principle, in cases of uncertainty, the Parties shall act in the best interest of the conservation of the species when considering proposals for amendment of Appendices I and II.*

These two formulations stress the importance of potential harm, cost-effectiveness and best interest of species as key to interpreting precaution.

## CITES and the precautionary approach

The precautionary principle started to gain acceptance in the 1980s, following its inclusion in international law to address marine pollution (Cooney, 2004). Several years before this, in 1975, CITES had come into force to address concerns over unsustainable international trade in wild species. The Convention lists species in three appendices:

- Appendix I to prohibit commercial international trade;
- Appendix II to regulate international trade through a permit system; and
- Appendix III for national governments to list species for which they wish the help of other parties to control their trade.

Neither the text of the Convention, nor the Berne Criteria adopted at the first meeting of parties to CITES in 1976 (Resolution Conf. 1.5) for inclusion of species in the Appendices, made any explicit mention of the precautionary approach. Nonetheless, the wording in both the Convention text and the Berne Criteria guided the parties to list species in Appendix I if they 'may' be threatened by international trade, and in Appendix II if trade 'may' become a threat. Indeed, for many species, the facts of their poor conservation status and of being in, or even possibly being in, international trade has often been sufficient to include the species in the Appendices, even though the international trade in question may not have been the primary driver of decline. The Convention defines international trade very broadly, as all forms of export, re-export, import or introduction from the sea. The Convention does not differentiate between the products of different forms of possible trade, such as hunting for meat or for other low-cost, high-volume products and high-cost, low-volume trophies. Therefore, although a precautionary approach was not specifically invoked in early CITES regulation, it can be retrospectively assessed to have followed a cautious approach, favouring the regulation of all international trade in the face of uncertainty over its impacts rather than maintaining the status quo, often despite a lack of clear evidence to support the need to regulate a specific form of international trade, such as trophy hunting. As a result, CITES is seen by many as an example of precaution in action (Dickson, 2000; Martin, 2000).

The Convention has allowed for non-commercial international trade in those specimens listed in Appendix I from early in its life, and explained procedures for dealing with hunting trophies of species listed in Appendix I through Resolution Conf. 2.11 (Rev) in 1979, and Resolution Conf. 9.21 (Rev. CoP13) in 1994. Since this time, the potential benefits of incentive-driven conservation have been further recognized (Hutton and Leader-Williams, 2003). This suggests that, in the face of uncertainty as to whether all forms of trade present a threat, restricting all international trade may not always be the most precautionary course of action. Parties to CITES recognized this apparent contradiction with the adoption of Resolution Conf. 8.3 on the Benefits of Trade in 1992, and of Resolution Conf. 9.24 on Criteria for Inclusion of Species in the Appendices in 1994, which specifically included the precautionary wording 'to act in the best conservation interest of the species', rather than a presumption in favour of increased restriction on trade. Given the evolution of conservation thinking, and the increasingly explicit use of the precautionary approach within CITES, our review seeks to question:

- how this guidance on precaution has been interpreted; and
- what lessons can be learned from this interpretation in order to better guide future conservation action and decision-making.

## TROPHY HUNTING

Trophy hunting can be extremely lucrative; record heads of spectacular rare species can command high prices, both in the form of trophy and licence fees, and of the daily rates charged for minimum safari lengths (Leader-Williams et al, 1996; see also Bhagwandas, 2005; Hunting Masters, 2005). In some respects, trophy hunting can also be viewed as a self-limiting form of harvest. By requiring quality trophies, trophy hunters can, in theory, automatically instigate a feedback loop for managers, in that taking too many males will diminish trophy quality, reducing the incentive to hunt that particular herd. Likewise, although high trophy fees might be expected to encourage managers to take a greater harvest, trophy fees will be affected by the laws of supply and demand in the long run. Hence, trophy fees are likely to decline as more trophy animals become available, as was the case with auction sales of white rhinos in South Africa (see *Game & Hunt*, 2004). Although there has been evidence and speculation regarding detrimental population impacts of trophy hunting and sex-biased hunting in terms of overharvest, population genetics and behaviour (Poole, 1989; Ginsberg and Milner-Gulland, 1994; Milner-Gulland et al, 2003), recent research has shown ways to overcome some of these concerns.

Studies of bighorn sheep *Ovis canadensis* and population modelling of lions *Panthera leo* have recommended that only post-reproductive males should be targeted by trophy hunters, as they have no further genetic contribution to make and their removal will cause little behavioural disruption to the population (Coltman et al, 2003; Whitman et al, 2004).

While Appendix I listings theoretically protect species from commercial international trade, several Appendix I species have continued to be shot as problem animals under national legislation in many range states. In such cases, importing states may still refuse to issue import permits for these species, based on their own unilateral import restrictions – the 'stricter domestic measures' provided for by Article XIV of CITES. This has particularly affected those species listed in Appendix I that are also included in the US Endangered Species Act (1973) (Hutton, 2000; Leader-Williams and Hutton, 2005). As a result, a potential source of conservation benefit that could have provided an incentive for landowners and farmers to tolerate these problem species may have been unintentionally removed. CITES has subsequently moved to recognize this situation, both for individual species, as well as more generically. Quotas were approved for trophy hunting of leopard in 1983 and for cheetah in 1992 from certain range states (Wijnstekers, 2003). More recently, trophy-hunting quotas were also approved for markhor in 1997 and for black rhinos in 2004, once evidence had become available of improved enforcement and of population recovery. More generically, the potential conservation benefits of trophy hunting have been recognized for a number of Appendix I listed species, through Resolution Conf. 9.21 on Quotas for Appendix I Species. As a consequence, a quota agreed at a Conference of Parties has served to reduce the justification for importing countries to question or refuse imports of Appendix I trophies.

# MARKHOR, TROPHY HUNTING AND PRECAUTION

## Taxonomy and ecology of markhor

Wild goats generally inhabit inaccessible mountain regions that have low primary productivity and that are unsuitable for growing crops (Poore, 1992). As the ancestors of domestic stock, adapted to climatic extremes and harsh conditions, the different isolated populations of wild goats represent unique gene pools, with important genetic diversity to be conserved for its potential contribution to the improvement of domestic stock. Furthermore, these species of wild goat are important for extractive uses such as hunting for food, medicine, skin or sport, and potentially useful for non-consumptive tourism. Nevertheless, in much of their range, grazing competition with domestic livestock is increasing and is compounded by habitat loss due to other causes, including disputes in sensitive border areas. In these harsh environments, wild goats are at risk from overexploitation due to their low reproductive rates compared with ungulates of similar body size, their high site fidelity, use of open habitats, and conspicuous rump patches (Hess et al, 1997).

**Table 4.1** *Taxonomy and geographical distribution of the sub-species of markhor* capra falconeri

| Sub-species | Common name(s) | Geographical distribution |
| --- | --- | --- |
| C. f. falconeri | Flare-horned markhor, Astor or Pir Pinjal markhor | India (Jammu and Kashmir) and Pakistan (Azad Jammu and Kashmir, Northern Areas and North West Frontier Province (NWFP)) |
| C. f. megaceros | Straight-horned sulaiman or Kabul markhor | Afghanistan and Pakistan (NWFP) |
| C. f. heptneri | Tadjik markhor | Tadjikistan (Dashtidjum district), Turkmenistan, Uzbekistan and possibly Afghanistan |

Note: C.f. chiltanensis is now recognized as a wild goat C. aegagrus.
Source: based on Shackleton (1997)

Markhor *Capra falconeri* are a form of wild goat from the same genus as domestic goats *C. hircus*. Although the taxonomy of wild goats is controversial, three sub-species of markhor are now generally recognized (see Table 4.1). Markhor are reported to twin and reach sexual maturity at about 30 months, with gestation of 135–170 days and longevity of 11–12 years (Nowak, 1999).

## Status of markhor in Pakistan

Pakistan is home to seven species and 11 sub-species of wild sheep and goat, and holds most of the global population of wild markhor *Capra falconeri*. The markhor has impressive spiral horns and has always been an important trophy for foreign hunters willing to pay large trophy fees to bag such animals (Johnson, 1997). Studies in Pakistan in the 1960s and 1970s indicated that markhor were severely threatened as their range had been significantly restricted and they survived only in discontinuous pockets (Roberts, 1969; Schaller and Khan, 1975). At the same time, the species was in demand by both international trophy hunters and by influential Pakistanis. In the early 1970s, Pakistan adopted conservation legislation through various provincial acts and ordinances. This legislation laid the foundation for three types of protected areas, and several areas were set aside for the protection of wild caprines such as markhor. However, due inter alia to their inaccessibility, these protection measures were poorly implemented (Shackleton, 1997), while the potential for generating revenue through non-consumptive tourism was limited due to the political instability of these areas.

## Initial listing of markhor in CITES Appendices

The international community became concerned over the continuing declines in markhor populations in the 1970s (see Table 4.2). As a result of these concerns,

**Table 4.2** *Chronology of events in approaches to conserving markhor*

| Year | Level | Authority | Status | Response to uncertainty or precautionary action |
|---|---|---|---|---|
| 1965 | Global | IUCN Red List | Indeterminate | |
| 1974 | National | Government of Pakistan | | Ban on hunting |
| 1975 | International biologist/ national | Schaller and Khan (1975) | Pakistan population estimate of <2000 straight-horned markhor | |
| 1975 | Global | CITES | Appendix I | Listing of straight-horned markhor |
| | | | Appendix II | Listing of other two markhor sub-species |
| 1975 | National/stricter domestic measures | US Endangered Species Act | Endangered | Listing of straight-horned markhor |
| 1984 | Local | Nawab | | Torghar programme conceived |
| 1985 | International biologist/ local community | Bellon (in prep.) | Torghar population estimate of <100 | |
| 1985 | Local/provincial | | | Torghar Conservation Plan implemented |
| 1986 | Global | IUCN Red List | Vulnerable | |
| 1992 | Global | CITES | Appendix I | |
| 1994 | Global | IUCN Red List | Endangered | Listing of other two markhor sub-species |
| 1994 | International biologist/ local community | Johnson (1997) | Torghar population estimate of 700 | |
| 1997 | International biologist/ local community | Frisina et al (1998) | Torghar population estimate of 1300 | |
| 1997 | International biologist/ local community | CITES | | Pakistan granted export quota of 6 markhor, with 2 for Torghar |
| 1999 | International biologist/ local community | Frisina (2000) | Torghar population estimate of 1680 | |
| 1999 | National/stricter domestic measures | US Endangered Species Act | | Review of endangered status |
| 2002 | Global | CITES | | Pakistan export quota increased to 12 markhor, with 4 for Torghar |
| 2004 | Global | IUCN Red List | Endangered (1996 assessment) | |

parties to CITES took the step in 1975 of listing all sub-species of markhor on CITES appendices. They sought to prohibit commercial trade in three sub-species (prior to their current taxonomic revision, as shown in Table 4.1), including the straight-horned markhor *C. f. megaceros*, through their listing on Appendix I. They also sought to regulate commercial trade in all other sub-species of markhor through their listing in Appendix II. In the early 1970s evidence had emerged from Pakistan of ongoing range reduction and population decline (Roberts, 1969), and the population of *C. f. megaceros* was estimated at less than 2000 individuals (Schaller and Khan, 1975). The reasons for their decline were reported as unmanaged use by nomadic herdsmen, grazing competition with domestic livestock, and interest from indigenous hunters seeking meat and foreign hunters seeking trophies (Schaller and Khan, 1975).

## The Torghar Conservation Project

In 1984, a private conservation initiative was started by local leaders in the Torghar Hills of Baluchistan, incorporating trophy hunting. Administration in the Torghar region since colonial times has been the joint responsibility of provincial government and leaders of the local tribes. Although recent legal changes have brought the administration back into the mainstream, it was only the local leaders who had the capacity to enforce tribal hunting laws. The local leaders supported the creation of the Torghar Conservation Plan in 1985, ten years after the original CITES listing (Johnson, 1997). The 1985 Plan initially instituted a total ban on markhor hunting and hired mountain hunters as game guards. At the same time, trophy hunts for a CITES Appendix II listed sub-species, the Afghan urial *Ovis orientalis cycloceros*, were used to generate income to support the programme and to provide benefits for the local owners of the mountain in the form of salaries for local game guards (Shackleton, 2001). Hence, trophy fees for urial were increased from a paltry US$100 per animal to US$1000 per animal in 1985.

Based on the early success of the Torghar Conservation Programme (TCP) in regulating nomadic hunting, the first trophy hunt for markhor was sanctioned by the tribal and provincial authorities in 1989 (Bellon, in preparation). The hunting of one to two markhor annually was allowed until the late 1990s, since when the quota has been increased to a possible four markhor per year. Hunting is limited to old males identified by the game guard and selected by the hunter (Johnson, 1997; Bellon, in preparation). During the first ten years of the project US$460,000 was raised from the sale of 20 urial and 14 markhor trophy hunts (Johnson, 1997).

Results from field surveys conducted in 1985, 1994, 1997 and 1999 indicated that the Torghar Hills population of straight-horned markhor had increased substantially since 1985, when only 56 individuals were thought to be present (see Table 4.2 and Figure 4.1). This 20-fold increase in population size over 12 years was reportedly due to a virtual elimination of unauthorized hunting, based initially on using income from trophy hunting of urial to employ local game guards (Johnson, 1997).

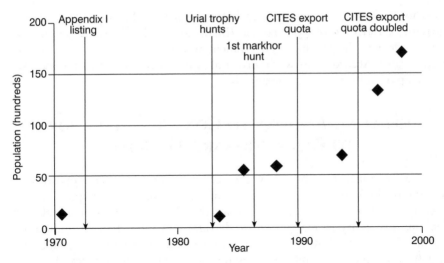

*Source:* chapter authors

**Figure 4.1** *Population numbers of markhor in relation to key actions taken to ensure their management in the Torghar Hills of Pakistan*

The majority of trophy hunters were originally from Europe, where stricter domestic legislation did not affect the import of trophies listed in Appendix I (Johnson, 1997). However, Americans were unable to obtain import certificates for markhor trophies during the 1990s because of stricter domestic measures applied under the US Endangered Species Act (see Table 4.2), jeopardizing some potential income for the community conservation programme (Johnson, 1997).

## CITES quotas for trade in markhor trophies

The difficulty in attracting international hunters to trophy hunt markhor prompted the national government of Pakistan to request an annual export quota for the species from CITES. In 1997, on the basis of results from the Torghar Conservation Programme and from other areas (CITES COP 10 Doc 10.84), Pakistan successfully requested a CITES export quota for its populations of Appendix I listed markhor (as shown in Table 4.2). The CITES parties approved an annual export quota of six animals for trophy hunting in 1997, provided that this benefited the conservation of the sub-species. The National Council for Conservation of Wildlife (NCCW), the CITES Authority of Pakistan, granted two permits to TCP and the remainder to the NWFP and Northern Areas. By 2002, the Torghar population of markhor had further increased to 1684 (CITES COP 12 Doc 12.23.2). Also in 2002, Pakistan's export quota was increased to 12 animals annually, of which four were awarded to TCP. This still represents a very conservative quota, as the size of the population in 2002 suggests that a sustainable harvest could comprise up to 18 markhor per year (Wegge, 1997). The trophy fee for the straight-horned markhor has now been set at US$25,000 per animal, while those for urial are currently set at US$8000 per animal (Bhagwandas, 2005). Of these fees, 20 per cent goes to the provincial government and the rest to the TCP (Bellon, in preparation). According to Woodford et al (2002), over 60 local tribesmen are now employed by TCP as game guards.

# RELATING ACTIONS TO CONSERVE MARKHOR TO PRECAUTIONARY THINKING

We now examine, retrospectively, the actions taken to conserve markhor in relation to the implicit use of the precautionary approach in response to the uncertainty surrounding factors such as: the ultimate drivers of population decline; the ability to manage those drivers; and the extent of population decline. We examine how precaution can operate at several institutional levels, and how its outcomes may vary under different circumstances. We also examine how there may be tensions between the different interests of conservation and development, and between local, national and international interests (see also Table 4.2).

## Legal and policy responses to uncertainty

### International responses

The straight-horned and two other sub-species of markhor were included in Appendix I of CITES in 1975, while other sub-species were initially only included in Appendix II (as shown in Table 4.2). The precautionary principle had not by then been widely articulated in international law (Cooney, 2004), and minutes of the CITES meetings do not indicate any explicit recognition of precaution in decision-making. However, the Appendix I markhor listings arguably indicate a precautionary approach, according the benefit of the doubt to the species. There was uncertainty surrounding the extent to which trade was a threat, and an Appendix I listing reverses the burden of proof. With such a listing, no trade is allowed except in very specific circumstances and on the basis that trade will not be detrimental to the species.

However, determining whether or not these decisions should be viewed as precautionary may depend on the value judgements of those making a retrospective examination of the decisions. In contrast to the original listing decisions, in 1997 and 2002 the parties approved an export quota for the Pakistani population of markhor. Some may interpret this as effectively reducing the level of precaution applied. Equally, others may interpret it as widening precautionary thinking to involve all parties to CITES in sanctioning a harvest level. For those whose value judgements equate extractive use with harm to the population (Hoyt, 1994), the most conservative and thus precautionary action would have been to refuse the quota in 1997 and 2002. Indeed, in 1999 some commentators recommended just that course of action in response to the US Fish and Wildlife Service (USFWS) review of the species listing under the

US Endangered Species Act (USFWS, 1999), based on the need to prevent any genetic impacts to the population. However, in 1997 there was clear evidence of a population recovery for the markhor, coinciding with the protection afforded by the TCP based on funding gained through trophy hunts (see Figure 4.1). This suggests that the less damaging, and more precautionary, approach was to approve the quota application, to generate further funding that could continue to support the key management action of patrolling by game guards, and so prevent the population going into even more of a potentially dangerous demographic and genetic bottleneck.

It is also important to note that the potential threats risked by granting a quota were reversible. Had the more controversial (for some) decision of granting a quota resulted in a population decline, the Conferences of the Parties in 1999 or 2002 could presumably have revoked the quota. In the event, based on evidence of the ongoing recovery of markhor, the approach in 2002 was to further increase a still conservative quota to allow exports of 12 trophies annually, and so provide further incentives for the cost-effective conservation of markhor in the best interests of the sub-species.

## National and provincial responses

Although hunting had generally been banned at the national and provincial levels in Pakistan, a remaining clause in the national legislation allowed the prime minister to license limited trophy hunting (Bellon, in preparation). Trophy hunting was carried out under tribal permit from 1987–89. When the TCP was conducting a single annual trophy hunt sanctioned by the provincial government in the early 1990s, the national government would not sanction export permits, apparently in accordance with the precautionary requirements of the existing Appendix I listing. Therefore, flexibility at the provincial level allowed the limited trophy hunting that supported the project, before it was clear that the approach would be successful in contributing to markhor conservation. Fortunately, this flexibility did not appear to lead to any misuse of funds by senior figures, as was alleged in the 1970s (Schaller and Khan, 1975).

## Local responses

The TCP arose through strong local leadership by Nawab Taimur Shah Jogezai (see Table 4.2). Local leaders recognized the threats faced by markhor and sought proactively to address these through sustainable and cost-effective measures agreed at community level. The local approach to uncertainty, including to uncertain environmental conditions such as the drought of the late 1990s and early 2000s, has arguably been precautionary in terms of limiting biological offtake. Uncertainty regarding success of the trophy hunting was addressed at a local level, first, by trophy hunting the more numerous urial, second, by only sanctioning a conservative quota of markhor, and third, through voluntary reduction of livestock numbers (Woodford et al, 2002). Equally, the precautionary quota setting might also have helped to restrict the supply of trophies and thus to maintain a high price (as for white rhino (*Game & Hunt*, 2004)).

## Conservation impacts of a precautionary approach towards markhor

The initial listing of straight-horned markhor in Appendix I may have resulted in only equivocal conservation benefits. On the one hand, hunting was rife and unregulated, and the listing may have helped bring unregulated hunting under control. Furthermore, the listing probably raised the profile of the issue and stimulated some monitoring. On the other hand, international trade was not the main threat facing markhor, and the Appendix I listing may have hampered conservation based on trophy hunting. Nevertheless, if it is retrospectively accepted that the initial listing of markhor represented a cautious response to uncertainty, it appears a justifiable, if not particularly effective, use of a precautionary approach. However, by the 1990s, restrictions invoked through CITES and stricter domestic measures imposed by the United States appear to have hindered rather than assisted the ongoing conservation of markhor.

It is therefore not always simple to determine the precautionary response: this may not be fixed and will depend heavily on context. Restricting trophy hunting may be the precautionary response in some circumstances, but may not be in others. In this instance, the demographic and genetic danger of allowing the population to decline further into a potentially dangerous bottleneck must be compared with the possible deleterious genetic effects of trophy hunting relatively few males (Coltman et al, 2003). The stance that trophy hunting should automatically be opposed or restricted on the basis of the precautionary principle, often invoked by those conservation and animal welfare groups opposed to hunting, ignores the potential benefits of trophy hunting (shown for markhor in Figure 4.1) and constitutes poor and inappropriate use of the principle.

## Socio-economic impacts of a precautionary approach towards markhor

The original Appendix I listing of markhor and the subsequent local hunting ban (see Table 4.2) are unlikely to have imposed onerous livelihood costs. At this time, only 56 markhor were estimated to remain in the TCP area, so it is unlikely that local families would then have derived any lasting benefit from use of the markhor. However, the development of the TCP has seen the programme make a real and locally important contribution to livelihoods. The initiation of the TCP developed a structure whereby the local community was able to benefit from protecting the population for a managed trophy harvest. Over the duration of the TCP, many families have benefited from income as game guards, to the extent that game guard salaries are now seen as a means of benefit sharing (Bellon, in preparation). However, the increase in wildlife populations raises the possibility of increased competition with livestock. According to one study, wildlife numbers are too low in most areas of northern Baluchistan for this to be an issue (Khan, 2003). However, in the Torghar area, local families have agreed to remove livestock and set aside part of their land for wildlife (Woodford et al, 2002). Furthermore, they have agreed that, even in livestock areas, they will maintain stock densities at the levels reached during the recent droughts. As these are apparently democratic decisions, it appears that the socio-economic benefits from the conservation of wildlife outweigh those from reducing wildlife numbers (Emerton, 2001; Leader-Williams and Hutton, 2005). However, the TCP has indicated that the benefits from trophy hunting wildlife will not lift local people out of poverty or contribute significantly to their development. To deliver sustainable development, the TCP must look to alternative sources of livelihood (Bellon, in preparation).

## Science and the precautionary principle in markhor conservation

Science can marshal and evaluate known facts and make predictions about the outcomes of possible actions based on past experience. But ultimately a precautionary approach is called into play when there is scientific uncertainty, and this approach inevitably involves value judgements coloured by the approaches to conservation favoured at the time. In this case, the remaining Torghar population of markhor began to recover in the mid-1980s following the local ban on hunting and initiation of protection measures ten years after their listing in Appendix I, as unmanaged hunting was brought under control by TCP activities. However, at the time of the listing, there was no guarantee that this would be the eventual outcome, as the major threat was local hunting (Ahmed et al, 2001). For example, following the listing of black rhino in Appendix I in 1977, it took 20 years and a major change of policy (to focus on small populations) before unmanaged hunting was brought under control (Leader-Williams, 2002). Views of what is or is not precautionary will be affected by culture and beliefs. Given that precaution is invoked when outcomes are uncertain, groups may differ in their perceptions of which actions will be precautionary and will lead to the desired outcome. This is exemplified by the different opinions expressed to the US Fish and Wildlife Service in response to the proposal for an export quota for the Torghar population of markhor (USFWS, 1997). One set of responses believed that approval of the quota would enhance the survival chances of the population, with the other group believing that the genetic make-up of the population could be compromised. Nevertheless, the final agreements regarding the approach to recovering markhor was driven by decisions reached in an open democratic manner at the local level.

While local participation in decision-making is important, science still has an important role. Science can be brought in after precautionary decisions to review the outcome, and can examine whether the circumstances have changed such that previous decisions require review through a process of adaptive management. As circumstances change, precautionary decisions should ideally be reviewed scientifically within a reasonable time frame, to ensure that appropriate action is being taken.

## Responding to changing circumstances in markhor conservation

Arguably, the sources of uncertainty surrounding conservation and management of markhor differed in 1975 and 1997 (see above). The CITES decisions on the markhor population of Pakistan in 1975 and 1997 adopted opposing approaches, by tightening and loosening export control, respectively. Therefore, on the evidence available at the time, both appear consistent with a precautionary approach by not postponing measures that were then believed to produce cost-effective conservation. The 1997 decision, necessary to satisfy stricter domestic measures in some importing countries, and so increase funds for paying game guards, was in line with Rio Principle 15 that advocates that precautionary measures be cost-effective. The parties have apparently responded to uncertainty in line with contemporary and pragmatic conservation thinking.

Our analysis suggests, therefore, that the outcomes of precautionary decision-making cannot be interpreted in a static fashion, but must take changing circumstances into account. For example, prohibiting trade appeared to be a precautionary response to a declining population in 1975. At the time, information on the threats faced by the markhor population was incomplete. Nevertheless, it seems reasonable to assume that, as one of the potential threats faced by this markhor population, banning trade appeared likely to reduce that threat. By contrast, when Pakistan requested a trophy-hunting quota in 1997, similar logic could have been invoked to agree that any threat to the population should be mitigated against. However, indiscriminate hunting had been brought under control using trophy-hunting revenue to pay sufficient game guards. Thus parties to CITES had implicitly to weigh up the risks of reducing support for the community conservation projects against the risks of unforeseen biological consequences of the limited trophy hunts, such as changes to genetic structure (Ginsberg and Milner-Gulland, 1994). On the basis of the information available, the parties accepted the quota proposal, presumably as being in the best conservation interest of the sub-species. However, a more transparent process could in future involve an explicit risk assessment procedure.

# LESSONS LEARNED FOR INTERPRETING AND IMPLEMENTING PRECAUTION IN BIODIVERSITY CONSERVATION

This review of the international regulation and local management needs of one population of an endangered sub-species throws up a number of lessons that would benefit from being examined across a wider range of taxa and situations. Our conclusions can be summarized as follows:

- Precautionary decisions may require different actions under different circumstances.
- The interpretation of what is, or is not, a precautionary action involves value judgements that should be sensitive to the local cultural context.
- A risk assessment process that explicitly addresses uncertainties could help to characterize and weigh the different threats, particularly for implementing innovative projects, where decisions can be coupled with a fall-back position should problems arise.
- International regulation should be responsive to local needs, in order to find mechanisms that ensure the survival of different local populations of species and sub-species that in turn make up the global population. The corollary of accepting this position may also be that the needs of local species populations may sometimes be compromised for the greater good.
- Retaining flexibility is important in drawing up policy and formulating legislation to enable authorities and institutions at local, national and international levels to respond to changing circumstances.
- Flexibility should nevertheless be sensitively incorporated into administrative frameworks, as it should not generate loopholes that can be exploited.
- Changing circumstances require that precautionary decisions should be reviewed and monitored for their impacts, in an adaptive management framework.
- Decision-makers need a framework for considering novel solutions when traditional approaches challenge the outcomes. In such situations, precaution may require a step-by-step approach with regular monitoring and the flexibility to abandon any novel approaches if this is required.

# REFERENCES

Ahmed, J., Tareen, N. and Khan, P. (2001) 'Conservation of Sulaiman markhor and Afghan urial by local tribesmen in Torghar Pakistan', *Lessons Learned: Case Studies in Sustainable Use*, Convention on Biodiversity website, www.biodiv.org/doc/case-studies/suse/cs-suse-iucn-pref.pdf

Bellon, L. (in preparation) *Sustainable Conservation: A Process or an Outcome? Lessons from the Conservation Programme in Torghar, Balochistan, Pakistan*

Bhagwandas (2005) 'Centre issues permits to hunt 93 rare animals', *Dawn: The Internet Edition*, 25 January. Available at www.dawn.com/2005/01/25/nat19.htm

Bond, I. (1994) 'Importance of elephant hunting to CAMPFIRE revenue in Zimbabwe', *Traffic Bulletin*, vol 14, pp117–19

Bond, I. (2001) 'CAMPFIRE and the incentives for institutional change', in D. Hulme and M. Murphree (eds) *African Wildlife and Livelihoods: The Promise and Performance of Community Conservation*, James Currey, Oxford, pp227–43

Caughley, G. and Gunn, A. (1996) *Conservation Biology in Theory and Practice*, Blackwell Science, Sunderland, Massachusetts

Caughley, G., Dublin, H. and Parker, I. (1990) 'Projected decline of the African elephant', *Biological Conservation*, vol 54, pp157–64

Coltman, D. W., O'Donoghue, P., Jorgenson, J. T., Hogg, J. T., Strobeck, C. and Festa-Bianchet, M. (2003) 'Undesirable evolutionary consequences of trophy hunting', *Nature*, no 426, pp655–58

Cooney, R (2004) *The Precautionary Principle in Biodiversity Conservation and Natural Resource Management: An Issues Paper for Policy-makers, Researchers and Practitioners*, IUCN Policy and Global Change Series, no 2, IUCN, Gland, Switzerland and Cambridge, UK

Dickson, B. (2000) 'Precaution at the heart of CITES?', in J. Hutton and B. Dickson (eds) *Endangered Species Threatened Convention: The Past, Present and Future of CITES*, Earthscan, London, pp38–46

Emerton, L. A. (2001) 'The nature of benefits and the benefits of nature', in D. Hulme and M. Murphree (eds) *African Wildlife and Livelihoods: The Promise and Performance of Community Conservation*, James Currey, Oxford, pp208–26

Frisina, M. R. (2000) 'Suleiman markhor (*Capra falconeri jerdoni*) and Afghan urial (*Ovis orientalis cycloceros*): population status in Torghar Hills, Balochistan Province, Pakistan', unpublished report to STEP and USFWS

Frisina, M. R., Woodford, M. H. and Awan, G. A. (2002) 'Habitat and disease issues of concern to management of straight-horned markhor and Afghan urial in the Torghar Hills, Balochistan Province, Pakistan', unpublished report to STEP and USFWS

Frisina, M. R., Woods, C. and Woodford, M. H. (1998) 'Population trend of Sulieman markhor (*Capra falconeri jerdoni*) and Afghan urial (*Ovis orientalis cycloceros*) with reference to habitat conditions, Torghar Hills, Baluchistan Province, Pakistan', report to the US Fish and Wildlife Service Office of International Affairs and to the Society for Torghar Environmental Protection

*Game & Hunt* (2004) 'White rhino sales down at KZN auction', *Game & Hunt*, August. Available at www.wildlifehunt.co.za/2004/august/auction.html

Ginsberg, J. and Milner-Gulland, E. J. (1994) 'Sex-biassed harvesting and population dynamics: implications for conservation and sustainable use', *Conservation Biology*, vol 7, pp611–17

Hess, R., Bollman, K., Rasool, G., Chaudhry, A. A., Virk, A. T. and Ahmad, A. (1997) 'Pakistan', in D. M. Shackleton (ed) *Wild Sheep and Goats, and their Relatives: Status Survey and Conservation Action Plan for Caprinae*, IUCN, Gland, Switzerland and Cambridge, UK, pp 239-60

Hoyt, J. (1994) *Animals in Peril: How Sustainable Use is Wiping Out the World's Wildlife*, Avery Publishing Group, New York

Hunting Masters (2005) *Markhor Hunting Community-Based Trophy Harvesting*, Markhor, Hunting Masters website, www.huntingmasters.com/markhor/

Hutton, J. (2000) 'Who knows best? Controversy over unilateral stricter domestic measures', in J. Hutton and B. Dickson (eds) *Endangered Species Threatened Convention: the past, present and future of CITES*, Earthscan, London, pp57–66

Hutton, J. and Leader-Williams, N. (2003) 'Sustainable use and incentive driven conservation: realigning human and conservation interests', *Oryx*, vol 37, pp 215–26

Johnson, K. A. (1997) 'Trophy hunting as a conservation tool for caprinae in Pakistan', in C. H. Freese (ed) *Harvesting Wild Species: Implications for Biodiversity Conservation*, John Hopkins University Press, Baltimore and London, pp393–423

Khan, A. G. (2003) *NASSD Background Paper: Rangelands and Livestock*, IUCN Pakistan, Northern Areas Progamme, Gilgit

LACS (2004) 'League Against Cruel Sports demand government action on trophy hunting', article available at www.bloodybusiness.com/trophy_hunting/govt_action.htm

Leader-Williams, N. (2002) 'Regulation and protection: successes and failures in rhinoceros conservation', in S. Oldfield (ed) *The Trade in Wildlife: Regulation for Conservation*, Earthscan, London, pp89–99

Leader-Williams, N. and Hutton, J. (2005) 'Does extractive use provide opportunities to offset conflicts between people and wildlife?', in R. Woodroffe, S. J. Thirgood and A. Rabinowitz (eds) *People and Wildlife: Conflict or Co-existence?*, Cambridge University Press, Cambridge, pp140–61

Leader-Williams, N., Kayera, J. A. and Overton, G. L. (1996) *Tourist Hunting in Tanzania*, IUCN, Gland, Swizterland and Cambridge, UK

Martin, R. B. (2000) 'CITES and the CBD', in J. Hutton and B. Dickson (eds) *Endangered Species Threatened Convention: The Past, Present and Future of CITES* Earthscan, London, pp29–37

Milner-Gulland, E. J. and Beddington, J. R. (1993) 'The relative effects of hunting and habitat destruction on elephant population dynamics over time', *Pachyderm*, vol 17, pp75–90

Milner-Gulland, E. J., Bukreeva, O. M., Coulson, T., Lushchekina, A. A., Kholodova, M. V., Bekenov, A. B. and Grachev, I. A. (2003) 'Reproductive collapse in saiga antelope harems', *Nature*, no 422, p135

Milner-Gulland, E. J. and Mace, R. (1998) *Conservation of Biological Resources*, Blackwell, Oxford

Murphree, M. (1993) *Communities as Resource Management Institutions*, Gatekeeper Series, no 36, International Institute for Environment and Development, London

Nowak, R. M. (1999) *Walkers Mammals of the World*, Sixth edition, John Hopkins University Press, Baltimore

Poole, J. H. (1989) 'The effects of poaching on the age structure and social and reproductive patterns of selected East African elephant populations', *The Ivory Trade and the Future of the African Elephant*, Ivory Trade Review Group, Queen Elizabeth House, Oxford, UK

Poore, D. (ed) (1992) *Guidelines for Mountain Protected Areas*, IUCN Gland, Switzerland and Cambridge, UK

Roberts, T. J. (1969) 'A note on *Capra falconeri* (Wagner, 1893)', *Z Saugetierk*, vol 34, pp238–49

Schaller, G. B. and Khan, S A (1975) 'Distribution and status of markhor *Capra falconeri*', *Biological Conservation*, vol 7, pp185–98

Shackleton, D. M. (ed) (1997) *Wild Sheep and Goats, and their Relatives: Status Survey and Conservation Action Plan for Caprinae*, IUCN, Gland, Switzerland and Cambridge, UK

Shackleton, D. M. (2001) 'A review of community-based trophy hunting programmes in Pakistan', unpublished report to the Mountain Areas Conservancy Project

Species Survival Network (2004) 'SSN Analysis of CoP 13 working documents. Draft Resolutions and Other Documents to be Discussed at the 13th COP to CITES', CITES 2004. Available at www.ssn.org/cop13/resolutions/Digest_Working_Doc_Table.pdf

USFWS (1997) 'Summary of US negotiating positions: Conference of the Parties to the Convention on International Trade in Endangered Species of Wild Fauna and Flora, Tenth Regular Meeting', *Federal Register*, vol 62, no 109, 6 June, pp31127–51

USFWS (1999) 'Endangered and threatened wildlife and plants: 90-day finding on petition to reclassify the straight-horned markhor population of the Torghar Region of Balochistan, Pakistan from endangered to threatened and initiation of status review for markhor', *Federal Register*, vol 64, no 184, 23 September, pp51499–51500

Wegge, P. (1997) 'Appendix I: preliminary guidelines for sustainable use of wild caprines', in D. M. Shackleton (ed) *Wild Sheep and Goats and Their Relatives: Status Survey and Conservation Action Plan for Caprinae*, IUCN, Gland, Switzerland and Cambridge, UK, pp365–72

Whitman, K., Starfield, A. M., Quadling, H. S. and Packer, C. (2004) 'Sustainable trophy hunting of African lions', *Nature*, no 428, pp175–78

Wijnstekers, W. (2003) *The Evolution of CITES*, Seventh edition, CITES Secretariat, Geneva

Woodford, M. H., Frisina, M. R. and Awan, G. (2002) *Habitat and Veterinary Concerns for the Management of the Suleiman Markhor* (Capra falconeri megaceros) *and the Afghan Urial* (Ovis orientalis cycloceros) *in the Torghar Hills Balochistan*, unpublished report to Torghar Conservation Project, www.virtualcentre.org/fr/ele/econf_02_faune/download/t2_08_torghar.pdf

# 5

# The Precautionary Principle in Impact Assessment: An International Review

*Graham Tucker and Jo Treweek*

## BACKGROUND AND OBJECTIVES

The precautionary principle is intended to promote actions that avoid serious or irreversible harm in advance of scientific certainty of such harm (Cooney, 2004). However, although widely accepted, practical incorporation of the principle into policy, law and environmental management has been marked by controversy and confusion.

The Rio Declaration (1992) firmly established the link between environment and development by stating that, 'in order to achieve sustainable development, environmental protection shall constitute an integral part of the development process and cannot be considered in isolation from it'. If environmental protection is to be an integral part of the development process, it is necessary to assess the environmental risks associated with human activities. Impact assessment (IA) is widely applied to predict the effects of proposed activities on the environment (UNECE, 1991). As such it can be an important component in a precautionary approach. IA can help implementation of the precautionary principle in many ways, not least by providing information about environmental effects and their likely significance. It forces proponents of new developments and activities to provide evidence that their proposals will be environmentally acceptable and provides a framework for discussion of possible harm and uncertainty. If properly applied IA provides opportunities to redesign proposals to avoid possible harm to sensitive biodiversity and promote alternatives that reduce risks. New developments in strategic environmental assessment will provide additional opportunities to avoid environmental harm at source, and to implement the precautionary approach for the benefit of biodiversity.

However, uncertainty is a characteristic component of most IAs, and their predictions can rarely be tested before development decisions are made. Therefore, while IA is an important tool for implementing the precautionary approach, the appropriate application of the precautionary principle within the IA process is also important.

## Objectives of the study

The chapter sets out to review the application of the precautionary principle in IA with respect to biodiversity and to provide recommendations on the appropriate application of the precautionary principle in IA with regard to biodiversity interests. It is based on two main analyses. First, a review of selected international project donor guidance on the application of the precautionary principle to IA, focusing primarily on environmental impact assessments (EIAs) of major infrastructure and development projects. Second, the identification and description of examples of IAs where uncertainty with regard to potential impacts was a significant issue, and where the precautionary principle was (or was not) applied in accordance with best practice guidance. The study was carried out as a desk exercise using available literature and internet information sources and consultations with some practitioners of IA.

# THE PRECAUTIONARY PRINCIPLE AND UNCERTAINTY IN IA

## The precautionary principle

An important and widely accepted property of the precautionary principle, explicitly stated in some definitions (for example Raffensperger and Tickner, 1999), is that the proponent of an activity should bear the burden of proof with regard to resolving uncertainty over possible impacts. Thus proponents of potentially environmentally damaging practices must demonstrate that their proposed activities are likely to be acceptable before they can go ahead; it is not incumbent on others to prove that the activities are harmful in order to have them stopped. The legal or policy requirement for a project proponent to carry out EIA and to provide decision-makers with the information they need in order to decide whether environmental impacts are acceptable therefore provides an important mechanism for implementing the precautionary principle.

## Impact assessment

IA may be applied at a project level to predict the environmental effects of a specific proposal (environmental impact assessment), or at a more strategic level to assess the environmental effects of proposed policies, plans or programmes (strategic environmental assessment or SEA). IA at either level may incorporate the results of specialist assessments of particular types of impact, for example assessments of impacts on human health or biodiversity.

IA is now mandatory in much of the world and is also required by international donor institutions, such as the World Bank, as part of their approval processes for major infrastructure and industrial developments projects (for example dams, railways, major trunk roads, airports, mining, oil extraction and pipelines). Such projects frequently have considerable biodiversity impacts (for example from direct habitat loss, or indirect effects of disturbance, pollution and habitat fragmentation). EIA and SEA have been recognized in the Convention on Biological Diversity and in other biodiversity related conventions as important tools for identifying, avoiding, minimizing and mitigating adverse impacts on biodiversity. This study focuses largely on project EIA for which there is more documented experience. However, SEA is becoming increasingly important as a mechanism for ensuring that environmental and social concerns are integrated with the development planning process and for reducing uncertainty earlier in the planning process.

IA is intended as a preventative mechanism to avoid or pre-empt adverse environmental effects that might be associated with a proposed development or new activity. However, if adverse environmental effects cannot be avoided, the IA process generally triggers measures to reduce or control adverse effects on the environment ('mitigation') or to provide compensation (also known as 'offsets'; see ten Kate et al, 2004) for unavoidable impacts.

Nevertheless, there is often limited capacity, especially in developing countries, to carry out comprehensive ecological evaluations (i.e. the identification and quantification of key ecological features such as threatened habitats and species, and biodiversity resources of socio-economic value) or to undertake reliable assessments of potential impacts. The main stages in an EIA are set out in Table 5.1. Although this implies a linear process, in practice EIA is iterative, with feedback and interaction among the various stages. Public consultations and participation with key stakeholders may also take place throughout (not just at the end).

Application of the precautionary principle in EIA is relevant in situations where: first, there is uncertainty about outcomes associated with proposed activities; and second, there is a reasonable risk that significant adverse impacts might occur. In practice all proposals subject to EIA are characterized by uncertainty to some extent. With respect to ecological issues, uncertainty may arise as a result of:

- inherent complexity of ecosystems;
- incomplete knowledge of ecosystem processes;
- lack of opportunity for experimental testing;
- lack of scope for comparative analysis;
- lack of long-term data sets; and
- lack of opportunity for testing the accuracy of predictions (Treweek, 1999).

**Table 5.1** *Potential sources of uncertainty associated with stages in EIA*

| | Stage | Main potential sources of uncertainty |
|---|---|---|
| 1. | Project screening | EIA screening criteria do not define environmental sensitivity. Limited experience of some types of proposal in some locations. Lack of knowledge of locations and distributions of important or vulnerable resources. Potential risks for biodiversity may be unknown. Risk of missing cumulative effects if proposals do not qualify for EIA due to insignificant effects when considered on a case-by-case basis |
| 2. | Scoping | Usually based on existing information, judgement or preliminary data. Important and sensitive ecological receptors, and/or potential impacts on them may be overlooked or underestimated |
| 3. | Consideration of alternatives | Alternatives are not examined in as much detail as the proposed project. Therefore predictions will be less reliable |
| 4. | Description of the project | Incomplete knowledge of future development and associated environmental changes (for example traffic levels following road construction) |
| 5. | Description of the environmental baseline | Inaccurate, incomplete or out-of-date information. Uncertainty over future events without project |
| 6. | Identification of the main impacts | Incomplete knowledge of ecological systems, including factors influencing habitat change and character, species' population levels and interactions between species. Indirect, cumulative and synergistic impacts may be overlooked or underestimated |
| 7. | Prediction of impacts | As 6 above |
| 8. | Evaluation and assessment of the significance of impacts | Incomplete knowledge of the status and value of habitats, species and other ecological receptors impacted |
| 9. | Consideration of mitigation measures | Incomplete knowledge of ecological systems and effectiveness of mitigation measures, especially where habitat restoration or species translocation measures are proposed |
| 10. | Public consultation and participation | Incomplete consultation and missing information |
| 11. | Environmental impact statement (EIS) presentation | May downplay environmental outcomes and risks where uncertainty remains |

*Note:* most stages depend on information from previous stages and therefore compound previous sources of uncertainty.

All the various stages in EIA involve a wide range of scientific and subjective considerations, any or all of which may be affected by uncertainty to different degrees. Table 5.1 identifies stages in EIA (up to the project decision stage) where uncertainty may occur. This provides a basis for determining where it might be appropriate to apply the precautionary principle within the EIA process.

It is difficult to appraise risks to the environment associated with proposals where uncertainty is a significant factor. To some extent IA is in itself a process of identifying and quantifying potential risks to the environment, which it generally does on the basis of incomplete information. Decision-makers and regulatory authorities determining consents for proposed activities must balance risks against uncertainty in determining whether it is appropriate to invoke the precautionary principle to withhold consent.

# REVIEW OF INTERNATIONAL REGULATIONS AND DONOR GUIDANCE ON EIAS AND THE PRECAUTIONARY PRINCIPLE

EIA is now mandatory in many countries and regions and is required by many project donor organizations. A significant amount of guidance has been produced on appropriate methods and 'best practice' (Spooner, 2000), including guidance produced by the Convention on Biological Diversity (CBD) as well as by major development agencies and funding bodies, such as the World Bank and European Commission. The chapter examines a number of international regulations and guidelines to establish whether any explicit advice is given on the application of the precautionary principle in EIA, especially relating to the potential causes of scientific uncertainty identified in the preceding section.

## Convention on Biological Diversity guidelines for EIA

The CBD incorporates the precautionary approach in its ninth preambular paragraph, which states that 'where there is a threat of significant reduction or loss of biodiversity, lack of full scientific certainty should not be used as a reason for postponing measures to avoid or minimize such a threat'.

Under Article 14 (Impact assessment and minimizing adverse impacts) the CBD requires each contracting party to:

> *introduce appropriate procedures requiring environmental impact assessment of its proposed projects that are likely to have significant adverse effects on biological diversity with a view to avoiding or minimizing such effects and, where appropriate, allow for public participation in such procedures.*

Subsequently the Conference of the Parties (COP) adopted *Guidelines for Incorporating Biodiversity-related Issues into Environmental Impact*

*Assessment Legislation and/or Processes and in Strategic Environmental Assessment* (CBD, Decision VI/7, A).[1]

The current guidelines focus on the screening and scoping stages, providing more limited advice about subsequent stages in the EIA process.

## Screening and scoping

The 2002 CBD guidelines provide a framework for the screening and scoping stages of EIA. This does not make any reference to the precautionary principle. However, by removing some of the uncertainty associated with screening and scoping, use of the guidance does reduce the need for a strong precautionary approach in later stages.

The proposed screening framework includes criteria (in Appendix 2) that can be used to allocate proposed projects to one of the following three categories:

- Category A: EIA mandatory. There is a legal basis for requiring EIAs relating to national legislation (for example on protected species and protected areas), international conventions and directives from supranational bodies, such as the European Union Habitats Directive (1992)[2] and the Birds Directive (1979).[3]
- Category B: the need for or the level of EIA is to be determined. In these cases there is no legal basis to require an EIA, but the proposed activity is such that significant impacts on biological diversity might be expected. Limited study may be needed to solve uncertainties or design mitigation measures.
- Category C: no EIA required. Applies to activities that are not covered in categories A or B, or are designated as category C after initial environmental examination.

This framework helps to clarify some of the principles involved in screening and, most importantly, it explicitly indicates that projects that may have a significant impact should be considered further, including if necessary further studies to solve uncertainties. To some extent this helps to alleviate the problem of screening being based on incomplete information. However, no clear advice is given about how to interpret the word 'may' and no explicit reference is made to the precautionary principle, although it would be highly appropriate to do so.

The guidelines also include a framework for scoping (identification of key issues and possible significant impacts to be investigated). While clarifying the key issues to be considered this process in itself should raise standards and thereby reduce uncertainty in assessments. Explicit guidance on procedures for minimizing and dealing with uncertainty is not provided, and there is no reference to the precautionary principle.

## Other stages in EIA

For the reporting and decision-making stages of an EIA the guidance does refer to problems with uncertainty and the application of the precautionary principle. In particular it notes that there is a problem with evaluating impacts and dealing with uncertainty when reporting the results of EIAs and making decisions based on them. As a result (paragraph 24) it is important to:

> *develop or compile biodiversity criteria for impact evaluation and to have measurable standards or objectives against which the significance of individual impacts can be evaluated. The priorities and targets set in the national biodiversity action plan and strategy process can provide guidance for developing these criteria. Tools will need to be developed to deal with uncertainty, including criteria on using risk assessment techniques,* precautionary approach *and adaptive management* [emphasis added].

The guidance also notes that:

> *Decision-making takes place throughout the process of EIA in an incremental way from the screening and scoping stages to decisions during data-collecting and analysis, and impact prediction to making choices between alternatives and mitigation measures and finally the decision between refusal or authorization of the project.*

Importantly it then goes on to note (in paragraph 31) that:

> *The precautionary approach should be applied in decision-making in cases of scientific uncertainty about risk of significant harm to biodiversity. As scientific certainty improves, decisions can be modified accordingly.*

This is a clear and explicit recommendation to follow the precautionary principle, but guidance on how the precautionary principle should be defined and applied is not given.

## Further CBD guidance

Proposals from the CBD executive secretary for further development and refinement of the CBD guidelines (UNEP/CBD/SBSTTA/9/INF/18) provide additional recommendations for EIA and SEA. Only one recommendation refers to the precautionary principle or suggests approaches for dealing with problems of uncertainty. Recommendation 26.3 suggests, on the basis of lessons learned from an important EIA case study of port development at Rotterdam (included in the Annex of case studies in the guidelines), that 'the application of the precautionary principle requires the assumption of the worst case scenario. This should be the starting point of departure for mitigation or compensation measures'.

## EC directives on environmental impact assessment

Rules for EIAs in European Union (EU) member states are laid out in the EC EIA Directive[4]. While directives are the controlling documents, member states have considerable discretion in implementing regulations, and these will vary. This review therefore focuses on Directive 97/11/EC. Compliance with the directive is required to obtain a European Investment Bank (EIB) loan.

The directive does not include any explicit reference to the precautionary principle, nor does it imply in any way that the principle should be followed. However, the directive does indicate (Article 1), that the 'Directive shall apply to the assessment of the environmental effects of those public and private projects which are *likely* to have significant effects on the environment' (emphasis added). The use of the word 'likely' here could be interpreted as a partial application of the precautionary principle in that the requirement for an EIA is not restricted to projects that are certain to have a significant effect. However, before an EIA is conducted, the knowledge and certainty of possible impacts is generally limited. Judgements of 'likely significance' therefore have to be made based on the type of activity proposed and its location in relation to important or sensitive environmental features and resources.

The main text of the directive does not refer to issues concerning scientific uncertainty, but Annex IV of the amended directive does require 'An indication of any difficulties (technical deficiencies or lack of know-how) encountered by the developer in compiling the required information'. This suggests that the proponent should document any sources of uncertainty in their assessment of baseline conditions and predicted impacts, providing an opportunity for the precautionary principle to be applied in the decision-making process if appropriate.

## World Bank guidance

The World Bank requires borrowers to undertake EIAs to examine the environmental risks and benefits associated with Bank lending operations. The EIA is part of project preparation and is therefore the borrower's responsibility. However, the Bank advises the borrower on the Bank's EIA requirements and reviews the findings and recommendations of the EIA to determine whether they provide an adequate basis for processing the project for Bank financing. The Bank's EIA[5] procedures are described in Operational Policy OP 4.01 (January 1999, revised August 2004)[6] and Bank Procedure BP 4.01 (January 1999, revised August 2004)[7]. This policy is considered to be the umbrella policy for the Bank's 'safeguard policies', which among others include Natural Habitats (OP 4.04). Additional guidance on EIA is given in the *Biodiversity and Environmental Assessment Toolkit* (Duke and Aycrigg, 2000).

There is no explicit mention of the precautionary principle in either OP or BP 4.01. The Bank undertakes environmental screening of each proposed project to determine the appropriate extent and type of EIA required. OP 4.01 classifies proposed projects into one of four categories, depending on the type, location, sensitivity and scale of the project, and the nature and magnitude of its potential environmental impacts. The categories are as follows:

- Category A: likely to have significant adverse environmental impacts that are sensitive, diverse or unprecedented.
- Category B: potential adverse environmental impacts on human populations or environmentally important areas – including wetlands, forests, grasslands and other natural habitats – are less adverse than those of Category A projects.
- Category C: likely to have minimal or no adverse environmental impacts. Beyond screening, no further EA action is required for a Category C project.
- Category F1: involves investment of Bank funds through a financial intermediary, in subprojects that may result in adverse environmental impacts.

No further guidance appears to be given in the OP or BP on how to decide if an impact is 'likely' (Category A), if the impact is 'minimal' (Category C), or if the project 'may' result in adverse environmental impacts (Category F1). It would seem highly appropriate to refer to the precautionary principle here, and as with the CBD guidelines, to recommend further investigations or a preliminary assessment to establish if impacts are likely where there is uncertainty.

The *Biodiversity and Environmental Assessment Toolkit* (Duke and Aycrigg, 2000) is aimed at EIA practitioners, agencies and other project stakeholders, and focuses on reviewing the rationale for including biodiversity considerations in EIAs, approaches for dealing with biodiversity in EIAs, and the implication of these considerations on the management of EIAs by the Bank. No explicit reference is made to the precautionary principle or to problems resulting from scientific uncertainty when conducting EIAs. However, advice is given that may help raise the standards of EIAs, thereby reducing scientific uncertainty.

In conclusion, although guidance on dealing with scientific uncertainty and the application of the precautionary principle would be appropriate with respect to World Bank advice on screening, scoping and impact assessment, none is given.

## Asian Development Bank guidelines for EIA

The Asian Development Bank (ADB) has produced *Environmental Assessment Guidelines*[8] that describe how to fulfil the requirements outlined in ADB's *Environment Policy and the Operations Manual on Environmental Considerations in ADB Operations.*

The ADB requires the environment to be considered at all stages of the project cycle from project identification through to implementation. However, the degree and scope of the environmental assessment requirements depends on the likely environmental impact of the project, which they categorize in a similar way to the World Bank. If necessary an initial environmental examination (IEE) is required to determine whether or not significant impacts that warrant an EIA are likely. This to some extent overcomes a basic uncertainty-related flaw with the EIA procedure, that an assessment would be required to establish whether or not there are impacts that need to be evaluated. However, the effectiveness of the procedure will depend on the adequacy of the IEE.

The ADB guidelines do not mention the precautionary principle, or provide advice on dealing with issues concerning scientific uncertainty.

# EXAMPLES OF THE APPLICATION OF THE PRECAUTIONARY PRINCIPLE IN IMPACT ASSESSMENT

There are limited documented examples of IAs that make specific reference to the application of the precautionary principle. Many see the application of IA in itself as a manifestation of a precautionary approach and do not see the need to ensure that the precautionary principle is applied within the IA process to benefit biodiversity. However, there are some notable examples where the precautionary principle has been invoked to delay development decisions pending acquisition of further information, or to require proponents to modify their proposals. This section summarizes some examples of IAs where the precautionary principle has clearly been applied. An example is also given of an application for consent to control predators of an endangered species, where the need for application of the precautionary principle was considered in the review process.

## Case Study 1: Project EIA for 'Parque Eólico do Alvão' (Alvão Wind Farm), Portugal – Precaution Incorporated by Further Studies

### Proponent
GAMESA Energia Portugal, S.A.

### The proposal
The proposed wind farm would be located in an area proposed for designation under the EU Habitats Directive as a Natura 2000 site.

### The regulatory process
The EIA was reviewed by the EIA Review Committee, which pointed out that there was an information gap about the area used by bats in the proposed location. Resolution 4.7 of the European Agreement on the Conservation of the Population of European Bats (2004), adopted in 2003, indicates that the parties should apply the precautionary principle in the development of wind farms due to uncertainty about the impacts of wind farms on bat populations.

## The decision
The EIA Review Committee advised (August 2004) postponement of the final decision to approve the wind farm due to this uncertainty. The Secretary of State approved (October 2004) the proposal in principle subject to presentation by the developer of a detailed study of bats in the development location, with a specified methodology, and approval of the study by the Nature Conservation Institute (within the Ministry of the Environment).

## Case Study 2: EIA for Voisey's Bay Mine and Mill, Canada – Uncertainty Addressed through Anticipation and Prevention

### Proponent
Voisey's Bay Nickel Company Ltd (VBNC), a subsidiary of Inco Ltd.

### The proposal
To develop a nickel, copper and cobalt mine/mill complex and related infrastructure to produce mineral concentrates at Voisey's Bay, northern Labrador, Canada. An EIA was produced (VBNC, 1997).

### The regulatory process
The project was subject to the Canadian Environmental Assessment Act (CEAA) (1992) and the Newfoundland Environmental Assessment Act (NEAA) (2000). An MoU (Memorandum of Understanding) was drawn up to allow harmonized EIA procedures and the involvement of two aboriginal peoples with a recognized land claim to the region. The MoU directed a panel set up to establish guidelines for the EIA to consider the following:

- capacity of renewable resources likely to be significantly affected by the project to meet the needs of present and future generations;
- extent to which biological diversity would be affected by the project; and
- extent of the application of the precautionary principle to the project.

The panel reviewed the extent to which the planning and design of the project addressed these three factors. To demonstrate VBNC's activities would not result in serious or irreversible damage, the panel asked it to take a conservative approach to its predictions, for example by using worst case scenarios. If there was great uncertainty about the seriousness and irreversibility of the effects of any project component, VBNC was required to reduce this uncertainty, correct the problem or suggest a viable alternative to that component.

### VBNC's position: 'anticipation and prevention'
VBNC interpreted the precautionary principle to mean 'anticipation and prevention', and instructed its designers to incorporate environmental information into all stages of their activities, for example to prevent pollution, deal with unplanned events, and develop monitoring and follow-up programmes.

VBNC also undertook to ensure the company's liability and insurance regime would hold it accountable for any damages.

To test its success in applying the precautionary principle VBNC asked:

- In design and operation has priority been given to strategies that avoid adverse environmental effects?
- Does control of deleterious outputs go beyond current emission standards?
- Have contingency plans addressed explicit worst case scenarios and included risk assessments and evaluations of the degree of uncertainty?
- Are monitoring programmes designed to ensure rapid response and correction where adverse effects are detected?
- Are appropriate liability and insurance regimes established to hold VBNC and its contractors accountable?

Responses to these questions were given in evidence submitted to the review panel.

### Innu Nation's position: 'if we wait and see it will be too late'
The Innu Nation wanted a stronger interpretation of the precautionary principle. It suggested that the panel should start with the hypothesis that the project would damage the environment and reject that hypothesis only under the weight of contrary evidence.

The Innu Nation stated that any action with long-term or irreversible consequences would preclude future options, contrary to the principles of sustainability. It asserted that adaptive management relies on a monitoring and mitigation approach that would violate both the precautionary and sustainability principles.

### The panel's position
The panel was instructed to consider the extent of the precautionary principle's application to the project in accordance with the Rio Declaration of 1992, to which Canada is a signatory, though the CEA Act provides no guidance on the application of the principle to EIA. The panel considered risks of serious or irreversible damage in accordance with the Rio (1992) definition of the principle by considering the:

- uncertainty about potential effects;.
- magnitude, duration and reversibility of potential effects; and
- extent and scale at which potential effects could impair biological productivity and ecosystem health.

The panel concluded (CEAA, 1999) that in many respects the proposal was relatively conventional, causing effects that could be predicted with reasonable certainty and using proven mitigation measures. It found no strong evidence that serious or irreversible adverse effects would occur and concluded that any uncertainty about this could be addressed by the measures recommended.

The panel recommended the proposal should go ahead subject to a number of recommendations. In particular the panel concluded that sufficient uncertainty remained about the effects of shipping through landfast ice and that this component of the project should not proceed until these questions were resolved to the satisfaction of the Labrador Inuit and the government.

## Case Study 3: New Quito International Airport EIA, Ecuador – Habitat Protection for a Possibly Extinct Species

### The proponent
'Quiport': a consortium made up of Canada's Aecon Group, Airport Development Corp. and Houston Airport System Development Corp.

### The proposal
Construction of a new international airport for Quito, Ecuador.

### The regulatory process
Funding for the project was sought from multilateral, bilateral and export credit agencies, and EIA was carried out according to World Bank standards and reviewed by a specialist independent review panel. The EIA identified that the proposed site was adjacent to the last remaining habitat for a possibly extinct hummingbird, the turquoise-throated puffleg (*Eriocnemis godini*). The lenders' review panel concluded that application of the precautionary principle was appropriate and that the proposed development should avoid direct impacts on the areas where the bird could possibly occur, if still in existence. The EIA recommended protection of steep-sided forested ravines adjacent to the proposed site, together with the establishment of an environmental protection area within the airport site that would help to buffer this habitat.

## Case Study 4: Application for Consent to use Poisoned Bait to Control Predators of an Endangered Bird in New Zealand

### The proponent
New Zealand Department of Conservation.

### The proposal
Application for a discharge permit for a substance called '1080' used to kill alien species (rats and mice) that pose a major threat to New Zealand's most threatened bird, the orange-fronted parakeet *Cyanoramphus malherbi* and also the nationally endangered mohua or yellowhead *Mohoua ochrocephala*.

Every three or four years New Zealand's beech forests have 'mast years' when trees shed literally kilos of seed per tree, causing population explosions of rats and mice, and their predators such as ferrets, stoats and cats. The latter feed on the eggs and young of the ground-nesting birds when other food runs out.

Applications of 1080 throughout the remaining habitat are used to prevent these population explosions of alien mammal species. However there is considerable public opposition to its use due to concerns about possible effects on aquatic ecosystems and potability of water supplies.

### The regulatory process

Where there is any risk that 1080 might enter the water supply, application for consent is subject to the requirements of New Zealand's Resource Management Act (1991). The consent authority must be satisfied that any adverse effects of the activity on the environment are 'minor' for the application to be considered without need for public notification.

In reviewing the application the decision-maker noted the importance of proposed poisoning operations for survival of the rapidly declining orange-fronted parakeet and mohua. The decision-maker also accepted the importance of meeting both national strategies for maintenance of biodiversity and international obligations. However, the adverse effects still had to be 'minor'. Due to uncertainty about all possible effects of 1080, a risk-based approach was taken. It was concluded that: first, it would be unlikely for 1080 to enter water in concentrations likely to result in any acute or chronic adverse effects on aquatic organisms; and second, that 1080 has a relatively short half life in most New Zealand soils and would degrade relatively quickly in water. No evidence was found in the literature that irreversible effects would be likely.

It was concluded that it was not necessary to invoke the precautionary principle with respect to possible environmental impacts of the toxin 1080. Despite some uncertainty, available evidence suggested that any effects would be short term and reversible. The highly threatened status of the two endangered bird species was a strong factor in the decision not to delay action in this case and the proposed application was consented.

## Case Study 5: Proposed Port Development at Dibden Bay, UK – Certain Damage and Uncertain Ecological Compensation

### The proponent
Associated British Ports (private company).

### The proposal
Construction of a major container shipping port, with a 1850m deep water straight line quay capable of taking six container ships simultaneously. A project of high economic importance for the UK.

The proposed location was 202ha of mudflat and open grazing land on the western shore of Southampton Water. The site and surrounding area is subject to international, national and local environmental designations. The foreshore is designated as a Ramsar Site (Wetland of International Importance) and a Special Protection Area (SPA) under the Birds Directive.[9] The adjacent waterway is designated as a Special Area of Conservation (SAC).

### The outcome and reasons

The proposal was turned down after a long public inquiry. Uncertainty about the adequacy and sustainability of proposed ecological compensation in relation to adverse effects on the integrity of European designated sites was a key factor.

Where designated sites will be affected by a development, it will only be permitted if there are no alternative solutions and where imperative reasons of overriding public interest can be demonstrated. If a proposal meets these criteria, member states must ensure that compensatory measures are undertaken to protect the coherence of the network of SPAs and SACs (Article 6(4) of the EU Habitats Directive[10]). In the UK, the government is committed to ensuring justified ecological losses are compensated by equivalent gains. However, the documented failure of previous ecological compensation attempts, combined with uncertainty about habitat creation and enhancement techniques, was a significant factor in the decision to apply the precautionary principle in this case and turn down the proposal.

## Case study conclusions

The case studies reinforce the relevance of the precautionary principle in EIA decisions where risks and uncertainty are high. The examples show how the implementation of the precautionary principle has helped to:

- reduce uncertainty;
- reduce risks to important biodiversity;
- resolve conflicts between stakeholder views;
- identify suitable alternatives; and
- require evidence of effective mitigation.

These examples also reinforce the need for the precautionary principle to be firmly embedded in policy and law and for clear guidance to be given about its interpretation. The Voisey's Bay example demonstrates clearly how different interpretations of the principle can be reached for the same proposal, resulting in very different conclusions about its acceptability.

## CONCLUSIONS

### Impact assessment embodies a precautionary approach

IA is an important mechanism for putting the precautionary principle into practice. The fact that project EIAs must be prepared by the proponent is in accordance with reversal of the burden of proof. IA provides an opportunity to assess the potential impacts of human activities on biodiversity and other environmental components, and can help identify opportunities and alternatives that avoid potential environmental damage at source, identify requirements for additional information and understanding, and specify requirements for mitigation or compensation.

### Impact assessments are constrained by uncertainty

IA is routinely constrained by scientific uncertainty. Often insufficient information is available, and proponents are frequently reluctant to invest time and money in the studies and data gathering necessary to reduce uncertainty to acceptable levels. Practitioners therefore have to deal with scientific uncertainty throughout the IA process, particularly for new project types in new locations. Despite this there appears to be very little guidance in EIA regulations and guidelines on dealing with such uncertainty and the appropriate use of the precautionary principle in such circumstances.

Inadequacies in information can have important effects at several particularly crucial stages in the EIA process. The first is the screening stage, when a decision is made on whether or not there are likely to be environmental impacts and, consequently, whether or not an EIA is required. For example, the screening process needs to determine the need for EIA based on limited knowledge and understanding of the affected environment. A key flaw in the EIA process is the difficulty of making reliable judgements about the need for EIA in circumstances where existing knowledge is limited. A strong precautionary approach would require EIA for every project. Otherwise some sort of appraisal is required to support screening decisions. This is generally based on knowledge of impacts known to be associated with certain activities, or the location of a proposal in relation to sensitive resources. Some EIA regulations and guidelines require preliminary investigations to be made if there is uncertainty (see CBD and ADB guidelines above). A similar problem applies with the scoping stage, when issues to be investigated in the EIA are identified.

There is also usually significant uncertainty in predicting the overall impacts of a proposed development. This is mainly because knowledge of ecosystem functioning is rarely adequate to make reliable predictions about outcomes for biodiversity or to suggest reliable mitigation measures. This is exacerbated by the compounding of uncertainty at previous stages and by the general failure to monitor or follow up on actual environmental outcomes to reduce uncertainty for future proposals. As a result, IA in practice tends to depend strongly on subjective judgement.

# Recommendations

## Apply the precautionary principle through the whole IA process

In accordance with the 2004 recommendation[11] of the International Association for Impact Assessment (IAIA) we recommend that the precautionary principle should be applied in IA in:

> *any situation where important biodiversity may be threatened, and there is insufficient knowledge to either quantify risks or determine whether effective mitigation could be implemented. Development consent should be delayed until best available information can be obtained in consultation with local stakeholders and experts and information on biodiversity is consolidated.*

The precautionary principle should be applied to anticipate and prevent impacts rather than relying on subsequent repair or compensation. Its effective application in EIA should involve:

- 'Preventative anticipation': taking action to safeguard the environment if necessary before scientific proof is available on the grounds that a delay in the action could cause irreversible damage to biodiversity and to society.
- Preliminary investigations where necessary at the EIA screening and scoping stage to establish whether an EIA is required and what issues should be addressed within it. If any uncertainty remains that there will be impacts then an EIA should be conducted. If at the scoping stage there is uncertainty regarding a potentially significant impact then it should be included within EIA.
- Use of the best available information as a basis for impact assessment and mitigation recommendations.
- Consultation with stakeholders and interested parties to ensure that current and future dependencies on the environment are understood.
- Measures to reduce uncertainty, particularly where risks to biodiversity or the environment are high (in accordance with a draft resolution on the precautionary principle submitted to the World Conservation Union – IUCN Third World Conservation Congress, November 2004 (but not adopted in this form), which stated that:
  *Subject to constraints of resources and capacity, application of the Precautionary Principle should include efforts to seek further information and reduce uncertainties, and reassessment of the decision in the light of new information.*
- Evaluation of risks taking into account the potential severity of impacts and their likelihood of occurrence: the precautionary principle to be particularly invoked to avoid impacts that are likely and significant, and unlikely but of potentially very high significance.
- Evaluation of risks on the basis of the worst case scenario where there is significant uncertainty in impact predictions.
- Consideration of environmental risks in the absence of the proposed project.

## Box 5.1 Applying the precautionary principle (based on draft guidance on biodiversity and EIA being produced in South Africa)

Practically, when required to make a decision, the following considerations with regard to biodiversity should be applied:

- When the affected ecosystem and/or species is critically endangered or endangered, and impacts thereon could be irreversible, and/or there is little prior experience or scientific confidence about the outcome – follow the strict precautionary principle. That is, impacts should be confined within the realm of complete reversibility, and only activities that have been shown to pose negligible risk to biodiversity should be permitted. Mitigation and/or offsets should totally and reliably compensate for impacts on biodiversity, and there should be no cumulative impacts on biodiversity.
- When the affected ecosystem and/or species is vulnerable, and impacts could be long term and significant, only those human-induced activities that pose low risk to biodiversity should be permitted. Impacts should be mitigated in full, and offsets or compensation provided to ensure that there is no net loss of biodiversity. The cumulative effect of impacts on the affected ecosystem and/or species should be minimal, and should not result in a change in threatened status to endangered. In addition, impacts and associated risks should not be such that they could jeopardize meeting targets for biodiversity conservation within that particular ecosystem.
- When the affected ecosystem and/or species is not threatened, human-induced activities that pose some risk to biodiversity should be permitted. However, impacts must be mitigated as far as practicable. Cumulative impacts on the affected ecosystem and/or species could be minor–moderate, but should not result in that ecosystem/and or species becoming threatened. In addition, impacts and associated risks should not be such that they could jeopardize meeting targets for biodiversity conservation within that particular ecosystem.

- Restriction or banning of activities whose impact on biodiversity remains uncertain and possibly serious.
- Building in safeguards for ecosystem viability so that we protect the future ability of the environment to provide ecosystem services.
- Use of safety margins in project design, siting and management when proposing a project of a type or in an area where there is significant uncertainty about environmental outcomes.
- Proportionality of response: action and expenditure to safeguard biodiversity now may be less costly than future action, such as if important life support systems are undermined, for example protecting mangroves now to provide future flood protection under sea level rise might be considerably cheaper than constructing hard defences in future.

- Duty of care: placing the onus of proof on those proposing to undertake an activity to demonstrate or provide reliable evidence that there will be no environmental harm.
- The implementation of compensation measures in advance of the project if there is significant doubt over their efficacy, and where potential impacts in their absence would be significant. The proponent must provide proof that adequate compensation has been provided before the project impacts that they are compensating for can take place. A judgement will, however, still need to be made on the long-term sustainability of the compensation, and the precautionary principle should be applied here if there is significant uncertainty regarding this.

### Improve monitoring and auditing of projects

IA in many countries, particularly at the project level, does not allow for follow-up or provide any opportunity for mitigation requirements to be enforced. Failure to do this undermines the accumulation of data and knowledge that can reduce uncertainty in IAs. This can jeopardize application of the precautionary principle. Decision-making authorities should make it a mandatory requirement for developers to monitor and publicly report on the environmental performance and outcomes associated with their projects. The CBD 2003 guidelines note the importance of monitoring and follow-up and most of the international finance institutions require follow-up as part of their procedures (UNEP/CBD/SBSTTA/9/INF/18).

This is particularly important where effective implementation of mitigation measures is critical to an acceptable environmental outcome. Clear evidence should be provided that recommended mitigation measures have been tried and tested and can be shown to be effective.

### Improve the rationale and clarity of decision-making

Applying the precautionary principle in IA, whether at the project or strategic level, requires clear communication and the development of a common understanding of the basis for decisions. Further guidance is required on establishment of thresholds for determining when significant effects are likely and under what circumstances a strong precautionary approach should be adopted (see Box 5.1).

IA processes need to define what is meant by 'high' and 'low' levels of uncertainty, irreversibility and impact. Technical analyses are important in defining these, but should not necessarily override stakeholder opinions and perceptions, particularly where there is a strong dependency on biodiversity to support livelihoods.

Through the assessment process, a determination should be made whether the extent of uncertainty regarding impacts, the likelihood of those impacts and their irreversibility means that the activities are unacceptable, thus dictating avoidance, or acceptable but requiring an adaptive management approach.

## ACKNOWLEDGEMENTS

We thank the following for their advice and assistance with the identification of case studies: Andrea Athanas, Steve Bonnell, Helen Byron, Leo Fietje, Julio Jesus and Maria do Rosario Partidario.

## NOTES

1    These CBD guidelines have also been recognized by the Convention on Wetlands of International Importance Especially as Waterfowl Habitat, (the Ramsar Convention) (1971), by Resolution VIII.9 (2002), which 'urges Contracting Parties to make use, as appropriate' of the CBD guidelines.
2    EC Directive on Conservation of Natural Habitats and of Wild Fauna and Flora (92/43/EEC).
3    EC Directive on the Conservation of Wild Birds (79/409/EEC).
4    European Commission Council Directive 97/11/EC of 3 March 1997 Amending Directive 85/337/EEC of 27 June 1985 on the Assessment of the Effects of Certain Public and Private Projects on the Environment, European Commission. Available at http://europa.eu.int/comm/environment/eia/full-legal-text/9711_consolidated.pdf
5    Referred to as 'environmental assessment' by the Bank.
6    See http://wbln0018.worldbank.org/Institutional/Manuals/OpManual.nsf/0/936 7A2A9D9DAEED38525672C007D0972?OpenDocument
7    See http://wbln0018.worldbank.org/Institutional/Manuals/OpManual.nsf/toc2/C4241D657823FD818525672C007D096E?OpenDocument
8    See www.adb.org/documents/guidelines/environmental_assessment/default.asp
9    See note 3, above.
10   See note 2, above.
11   Final draft available at www.iaia.org.

## REFERENCES

CEAA (1999) *Voisey's Bay Mine & Mill Environmental Assessment Panel Report* Canadian Environmental Assessment Agency, Hull. Available at www.ceaa.gc.ca/panels2/voisey/report/2_e.htm

Cooney, R. (2004) *The Precautionary Principle in Biodiversity Conservation and Natural Resource Management: An Issues Paper for Policy-makers, Researchers and Practitioners*, IUCN Policy and Global Change Series, no 2, IUCN, Gland, Switzerland and Cambridge, UK

Duke, G. and Aycrigg, M. (2000) *Biodiversity and Environment Assessment Toolkit*, World Bank Group. Available at http://lnweb18.worldbank.org/ESSD/envext.nsf/48ByDocName/ToolsBiodiversityandEnvironmentalAssessment

ten Kate, K., Bishop, J. and Bayon, R. (2004) *Biodiversity Offsets: Views, Experience and the Business Case*, IUCN, Gland, Switzerland and Insight Investment, Cambridge, UK

Raffensperger, C. and Tickner, J. (1999) *Protecting Public Health and the Environment: Implementing the Precautionary Principle*, Island Press, Washington, DC

Spooner, B. (2000) 'Review of the quality of EIA guidelines, their use and circumnavigation', *Environmental Planning Issues EPI 19*, IIED Environmental Planning Group, International Institute for Environment and Development, London

Treweek, J. (1999) *Ecological Impact Assessment*, Blackwell Scientific Publications, Oxford

UNECE (1991) *Policies and Systems of Environmental Impact Assessment*, United Nations Economic Commission for Europe, Geneva

VBNC (1997) 'Voisey's Bay Mine/Mill Project environmental impact assessment', Voisey's Bay Nickel Company, St John's, Canada

# Section Two

# National Experience in Applying the Precautionary Principle

# 6

# The Evolution and Impact of Precautionary Fisheries Law and Policy in Australia: An Environmental NGO Perspective

*Glenn Sant*[1]

## INTRODUCTION

The precautionary principle has been adopted widely in the rhetoric of fisheries management internationally. Its interpretation, application and impact varies significantly. In Australia, the principle was first adopted formally as part of overall environment policy in 1992 through the National Strategy for Ecologically Sustainable Development (ESD) (Commonwealth of Australia, 1992) and the Intergovernmental Agreement on the Environment (IGAE)[2]. It was incorporated into Commonwealth fisheries legislation in 1997. TRAFFIC Oceania was closely involved in the drive to include the principle in fisheries legislation and continues to be a strong advocate of its application.

This chapter explores the adoption, interpretation and application of the precautionary principle in Australia's Commonwealth-managed fisheries[3] (see Figure 6.1). An attempt is then made to assess whether the application of the principle is making an impact on the achievement of fisheries management objectives.

In Australia the precautionary approach is usually used to mean the implementation or application of the precautionary principle (DEH, 2001; FRDC, 2004; AFMA, 2004). That usage has been adopted here.

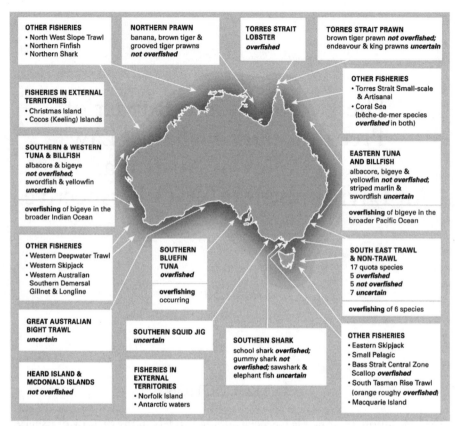

*Notes:* **Overfished**: a fish stock with a biomass below a prescribed threshold or limit reference
**Overfishing**: the amount of fishing exceeds a prescribed level or limit reference
**Uncertain**: a fish stock that might be not overfished or subject to overfishing, but for which there is inadequate or inappropriate information to make a reliable assessment of its status

*Source:* Caton and McLoughlin (2005)

**Figure 6.1** *Map of Commonwealth Fisheries*

## COMMONWEALTH FISHERIES

The Australian Fisheries Management Authority (AFMA) is a statutory authority responsible for the day-to-day management of Commonwealth fisheries. It was established under the Fisheries Administration Act, 1991 (FAA) and its activities are underpinned by the Fisheries Management Act, 1991 (FMA). AFMA is overseen by a board of directors with management, research, fishing industry, financial and policy expertise. AFMA's partnership approach to management is reflected in the broad stakeholder composition of Management Advisory Committees (MACs) that provide fishery-specific advice to the AFMA Board.

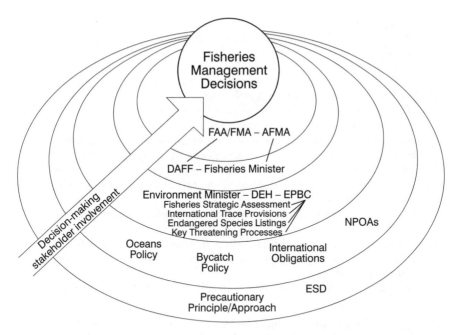

**Figure 6.2** *Representation of levels of influence on decision-making*

AFMA manages 21 domestic fisheries and is responsible for certain international fisheries matters including illegal foreign fishing and managing high seas fishing by Australian operators. A number of Commonwealth fisheries are based on migratory stocks that are under the jurisdiction of regional fisheries management organizations (RFMOs) of which Australia is a member.

## LEGISLATIVE AND POLICY REQUIREMENTS

AFMA's application of the precautionary principle is required by Commonwealth fisheries legislation, requirements of the Environment Protection and Biodiversity Conservation Act, 1999 (EPBC Act) and commitments arising from Australia's ratification of various international fisheries conventions and its support for a wide range of international 'soft law' relating to fisheries management. Taken together, these impose an overwhelming imperative on AFMA to apply a precautionary approach to fisheries management. The legislation, policies and agencies influencing AFMA's application of the precautionary principle are presented in Figure 6.2.

### AFMA's legislative objectives

The FMA and the FAA specify AFMA's objectives. These have been amended several times since the Acts took effect in 1991 and currently read as follows in the FMA (amendments are italicized):

*3 Objectives*

*(1) The following objectives must be pursued by the Minister in the administration of this Act and by AFMA in the performance of its functions:*

*(a) implementing efficient and cost-effective fisheries management on behalf of the Commonwealth; and*

*(b) ensuring that the exploitation of fisheries resources and the carrying on of any related activities are conducted in a manner consistent with the principles of ecologically sustainable development and the exercise of the precautionary principle, in particular the need to have regard to the impact of fishing activities on non-target species and the long-term sustainability of the marine environment; and*

*(c) maximizing economic efficiency in the exploitation of fisheries resources; and*

*(d) ensuring accountability to the fishing industry and to the Australian community in AFMA's management of fisheries resources; and*

*(e) achieving government targets in relation to the recovery of the costs of AFMA.*

*(2) In addition to the objectives mentioned in subsection (1), or in section 78 of this Act, the Minister, AFMA and Joint Authorities are to have regard to the objectives of:*

*(a) ensuring, through proper conservation and management measures, that the living resources of the AFZ [Australian Fishing Zone] are not endangered by over-exploitation; and*

*(b) achieving the optimum utilisation of the living resources of the AFZ; and*

(c) ensuring that conservation and management measures in the AFZ and the high seas implement Australia's obligations under international agreements that deal with fish stocks;

*but must ensure, as far as practicable, that measures adopted in pursuit of those objectives must not be inconsistent with the preservation, conservation and protection of all species of whales.*

The amendment to objective 3(1)(b), known as the ESD objective, requiring AFMA to pursue the exercise of the precautionary principle, was made in 1997. The amendment reflected the community's desire to improve the effectiveness of fisheries management from an ESD perspective. The legislation relies on the definition of the precautionary principle contained in the IGAE:

*Where there are threats of serious or irreversible environmental damage, lack of full scientific certainty should not be used as a reason for postponing measures to prevent environmental degradation. In the application of the precautionary principle, public and private decisions should be guided by:*

*(i) careful evaluation to avoid, wherever practicable, serious or irreversible damage to the environment; and*

*(ii) an assessment of the risk-weighted consequences of various options.*

The FAA and FMA mandate AFMA to actively pursue sustainability and to use the precautionary principle. Most other Australian legislation that includes references to ESD simply sets sustainability as an objective, without prescribing that actions be consistent with the principles of ESD and/or the precautionary principle (Gullett, 2005). As discussed below, even the EPBC Act is less rigorous than the fisheries legislation in its emphasis on the precautionary principle.

## The EPBC Act

The EPBC Act operationalizes the IGAE, the National Strategy for ESD and the 1996 National Strategy for the Conservation of Australia's Biological Diversity. The Act is administered by the Department of Environment and Heritage (DEH). The objectives of the Act include the promotion of ESD, which is defined to include the application of the precautionary principle. The Act uses, essentially, the IGAE definition (see above) but excludes the two points on guidance for application.

The EPBC Act contains provisions for Strategic Assessment of Commonwealth fisheries (Section 10) and requires (Part 13A) the sustainability of native fish species to be assessed in order for them to be exported legally from Australia. Most Commonwealth fisheries have a significant export component. All marine species were exempt from scrutiny under the export provisions of the previous act. The legislative change to ensure greater scrutiny of marine species was brought about through pressure from non-governmental organizations.

The Act also provides for the 'listing' of threatened species, including fish species. Listing may trigger the development of a Recovery Plan or a Threat Abatement Plan.

The EPBC Act requires that the Minister for the Environment and Heritage:

> *must take account of the precautionary principle in making a decision listed in the table in subsection (3), to the extent he or she can do so consistently with the other provisions of this Act.*

This requires that the Minister consider the principle but does not require that decisions be made in accordance with the principle. Further, this requirement does not apply to all decisions taken by the Minister under the EPBC Act. Notably, the requirement does not apply to decisions relating to Strategic Assessment of Commonwealth fisheries but does apply to provisions determining whether native species taken in Commonwealth fisheries may be legally exported from Australia (Nevill, 2004).

Decisions on Strategic Assessment of Commonwealth fisheries and on allowing exports of species taken in these fisheries are based on assessments against the *Guidelines for the Ecological Sustainability of Fisheries* (the Guidelines).[4] The Guidelines were developed through an extensive consultation process with the outcome reflecting the community's interest in ensuring ESD in fisheries. Overall, the Guidelines require that:

- the management regime of a fishery be strategic, transparent, developed through a consultative process and enforced;
- a fishery be managed and conducted in a way that ensures the harvest of target and by-product species (non-target species that are kept and sold) is sustainable (Principle 1); and
- fishing operations be managed in a way that minimizes impacts on the structure, productivity, function and biological diversity of the ecosystem (Principle 2). (DEH, undated)

The Guidelines refer to 'precautionary management actions', 'precautionary recovery strategies' and the precautionary approach, and rely on the following definitions:

- *Precautionary approach – used to implement the precautionary principle. In the application of the precautionary principle, public and private decisions should be guided by:*
  - *careful evaluation to avoid, wherever practicable, serious or irreversible damage to the environment; and*
  - *an assessment of the risk-weighted consequences of the various options.*
- *Precautionary principle – the lack of full scientific certainty should not be used as a reason for postponing a measure to prevent degradation of the environment where there are threats of serious or irreversible environmental damage.*
- *Precautionary recovery strategy – management and operational strategy, designed to increase numbers within the stock, that incorporates the precautionary approach and includes mechanisms to avoid or mitigate adverse ecosystem effects.*

Despite the fact that the Minister for the Environment and Heritage is not required to consider the precautionary principle in taking decisions on Strategic Assessment of fisheries, the Guidelines on which DEH formulates its ministerial advice explicitly take the principle into account. Further, the definition of the precautionary approach used in the Guidelines includes the two guiding principles of the IGAE definition excluded from the EPBC Act definition of the principle.

## Policy

Australia's Oceans Policy (Commonwealth of Australia, 1998) aims to establish 'a framework for integrated and ecosystem-based planning and management for all of Australia's marine jurisdictions'. The Policy provides guidance for the application of the precautionary principle in implementing management arrangements for Australia's oceans:

- *If the potential impact of an action is uncertain, priority should be given to maintaining ecosystem health and productivity.*

- *Incomplete information on possible impacts should not be used as a reason for postponing precautionary measures intended to reduce or avoid unacceptable levels of change or to prevent serious or irreversible environmental degradation of the oceans.*
- *In the application of the precautionary approach, public and private decisions should be guided by:*
  - *careful evaluation to ensure that changes arising from a use or uses remain within limits considered acceptable to avoid, wherever practicable, serious or irreversible damage to the environment; and*
  - *assessment of the risk-weighted consequences of various options.*
- *If there is a risk of serious and irreversible environmental damage resulting from an ocean use, that use should be permitted only if the damage can be mitigated, or it is limited in its extent, and there is an overriding net community benefit from the use:*
  - *the higher the risk of unacceptable levels of change or of serious or irreversible environmental damage, the more conservative should be the measures required to reduce that risk.*
- *Ocean users carry a responsibility to assure the ecological sustainability of their operations and an obligation to identify and implement precautionary measures.*

While AFMA is responsible for day-to-day management of fisheries, the Commonwealth Department of Agriculture, Fisheries and Forestry (DAFF) has responsibility for development of overarching fisheries management policy. The implementation of the FAA and the FMA and the consequent creation of AFMA, arose from a Commonwealth Policy Statement in 1989 (Commonwealth of Australia, 1989). The precautionary principle had not been recognized as part of Australia's environment policy at that time and was not reflected in the document. The statement served as the basis of Commonwealth fisheries policy until 2003 when the government released *Looking to the Future: A Review of Commonwealth Fisheries Policy* (DAFF, 2003). The Review did not result in any changes to the implementation of the precautionary principle in Commonwealth fisheries. It did, however, identify a number of issues with respect to the implementation of the principle. These are discussed below.

Another policy of relevance to the ESD objective is the Commonwealth Policy on Fisheries Bycatch (Commonwealth of Australia, 2000). This implemented the bycatch initiatives contained in Australia's Oceans Policy and has resulted in the development of bycatch action plans for all major Commonwealth fisheries.

The National ESD Reporting Framework for Australian Fisheries (Fletcher et al, 2002) was developed largely in response to the requirement for fisheries to be assessed under the EPBC Act. The Framework provides a format for documenting how a fishery contributes positively and negatively to ESD in both the short and long term. The framework does not in itself promote the adoption of a precautionary approach to management.

## International obligations

Australia has ratified a number of international conventions and has endorsed a range of 'soft laws' with implications for fisheries management that impose a legal or moral obligation to act in accordance with the precautionary principle.

From a fisheries management standpoint the two key conventions ratified by Australia are the United Nations Convention on the Law of the Sea (UNCLOS) and the UN Fish Stocks Agreement (UNFSA)[5]. While UNCLOS pre-dates the broad acceptance of the precautionary principle, it is arguable that the provisions of the convention provide for acceptance of the precautionary approach (Freestone, 1999; Cooney, 2004). Further, it is considered by some that decisions of the UNCLOS dispute resolution body, the International Tribunal for the Law of the Sea (ITLOS), provide some indication that ITLOS is prepared to support application of the principle (Marr, 2000). Australia and New Zealand appealed to the precautionary principle in support of their southern bluefin tuna (SBT) case against Japan in ITLOS.[6]

The UNFSA explicitly (Article 6 and Annex 11) requires a precautionary approach to fisheries management of straddling stocks and migratory species by its signatories. This obligation extends to the management approach taken to these stocks in national waters and in attempts to manage high seas or straddling stocks through mechanisms such as RFMOs or bilateral agreements.

Australia has also ratified the Convention on Biological Diversity, the Convention on International Trade in Endangered Species of Wild Fauna and Flora, the Convention on Migratory Species and the Agreement on Conservation of Albatrosses and Petrels. Each of these either explicitly or through decisions taken under them, appears to support the application of the principle.

Of the regional fisheries conventions and agreement signed by Australia, only the Convention on the Conservation and Management of Highly Migratory Fish Stocks in the Western and Central Pacific Ocean (2000, not yet in force) explicitly requires the application of the precautionary approach. This does not necessarily imply that the precautionary principle is not invoked in other RFMOs of which Australia is a member. These include the Commission for the Conservation of Antarctic Marine Living Resources (CCAMLR), the Commission for the Conservation of Southern Bluefin Tuna (CCSBT) and the Indian Ocean Tuna Commission (IOTC).

CCAMLR is an example of where it is apparent that, despite its convention having been drawn up well before the development of the precautionary principle, documents outlining CCAMLR's approach to management stress the adoption of a precautionary approach heavily (see for example Kock, 2000). It must be said, however, that there is less evidence of the acknowledgment of this approach in the deliberations of the CCSBT or IOTC.

Australia has been an active participant in and supporter of various voluntary agreements developed under the auspices of the UN Food and Agriculture Organization (FAO). These include the FAO Code of Conduct for Responsible Fisheries (FAO, 1995) and the various technical guidelines developed to assist implementation of the Code. The Code itself draws heavily on the application of a precautionary approach and the technical guidelines, *Precautionary Approach to Capture Fisheries and Species Introductions* (FAO, 1996), provide explicit advice on implementation of the precautionary approach. The application of the precautionary principle is also reflected in International Plans of Action (IPOAs) developed in accordance with the Code. Australia is developing national plans of action in response to these IPOAs.[7]

# INTERPRETATION

There is general concurrence across the various agencies in the definition of the precautionary principle to be used in relation to fisheries management. In this section the interpretation of that definition is examined with reference to: academic literature; published statements by those responsible for developing and applying policy based on it, namely DAFF, AFMA and DEH; examples of its application by AFMA and by those 'auditing' AFMA's performance, DEH and BRS; and case law.

## Academic literature

Gullett (2005) examines the IGAE formulation of the precautionary principle, as applied in Australian fisheries. His findings are that:

> *This formulation does not provide a strong mandate for the use of precaution in environmental management. This is because the measures that are needed to give effect to the principle are not clearly spelled out. There is only an instruction about what should* not *be done. Further, this formulation utilizes preventive rather than precautionary phraseology. It focuses on responding to risk (including 'serious' and 'irreversible' damage) rather than* uncertainty, *which is the essence of the principle.* (Gullett, 2005)

The IGAE definition establishes its threshold as 'where there are threats of serious or irreversible environmental damage'. Gullett discusses the implications of this threshold. He finds that the threshold:

> *calls for response to threats involving a certain degree of evidence of the two elements of 'risk' – likelihood of occurrence and severity of consequences. This suggests that a high level of scientific understanding or proof is required before the principle can be invoked, thus limiting the ability to take anticipatory action before the threshold of 'threat' is reached. This limits action to situations when there is knowledge that a dangerous outcome is*

> *possible (or probable) rather than when there is uncertainty or only some indication that environmental harm may occur. As such, the IGAE sets out a high threshold for the application of the precautionary principle and consequently provides little support for precautionary, as opposed to preventative, decisions.* (Gullett, 2005)

Gullett's interpretation of the IGAE definition raises some interesting questions, the answers to which would appear to be fundamental to AFMA, which is charged with exercising the precautionary principle and to those assessing how well AFMA is discharging that responsibility. These questions include:

- What constitutes a 'serious or irreversible threat' (the threshold question)?
- Does the definition impose a burden of proof?
- If so, on whom does the burden of proof of such threats fall?
- If the 'serious' or 'irreversible' threats are established, or even if the lower threshold of 'there is sufficient uncertainty about the likelihood and consequence of such risk to warrant a precautionary approach' is accepted, what constitutes a sufficiently precautionary response?

The following sections may shed some light on whether these questions have been addressed by AFMA and its 'auditors' and whether legal challenges to the exercise of the principle have clarified any of these issues.

## Statements of interpretation

### AFMA

There is no indication that AFMA has considered these questions to inform their application of the principle. AFMA has provided no guidance to its MACs or stakeholders generally on how it interprets or exercises the precautionary principle. AFMA's latest Annual Report (AFMA, 2004) raises the question as to whether AFMA actually understands where the principle should be applied. The report claims that AFMA is:

> *leading in Australia's approach to the implementation of ecosystem based approaches to fisheries management. The central elements of this approach are the management of impacts of fishing on target species, non-target species and the broader marine environment. For target species, AFMA is taking a precautionary approach to protecting Australia's fish stocks in keeping with one of its key objectives of ensuring a sustainable resource into the future.* (AFMA, 2004)

This statement either mistakenly or deliberately, implies that the precautionary approach is only being applied to target species. Such an interpretation of objective 3.1(b) of the FMA cannot be sustained.

## DEH

In the explanatory literature surrounding its *Guidelines for the Ecologically Sustainable Management of Fisheries*, DEH made no attempt to address how it interprets or applies the precautionary principle for the purpose of assessing fisheries. Stakeholders are left to wonder, for example, how DEH would determine whether a 'recovery strategy' met its definition of a 'precautionary recovery strategy'. DEH's own definition of the precautionary principle, as stated above, require that such a strategy incorporates the precautionary approach. This suggests that those assessing recovery strategies would need a baseline definition of 'serious or irreversible damage' and that each strategy would be determined on the basis of an assessment of the risk-weighted consequences of various recovery strategies.

## DAFF

The 2003 review of Commonwealth fisheries policy (DAFF, 2003) acknowledged criticism that management policy had not adopted 'sufficiently precautionary measures in managing Commonwealth fisheries resources' and that the 'biological assessment of Commonwealth-managed fisheries shows an increase in the number of overfished fisheries' (DAFF, 2003). In response, the review noted that 'The Government and AFMA must seriously consider the implication of this increase in overfished fisheries and, in particular, consider the application of a precautionary approach'. The outcomes of the review included a commitment that 'AFMA will implement the precautionary approach'. In making this commitment the review noted that 'the collection of quality data and information to support the objective of improving the effectiveness (including cost-effectiveness) of management should be a priority'. Given that AFMA has a legislative responsibility to implement the precautionary approach, and given the apparent deterioration in the status of fish stocks under its watch, it might have been expected that the review would consider whether AFMA had been applying the precautionary approach. It made no attempt to do so. Instead, its response to this situation implies that a lack of information is to blame for the failure to take sufficiently precautionary action. This suggests a complete misunderstanding of the principle and its application.

It is unfortunate that the review seems to have confused rather than clarified the Commonwealth's interpretation of the principle since it also identified stakeholder demands for more effective implementation and accountability by AFMA against the basic principles of its legislative objectives, especially the precautionary principle, in decision-making. The review made no attempt to provide policy guidance on how to interpret and apply the approach. Instead the government has committed to amending the legislation to provide better expression of the concept of ESD by incorporating the ESD definition in the EPBC Act into the FMA.

### Bureau of Rural Sciences

The Bureau of Rural Sciences (BRS) produces fishery status reports to provide governments, industry and the community with an independent overview of the status of fish stocks in fisheries managed by AFMA. These reports are the primary means by which DAFF judges AFMA's performance in meeting its ESD objective. Despite its focus on that objective, the BRS does not explicitly assess whether the management measures adopted are indicative of the exercise of the precautionary principle. In its latest report (Caton and McLoughlin, 2005), the BRS included this statement of its interpretation of AFMA's use of the precautionary approach:

> *AFMA needs timely scientific, economic, industry and manage-ment advice on which to base sound fisheries management. Where there are gaps in the information, AFMA is required to apply a precautionary approach when making decisions. In practice, this means that AFMA must act on the best available information to protect the resource and take steps to reduce any uncertainty about, or risk to, that resource.* (Caton and McLoughlin, 2005)

Overall, the public expressions of what the precautionary principle implies confuse rather than clarify.

## Application

### AFMA

AFMA frequently invokes the adjective of 'precautionary' in its description of management measures. In many cases such measures reflect the setting of a catch or effort limit in the face of no information. This is somehow viewed as 'precautionary' compared to the alternative of no limit. However, implementa-tion of a limit is not in itself precautionary in the sense required by the precautionary principle even though it may, by chance rather than design, provide some protection. A more precautionary strategy in the face of uncer-tainty may be to allow fishing only in order to reduce the uncertainty, for example by implementing a research survey. In other cases, for example where stocks are regarded as overfished, reductions in catch are promoted as being precautionary. Again such reductions may reduce the impact but unless carefully assessed against a rebuilding strategy may not be sufficiently precau-tionary to allow stock recovery. A case in point here is the stock of eastern gemfish *Rexea solandri*. While management has restricted catch of this stock to a bycatch for over a decade, there is no sign of recovery. According to the BRS 'significant numbers of adults and juveniles continue to be taken as bycatch, which could jeopardize rebuilding of the stock, so more stringent management measures to protect spawning aggregations and juvenile fish are required' (Caton and McLoughlin, 2005). Conservation groups have previ-ously recommended the implementation of area closures to protect the winter spawning run of gemfish, but to no avail.

### DEH

The DEH assessments of Commonwealth fisheries conducted to date shed little light on how judgements as to compliance with the precautionary aspects of their guidelines are made. This raises questions as to whether such judgements are consistent across fisheries and over time. DEH has stated '[i]n general, fisheries submitted for assessment have shown a good understanding of the need for ecologically sustainable management. Fisheries that lack information on their impacts are generally managed with appropriate precaution, and a number of jurisdictions are undertaking risk assessments to inform their management' (DEH, undated). The question is, what does DEH judge to be appropriate precaution and how does it exercise that judgement?

## BRS

BRS (Caton and McLoughlin, 2005) uses the term 'precautionary' to describe a number of management measures taken by AFMA. For example, BRS states that AFMA uses 'a precautionary initial total allowable catch of 1000t shell weight' in the Bass Strait Central Zone Scallop Fishery. In such cases it remains unclear whether BRS has made its own expert assessment that such a measure is in fact precautionary, that is, consistent with the exercise of the precautionary principle or whether it is using, the term, as AFMA appears to, in its more generic sense.

On occasion, BRS does counsel the need for a 'precautionary approach'. For example in relation to the Southern Squid Jig Fishery, the report (Caton and McLoughlin, 2005) says, 'at present, scientists are unable to determine a TAC [total allowable catch] based on biological and ecological evidence. Any TAC or jig-effort limits applied in the near future will have to be determined from management needs and consideration of the precautionary principle'. Similarly, in relation to SBT the report states, '[f]rom the point of view of stock security, the precautionary approach would suggest a focus on the reality of the seriously reduced spawning stock'.

In the absence of a shared understanding of the precautionary principle across agencies and stakeholders there is little likelihood that such counsel will be effective.

## Case law

Many of AFMA's decisions are subject to merit review through the Administrative Appeals Tribunal (AAT) and can ultimately be challenged in the Federal Court. There is a considerable body of case law in relation to AFMA's fisheries management decisions and in particular the application of AFMA's objectives. In some cases AFMA's application of the precautionary principle has been the subject of consideration. Gullett (2005) has considered the case law available on the application of the precautionary principle in Australia, particularly as to whether the courts and tribunals required that the threshold test be met, that is, whether there needed to be proof that there was a 'serious or irreversible threat'. Gullett points to a decision by the AAT in a case between a fisher and AFMA.[8] In that case the AAT decision suggested that AFMA can lawfully pursue the precautionary principle where it has not established that there is a 'serious or irreversible threat' and that uncertainty alone can meet the threshold of IGAE definition. This AAT decision was appealed to the Federal Court and upheld.

This interpretation provides a strong basis for AFMA's application of the principle in the face of the considerable uncertainty that persists in its fisheries. The adoption of a precautionary approach, together with the introduction of research and data collection to reduce the uncertainty over time and the adoption of adaptive management, would seem to be a defendable management approach.

# IMPACT

There are a number of indicators that could be used to detect whether the incorporation of the precautionary principle into AFMA's objectives has advanced the goal of ecological sustainability in Australia's marine environment. Some of these are examined below.

## Stock trends

Neither of the fisheries 'audit' processes conducted by BRS and DEH, provide an explicit assessment of AFMA's exercise of the precautionary principle and its impact on achievement of ESD in fisheries.

BRS status reports do provide an indication of trends in the status of stocks of 'primary' species over time. These species are generally target or by-product (retained) species. The status reports do not attempt to assess the status of bycatch species in Commonwealth fisheries, although some discussion of broader environmental impacts of each fishery, including bycatch, is included.

It is eight years since the precautionary principle was incorporated in the legislation. At a minimum, it would not seem unreasonable to expect that stock status would have stabilized or improved since that time. Unfortunately the number of stocks assessed as overfished continues to increase. In 1997, four species were assessed as overfished. By 2004 this had risen to 17. During that time the status of only three species previously assessed as 'overfished' had improved to 'not overfished'. The status of 40 species remains uncertain (Caton and McLoughlin, 2005).

BRS notes that some of the changes in status over time reflect more accurate assessments based on new information. Thus, species classed as 'uncertain' two years ago may now be classed as 'overfished' based on new information. However this does not reduce the significance of the number of stocks overfished. Application of the precautionary approach in the presence of uncertainty (in this case a lack of information) should have seen the implementation of measures sufficient to ensure that the species did not become overfished.

BRS defines an overfished stock as a 'stock with a biomass below the limit reference'. If one assumes that such a stock constitutes a threat of serious or irreversible environmental damage, then a lack of information cannot be used as a 'reason to postpone measures to prevent environmental degradation'. AFMA, and the Commonwealth, argue that they have not postponed such measures and that in relation to the nine overfished stocks directly under AFMA's control 'steps have been taken to help the stocks recover'. Two of those stocks have been classed as overfished for 14 years. Seven have become overfished since the introduction of AFMA's legislative responsibility to exercise the precautionary principle. This suggests that the approach to stock recovery taken by AFMA has not been sufficiently precautionary to provide for stock rebuilding and that its management strategies for stocks not previously believed to have been overfished has not been sufficiently precautionary to prevent overfishing.

A further eight species under AFMA's jurisdiction are considered overfished. Three of these are tuna stocks that also come under the jurisdiction of RFMOs (the CCSBT, the IOTC and the newly-formed Western and Central Pacific Fisheries Commission). Another, a straddling orange roughy stock, is managed bilaterally with New Zealand, and four are managed jointly with the Queensland Government and Torres Strait islanders under the Torres Strait Fisheries Act, 1984. While it is true to say that AFMA cannot be held solely responsible for the status of these stocks, this does not mean that AFMA can abrogate its responsibilities to take precautionary action where it is justified. As noted above, the UNFSA imposes obligations on its members to apply the precautionary approach to management of straddling stocks and highly migratory species. This, together with AFMA's legislative objectives, should ensure that AFMA adopts what it believes to be a precautionary approach to fishing for those portions of highly migratory and straddling stocks within its national waters and fishing by its vessels of those stocks on the high seas, regardless of whether bilateral and multilateral negotiations support that level of precaution.

In the case of the three overfished tuna species, the Australian Minister responsible for fisheries has argued that 'by itself, Australia has no control over these stocks of highly migratory species and international action is required' (Macdonald, 2005). As the case of SBT shows, such action can be a long time coming. The CCSBT global total allowable catch for SBT has remained steady since 1989[9] despite increasingly pessimistic assessments of the status of the stock and the strong likelihood that there has been recruitment failure. Australia's allocation of the CCSBT TAC has also remained stable at 5265 tonnes. AFMA's statutory management plan for SBT provides for AFMA to set its TAC for SBT no higher than its allocation from CCSBT. The plan does not preclude AFMA from setting a TAC for its operators of less than the CCSBT allocation but AFMA has not done so.

The situation with respect to bycatch species is even less clear with stock assessments generally not being conducted for these species. A recent meeting of environment members, generally drawn from non-governmental conservation agencies, on AFMA's Management Advisory Committees identified a range of bycatch issues (seabirds, seals, dolphins, sharks) as key outstanding issues to be addressed by AFMA.

## EPBC Act assessments

The impact of the introduction of the DEH assessments of Commonwealth fisheries against sustainability criteria including the exercise of the precautionary principle is really yet to be seen. To date, no Commonwealth fishery has failed to have its management arrangements accredited under the Strategic Assessment provisions of the EPBC Act. Further, no native species taken from Commonwealth fisheries has been excluded from export on the grounds that its management does not meet the sustainability guidelines (Part 13A). However, the Minister for the Environment and Heritage has in each case made a number of recommendations for improvements. In seven of the eleven Commonwealth fisheries assessed so far the minister has made provisional decisions in relation to Part 13A approvals by approving fisheries as Wildlife Trade Operations.[10] DEH will reassess fisheries every five years, or sooner if classified as a Wildlife Trade Operation. Action taken by the fishery in response to DEH recommendations or conditions will be assessed at that time. This process provides for continuous improvement in ensuring sustainable fisheries.

## Nominations for listing

There are currently seven species taken by Commonwealth fisheries that have been nominated, under Section 179 of the EPBC Act, for listing as threatened species. Four of these species, SBT *Thunnus maccoyii*, orange roughy *Hoplostethus atlanticus*, school shark *Galeorhinus galeus* and gemfish *Rexea solandri* are, or were, target stocks in Commonwealth fisheries. Each is classified as 'overfished' by the BRS. The remaining nominated species are three species of dogfish (*Centrophorous harissoni*, *C. moluccensis* and *C. uyato*), which had been taken as by-product in large quantities in the South East Trawl Fishery.

The nomination of these species for listing as critically endangered or vulnerable demonstrates that there are concerns in the community that the current application of Commonwealth fisheries legislation, despite the requirement that the precautionary principle be exercised, is failing to protect or rebuild these fish stocks. Whether or not these concerns are justified is currently under consideration by the Threatened Species Scientific Committee that advises the Minister for the Environment and Heritage.

## Developments in management

There is a range of developments in management approaches in AFMA that are consistent with the spirit, if not the letter, of the precautionary principle. These include development of more rigorous statutory management plans and bycatch action plans, adoption of adaptive management techniques, and development of strategic data plans. However, the most significant development in terms of improving AFMA's capacity to legitimately claim that it takes a risk-weighted approach to developing appropriately precautionary responses to management issues is the undertaking of ecological risk assessments (ERAs) for each Commonwealth fishery. This programme commenced in 2001 and will be completed by 2006. AFMA intends that these assessments will be an integral part of the future management of each fishery and is developing an ecological risk framework to provide a process for responding to the results of the ERAs. The challenge for AFMA will be to determine quantitatively the extent of the management measure (for example the reduction in catch or effort, the extent and location of closed areas) that equates to an appropriately precautionary response.

There is little doubt that the DEH assessment processes have hastened the development and application by AFMA of this comprehensive risk assessment framework. The fact that an ERA was underway for each Commonwealth fishery at the time that DEH conducted its assessments was a significant factor in providing DEH with confidence that AFMA would be in a position to ensure that, in the medium to longer term, fisheries were not having an unacceptable impact on the environment.

## CONCLUSIONS

Overfishing and a lack of information on fish stocks and on the marine environment continue to dog fisheries management in Australia. This situation is unlikely to be overcome quickly. The reality is that fisheries management will continue in an environment of considerable uncertainty. The current state of fisheries in Australia, and elsewhere, is the legacy of poor decisions taken in the face of uncertainty. Only the application of a precautionary approach is likely to deliver a different future. There is no doubt that the precautionary principle is well entrenched in Commonwealth fisheries legislation and policy in Australia. It is widely preached by those involved in fisheries management and those assessing the effectiveness of that management. The available evidence indicates, however, that there has been no demonstrably positive impact on the status of fish stocks and their ecosystems since the adoption of the precautionary principle. Rather, since its introduction in 1997, the precautionary principle has not prevented the deterioration in the status of primary species in Commonwealth fisheries. At this point there is simply no basis on which to make a judgement about its impact on bycatch species or marine ecosystems. Questions remain therefore as to whether the principle is being applied and, if it is, whether the level of precaution is sufficient.

The incorporation of the principle in the FMA and the development of the EPBC Act reflected growing community and stakeholder awareness and acceptance of the need for a precautionary approach. These legislative changes have laid the foundations for the implementation of the precautionary principle in Australian fisheries management. This foundation is being strengthened through initiatives such as the ERAs and through an apparent willingness of the courts and tribunals to take an approach to the threshold question of whether 'serious or irreversible threats' exist, which appears to err on the side of the fish.

What is required now is a shared understanding of the meaning and application of the precautionary approach to be developed. This will require, firstly, an enunciation of the precautionary principle based on the current national and international thinking, a clear explanation of how the principle will be applied (the precautionary approach) and opportunities for public debate. Secondly, there is a need for a framework that provides guidance on establishing the appropriate level of precaution when implementing management measures. The framework could, for example, be based on fishery-specific decision trees with higher levels of risk and uncertainty directing non-discretionary, precautionary decisions. In order for the precautionary principle not to be invoked, this framework must put the onus on AFMA and the fishing industry to demonstrate that 'serious or irreversible threats' are not occurring or that the level of uncertainty of such threats arising is acceptable. In other words, the burden of proof must fall squarely with the resource user. This would represent a change from current management practice where fishing continues unless stakeholders, such as environmental non-governmental organizations, prove the need for a reduction.

Countries considering the explicit adoption of the precautionary principle in fisheries management can learn from Australia's experience. This assessment suggests that the most important lesson is that the adoption of the approach requires the development of a framework for implementation. Guidance is required on how the principle will be applied. This will provide certainty for stakeholders, ensure consistency in application and provide a basis for determining if the way in which the principle is being applied is delivering better conservation outcomes.

# NOTES

1   The content of this chapter is the result of extensive discussions with and input from a number of colleagues.
2   The Intergovernmental Agreement on the Environment was agreed between the Australian commonwealth and state/territory governments. A copy is available at www.deh.gov.au/esd/national/igae/
3   Management of marine fisheries in Australia is the responsibility of seven state and territory governments and the Commonwealth government. Generally, the states/Northern Territory have responsibility for species within three nautical miles (nm) of the coast and the Commonwealth manages those outside those waters to the limit of the Australian Fishing Zone (200nm). Under Australia's Offshore Constitutional Settlement (OCS) alternative jurisdictional arrangements have been agreed to maximize the management of some species across their range.
4   The Guidelines are available at www.deh.gov.au/coasts/fisheries/guidelines.html
5   The 1995 Agreement for the Implementation of Provisions of the United Nations Convention on the Law of the Sea of 10 December 1982 relating to the Conservation and Management of Straddling Fish Stocks and Highly Migratory fish Stocks.
6   Proceedings can be found at www.itlos.org/start2_en.html

7 Members of the FAO have developed IPOAs for seabirds, sharks, fishing capacity and illegal, unreported and unregulated fishing (IUU fishing). Details can be found at www.fao.org/fi/default.asp. Australia has developed a National Plan of Action (NPOA) for the conservation and management of shark and is developing NPOAs for seabirds, fishing capacity and IUU fishing.

8 Ajka Pty Limited v. the Australian Fisheries Management Authority, AAT Nos S1998/320 and S1998/321.

9 The TAC has been increased in recent years to accommodate new members of the CCSBT. However this has not affected the quantum of the allocation to Australia and the other two original members of the Commission, Japan and New Zealand.

10 More information can be found at www.deh.gov.au/coasts/fisheries/index.html

# REFERENCES

AFMA (2004) *Annual Report 2003–04*, AFMA, Canberra

Caton, A. and McLoughlin, K. (2005) *Fishery Status Reports 2004: Status of Fish Stocks Managed by the Australian Government*, DAFF, Canberra

Commonwealth of Australia (1989) *New Directions for Commonwealth Fisheries Management in the 1990s. A Government Policy Statement*, AGPS, Canberra

Commonwealth of Australia (1992) *National Strategy for Ecologically Sustainable Development*, AGPS, Canberra

Commonwealth of Australia (1998) *Australia's Oceans Policy*, vol 1, Environment Australia, Canberra

Commonwealth of Australia (2000) *Commonwealth Policy on Fisheries Bycatch*, AFFA, Canberra

Cooney, R. (2004) *The Precautionary Principle in Biodiversity Conservation and Natural Resource Management: An Issues Paper for Policy-makers, Researchers and Practitioners*, IUCN Policy and Global Change Series, no 2, IUCN, Gland, Switzerland and Cambridge, UK

DAFF (2003) *Looking to the Future: A Review of Commonwealth Fisheries Policy*, DAFF, Canberra

DEH (2001) *Guidelines for the Ecologically Sustainable Management of Fisheries*, Environment Australia, Canberra

DEH (undated) *Managing Australia's Fisheries for a Sustainable Future*, DEH, Canberra

FAO (1995) *Code of Conduct for Responsible Fisheries*, FAO, Rome

FAO (1996) *Precautionary Approach to Capture Fisheries and Species Introductions*, FAO Technical Guidelines for Responsible Fisheries, no 2, FAO, Rome

Fletcher, W. J., Chesson, J., Sainsbury, K. J., Hundloe, T., Fischer, M., Smith, A. D. M. and Whitworth, B. (2002) *National ESD Reporting Framework for Australian Fisheries: The 'How To Guide' for Wild Capture Fisheries*, version 1.01, FRDC Report 2000/145, FRDC, Canberra. Available at www.fisheries-esd.com/c/implement/implement0200.cfm

FRDC (2004) *Annual Report 2003–04*, FRDC, Canberra

Freestone, D. (1999) 'International fisheries law since Rio: the continued rise of the precautionary principle', in A. Boyle and D. Freestone (eds) *International Law and Sustainable Development: Past Achievements and Future Challenges*, Oxford University Press, Oxford

Gullett, W. (2005) 'The threshold test of the precautionary principle in Australian courts and tribunals: lessons for judicial review', in R. von Schomberg, E. Fisher and J. Jones (eds) *The Precautionary Principle and Public Policy*, Edward Elgar Publishing (in press)

Kock, K.-H. (2000) *Understanding CCAMLR's Approach to Management*, Commission for the Conservation of Antarctic Marine Living Resources. Available at www.ccamlr.org/pu/E/e_pubs/am/text.pdf

Macdonald, I. (2005) *HSI Off the Mark in Fisheries Criticism*, media release, Senator, the Hon. Ian Macdonald, Minister for Fisheries, Forestry and Conservation, 24 March

Marr, S. (2000) 'The southern bluefin tuna cases: the precautionary approach and conservation and management of fish resources', *European Journal of International Law*, vol 11, pp815–831

Nevill, J. (2004) 'Australian ocean management and the precautionary principle (draft)'. Available at www.ids.org.au/~cnevill/marinePrecautionaryPrinciple.doc

# 7

# Protection of Sea Turtles: Putting the Precautionary Principle into Practice

*Rolando Castro*

## BACKGROUND

Costa Rica is known worldwide for its impressive biological diversity as well as its dedication to conservation. It is perhaps the Latin American country that has the most developed environmental legislation. For instance, Costa Rica's Constitution was amended in 1994 to grant every person the right to a healthy and ecologically balanced environment. The same year, Congress ratified the Convention on Biological Diversity (CBD), one of the first international agreements to contemplate the precautionary principle. Under Article 7 of the Costa Rican Constitution, all international treaties duly ratified by Congress become part of the domestic legal framework, and take precedence over national laws.

In April of 1998, Costa Rica enacted its Biological Diversity Law. This was based on the CBD. Article 11 of this law introduced the precautionary principle. This principle is also referred to in this law as *in dubio pro natura*, a Roman law principle for environmental protection that asserts that, in case of doubt, any decision should favour the protection of nature.

Within this legal framework, it is important to consider how and to what extent the precautionary principle can be put into practice to achieve effective environmental protection. This paper examines a case where citizen groups used the precautionary principle to challenge a controversial regulation that allowed the killing of green sea turtles in Costa Rica.

## SEA TURTLES IN COSTA RICA

Because of their strategic location in the Central American isthmus, Costa Rican shores are blessed with nesting populations of five of the seven existing species of sea turtle.

One of these is the green sea turtle *Chelonia mydas*, a species that is listed as endangered in the IUCN Red List of Threatened Species (IUCN, 2004). Green sea turtles may require several decades to reach reproductive maturity (Boulon and Frazier, 1990; Hirth, 1997). The World Conservation Union assessment highlights:

> *extensive subpopulation declines in all major ocean basins over the last three generations as a result of overexploitation of eggs and adult females at nesting beaches, juveniles and adults in foraging areas, and, to a lesser extent, incidental mortality relating to marine fisheries and degradation of marine and nesting habitats. A 48 per cent to 67 per cent decline in the number of mature females nesting annually over the last three generations was also documented worldwide.* (IUCN, 2004)

Every year between June and September, gravid females migrate to the 35km of beach between Parismina and Tortuguero on Costa Rica's Caribbean coast. This area is one of the most important nesting sites for this species in the world, and the largest in the Western Atlantic Ocean. Studies of migratory periodicities show that the turtles return faithfully to this beach to lay their eggs at intervals of two or three years, continuing a cycle of life that has perpetuated for centuries (Opay, 1998).

The Caribbean Conservation Corporation (CCC) was established in 1959 to study and protect Caribbean green turtles in Tortuguero (TNP, undated). The Tortuguero National Park (TNP) was formally created in 1975 to protect this important nesting site and the green turtle. To provide further protection, the National Parks System Law of 1977 prohibited the capture of sea turtles inside these protected areas. The green turtle was first deemed reduced or threatened in 1993 under domestic law[1] and later, in 1997, it was declared in danger of extinction.[2]

The green sea turtle has traditionally been hunted by Caribbean communities for meat, fat and eggs. As a result, the turtle population is believed to have come perilously close to extinction in the 1960s when some estimate that nearly every female turtle arriving to nest in Tortuguero was illegally taken for turtle soup for the export market, and for meat and eggs for the local market (TNP, undated).

Faced with this reality and in a attempt to regulate and limit turtle hunting, in 1982 the Costa Rican Government enacted a regulation officially establishing a quota of 1800 for the annual capture of green sea turtles in Costa Rica's near-shore waters. The regulation required that the turtles be butchered at state-regulated slaughter houses, and their meat sold only within the country. The regulation had the effect of significantly reducing the permitted level of harvest from the actual level of harvest observed at the time it entered into force. However, by the late 1990s high rates of poaching meant that the number of green turtles being killed each year was actually many times higher than this legal limit, thereby putting unacceptable pressure on the already fragile population. While the law permitted turtle hunting in some of Costa Rica's waters, poaching also took place in the protected areas where such hunting was strictly prohibited.

## I'll see you in court

In the light of this, sea turtle conservation groups, environmental non-governmental organizations and some ecotourism hotels from Tortuguero,[3] requested INCOPESCA – the Costa Rican Fisheries Authority (Instituto Costarricense de Pesca y Acuacultura) – to amend this regulation and prohibit all harvesting of green turtles. They were unsuccessful in their attempt. In May of 1998 the groups filed a lawsuit to challenge the regulation before the Constitutional Court, a branch of the Costa Rican Supreme Court.

Since its creation in 1989, this court has resolved very important environmental cases, and Constitutional Court jurisprudence has made a significant impact on environmental legislation. This, despite the fact that Costa Rica is a civil law country where written law takes precedence over case law.

The lawsuit argued that the Costa Rican regulation that permitted hunting of an already endangered species was incompatible with the Costa Rican Constitution and with its conservation obligations under many of the international agreements to which Costa Rica was a signatory. Among these was included the Inter-American Convention for the Protection and Conservation of Sea Turtles (1996, came into force 2001). The objective of this Convention is to promote the protection, conservation and recovery of sea turtle populations and of the habitats on which they depend, based on the best available scientific evidence, taking into account the environmental, socio-economic and cultural characteristics of the parties (Article 2). Also cited in support of this case were CITES, the CBD, the Convention on Nature Protection and Wildlife Preservation in the Western Hemisphere (1940), and the Convention for the Conservation of Biological Diversity and Protection of Priority Protected Areas in Central America (1992).

The petitioners further argued that the quota that permitted the taking of 1800 turtles per nesting season was established arbitrarily and was not based on adequate science. Capturing breeding adults such as those in the Costa Rican near-shore waters is likely to have very serious long-term impacts on sea turtle populations because turtles take decades to mature and females only nest every two, three or more years. The consequences of a dwindling adult population at such a significant nesting site would be felt for generations and across oceans (AIDA, 2004).

Despite the fact that INCOPESCA licensed commercial fishermen to hunt 1800 green sea turtles per year, the agency could point to no research to support the sustainability of that figure; thus, the agency did not know whether the allowed take was harming the population. The fact that the agency established a quota with no scientific basis highlighted the serious lack of information for the management of this species within the agency (Opay, 1998).

Moreover, there was no evidence that scientific research was being conducted to study how the population of green turtles was responding to this type of management, despite the fact that these permits had been issued for 15 years.

Furthermore, lax enforcement by governmental authorities led to the death of many more than the permitted number of turtles each year. In 1997, CCC researchers documented the illegal taking of 1700 turtles from Tortuguero Beach alone (EMS, 2004). As a result, CCC estimated that approximately 7000 individuals were being taken per nesting season.[4] The existence of a legal market meant that turtles caught illegally could also be sold openly.

Finally, the petitioners argued that much of the take was harvested from beaches in the Tortuguero National Park where turtle hunting is strictly forbidden. While Costa Rican law prohibits the hunting of turtles within the TNP, INCOPESCA was issuing permits to fishermen in the knowledge that very few turtles were present outside the park and that the fishermen were likely to cross park boundaries (Opay, 1998).

Because there was uncertainty as to how this 'legal' exploitation of the green turtle was affecting the ecological equilibrium of the species, the petitioners invoked the precautionary principle and asked the Court to nullify the regulation as a means to prevent the extinction of the green turtles. The petitioners emphasized the fact that green turtles are listed as endangered species in the Red List of Threatened Species established by IUCN and under the Costa Rican Wildlife Law. Furthermore, like all other sea turtle species, the green turtle is listed in Appendix I of CITES, which means that the parties have judged they are threatened with extinction.

INCOPESCA's defence in court was based on the argument that the agency did not have actual scientific proof that any marine species in the Costa Rican exclusive economic zone were facing extinction. It is worth noting that this is precisely the form of argument that the precautionary principle seeks to counter. They claimed that all the efforts of the institute were aimed at preventing such extinctions through the implementation of the regulation.

The General Attorney's Office (Procuraduría General de la República) is always a party in Costa Rican cases in which the constitutionality of a law or regulation is being challenged. In its briefs to the Court, this office supported the petitioners' arguments and asked the Constitutional Court to set an example that would save the green turtle from extinction. The office concluded that the take of such a large number of turtles did not appear to be consistent with a sustainable development policy.

Furthermore, an *Amicus Curiae* presented by the Costa Rican Ombudsman (Defensoría de los Habitantes de la República) was highly influential in the case. This institution is charged with balancing and controlling the environmental and social impacts of decisions taken by public authorities, so its position was critical. It was the consideration of the Ombudsman, that the precautionary principle:

*mandates that the interpretation of the law and the behaviour of the administration should be carried out using environmental protection as the main goal and not to threaten the marine resources as in this case.*

The Ombudsman also added that the Wildlife Law and CITES both state that the use or trade of endangered natural resources such as the turtles should be subject to very strict regulation and only be permitted in exceptional cases. They argued that these requirements were not met in this case because the regulation was very broad and was not based on technical studies that could justify the take.

While CITES applies only to international trade and does not involve any obligations to limit harvest within states, the recognition by CITES parties that the green turtle was threatened with extinction was used by both petitioners and supporters as an argument to require maximum protection measures.

## A HISTORIC RULING

With all these different arguments and important jurisprudence to define, the decision of the Court was eagerly awaited by different sectors. Finally the decision was issued by the Constitutional Court on 19 February 1999.[5] Among other important aspects, the Court ruled:

*Articles 7, 50 and 89 of the Constitution have been violated for non-compliance with the protection established by international conventions, leaving unprotected the right to a healthy environment, and specifically the right to an ecologically balanced environment. These require preventive measures to avoid the extinction of the species, and a responsible attitude by the competent authorities. Furthermore, this off-take is not even allowing the turtles to reproduce, implying the total extinction of this species from our coast. This is a species which does not even belong to us, but comes to nest on our shores. This thus violates the constitutional rights that protect the environment, as future generations also have the right to experience and appreciate the same ecosystem as we do today.*

*Violation of article 7 of the Constitution is also evident because international conventions have been contradicted. This regulation allows hunting of green turtles for consumption and trade without sufficient scientific basis to indicate that it is feasible to do so, leaving the turtles irresponsibly unprotected. The sole existence of doubt about the turtles' survival possibilities makes this regulation unconstitutional, according to the principle 'in dubio pro natura'. According to this principle, uncertainty about the harm that could be caused to the ecological equilibrium is, alone, enough to require its protection; and the requirement is even stronger when there are scientific studies indicating the maximum level of protection is required.*

The Constitutional Court recognized that the regulation protected the green sea turtle for the first time, authorizing a certain level of take without any previous scientific study on the potential risk to the species. The Court considered that the regulation permitting turtle hunting should be abolished since the turtle was declared in danger of extinction under domestic law.

In the end, the Constitutional Court decided to annul the regulation permitting the take of 1800 green turtles. Subsequently, INCOPESCA published a resolution stating that hunting and commerce of the green turtle were prohibited.[6] As a result Costa Rica's green sea turtle fishery is now officially closed.

This was an extremely important ruling because it was the first time that the Court upheld the constitutional right to an ecologically balanced environment. It differed from previous cases where arguments had been based on the right to a healthy environment, with the focus being on the impact on human health rather than biodiversity and ecosystem protection.

The precautionary principle was thus, for the first time, invoked by the Court as one of the means to grant such rights. This is perhaps one of the most important outcomes of this case. The fact that the Court ruled that Costa Rica is required to comply with all international conventions to which it is a signatory is also worth pointing out. These are legally binding and must be implemented through domestic law and policy.

## SOCIO-ECONOMIC IMPACTS OF THE BAN

An important evaluation that was carried out before this case went to court was the socio-economic implications of the case. On the one hand, many fishermen made a living from green sea turtle hunting, and green sea turtles were an important source of protein for the inhabitants of the Caribbean Coast of Costa Rica. On the other hand, people in Tortuguero – mostly former turtle fishermen – today make a good living from ecotourism that is dependent on the protection of the turtles.

Since the 1980s, tourists have been visiting Tortuguero to observe nesting turtles and other wildlife. Since 1993, Tortuguero villagers have been prohibited from taking any green turtles, even for subsistence use. Efforts to develop an alternative income source for former turtle users were initiated by CCC and the Costa Rican National Park service in 1990 with the establishment of a tour guide training programme. Tourists wishing to see nesting turtles at night must now be accompanied by a licensed tour guide (Troëng, Chamorro and Silman, 2002). Today, Tortuguero receives close to 33,000 visitors a year, and the gross revenue from marine turtle tourism in Tortuguero – which provides 265 jobs – is estimated at almost US$7 million a year (Troëng and Drews, 2004). Tourists pay considerable fees to local guides to watch sea turtles nest on Tortuguero Beach, and it appears that here sea turtles are more valuable to villagers alive than cooked up in a stew (Caribbean Conservation Corporation, 1999).

From a socio-economic perspective the ban on harvesting has had winners and losers. The villagers and the thriving tourism industry in Tortuguero had a great deal to gain from the prohibition of turtle hunting. The fishermen who lost out were mostly from the Port of Limón, and if they were to come to Tortuguero National Park area to illegally catch the turtles, they would be affecting the local Tortugueran economy.

## CONSERVATION IMPACTS OF THE BAN

It is important to analyse the results that the prohibition of green turtle harvesting has had in relation to the situation that prevailed before the application of the precautionary principle. According to research data, the ban on green turtle fishing together with increased enforcement are likely to have diminished hunting and increased adult turtle survivorship in Costa Rica since 1999 (Troëng and Rankin, 2005).

Additionally, although cooperation between conservationists and turtle fishermen in Limón has traditionally been limited, due to opposing views on turtle exploitation, after the court ruling communication between them increased. As the affected parties, they began to organize themselves and demand an alternative solution for their livelihoods. Some of the petitioners met with the fishermen and both asked the government to provide compensation to the turtle fishermen for the first nesting season. Also, a joint awareness campaign to protect green turtles from illegal fishing, using posters and TV advertisements, was also conducted by the petitioners and the fishermen. Possible cooperative projects for the fishermen were identified, including the construction of a processing plant for seafood products, turtle watching by boat, a nesting beach conservation project, construction of a museum/visitor centre, and education programmes for fishermen about sea turtles and sustainable fishing techniques (Silman et al, 2002).

In the long term, it should be noted that it will be important to carefully assess and manage the potential negative impacts on the ecosystem of tourism to the area.

## CONSISTENCY OF APPLICATION OF THE PRECAUTIONARY PRINCIPLE BY THE CONSTITUTIONAL COURT

This case study provides the opportunity to assess whether the Constitutional Court has been applying the precautionary principle consistently in other cases involving natural resources management.

A review of the jurisprudence of the Constitutional Court reveals that one of the first applications of this principle was in a case involving protected areas. In that case, the Court ruled:

> *In the protection of our natural resources should exist a preventive approach, in other words, if the degradation is to be minimized, it is necessary that precaution and prevention will be the dominant principles... One should keep in mind that we are in a field of Law where the most important laws are those that can prevent all kinds of damage to the environment since there are no laws that can repair afterwards the damage already inflicted to the environment. This preventive approach is even more urgent in the case of a developing country.[7]*

In another case, referring to environmental impact assessment (EIA), the Court stated that a prior EIA is the ideal technical instrument for fulfilling the precautionary principle on environmental issues.[8] In another case, this tribunal ruled that the actions taken by public authorities to protect the environment were insufficient as they did not prevent negative impacts on the environment according to the precautionary principle.[9]

The precautionary principle has also been used in a ruling on measures to control shark finning. A case was brought to the Constitutional Court calling for precautionary measures to be implemented since the government was allowing shark fins to be landed without effective controls. The practice of shark finning is known worldwide to be a wasteful and unsustainable practice causing severe declines in shark populations. The Court ruled that there was an unjustified delay by the customs authorities in applying precautionary measures to control the landing of shark fins by foreign vessels.[10]

However, a different approach has been taken in a case concerning the construction of high tension power lines. In this case the Court did not apply the precautionary principle to restrict construction, because it argued that it was not clear that the health of the people and the integrity of the environment were under a real and imminent threat.[11]

Recently, a case was brought to the Court challenging 'sport hunting permits' established under the Wildlife Law.[12] The case was presented by the Ombudsman and is based on similar arguments to those used in the green sea turtle case: the absence of scientific research regarding the status of wildlife populations that would be necessary to justify that hunting does not comply with the preventive and precautionary criteria included in the Biological Diversity Law. The case is being studied by the Court and it will be very interesting to observe how the precautionary principle will be applied to an activity that in some other parts of the world is considered a conservation tool.[13]

## CONCLUSIONS

This case study illustrates a situation where the precautionary principle was used to its extreme, to entirely prohibit the consumptive use of a species. The evidence of the endangered status of the green sea turtle worldwide, and the poor management practices being used in Costa Rica, justified calling on the precautionary principle as a 'lifesaver' for the green sea turtle population and for the local economy of Tortuguero.

For Costa Rica, as a civil law country, one of the most important achievements of the case was the strong acceptance of the precautionary principle. This is all the more impressive as the precautionary principle is a very innovative approach, and judges and public authorities are often reluctant to switch the burden of proof in cases where there is lack of evidence, as they did in this case. This application reflects the Court's demonstrated willingness to apply the precautionary principle in a range of cases relating to natural resources. The reasons for the refusal of the Court to require the more precautionary strategy in the case of the high tension power lines is not clear. Perhaps people are more sensitive to risks to the environment than risks to health. Alternatively, criteria for applying the precautionary principle could vary with the individuals sitting in the Court.

For a developing country, it is not always feasible to base decisions on the best scientific information available, which could be seen as a limitation on the scope for applying precautionary measures. Nevertheless, the precautionary principle offers an opportunity for countries to require the proponents of use of a specific natural resource to bear the cost of research necessary in order to ensure that its use is sustainable. This case could also be of importance in other countries where similar conditions exist and where lack of financial or technical resources is typically used as justification to avoid taking precautionary measures to protect natural resources.

Environmental groups and even public institutions have been using the precedent of the green sea turtle case and the interpretation of the precautionary principle as applied by the Court to question management practices in relation to natural resources that are conducted in the absence of scientific criteria. Obviously, there are some cases where this is not feasible, such as artisanal fisheries. However, when dealing with endangered species or fragile habitats, the precautionary principle constitutes a powerful tool for applying immediate and strong protection measures.

# NOTES

1   Decreto Ejecutivo No 22545–MINAE of 30 August 1993.
2   Decreto Ejecutivo No 26435–MINAE of 30 October 1997.
3   This group included the Caribbean Conservation Corporation (CCC), Sea Turtle Restoration Programme (PRETOMA), the Environmental and Natural Resources Law Centre (CEDARENA), the Interamerican Association for Environmental Defense (AIDA), Fundación Neotrópica and the World Society for the Protection of Animals (WSPA).
4   During the Central American Marine Turtle Workshop, which convened in Tortuguero at the end of September 1997, an exercise was undertaken to calculate the level of poaching over a period of two nights during the workshop. The

estimate was based on beach surveys conducted in the early morning hours. The evidence suggested that more than 150 turtles were taken from the beach during these two nights alone (Opay, 1998).

5   Resolución No 01250-99 of 11h24 of 19 February 1999.
6   Resolución No 92, *La Gaceta 78*, 23 April 1999.
7   Resolución No 5393 of 27 October 1995.
8   Resolución No 6322 of 3 July 2003.
9   Resolución No 2481–2002.
10  Resolución No 2140–2004.
11  Resolución No 2219–99 of 24 March 1999.
12  Case No 04–007573-0007.
13  IUCN Resolution RECWCC093, available at www.iucn.org/congress/members/ adopted_res_and_rec/REC/RECWCC3093-%20REC007%20-%20REV1%20 Final.pdf

# REFERENCES

AIDA (2004) *Costa Rica Turtles*, Interamerican Association for Environmental Defense (AIDA), www.aida-americas.org/aida.php?page=70&lang=en

Boulon, R. H. and Frazier, N. B. (1990) 'Growth of wild juvenile Caribbean green turtles, *Chelonia mydas*', *Journal of Herpetology*, vol 24, pp441–45

Caribbean Conservation Corporation (1999) *Lawsuit Victory Halts Legal Killing of Green Sea Turtles in Costa Rica*, press release, Caribbean Conservation Corporation, 11 March. Available at www.cccturtle.org/news/n_harvest.htm

EMS (2004) *Costa Rican Constitutional Court Rules Customs Department Violating Constitution for Failure to Resolve Illegal Shark Fin Landings*. Available at www.ems.org/nws/2004/06/11/costa_rican_court

Hirth, H. F. (1997) 'Synopsis of the biological data on the green turtle *Chelonia mydas* (Linnaeus 1758)', United States Fish and Wildlife Service. *Biological Report*, vol 97

IUCN (2004) *2004 IUCN Red List of Threatened Species*, IUCN Species Survival Commission. Available at www.redlist.org

Opay, P. (1998) 'Legal action taken to stop the hunting of green turtles in Costa Rica', *Marine Turtle Newsletter*, no 79, pp12–16

Silman, R., Rankin, D., Arauz, R. and Troëng, S. (2002) 'Ban on green turtle fishing results in increased cooperation between fishermen and conservationists', in A. Mosier, A. Foley and B. Brost (compilers) *Proceedings of the Twentieth Annual Symposium on Sea Turtle Biology and Conservation*, National Oceanic and Atmospheric Administration Tech Memo, NMFS-SEFSC-477

TNP (undated) *Costa Rica 'Region of the Turtles'*, Tortuguero National Park (TNP). Available at www.cccturtle.org/tortnp.htm

Troëng, S., Chamorro, E. and Silman, R. (2002) 'Ban and benefits: Tortuguero at 2000', In A. Mosier, A. Foley and B. Brost (compilers) *Proceedings of the Twentieth Annual Symposium on Sea Turtle Biology and Conservation*, National Oceanic and Atmospheric Administration Tech Memo, NMFS-SEFSC-477

Troëng, S. and Drews, C. (2004) *Money Talks: Economic Aspects of Marine Turtle Use and Conservation*, WWF International, Gland, Switzerland

Troëng, S. and Rankin, E. (2005) 'Long-term conservation efforts contribute to positive green turtle *Chelonia mydas* nesting trend at Tortuguero, Costa Rica', *Biological Conservation*, vol 121, pp111–16

# 8

# Application of the Precautionary Principle in Judicial and Administrative Decisions about Argentinian Biodiversity: A Case Study

*Maria Eugenia Di Paola and Natalia Machain*

## INTRODUCTION

This chapter examines the application of the precautionary principle in relation to biodiversity and natural resource management in Argentina. It is based on an examination of legislation and policy, specific administrative and judicial decisions, and attitudes toward the precautionary principle among decision-makers. It seeks to draw insights and conclusions about the impacts of the precautionary principle in Argentina and barriers to its effective implementation.

The chapter begins by setting out the basic structure of government in Argentina, before going on to examine the incorporation of the precautionary principle in relevant law. The study then introduces the process of judicial decision-making in Argentina by analysing cases that have involved the precautionary principle and highlighting major trends. It then discusses some administrative decisions relating to various subject areas, and analyses different approaches taken by administrative authorities in relation to the principle. Finally, the chapter presents some insights and conclusions.

The discussion of administrative decisions and attitudes is based on a series of interviews carried out by the authors with authorities from federal administrative offices, on the application and use of the precautionary principle or precautionary approach in each field, between August and November 2004. Relevant judicial decisions were sought from several Argentine jurisdictions.

## STRUCTURE OF THE GOVERNMENT OF THE REPUBLIC OF ARGENTINA

The Argentine Republic is a federally organized country with four levels of government: nation, provinces, municipalities and the City of Buenos Aires; and three powers: executive, legislative and judicial. Section 24 of the National Constitution establishes that the provinces have sovereignty over the natural resources located within their territory. The provinces are therefore responsible for and have legal jurisdiction over environmental issues. Nevertheless, the National Congress is competent to enact legislation in a number of relevant areas. In particular, it is responsible for establishing minimum standards for environmental protection (Section 41). The provinces may then complement these with their own stricter regulations. The National Congress is also responsible for enacting legislation that addresses international, interprovincial and interjurisdictional trade, as well as criminal, civil, commerce, mining and labour codes (Section 75), and any legislation that relates to the harmonized growth of the nation.

The federal departments that have primary responsibility for environment-related issues are the Secretariat of Environment and Sustainable Development (SAyDS) of the Ministry of Health and Environment (which is responsible for environmental protection, sustainable development, and the rational use and conservation of natural resources); the Secretariat of Agriculture, Livestock, Fisheries and Food (SAGPyA), which is composed of several departments that monitor and regulate different areas under the control of the Secretariat, including, agriculture, aquaculture, farm activities, livestock, fishing activities, food quality, forestation and genetically modified organisms (GMOs); and the Administration of National Parks (APN), a division of the Secretariat of Tourism, which is responsible for all aspects of national parks and national protected areas throughout the country.

Another important body, which is a coordination body that comes under the Federal Environmental System, is the Environmental Federal Council (COFEMA), which brings together and coordinates all the activities of the environmental authorities of the nation, provinces, and the City of Buenos Aires in relation to environmental policy in the country.

## RELEVANT APPLICABLE LAW IN ARGENTINA

Argentina has signed and ratified various international agreements that reflect or incorporate the precautionary principle. The most important, in the biodiversity context, is the Convention on Biological Diversity (CBD),[1] which includes a version of the precautionary principle in its Preamble. SAyDS is the authority responsible for overseeing implementation of the CBD, and has incorporated the precautionary principle into the National Biodiversity Strategy (2003 – see below). Argentina is also a signatory to CITES,[2] which regulates trade of listed specimens of wild animals and plants in order to safeguard certain species from overexploitation. The precautionary principle has been adopted by the parties to CITES to guide listing decisions (Resolution Conf. 9.24 (Rev. CoP13)). All parties must obtain and present a pertinent document to import or export a CITES-listed specimen. The legal authority responsible for the enforcement of the country's obligations under this instrument is SAyDS.

While the National Constitution contains no explicit mention of the precautionary principle, Section 41 states that the inhabitants of Argentina are entitled to a healthy environment and have a duty to preserve it. The authorities must guarantee the exercise of this right, the rational use of natural resources, the protection of the natural and cultural heritage, the conservation of biological diversity, and provide environmental information and education.

In 2002, the National Congress started enacting laws that included minimum standards for environmental protection, as provided for in the Constitution. Although there is at present no minimum standard law on biodiversity, the General Environmental Law (GEL) (2002) includes environmental principles and, specifically, the precautionary principle (in Section 4):

> *When there exists danger of serious or irreversible damage, the lack of information or scientific certainty should not be used as a reason to postpone the adoption of efficient measures – depending on cost – to prevent degradation of the environment.*

According to Section 41 of the National Constitution, this law must be applied by the three powers (executive, legislative and judicial) at all levels (national, provincial and municipal). Therefore, in the case of uncertainty, decision-makers must apply the precautionary principle. The GEL also includes a provision for compulsory environmental impact assessment (EIA) of those projects or activities that may lead to a significant degradation of the environment or any of its components.

The National Law of Conservation of Wild Fauna (1981)[3] established that in the regulation and application of this law, authorities must respect the balance between the economic, cultural, farming, recreational and visual benefits of wild fauna for mankind, but give due preference to conservation in all cases, as the main guiding principle for all administrative acts (Section 2). In case of doubt, conservation must prevail as the principal criteria. The more vulnerable a species is, the more restricted its use. Section 2 underpins the whole system created by this law in order to frame the management of species and their use. The law establishes the necessary conditions for prior authorization by the enforcement authority for situations including any projects in natural places that may have an effect on wild fauna, introduction of a new alien species into the country, and use of poison and toxic products.

The idea of the precautionary principle is therefore not new in Argentina, and even before passing of the GEL the judiciary applied the principle based on the CBD (see *Copetro*, below). However, its reception in GEL as an explicit

– and we consider mandatory – principle to guide policy interpretation and application of the law is indeed new.

# JUDICIAL DECISIONS

Both federal and provincial judges, in a wide range of cases, have used the precautionary principle over the past decade. The first judicial decision to mention the precautionary principle in Argentina was the *Copetro*[4] case in 1995. In this case, the civil and commercial court of appeals applied the precautionary principle, citing the CBD, in support of the finding that a party that generated air pollution had an obligation to correct the environmental damage it had caused.

It appears that Argentine judicial decisions apply the precautionary principle, as set out in the CBD and in the GEL, not only reactively (to stop activities) but also proactively (to require particular actions). Judges used the precautionary principle to stop potentially damaging activities in the *Villavar*[5] case in 2003, where a federal court of appeals decided that the precautionary principle supported the suspension of mining work that might affect the environment, biological diversity and human health. Here a mining company was ordered to stop all mining of the Esquel Cord, until it complied with the EIA process required under provincial law. In *Verzeñassi*[6] (2004), the court of Entre Rios ordered the executive authority of the province of Entre Rios not to apply a decree that authorized the felling of native forest and repealed a declaration of environmental emergency covering the native forest in the province. The court cited the CBD and the principles of prevention, precaution and of sustainability set out in the 2002 GEL, and required the provincial authority to develop an environmental impact assessment that conferred certainty of adequate protection.

The judiciary has used the principle in a proactive sense in several recent cases. In *Figueroa*[7] (2004), the Rio Negro court of appeals applied the precautionary principle to justify the adoption of urgent and corrective measures to address pollution in a body of water. The court ordered industries and the municipality to implement specific actions, including building of effluent treatment facilities and carrying out of interdisciplinary studies and EIA. In *Barragán*[8] (2003), an appeal court in the City of Buenos Aires used the precautionary principle together with the principle of prevention to justify requiring a highway company to take measures to mitigate possible damage to human health caused by noise from a highway. Measures required included development of a technical environmental impact study and an environmental adaptation plan.

In many cases, the precautionary principle is not used as an absolute barrier to activities, but as a basis for requiring that uncertainty or the level of possible threat be reduced before activities are allowed to proceed, through, for instance, requiring EIA or further scientific studies (see the cases of *Verzeñassi* and *Barragán*, above). In *Asociación Usuarios*[9] (2003), the federal court of appeals halted the installation of cables and required a mitigation plan for any environmental and health damage from an electric substation. The bases of these two decisions were related to concerns about the long-term health impacts of the electromagnetic radiation emitted by an existing electric substation and the future installation of cables. The precautionary principle was used by the court to analyse the evidence.

As can be seen in many of the cases described above, judicial decisions often use the precautionary principle in tandem with other principles of environmental law. In particular, judges tend to use both the prevention and the precaution principles together to act when there is uncertainty as to future damage, and these are often linked with the principles of sustainability, environmental liability and the right to a healthy environment.

The precautionary principle, along with other legal tools, has been applied in a wide variety of situations and types of decisions, and has led to the adoption of a number of specific decisions. However, it appears that its use in situations with similar characteristics can lead to divergent decisions. For an illustration of this, it is possible to compare the cases of *Asociación de Usuarios* and *Castellani*[10] (2003). In the former, described above, despite the lack of any positive evidence of damage to health or the environment, an activity (installation of cables), was stopped and mitigation measures ordered. In the latter, the plaintiffs argued that installation of cellular phone antennas should not proceed until scientific bodies could certify that there was no risk or danger to human health, or to the right to a healthy environment. The provincial court found that there was no evidence of risk or damage posed by the installation of cellular phone antennas, and no basis for barring their installation. However, one of the judges established a dissenting opinion, citing the precautionary principle, considering there was real uncertainty regarding the effects of radiation emissions.

Given the innovative condition of the application of the principle in terms of the judicature, it can be concluded that at present these decisions form part of an ongoing and unavoidable process to construct a clearer concept. This process is reinforced by its reception and treatment by the administrative authorities, as can be observed in the *Ficchi* case.[11] This was a judicial decision of the federal court of Mar del Plata, in the province of Buenos Aires, in which the plaintiff asked the court to declare a resolution of SAGPyA unconstitutional and arbitrary. This resolution established fishing quotas and closed seasons for fishing of Argentinian hake *Merluccius hubbsi*, based on the application of the precautionary principle. The court upheld the legality and reasonableness of the administrative decision and denied injunctive relief.

## ADMINISTRATIVE DECISIONS

Understanding the concrete impact of the precautionary principle requires going well beyond an analysis of law and judicial cases, to an examination of the administrative decisions that impact on biodiversity. This section analyses the administrative decisions of the national government pursuant to the competencies already mentioned, and involving the various departments described above.

One of the most important questions regarding the application of the precautionary principle is whether it should be mandatory or discretionary for decision-makers in Argentina. The precautionary principle can be viewed as one tool for resolving the age-old conflict between an activity and its effects on human health or on the environment and its components, in the specific factual situation of lack of certainty or information. According to the legal framework, it appears that the precautionary principle is one of a body of principles, whose main objectives are conservation and protection, which act as a guide for environmental policies and interpretation of the law (see GEL). It is clear that in all cases where the fact situation indicates there is the danger of serious and irreversible damage, and there is a lack of information or scientific certainty, the precautionary principle must be applied as a *mandatory* principle. Taking into account that there exist other overarching principles within the legal framework, the precautionary principle is part of a new vision of environmental issues and decisions, which balances different priorities and interests to resolve the potential conflicts between development activities and the environment/human health.

We now turn to review the application of the precautionary principle in administrative decisions on different issues and by diverse authorities.

## Biodiversity and wild species

The National Biodiversity Strategy (NBS),[12] a resolution of the SAyDS, deals with obligations deriving from the CBD. The text of the resolution includes various provisions, which reflect the precautionary principle, such as provisions on:

- promoting a new law of minimum standards to guarantee sustainable use of biological resources; this new law should require an EIA and management of all projects that may include use of natural resources;
- applying the precautionary principle to the prevention and control of alien and invasive species; and
- a general requirement for an EIA for all those public and private projects that may affect biological diversity.

While the NBS is a general administrative guideline, its application in concrete situations will require specific administrative decisions.

With respect to the conservation of wild fauna, SAyDS is the national enforcement authority of the National Law of Conservation of Wild Fauna, and of the international agreements on conservation. As set out above, relevant obligations to apply the precautionary principle derive from these and other instruments. Relevant administrative decisions include SAyDS Resolution No 62/1986, which suspends the exportation of all living species of native mammals, birds and reptiles, except those bred in captivity, those considered by law to be harmful or invasive species, or those subject to specific regulation considered by the same authority. These measures can be considered as a concrete application of the precautionary principle as reflected in the National Law of Conservation of Wild Fauna.

In relation to sustainable use and management of wild species, SAyDS also has administrative power. Its national programme includes management of specific species, establishing quotas or controls on trade and hunting, conservation of habitats, and experimental quotas for capture. It does not include an environmental risk study. Nevertheless, for the concrete implementation of this programme, it develops scientific studies to justify the adoption of different measures. Based upon the new information, regulations are updated periodically. The decision process involves scientific information and application criteria. The Secretariat receives scientific information from specialized official institutes (depending on each case), as well as from local universities. After an integrated analysis of the information, the authorities include the criteria and principles derived from the National Law of Conservation of Wild Fauna in order to justify the decisions adopted with regard to natural resources management.

Regarding the introduction of exotic species, the Secretariat has established a system requiring an EIA to assess the potential introduction of an invasive species. It includes evaluating potential impacts, including health risks for plants and animals, as well as economic and productive risks (Resolution No 376/97). According to interviews with enforcement authority officials, the resolution was established to deter clandestine behaviour. At present, only one request for permission has been submitted (ostrich) but the applicant abandoned the presentation after the Secretariat requested further information.

Among the major problems surrounding these programmes and functions of SAyDS are enforcement and coordination between departments and provincial authorities. These are important current issues in the legal system in Argentina, and imply major obstacles for the implementation and effectiveness of the legal framework and its provisions, including the precautionary principle.

Moreover, the authorities claim that the main barrier to implementing a precautionary approach to natural resource management and biodiversity conservation are productive activities that may directly impact biodiversity. Farming activities, such as GMO production or monocultivation, have been cited in Argentina in relation to discussions on impact on habitats of wild species.

We now consider the application of the precautionary principle, together with other tools, which could be used to make implementation effective.

## Fisheries

Law 24,922 of the Federal Fisheries Regime establishes a system by which the competent authority grants fishing quotas based on maximum permissible catch. This is defined by considering the maximum sustainable product of each species. The determination of the maximum permissible catch is based upon scientific studies made by the National Institute of Fishing Research and Development (INIDEP).

SAGPyA is responsible for enforcing fishing policies, conservation and ordering of resources, even on the high seas. Likewise, the Federal Fisheries Council (CFP) – created by federal law and composed of the maritime provinces, the Fisheries Secretary, SAyDS, the Ministry of Foreign Affairs and the national executive power – carries out important functions that form the basis on which SAGPyA acts. Among its functions are establishing fishing policy, promoting research and establishing the maximum permissible catch per species. Therefore, although the CFP is the only organ legally entitled to establish fishing quotas and national fisheries policy, the law has established a system for resource administration in which these two organs share different faculties.

Law 24,922 of the Federal Fisheries Regime makes no mention of the precautionary principle. However, it should be interpreted consistently with GEL, and application of the law should therefore take into account the prevention and precautionary principles in the determination of maximum sustainable fishing quotas. At present, there are significant problems related to fishing in Argentine waters associated with economic pressure and interests, and deficient enforcement, which have led to overfishing. One of the major problems comes from incomplete and unsystematic compliance with the quotas created by the authorities. In this sense, while it is possible to find diverse resolutions from both SAGPyA and CFP, there is currently a lack of unified and coherent national policy on this issue.

Two decisions by SAGPyA and CFP can be quoted as examples of the recognition of the precautionary principle or approach to fishing activities. First, through Resolution No 8/2002, SAGPyA restricts fishing activities of a protected species, *Merluccius hubbsi*, currently declared to be in a state of emergency. This resolution uses the precautionary principle. At the time the resolution was passed, INIDEP had not completed the scientific research to accurately establish the maximum permissible catch that would not alter the effects on, and the exploitation pattern of, the species. The judiciary sustained the legality and reasonableness of the administrative decision and, in particular, the application of the precautionary principle (see judicial case *Ficchi*).

According to interviews conducted, the CFP takes into account the precautionary principle. In accordance with the exchange of information carried out with authorities from CFP, the GEL has brought new concepts to the council, and the interaction with SAyDS (as one of the members of the council) has been fundamental to the incorporation of the concepts of prevention and precaution in the work of the CFP. CFP decisions must be based on scientific information provided by INIDEP. Nevertheless, whenever there is insufficient information to fix the maximum permissible catch per species for a certain period, CFP contemplates the possibility of implementing special management measures and temporarily closed seasons. In some cases of doubt, a lower level of capture is always considered based upon the application of the precautionary principle.

Second, the interesting administrative case of *Variado Costero*, from the south of the Province of Buenos Aires demonstrates the potential of an ecosystem management approach, which includes implicit use of the precautionary approach. In the area of the south coast of the Province of Buenos Aires, INIDEP carried out research showing that while most of the coastal species were fished on a large scale, this ecosystem had a high level of reproduction of many species of fish and concentration of young. It revealed that catches and the number of ships in the area had increased in recent years and that most of the species now showed signs of overexploitation. INIDEP suggested placing limits on fishing during the reproductive season within the area, based upon these preliminary studies. It was clear that the problem was not setting a lower maximum catch for some species, but treating the area with a precautionary vision and as an interactive whole.

In addition, in the coastal zone many communities depend exclusively on fishing for survival and would be highly affected if a total closed season was established. The CFP wanted to establish an integrated management area rather than diverse resolutions on maximum permissible catches per species. Therefore, CFP No 53/2004 established a closed season at a certain time of year and a specific management zone for conservation, considering the necessity of fishing activity in the area, and taking into account the need for precaution in responding to the new information, in order to prevent damage to this ecosystem. Moreover, the CFP asked the INIDEP to update the information to establish the next closed season.

It can be seen that the precautionary principle has in fact produced specific protection, and that without it the result in each case would have been different. It can be concluded that even in those cases in which the application of the precautionary principle may be conflicting in terms of limitation (temporal or not) of an economically important activity, when the authority is convinced of its duty and takes the political decision to apply the principle in cases of uncertainty or lack of information, the tool is effective in relation to its stated goal.

Nevertheless, and considering the reality of marine resources in Argentine waters, it seems clear that the use of the principle would be greater if a coherent policy and integrated implementation of the principle existed in all cases with these characteristics in a long-term perspective, together with an ecosystem-level vision of the problem.

## Protected areas

The system established by the National Law on Protected Areas 22,351 is based upon the idea of conservation, but there is no explicit mention of the precautionary principle. Nevertheless, it must be taken into account that Resolution No 16/1994 of the National Parks Administration (APN) requires EIA in the administrative area, by which the performance of an EIA is established as a duty for the execution of public or private projects within the areas covered by the law.

The authority may permit hunting and fishing only when there are biological, scientific or technical reasons for doing so. Both activities can be used for control and eradication of invasive species.

## Forestry

Law 25,080 on forestry projects requires EIA to assess forestry projects affecting native and exotic species. For all projects, this regulation requires an EIA study involving the SAGPyA enforcement authority and SAyDS. At present, interaction between these two organizations has not been implemented, so the SAGPyA is the only authority involved in project evaluation.

## GMOs – agricultural activities

Even though this legal framework does not specifically refer to the precautionary principle, it includes a risk assessment system. The regulations (Law 20,247 on seeds and phytogenetic creations and Law 13,636 on veterinarian products, supervision, creation and commercialization, and specific regulations) provide a legal framework for the decisions of the SAGPyA regarding approval or rejection of applications for release into the environment and/or trade of GMOs. Argentina has not yet ratified the Cartagena Protocol.

National authorities currently tend to use a less stringent application of the precautionary principle in those decisions that can affect trade. Because of the importance of the economic production involved, they take the approach that scientific uncertainty should be subject to a specific time limit so as to prevent the erection of trade barriers.

# ATTITUDES TOWARD THE PRECAUTIONARY PRINCIPLE AMONG ADMINISTRATIVE AUTHORITIES

The interviews conducted revealed that the various authorities are aware of the legislation supporting the existence of the precautionary principle in the Argentine legal system. As a result of the GEL, they recognize the application of the principle in decisions regarding environmental policy.

Nevertheless, there was a strong contrast between authorities that recognize the need for this tool, and those that view it as a possible barrier to economically important activities in the country. The authorities that are using scientific prevention criteria for the management of natural resources appeared to be more receptive and less fearful of the principle. By contrast, concern was expressed by other administrative authorities that the application of the principle cannot be unlimited in time. This position is more evident among those authorities responsible for decision-making about activities that are presently the subject of controversy, such as the release into the environment and trade of GMOs and their respective activities, or demands for the labelling of products containing GMOs.

Overall, however, it is clear that the economic effects of administrative decisions on economically important activities such as agriculture or fishing play a vital role when limiting the exploitation or the use of a natural resource. Effective application of the principle is likely to require an integrated environment protection policy built on consensus, which takes into account all the factors involved in the use and management of the resource it seeks to protect.

## Insights and Conclusions

The precautionary principle is now part of the Argentine legal system. It has been used and applied in environmental decision-making in various government departments with powers for conservation, environment and biodiversity, and is an important principle recognized by the judiciary. On the basis of analysis of decisions and interviews, a range of insights and conclusions can be drawn about the implementation of the principle in Argentina and barriers to implementation:

- The precautionary principle has been incorporated into Argentine environmental legislation, and must be applied in the interpretation of environmental legislation in general.
- Because it is new, an ongoing process of development, construction and understanding of a definition of the precautionary principle can be observed among the different authorities and the judiciary. In consequence, while there is general agreement on its existence as an obligation, the conditions for its application are uncertain.
- The precautionary principle does not work alone, but may be used by the judiciary in tandem with principles of prevention, sustainable development, the right to a healthy environment and environmental liability. Nevertheless, a better definition of and clarity on the precautionary principle are likely to result in more specific and convincing application.
- In some judicial cases, the precautionary principle has been applied to resolve conflicts, by leading to decisions requiring the carrying out of an impact study or risk assessment, or other research that may clarify the lack of certainty or information. It has not necessarily been interpreted to mean activities must be indefinitely prohibited. The principle can be applied until more information and concrete data allow the adoption of a decision.
- Judicial decisions have provided fundamental contributions in developing conceptions of the appropriate use of the precautionary principle. This is particularly important because overall the executive branch of government tends not to be coherent and proactive.
- Two basic attitudes to the precautionary principle among administrative decision-makers can currently be observed. One is receptive of its application under conditions of lack of information and uncertainty, and

envisaging its use for concrete measures on use and management of natural resources. The other reflects a fearful position regarding the principle's application, envisaging its use as a barrier to trade or as a limit on economically important activities.

- Despite this fear the facts suggest that application of the precautionary principle, including as applied by the authorities who must decide on issues of economic importance, has not constituted a real limitation for the development of these same activities. For instance, the precautionary principle is part of the policy framework for risk management for GMOs, and the GMO-related agrofood sector is one of the most productive in Argentina. This shows a concrete need to define criteria for the application of the precautionary principle.

- There is little policy coordination between relevant departments, leading to different conceptions of and attitudes toward the precautionary principle in different departments (for example sustainable development versus agriculture). This leads to lack of coordinated policy, decision-making and action on threats to biodiversity. In addition, policy differences between levels of government and the lack of a minimum standards law on biodiversity may complicate the scenario.

- Implementation of the precautionary principle requires analysis and improvement of enforcement and compliance mechanisms, such as through an indicators system of enforcement and compliance on biodiversity issues. Such a system, not currently developed in Argentina, would provide tangible indicators of progress toward the implementation of the precautionary principle to secure protection and conservation of biological diversity.

## NOTES

1  Approved by National Law 24,375 and ratified on 22 November 1994.
2  Approved by National Law 22,344 and ratified on 8 January 1981.
3  National Law 22.421, B.O. 03/12/1981.
4  Almada, Hugo c/ Copetro SA and others; Iruzu, Margarita c/ Copetro SA and others; Klaus, Juan c/ Copetro SA and others, which began in 1993. Decision by the Court of Appeals C.1° Civ and Com. La Plata, Sala 3°, 02/09/1995.
5  Villavar, Silvana Noemí c/ Province of Chubut and others s/ Injunctive Relief, First instance – Esquel – Province of Chubut 02/19/2003.
6  Verzeñassi Sergio Daniel y otro c/ Superior Gobierno de la Provincia de Entre Ríos s/ Acción de Amparo Ambiental, First Instance Court of Paraná III – Paraná – Entre Ríos, 06/03/2004.
7  Figueroa, Eusebio Sebastián and others s/ Injunctive relief, Labor and Contentious Administrative Court – City of Cipoletti – Province of Rio Negro (it is a Court of Appeals), 07/08/2004.
8  Barragán, José Pedro c/ GCBA and others s/ Injunctive relief, First Instance/Court of Appeals – Contentious Administrative Court – II – City of Buenos Aires, 2003.
9  Coordinator Association of Users, Consumers and Taxpayers c/ ENRE – EDESUR s/ Finish with the cables' work and transferring of the transformation station, Federal Court of Appeals – II – La Plata – Province of Buenos Aires, 07/08/2003.

10 Castellani, Carlos Edgardo and Others – Injunctive Relief – Appeal – Repeal and Unconstitutionality Resources, Superior Court of Justice of the Province of Cordoba Argentina – 03/11/03.
11 Ficchi, Francisco José c/ SAGPyA s/ Injunctive Relief, First Instance – Second Federal Court – Secretariat 1º – Mar del Plata, Province of Buenos Aires, 08/11/2003.
12 National Resolution SAyDS No 91/03.

# REFERENCES

The following publications were consulted for this chapter, though none have been directly quoted from or cited in the text.

Bec, E. R. F. and Horacio, J. (2004) 'Los 12 problemas ambientales que más preocupan a las empresas', *Gerencia Ambiental*, Año 11, no 107, pp417–20
Cooney, R. (2003) *The Precautionary Principle and Parks Management: Science, Uncertainty, Communities and Conservation*, report of panel discussion at the IUCN Worlds Parks Congress, September 2003, Durban, South Africa. Available at www.pprinciple.net
Cooney, R. (2004) *The Precautionary Principle in Biodiversity Conservation and Natural Resource Management: An Issues Paper for Policy-makers, Researchers and Practitioners*, IUCN Policy and Global Change Series, no 2, IUCN, Gland, Switzerland and Cambridge, UK
Daneri, J. (2004) 'El principio precautorio y las plantas de celulosa en la cuenca del río Uruguay', *Suplemento de Derecho Ambiental*, FARN – La Ley, Año XI, no 1
Di Paola, M. E. and Kravetz Diego, G. 'Invasive alien species: legal and institutional framework in Argentina', in M. L. Miller and R. N. Fabian (eds) *Harmful Invasive Species: Legal Responses*, Environmental Law Institute, pp71–87
Estrada Oyuela, R. and Aguilar, S. (2003) 'El principio o enfoque precautorio en el Derecho Internacional y en la Ley General del Ambiente', *Suplemento de Derecho Ambiental*, FARN – La Ley, Año X, no 4
FARN and IUCN (2004) *Minimum Standards of Environmental Protection – Recommendations for their Implementation*, FARN and IUCN, Buenos Aires
Goldemberg, I. and Cafferatta, N. A. (2002) *El Principio de Precaución*, Jurisprudencia Argentina, T. IV, pp 1442–56
Iribarren, F. and Lichtschein, V. (2004) *Ley de Conservación de la Fauna Comentada*, Centro de Estúdios sobre Agricultura y Recursos Naturales (CEARN), Buenos Aires
Juli, A. and Birchall, N. (2002) 'Case Notes on Spray-Tech v. Hudson (Ville)', *Review of European Community and International Environmental Law*, vol 11, no 1, pp104–106
Orona, C. F., Giardina, E. B. and Cimato, M. del P. (2003) 'Viabilidad de la aplicación del princípio de precaución en nuestra actividad jurisdiccional y como elemento integrante del proceso de toma de decisiones', *Suplemento de Derecho Ambiental*, FARN – La Ley, Año X, no 5
Precautionary Principle Project (2004) *Managing Uncertainty: Risk and the Precautionary Principle in Biodiversity Conservation and Sustainable Use*, final report for workshop held as part of the Fourth Regional Session for Africa of the Global Biodiversity Forum, Southern and Eastern Africa, Tanzania, 9–11 June. Available at www.pprinciple.net

Precautionary Principle Project (2004) *The Precautionary Principle in Natural Management and Biodiversity Conservation*, final report for workshop held as part of the Fourth Regional Session for Asia of the Global Biodiversity Forum, Southeast Asia, Manila, The Philippines, 20–23 June. Available at www.pprinciple.net

Sands, P. (1995) *Principles of International Environmental Law*, First edition, Manchester University Press, Manchester and New York

Scholtz, W. (2002) 'The precautionary principle and international trade: conflict or reconciliation?', *South African Journal of Environmental Law and Policy*, vol 9, pp163–75

Segger, M.C., Borregaard, N., Mindahi, B., Muñoz, S. and Salvador, D. (2003) *Social Rules and Sustainability in the Americas*, International Institute for Sustainable Development, Winnipeg

Von Moltke, K. and Ryan, D. (eds) (2001) *Medio Ambiente y Comercio: El Caso Mercosur y los Princípios de Winnipeg*, informe de trabajo, División de Medio Ambiente, Departamento de Desarrollo Sostenible, Banco Interamericano de Desarrollo

Walsh, J. R. (2004) 'Major infrastructure projects, biodiversity and the precautionary principle in the case of the Yaciretá Dam and Iberá Marshes', *Review of European Community and International Environmental Law*, vol 13, no 1, pp61–71

Wanhua, Y. (2002) 'Environmental provisions in the WTO agreements and their implications', *Review of European Community and International Environmental Law* vol 11, no 3, pp314–327

# 9

# Preventing Alien Invasions: The Precautionary Principle in Practice in Weed Risk Assessment in Australia

*Tim Low*

## INTRODUCTION

The precautionary principle can play a key role in preventing the entry of invasive (alien) plants and animals into a country. All over the world, alien invaders have a serious impact on biodiversity, resource conservation, agriculture and human health. This chapter examines Australia's approach to controlling the entry of potentially invasive plants through the weed risk assessment process, among the most precautionary control systems for invasive species in the world.

## EXPLAINING WEED RISK ASSESSMENT

Weed risk assessment (WRA) was introduced in 1997 as a regulatory measure to reduce the flow of new weeds into Australia (Low, 1999; Baskin, 2002; Walton, 2001). It is a government screening process to predict which new imported plants will become weeds. It operates on a precautionary principle: under WRA some new plants are banned because they *might* become weeds.

Weeds are a very serious problem for Australia (and other countries), and cost billions of dollars each year. They do great harm to agriculture and to the environment. Most weeds are plants that were deliberately imported to serve some purpose. Of Australia's 20 worst weeds (so-called 'Weeds of National Significance'), 16 were deliberately imported from other countries. Major weeds include plants that have been brought into the country for every possible reason: food, medicine, timber, shade, ornament, lawn, livestock feed, birdseed, aquarium decoration, salinity reclamation and so on. One government study found that ten new weeds were appearing in Australia each year and that of these, 65 per cent had been imported as garden plants (Groves, 1998). Weeds can rarely be eradicated and their introduction represents an irreversible harm. Most of them are no longer widely used for their original purpose and today, their introduction is regretted. Some weedy plants are still grown by gardeners (often from ignorance), but alternatives are available.

New plants are still imported (mainly as seeds) and some of these will become weeds in future. Because weeds are such an immense problem, the Australian Government now restricts the entry of new plants by applying a precautionary approach: plants considered likely to become weeds in Australia are prohibited, even though it is accepted that not all of them might become weeds.

In the past the Australian Quarantine and Inspection Service (AQIS) kept a list of prohibited plants. This list consisted of weeds that caused problems overseas but that were not found in Australia. If a plant was not on that list, and not closely related to a plant on that list, it could be imported. There was also a large list of plants already approved for introduction.

These lists are still used, but in 1997 AQIS introduced WRA (Pheloung, 1996; Walton and Ellis, 1997; Low, 1999; Baskin, 2002; Pheloung, 2001; Walton, 2001). It incorporates two extra processes. The first of these is the administration of a questionnaire that includes a series of 49 questions (Walton and Ellis, 1997; Pheloung, 2001). These are asked about any new plant that someone wants to import, if it is not on either of the two lists. Questions include: does the plant form dense thickets? Is it spread by animals? Is it a weed somewhere else? Most of the questions are taken to be possible indicators of weediness. Some of the questions are thought to indicate a low risk of weediness. Plants receive a score depending upon the answers generated (most questions get one point for 'yes', while those indicating low weediness reduce the score). If a plant scores zero or less it is allowed in. If it gets more than five points it is denied entry. If it scores one–five it must be evaluated further under a third process that has yet to be put in place/agreed upon/implemented.

Further evaluation in most cases is likely to begin with a search for more information about the plant. This may lead to a new score of zero or more than five, in which cases the plant will be accepted or banned accordingly. If the score remains in the one–five range then even further evaluation will be required, and this will rely more on a cost–benefit analysis than a precautionary approach.

An importer is not charged for the first two stages of WRA, but is charged for the third (or will be, when it is developed). The government does not impose full cost recovery because a high cost could encourage plant smuggling.

Whenever a plant is denied entry because of WRA questions, the precautionary approach acts to prevent irreversible harm (weeds can seldom be eradicated once they spread). WRA keeps out plants that seem *likely* to become weeds, with no certainty that they will. The rights of importers are curtailed by a process of prediction. The general presumption in favour of development (the right to import) is subordinated to the principle of precaution, and with no apparent consequences for equity.

Australia's WRA has won praise from international weed experts as the most effective system in the world for keeping out weeds. It has been adopted (with modifications) by New Zealand and has attracted interest from other countries. It targets environmental weeds as much as economic weeds and thus benefits biodiversity as well as people.

## SCIENTIFIC BASIS

According to the guidelines developed for applying WRA (Walton and Ellis, 1997), 'the weed assessments ... scientifically determine pest risk and the process used is transparent'. Australia is an active member of the WTO. The World Trade Organization Agreement on the Application of Sanitary and Phytosanitary Standards, 1994 (SPS Agreement), designed to stop nations from using quarantine rules as a guise to block trade, insists that any processes for restricting imports be scientifically sound. Australia is often accused of misusing quarantine to protect its farmers from cheap imports, and the need for a scientific process is well recognized.

Plant importers have no say in how WRA is applied. If they had an influence over WRA it would no longer appear to be scientifically sound. But because the process is simple and transparent there are few complaints about the way in which the WRA questions are asked and answered.

The validity of WRA was established by testing the questions against 370 plant species already found in Australia. These included economic and environmental weeds, as well as other useful plants (Pheloung, 1996, 2001). The system rejected 100 per cent of the serious weeds it was tested against and 84 per cent of the minor weeds. It rejected 7 per cent of non-weedy plants. It performed better than two earlier questionnaire systems devised by government weed experts that were also tested (Pheloung, 1996; Walton and Ellis, 1997). The system was refined with the help of scientists from 13 organizations in Australia and New Zealand (Walton and Ellis, 1997).

Australia has been a leader in advancing the science of weed risk assessment. It held the First International Workshop on Weed Risk Assessment in 1999, and papers from this workshop (and other contributions) were later published by Australia's foremost science group, the Commonwealth Scientific and Industrial Research Organisation (CSIRO) in a book entitled *Weed Risk Assessment* (Groves et al, 2001).

Many of the WRA questions assume that weediness can be predicted from the properties of a plant. This assumption has been questioned (Groves et al, 2001; Low, 2002). As Lonsdale and Smith (2001) note: 'There is a range of views on whether there are certain ecological traits of organisms that might confer high invasive potential'. Earlier suggestions that weeds share certain properties such as continuous seed production and short life cycles (Baker, 1965) have been invalidated (Williamson, 1996). But some recent studies suggest that a limited range of properties may indicate invasiveness (Groves et al, 2001), although not necessarily on the scale implied by WRA. Some questions in WRA may not target likelihood of weediness so much as attributes that prove especially undesirable if a plant does become weedy. For example, plants with tubers or bulbs earn a point, not, it seems, because of evidence that they become weedy more often, but because 'Plants from this group can be particularly difficult to eradicate' (Walton and Ellis, 1997).

When a modified form of WRA was tested recently in Hawaii (Daehler et al, 2004), several plants that are weeds in Australia (in regions with a similar climate to that of Hawaii) scored as non-weedy. However, this failing may reflect poor application of WRA rather than the limits of prediction. Differing opinions about the prediction of weediness are canvassed in *Weed Risk Assessment* (Groves et al, 2001).

Other questions asked under WRA are less open to doubt. These include questions about whether the climate where the plant grows naturally matches the climate in Australia, and the history of the plant as a weed overseas. A plant that is weedy overseas and well suited to Australia's climate could be expected to become a weed in Australia. Questions about pollination are also sound. A plant that can self-fertilize can spread from one imported individual, whereas a species that needs a special pollinator may not spread at all if that pollinator is absent.

The science underlying WRA is not strongly established, yet there is no better science to turn to, and no better method in use anywhere in the world. Low (2002) questioned the idea of predicting weediness from plant characters but nonetheless decided that 'Weed Risk Assessment does have merit because it captures the one highly predictive value – weediness in one part of the world is often matched by weediness elsewhere'. The system works best when considering plants that have already been cultivated for long periods somewhere else. Any system that keeps out large numbers of plants will keep out some weeds, whether or not the science is sound. However, those who cannot import these plants are likely to criticize the science. This has happened in Australia, and is explained later on in this chapter.

WRA provides a striking example of the precautionary principle operating in a setting of scientific uncertainty. The science does not produce definitive answers, yet decisions to ban plants are still made, because a commitment to precaution guides the process. This is justified by the immense and irreversible harm that many weeds cause.

## LEGAL AND POLICY BASIS

The importance of keeping out new weeds is stated in the National Weed Strategy, introduced by Australia's Commonwealth and state governments in 1997 (revised 1999) to 'reduce the impact of weeds on the sustainability of Australia's productive capacity and natural ecosystems' (Commonwealth of Australia, 1999). The strategy has four principles, two of which justify WRA:

*2. Prevention and early intervention are the most cost effective techniques that can be deployed against weeds.*

*3. Successful weed management requires a coordinated national approach which involves all levels of government in establishing appropriate legislative, educational and coordination frameworks in partnership with industry, landholders and the community.* (Commonwealth of Australia, 1999)

Objective 1.1 of the strategy is 'To prevent the introduction of new plant species with weed potential'. The timetable for meeting this objective was set out in *National Objectives and Targets for Biodiversity Conservation, 2001–05* (Commonwealth of Australia, 2001; Spafford Jacob et al, 2004b). The following goals were accepted as national responsibilities:

*Target 4.1.1: By 2001, the import of all new live organisms is subject to a risk-based assessment process that identifies the conditions necessary to minimise threats to the environment.*

*Target 4.1.2: By 2001, no new non-native species are deliberately introduced into Australia unless assessed as being of low risk to the environment.* (Commonwealth of Australia, 2001)

WRA is administered by AQIS. All plants and animals brought into Australia must be declared to AQIS, which is obliged by the Quarantine Act (1908) to keep out pests. Australia's quarantine system is acknowledged internationally as one of the strictest in the world.

AQIS sits within the Department of Agriculture, Fisheries and Forestry. Its sole responsibility is to inspect imports and exports and to certify exports. Another unit within the same department, Biosecurity Australia (BA), produces import risk analyses and develops quarantine policies.

The precautionary principle as a more general guide was endorsed in the 1992 Australian Intergovernmental Agreement on the Environment (IGAE). IGAE states that 'In the application of the precautionary principle, public and private decisions should be guided by: careful evaluation to avoid, where practicable, serious or irreversible damage to the environment; and an assessment of the risk-weighted consequences of various options'. It is also included in the Commonwealth Environment Protection and Biodiversity Conservation Act (Fisher and Harding, 2001).

Government officials have recently begun discriminating between a 'precautionary principle' and a 'precautionary approach', which is their preferred concept (Pheloung, personal communication). Australia, as a major exporter of farm goods, is concerned by European nations, notably France, invoking the 'precautionary principle' to ban genetically modified crop strains and beef imports. As noted by Gebbie and Bowen (2000), 'Australia is concerned that the push to have a "precautionary principle" in the food safety area could result in subjective factors such as consumer perceptions replacing more objective technical and scientific factors in risk management decisions'. The 'precautionary principle' as defined by Gebbie and Bowen (2000) is more risk averse, with nations banning genetically modified crops because citizens fear there might be a risk, even though the evidence is very limited. By this definition WRA operates on a 'precautionary approach' because it only bans those plants that possess several characteristics deemed as weedy. If it adopted a 'precautionary principle' as defined by Gebbie and Brown, very few plants would pass through WRA because there would always be a slight risk of them becoming weeds. The distinction between a 'principle' and an 'approach' is not followed within this chapter, in which the two expressions are used interchangeably.

Under the SPS Agreement nations have a sovereign right to establish their own appropriate levels of protection against risk. That level may be higher than that reflected in existing international standards. Australia, as an island nation free of many diseases and pests, often applies a higher level of protection than other nations. WRA is one example of this. Australia is one of the few countries that applies a 'guilty until innocent' (precautionary) approach towards live imports, unlike most nations, which treat imported plants and animals as innocent until proven guilty.

## IMPACTS OF INTRODUCING WRA

WRA has kept out many hundreds of plants, including species known to be weeds overseas, for example *Melica clypteata*, a widespread poisonous grass (Walton, 2001). During 2002–03, for example, 320 plant species were refused entry to Australia (Senate Environment, Communications, Information Technology and the Arts References Committee, 2004). Because of the precautionary nature of WRA, it is impossible to know how many of the excluded plants would have become weeds, or how seriously weedy they would have become. But no one doubts that WRA has kept out weeds, including agricultural and environmental weeds. The benefits to Australia (in the long term) include more productive agriculture, less herbicide use and less harm to national parks. These benefits might not be large in most situations because there are already many weeds blighting farms and forests, and extra species might not significantly increase costs or harm, except in particular situations.

The perceived disadvantage of WRA is that useful plants are kept out, merely on the suspicion that they might become weeds. The socio-economic costs of introducing WRA were not taken into account when it was introduced. But it was brought in after tens of thousands of plant species had already been introduced, at a time when most groups in society had enough plants to meet their needs.

WRA has especially limited the freedom of two groups: the nursery industry and pasture researchers. The nursery industry is today supportive of WRA, the pasture sector less so.

Gardening is very popular in Australia, and the nursery industry is large, with an annual turnover of more than US$1 billion (Virtue et al, 2004). More than 10,000 ornamental plant species are already available in Australia, yet many nurseries seek new plants to sell because market research shows that many customers want something new. But only a small number of nurseries in Australia import plants directly from overseas, and it appears that market needs can be met from the existing pool of species plus the new imports that WRA permits. The main organization representing nurseries, the Nursery and Garden Industry Australia (NGIA), supports WRA.

WRA has proved more problematic for pasture workers than the nursery trade, and their concerns are considered in the next section.

## CRITICISMS OF WRA

Attacks on WRA or its application have come from pasture scientists, conservationists and weed experts. Pasture workers say that WRA may be too restrictive and precautionary, unlike conservationists and weed scientists, who argue that it is not applied strictly enough. These criticisms are considered in turn.

### Too precautionary

Virtue et al (2004) have voiced the apprehension of pasture scientists: 'there are some current concerns that potentially high-value, new agricultural species are subsequently being missed due to a precautionary approach to plant introductions to Australia'.

Pasture researchers import foreign grasses and legumes for planting by farmers as food for cattle and sheep. They have brought many serious weeds into Australia (Lonsdale, 1994; Low, 1997) and WRA was introduced partly to curtail them. Pasture plants regularly become weeds because they are expected to behave like them. Unlike other introduced plants they are required to form reproducing populations, and under the harsh conditions of grazing. Because of concerns about weediness, and because recent pasture research has not met the full expectations of farmers, funding for pasture work, especially in northern Australia, has declined. Most funding today is devoted to research on pasture plants for salinated soils in southern Australia.

Salinity is emerging as a major problem for Australia. It is likely to cost the nation more than US$2 billion, and to affect 13.6 million ha in temperate Australia by 2050 (Virtue et al, 2004). Vast deposits of underground salt are rising to the surface in places where trees and shrubs have been cleared and replaced by annual crops. Salinity researchers are testing salt-tolerant plants to grow in salt-affected soils. They also want deep-rooted perennial plants to lower the water table in areas where salt may rise in future. Most of the lands threatened by salinity are used for grazing, and the goal is to find a wide range of highly productive pasture and browse plants for these areas (Virtue et al, 2004). New perennials are unlikely to be grown widely 'unless they are also profitable compared with currently available options' (Ewing, 2004). Imported plants are likely to offer the best prospects (although native species have not been adequately tested), and a wide range of species is wanted.

Salinity researchers have been stopped from bringing in promising plants by WRA. Several papers have been published that voice concerns that WRA is too restrictive towards salinity plants (Smith, 1999; Emms et al, 2004; Ewing, 2004; Gordon, 2004a, b). None of these papers calls for its abolition but they do propose changes, sometimes of a profound nature. Salinity research across Australia is conducted by the Cooperative Research Centre for Plant-based Management of Dryland Salinity (CRC), which includes as members all the universities and government units that do salinity research.

It has been argued that WRA, if ever it was applied too strictly, might produce poor conservation outcomes in Western Australia, where many rare native plants are threatened by the spread of salinity (Ewing, personal communication). If farmers are denied access to profitable new plants then most of them will not address salinity properly and the problem will worsen greatly. Native salinity plants could lessen the problem but they are less likely to return a profit.

However, the core problem here is one of unrealistic expectations of the land. In the past, farmers have earned income by overexploiting their land and now they wish to maintain that level of income while repairing their land. The question: 'Should we let in weedy plants to solve salinity?' may pose a false choice. Even if farmers get all the plants they want they might not sow them on a large enough scale. The world's best salinity plants are unlikely to be very profitable in the poor soils in Western Australia. The most likely outcome is that farmers will undertake limited plantings. Australia may end up with more weeds as well as more salinity.

Pasture researchers are more willing today to admit that pasture plants often become weeds. When WRA was introduced they considered two of the WRA questions to be unfair. Grasses and nitrogen-fixing woody plants both earn a point as indicators of weediness. All of the plants introduced by pasture agronomists are grasses or legumes (nitrogen-fixing plants). Grasses are the main food of cattle and sheep, and legumes supply protein.

A more general claim is that WRA is rejecting too many plants (Smith, 1999). Pasture researchers are surely correct in saying that WRA is rejecting some plants that would not become weeds, and by pushing this point they are pressuring the government to weaken the precautionary approach that underpins WRA. One proposal is to raise the entry score so that plants scoring one (or slightly higher) are allowed in.

A more explicit attack on the precautionary principle has come from a student of economics, Cheryl Gordon: 'A precautionary approach to plant introductions ensures the prevention of irreversible harm, but promotes the likelihood that species which offer substantial benefits to society will be denied import access' (Gordon, 2004a). She emphasizes salinity plants as 'plants that appear to warrant an introduction process which is not precautionary in nature' (Gordon, 2004b). She has argued instead for an 'economic approach' or cost–benefit analysis. Plants should be allowed in if the economic benefits outweigh the costs. However, this approach is not supported by salinity researchers at the organizational level.

Gordon presents an important criticism of the precautionary principle as it applies in WRA. Surely a plant promising great benefits should not be banned just because it might become an occasional weed? In reality, the choice is rarely this clear, and the economic or cost–benefit approach raises more conceptual problems than it solves. First, the benefits of new plants are often overstated by those who stand to profit from them, or by those who have invested a career in studying them. Second, weed costs are impossible to predict or calculate in advance. And when environmental harm is involved there is no acceptable way of measuring it. After a plant becomes a weed it is likely to remain in the landscape forever, and any cost–benefit analysis conducted today may lack meaning in a thousand years time. The economic approach can also lead to unfair outcomes because the benefits and costs of a plant usually flow to different sectors, and there is no accepted way to make those who benefit from a plant pay those who bear the costs. By focusing on an economic approach one may also fail to consider that substitutes for the imported plant may already exist within the country – a critique that applies in force to salinity plants (Semple et al, 2004).

In any event, the Australian quarantine service has a policy of not assessing the merit of imports when the quarantine risk is high. Virtue et al (2004) claim that, because of the SPS Agreement, 'Economic benefits cannot be considered in making decisions (to avoid protectionist trade barriers) and hence the potential advantages of new plant species imports cannot be considered'.

That said, the WRA process does shift from a precautionary approach to a cost–benefit analysis if plants obtain a score of one to five. To date, hundreds of plants have fallen into this category but none has been evaluated further. The intermediate score obtained by these plants suggests they might become weeds, but not with enough confidence to justify an outright ban. The quarantine service has so far failed to release any guidelines for evaluating these plants, leading one salinity researcher to complain that this category has, in practice, become a second 'reject' category (Ewing, 2004), a situation that pleases many weed experts. Nursery importers have not pushed this option because it is likely to involve field or glasshouse trials funded by the importer (Walton and Ellis, 1997), but salinity researchers do want their plants assessed. The first stage in the process may involve a search for more information about the plants to see if their scoring under WRA changes. If they reach six or more they will be prohibited (Walton, personal communication). But if the score remains between one and five, and field tests show that a plant has significant economic benefits but also behaves as a minor weed, it is likely to be allowed in, provided the expected benefit is considerably greater than the anticipated cost (Walton, personal communication). Some decisions are likely to prove controversial, and some tests are likely to provoke criticism as inadequate.

## Not strict enough

A range of criticisms of WRA from the opposite perspective argue that is it not strictly enough applied, with failings in its scope or application.

### A major loophole exempts 125,000 plant species from WRA

Almost half of the world's plant species, estimated at 125,000 species, including 4000 known weeds, are exempted from WRA because of a major loophole (Spafford Jacob et al, 2004a, b). This loophole only became public knowledge in 2003, six years after WRA was introduced. It does not represent a shortcoming of WRA, but rather a failure to apply WRA properly.

The loophole has arisen for the following reason. In the days before WRA was introduced, pasture researchers imported seeds of various grasses for research. At that time no one gave any real thought to whether the grasses would become weeds; the only concern was that imported seeds might harbour impurities, such as fungal infections (Low, 2003; Spafford Jacob et al, 2004a). So AQIS devised a set of protocols, outlining the treatments and standards to be met by anyone importing the seeds. To save time and trouble for AQIS and their clients, AQIS declared that the protocols developed for one species would apply to closely related plants (in the same genus). Once these protocols had been developed, the whole genus was placed on the list of permitted plants. The same process was applied to garden and forestry plants. Once a protocol was developed for one species, the whole genus usually ended up on the white (permitted) list.

When WRA was introduced it was recognized that these plants did not belong on the list of permitted plants. However, a decision was made to keep them there until each genus could be assessed, after which those species that already occurred in Australia would go on to the permitted list and others would be removed. This assessment was to be completed by 2001, but so far only one genus has been assessed (Spafford Jacob et al, 2004a).

Government weed experts point out that this loophole represents an embarrassing failure of weed policy. It makes a mockery of international praise for WRA. It means that nurseries and pasture scientists are still free to import a majority of the plants they want without any screening. The failure to close the loophole has been heavily criticized by the two conservation groups with a strong focus on pest issues, World Wide Fund for Nature (WWF) Australia and the Invasive Species Council (Low, 2003; Glanznig et al, 2004). WWF Australia funded two government weed experts of international reputation and a university expert to critique the loophole (Spafford Jacob et al, 2004a). In July 2004 Senator Ian MacDonald, the minister responsible for WRA, denied there was any loophole. In the federal election held in October 2004 the loophole became a minor election issue, with the main opposition party, the Australian Labour Party, implying it would remove it. The Labour Party failed to win the election. In December 2004 a senate inquiry on invasive species, representing the government and opposition, delivered a report that also criticized the loophole and urged that it be closed 'urgently' (Senate

Environment, Communications, Information Technology and the Arts References Committee, 2004). Soon afterwards, Senator Ian Macdonald responded by promising that 4000 overseas weeds, which can legally be imported into Australia via the loophole, would soon be placed on the prohibited list, and said the loophole itself would probably be closed by the end of 2006.

Why will the government not close the loophole immediately? Weed experts with an insight into this issue say that the staff are overworked with their time devoted to 'more serious' matters including risk analyses of imported fruits; staff fear the extra workload that will arise when the loophole is removed. There is no evidence to suggest political interference from those importers who benefit from the loophole, although the arm of government responsible for WRA, Biosecurity Australia, seems reluctant to upset them. One expert said that BA lacks any botanists on its staff, and does not understand the urgency and seriousness of weed issues.

## WRA disregards weeds already in the country

Many foreign plants in cultivation are thought to be 'sleepers' (Low, 1999; Baskin, 2002), which means they are not very weedy today, but may become so in future. For example, pampas grass was not a weed for a hundred years because all the plants in gardens were female. When a new colour form was imported – a hermaphrodite – the plants began setting seed and pampas grass became a serious environmental weed. Many of the garden plants grown in Australia probably lack enough genetic diversity to produce healthy seeds. They are struck in nurseries as clones from an original introduction. Weed experts fear that an importer bringing in new stock could unleash a new weed problem.

AQIS has almost no power to prevent this. Australia is a signatory of the WTO SPS Agreement. Under this agreement weeds (and other plants) already in a country may only be banned if they are limited in distribution and subject to an 'official control programme', or if an importer wants to introduce a new strain that differs genetically in such a way that it poses a greater weed risk than existing strains. The SPS Agreement was worded like this to stop countries from creating barriers to trade disguised as quarantine rules (Virtue et al, 2004). A new example of a garden plant could create a weed problem even if it was not a new strain. It might only need to be a different gender. Weed experts agree there may be many sleeper weeds in this category. The SPS Agreement effectively stops governments from applying the precautionary principle in this situation.

## Answers can be omitted or skewed

WRA includes 49 questions but only ten need be answered. That is because information about new plants is often lacking. Nurseries often import obscure plants about which many questions cannot readily be answered, for example, is it unpalatable to grazing animals, toxic to animals, a fire hazard, shade tolerant, dependent on specialist pollinators, self-fertile? Does it grow on infertile soil? Officers assessing plants rely largely upon plant identification texts (regional floras) that seldom answer these questions.

Here is a serious limitation of WRA. The less that is known about a plant the less certain one can be about its weed risk. Answers to most of the questions could probably be obtained by contacting overseas experts, but this would be time consuming, and the WRA rules do not require it.

WRA is meant to be transparent and scientifically sound, but because only ten of the 49 questions need be answered, a bureaucrat could obtain the outcome they wanted if they ignored certain questions by claiming lack of knowledge. Some of the questions also allow for subjective interpretation. How is 'infertile soil' defined? Is a plant that grows on sandstone a plant of infertile soils? Or does it only meet that criterion if some book or article specifies 'infertile' soil? If a plant has small brightly coloured fruit can one deduce that it is 'bird dispersed' or is more concrete evidence needed?

**No third tier has yet been developed**

As noted above, the third tier of WRA has yet to be developed, leading to criticism from pasture researchers that plants requiring further assessment are effectively banned.

# WRA AS AN EXAMPLE OF PRECAUTION

WRA is designed to address a very specific question, about which there is uncertainty: will a new plant that someone wants to bring into Australia become a weed? WRA does not provide a definite answer to this question, but provides an indication (a numerical score) that determines if the plant should be admitted into the country. It works in situations where there is epistemological uncertainty (plants can usually be scored even when information about them is inadequate), and when there is ontological uncertainty (plants are banned without proof they will become weeds).

WRA is an example of the precautionary principle operating successfully on a limited scale to prevent economic and environmental harm. It has won support (sometimes qualified) from those sectors of society whose freedoms are most curtailed by it: the nursery industry and salinity researchers.

The degree to which WRA is precautionary depends very much upon the plant being assessed. If a plant is a weed in other countries, and Australia offers ideal conditions for that plant, then the weed risk is very high, and the level of uncertainty is low. In this situation a ban applied under WRA relies on common sense, or the principle of preventative action (Cooney, 2004), as much as on a precautionary approach (although the imposition of a ban counts as a precautionary action). If a plant is not known to be a weed anywhere, but is closely related to well-known weeds (for example it is a species of thistle) then the level of uncertainty is higher. If a plant is not known to be a weed anywhere in the world, and has no weedy relatives, then the level of uncertainty is much higher. The operation of a precautionary principle is strongest when plants in the latter category are banned.

The degree to which WRA is precautionary also depends upon the score a plant gets. If a plant goes through the questions and gets an ambiguous score of one to five it requires further assessment, paid for by the importer. The assessment guidelines have yet to be developed but will operate on a cost–benefit analysis and not on a strict precautionary approach (Walton, personal communication). This means that a plant that is highly useful but also slightly weedy will probably be admitted. WRA thus moves from a completely precautionary approach when the risk is high, to a cost–benefit approach when the risk is less obvious, provided that the benefit seems substantial.

But until the guidelines are released, plants that score between one and five are effectively banned. When the guidelines appear, nurseries are unlikely to pursue this option because of the cost, but salinity researchers will. The slow development of guidelines, and the cost to the importer, contribute to the precautionary operation of WRA by imposing a brake on importers.

WRA may prove most effective at keeping out certain weedy garden plants. But some of the plants imported by nurseries will still become weeds (because prediction is limited), and some of the plants imported for salinity will also become weeds (for the same reason, and also because some plants with low scores will be allowed in). WRA will not keep out all weeds, and may not keep out most weeds, but it will stop some weeds, and that is where its value is to be found.

WRA is perhaps the best system possible in a world in which trade and individual freedoms (including the right to import) are so highly valued. However, a better system would require an importer to demonstrate some public benefit before a plant could be considered for importation. Far fewer garden plants would then enter (because Australia, like most countries, has enough garden plants) and fewer weeds would be imported among them.

## IMPLICATIONS FOR OTHER NATIONS

A precautionary approach should always be applied when species are introduced to new places. History is replete with examples of supposedly beneficial plants and animals wreaking disaster, for example the shrubs and trees taken to South Africa to re-clothe denuded lands (now threatening the Cape Town water supply), the rabbits and foxes brought to Australia (causing erosion and extinction), and the ornamental miconia tree planted in Tahiti, (where it now dominates 70 per cent of the landscape) (Bright, 1998; Low, 1999; Baskin, 2002). Hundreds of similar examples can be given. Recent concerns about genetically modified plants often highlight the weed risk they may pose.

Foreign species should always be considered guilty until proven innocent. But most nations treat them as innocent until proven guilty. It is true that most foreign species do little harm, but the grief brought by one rogue species often exceeds the benefit bestowed by many harmless species. This holds especially true of garden plants, pet fish and pet birds. The benefits they provide are mainly only aesthetic, harmless alternatives are readily available, yet the costs they incur when problems arise are often massive, and include both economic and environmental harm.

Precautionary quarantine rules for plants and animals would benefit all nations. All countries are harmed by weeds, including deliberately introduced plants, and some form of risk assessment applied to plants would prove beneficial everywhere. Australian weed scientists are working with the UN Food and Agriculture Organization (FAO) to develop a simplified form of WRA for use by other countries, especially those with limited resources. A key component will be a CD-ROM containing a list of all the world's weeds, which helps provide an answer to the most important WRA question: is the plant a weed somewhere else? If WRA was introduced into several countries, information could be shared among relevant quarantine officers, reducing everyone's workload.

WRA is likely to prove most acceptable in countries where the public understands the weed problem. In Australia, importers who are restricted by WRA may resent their loss of freedom, but they accept that weeds are a problem. Importers in other countries may not hold the same view. In many countries a national programme to introduce WRA would also need a publicity campaign, targeting key groups (plant importers, conservation groups, relevant government departments) to explain the weed problem and the need for action.

WRA could prove very contentious if economically important plants were banned. Some aid organizations, notably the World Seed Program, controversially promote the planting of weedy shrubs and trees in third world nations for firewood and stock feed (for example *Prosopis juliflora*, *Leucaena leucocephala*, *Acacia nilotica*, *Gleditsea triacanthos*). These fast-growing plants can benefit local communities and biodiversity by reducing pressure to clear dwindling forests, but they also harm communities and biodiversity by invading land and stalling regeneration. They are a quick remedy that imposes long-term costs that are seldom recognized by those promoting them. Under WRA the import of such plants, if they were new, would be challenged, and consideration would be given to both the potential problems they cause and local alternatives. While WRA will not solve all weed problems, that alone would be worthwhile.

# REFERENCES

Baker, H. G. (1965) 'Characteristics and modes of origin of weeds', in H. G. Baker and G. L. Stebbins (eds) *The Genetics of Colonising Species*, Academic Press, New York

Baskin, Y. (2002) *A Plague of Rats and Rubbervines*, Island Press,Washington, DC

Bright, C. (1998) *Life Out of Bounds: Bioinvasion in a Borderless World*, W. W. Norton and Co, New York

Commonwealth of Australia (1999) *National Weed Strategy*, Commonwealth of Australia, Canberra

Commonwealth of Australia (2001) *National Objectives and Targets for Biodiversity Conservation: 2001–05*, Environment Australia, Canberra. Available at www.deh.gov.au/biodiversity

Cooney, R. (2004) *The Precautionary Principle in Biodiversity Conservation and Natural Resource Management: An Issues Paper for Policy-makers, Researchers and Practitioners*, IUCN Policy and Global Change Series, no 2, IUCN, Gland, Switzerland and Cambridge, UK

Daehler, C., Denslow, J. S., Ansari, S. and Kuo, H. (2004) 'A risk-assessment system for screening out invasive pest plants from Hawaii and other Pacific Islands', *Conservation Biology*, vol 18, no 2, pp360–68

Emms, J., Virtue, J. G., Preston, C. and Belloti, W. D. (2004) 'Do all legumes pose the same weed risk? Development of a method to evaluate the risk of introduced legumes to temperate Australia', in B. M. Sindel and S. B. Johnson (eds) *Weed Management: Balancing People, Planet, Profit*, 14th Australian Weeds Conference: papers and proceedings, Weed Society of New South Wales, Sydney, pp105–108

Ewing, M. A. (2004) 'New perennial plant options needed to transform agriculture and manage salinity', in Sindel, B. M. and Johnson, S. B. (eds) *Weed Management: Balancing People, Planet, Profit*, 14th Australian Weeds Conference: papers and proceedings, Weed Society of New South Wales, Sydney, pp27–32

Fisher, L. and Harding, R. (2001) 'The Precautionary Principle in Australia' in T. O'Riordan, J. Cameron and A. Jordan (eds) *Reinterpreting The Precautionary Principle* Cameron May, London, pp215–233

Gebbie, D. and Bowen, B. (2000) 'Does the SPS Agreement need a precautionary principle? The case of food safety', in *Quarantine and Market Access – Playing by the WTO Rules*, Biosecurity Australia, Canberra

Glanznig, A., McLachlan, K. and Kessal, O. (2004) *Garden Plants that are Invasive Plants of National Importance: An Overview of their Legal Status, Commercial Availability and Risk Status*, WWF Australia, Sydney

Gordon, C. K. (2004a) 'Reduces salinity v extra weeds – how can we decide?', in *Salinity Solutions*, CD ROM of proceedings of the Salinity Solutions Conference 'Working with Science and Society', 2–5 August, Bendigo, Victoria

Gordon, C. K. (2004b) 'Without expected benefits, is weed assessment a frustrating search for the wrong needle in the wrong haystack?', in B. M. Sindel and S. B. Johnson (eds) *Weed Management: Balancing People, Planet, Profit*, 14th Australian Weeds Conference: papers and proceedings, Weed Society of New South Wales, Sydney pp33–38

Groves, R. H. (1998) *Recent Incursions of Weeds to Australia 1971–1995*, CRC for Weed Management Systems, Adelaide

Groves, R. H., Panetta, F. D. and Virtue, J. G. (2001) *Weed Risk Assessment*, CSIRO Publishing, Canberra

Lonsdale, W. M. (1994) 'Inviting trouble: introduced pasture species in northern Australia', *Australian Journal of Ecology*, vol 19, pp345–54

Lonsdale, W. M. and Smith, C. S. (2001) 'Evaluating pest-screening systems – insights from epidemiology and ecology', in R. H. Groves, F. D. Panetta, and J. G. Virtue (eds) *Weed Risk Assessment*, CSIRO Publishing, Canberra

Low, T. (1997) 'Tropical pasture plants as weeds', *Tropical Grasslands*, vol 31, pp337–43

Low, T. (1999) *Feral Future: The Untold Story of Australia's Exotic Invaders*, Penguin, Melbourne (republished by the University of Chicago Press, 2002)

Low, T. (2002) 'Why are there so few weeds?' in H. Spafford Jacob, J. Dodd and J.H. Moore (eds) *13th Australian Weeds Conference Papers & Proceedings*, Plant Protection Society of Western Australia, Perth, pp1–6

Low, T. (2003) 'Gaping holes in the weed screen', *Feral Herald*, vol 1, no 3, pp 1–3. Available at www.invasives.org.au/downloads/feralherald3.pdf

Pheloung, P. (1996) 'Predicting the weed potential of plant introductions', in C. R. Shepherd (ed) *Proceedings of the Eleventh Australian Weeds Conference*, Weed Society of Victoria, Frankston, pp458–461

Pheloung, P. (2001) 'Weed risk assessment for plant introductions to Australia', in R. H. Groves, F. D. Panetta and J. G. Virtue (eds) *Weed Risk Assessment*, CSIRO Publishing, Canberra, pp83–92

Semple, B., Cole, I. and Koen, T. (2004) 'Exotic vs. native salt-tolerant species: our choice now but a potential burden for future generations?' in *Salinity Solutions*, CD-ROM of proceedings of the Salinity Solutions Conference 'Working with Science and Society', 2–5 August, Bendigo, Victoria

Senate Environment, Communications, Information Technology and the Arts References Committee (2004) *Turning Back the Tide – the Invasive Species Challenge*, report on the regulation, control and management of invasive species and the Environment Protection and Biodiversity Conservation Amendment (Invasive Species) Bill 2002, The Senate, Canberra

Smith, C. S. (1999) 'Studies on weed risk assessment', unpublished MAppSc thesis, University of Adelaide

Spafford Jacob, H., Randall, R. P. and Lloyd, S. G. (2004a) *Front Door Wide Open to Weeds: An Examination of the Weed Species Permitted for Import Without Weed Risk Assessment*, WWF Australia, Canberra

Spafford Jacob, H., Randall, R. P., Lloyd, S. G. and King, C. (2004b) 'Quarantine law loophole: an examination of the known weed species permitted for import without weed risk assessment', in B. M. Sindel and S. B. Johnson (eds) *Weed Management: Balancing People, Planet, Profit*, 14th Australian Weeds Conference: papers and proceedings, Weed Society of New South Wales, Sydney, pp684–689

Virtue, J. G., Bennett, S. J. and Randall, R. P. (2004) 'Plant introductions in Australia: How can we resolve "weedy" conflicts of interest?' in B. M. Sindel and S. B. Johnson (eds) *Weed Management: Balancing People, Planet, Profit*, 14th Australian Weeds Conference: papers and proceedings, Weed Society of New South Wales, Sydney, pp42–48

Walton, C. S. (2001) 'Implementation of a permitted list approach to plant introductions to Australia', in R. H. Groves, F. D. Panetta and J. G. Virtue (eds) *Weed Risk Assessment*, CSIRO Publishing, Canberra, pp93–98

Walton, C. and Ellis, N. (1997) *A Manual for Using the Weed Risk Assessment System (WRA) to Assess New Plants*, Australian Quarantine and Inspection Service, Canberra

Williamson, M. (1996) *Biological Invasions*, Chapman and Hall, London

# Making Decisions about Uncertain Threats: Precaution, Prohibitions and Adaptive Management

# 10

# Making the Precautionary Principle Work for Biodiversity: Avoiding Perverse Outcomes in Decision-making Under Uncertainty

*Brendan Moyle*

## INTRODUCTION

The precautionary principle is a recent regulatory instrument. It was developed for application in situations where threats of serious environmental damage exist. The principle is enshrined in many international treaties. Nonetheless, it has been defined and applied differently, and with varying degrees of weight, across different international treaties. For the purposes of the current study, we shall use the definition and scope by which it was adopted at the 1992 Rio Conference and the 1992 Convention on Biological Diversity. These definitions established that the principle can be applied to biodiversity conservation.

One area where the precautionary principle has been applied is the sustainable use of wildlife. While not all uses of wildlife generate conservation benefits; the sustainable use of wildlife can nonetheless be employed as a conservation strategy. The implementation of sustainable use as such a strategy can, however, be hindered by environmentalists arguing that use contravenes the precautionary principle. This was demonstrated in a recent World Wide Fund for Nature (WWF) report on marine turtles, which argued that consumptive use violated the precautionary principle (Troëng and Drews, 2004). In other words, the precautionary principle was used to choose between competing conservation strategies.

The application of the precautionary principle to biodiversity conservation is a novel departure from its original intent. Early applications of the precautionary principle were found in treaties dealing with hazardous substances. In other words, the precautionary principle originated from an *industrial context*. An example of this can be found in the Declaration of the Third Ministerial Conference of the North Sea in the early 1980s, which defined it as:

> *action to avoid potentially damaging impacts of substances that are persistent, toxic and liable to bioaccumulate even where there is no scientific evidence to prove a causal link between effects and emissions.* (Haigh, 1993)

Nonetheless, the use of the precautionary principle in a biodiversity context followed quickly.

The distinction between the industrial context and the biodiversity context is important. In an industrial context, such as in the case of hazardous substances, there is only one potential source of harm. The threat appears only in a 'business-as-usual' context. A similar case could be made for introducing new organisms into a country. The alternative strategy of 'not introducing the organism' does not create a new potential source of environmental harm.

In the biodiversity context, however, threats can arise as a result of any number of management scenarios. Adopting one management regime may simply result in the species being shifted on to an alternative path to extinction. For instance, if sustainable harvests of marine turtles are prohibited under the precautionary principle (to avoid the threat of overharvest), it does not follow that *no* new threats are created as a result. Impoverished human communities may be provoked to indiscriminately poach turtles and their eggs. Nesting sites on beaches may be destroyed as developing countries create more commercial tourism developments (for example beachside hotels). Economic arguments that support the use of the precautionary principle in the case of hazardous substances do not necessarily extend to biodiversity.

This chapter examines the value of the precautionary principle in the context of biodiversity conservation. It will seek to show that the precautionary principle can lead to adverse conservation outcomes. For this reason, the precautionary principle needs to be allied with other decision rules. These are elaborated in a discussion of scenario planning.

# THE PRECAUTIONARY PRINCIPLE

The precautionary principle is a multi-disciplinary concept. Rather than belonging to any single discipline it has become embedded in legal, economic and scientific policies. This chapter examines it from an economic analysis perspective. This is because economists have a long history and widespread experience of research into decisions affected by risk and uncertainty.

## Economic interpretation

From an economic point of view, the precautionary principle has three main elements. The first two pertain to the appropriate setting for applying the precautionary principle. First, it is a management approach applicable where threats are *uncertain*. It is not an approach that is applicable to situations of *risk*. Second, the outcome of favouring one strategy over another must (potentially) be irreversible and costly. The precautionary principle is inappropriate for managing trivial and easily reversed costs. The third element concerns the impact of the precautionary principle. This shifts the burden of proof to the party advocating the policy or course of action associated with the irreversible cost. For instance, it would be up to the polluter to prove that an emission is safe. Others do not have to prove that it is unsafe.

## Risk and uncertainty

Economic analysis based on the method set out in 1921 by Frank Knight distinguishes risk from uncertainty. In both cases, agents do not know (with certainty) what outcome will occur in the future. With risk, however, it is possible to estimate and agree upon two things. First, the various possible outcomes can be fully described. Thus, decision-makers have complete information on the range of possibilities in front of them. Second, with risk, probabilities are known objectively and can be assigned to each outcome.

Given defined outcomes and known probabilities, this means that each decision can be expressed in terms of an *expected pay-off*. An expected pay-off has three basic elements: first, a value is attributed to each possible outcome; the likelihood that each of these outcomes will occur as a result of the action of the agent is then measured; if the agent is risk averse, then pay-offs are discounted further. For instance, banks usually face a *liquidity risk*, caused by depositors withdrawing their funds. The pattern of withdrawals is (outside of bank runs) easy to estimate. As such, the bank can estimate the expected pay-off from holding a given proportion of deposits as reserves.

Where risks are sufficiently well known, any decision can be reduced to an expected pay-off. Consider a gamble involving a fair coin toss. On a heads, the player will win US$20. On a tail, the player will lose US$10. Assuming the player is risk neutral (that is, they neither avoid nor seek risky actions), then the expected pay-off is simply:

$$0.5 \times (US\$20) + 0.5 \times (US\$-10), \text{ or } US\$5$$

Uncertainty has two main sources. Uncertainty may be caused by ignorance, such as in the case where all the potential outcomes cannot be fully described. Furthermore, events that no one anticipated may occur. For instance, the effect of CFCs on the ozone layer was not known when these chemicals were adopted for coolant and refrigeration purposes. Given that the range of outcomes is not known, assigning probabilities to each event is fraught with problems. This is exacerbated by the fact that uncertain events typically occur infrequently. This means there is little or no history that can be drawn on to predict probabilities.

Pure uncertainty occurs where outcomes are known, but probabilities cannot be assigned. This is approximated by having a panel of experts whose predictions are very diverse and where there is little agreement about the underlying probabilities.

Decision-making in the face of uncertainty is not amenable to an expected pay-off approach. To start with, not all outcomes are accounted for. This means the probability of each outcome must be in error or *biased*. This ensures that decisions based on expected pay-off rules will be suboptimal. That is, they will in general lead managers to make imprudent decisions. The problem of unaccounted for, surprising outcomes was poignantly illustrated during the oil price shocks of the 1970s. A number of projects based on expected pay-off rules became unprofitable. For example, a joint venture between Shell and Gulf Oil to build a high temperature reactor lost £300 million.

While an expected pay-off approach may be suboptimal, there still remains a possibility of surprising gains. In other words, might the problem of costly surprises be offset by surprising gains (windfalls and the like)? Nonetheless, if costly surprises are more frequent and/or severe than the surprising gains, the expected pay-off approach will be biased. By selecting strategies that have a high expected pay-off – but are associated with surprising and unanticipated losses – irreversible outcomes are more frequently observed. Thus the precautionary principle would seem justified in its original context. The threat of (say) hazardous substances could be argued to have more 'down-side' danger than 'up-side' possibilities. The precautionary principle thus argues that an expected pay-off framework will be insufficient to deal with the costs of surprises. This point is entirely reasonable.

The second element of the precautionary principle is the emphasis on serious (usually irreversible) costs. Again this is reasonable, because as Henry (1974) shows, irreversibility causes decision-makers to favour this 'irreversible' strategy more often than they should. Intuitively, options are also valuable but if an irreversible outcome occurs, these valuable options will be lost. Hence, application of the precautionary principle should mitigate this source of inefficiency.

The third element is the allocation of costs. As noted above, the burden of proof is shifted to the party that is likely to create the risk of an irreversible harm. This could be regarded as efficient under certain conditions. In economic terms, an appropriate distribution of the risks would minimize total costs. Total costs incorporate direct monetary effects as well as indirect effects – such as lowered life expectancies as a result of exposure to harmful pollutants. This in turn provides an economic rationale for using the precautionary principle as a vehicle for intergenerational equity. If current generations can bear the risk at lower cost (by proving that the action is safe) than future generations can (that is, mitigation of the harm), then it is appropriate for current generations to bear the risk. This, however, carries the auxiliary assumption that there are no income effects. If future generations are much wealthier than current generations, it may be that they can bear this risk more easily.

# THE PRECAUTIONARY PRINCIPLE AND CONSERVATION

## Example: swiftlet nests

In 1994 Italy proposed that several species of swiftlets (*Collocalia* spp, the Southeast Asian species that form the basis of the birds' nest trade) be up-listed to Appendix II of CITES. This proposal was based on several indications of declines in local populations. The most influential, however, was a reported 85 per cent decline at the Niah caves, Malaysia, between 1935 and 1990. Allied to this proposal was a TRAFFIC report indicating a range of potential conservation problems that may have been occurring alongside an expansion in the trade of swiftlet nests (Er et al, 1995).

This proposal was justified implicitly in terms of the precautionary principle. The Appendix II listing could be seen as a precaution against possible decline, where harvest carried the potential risk of extirpating meta-populations (Er et al, 1995). Declines at some sites did not demonstrate that the species were threatened overall, and indications of 'potential conservation problems' do not prove these problems are actually occurring.

An Appendix II listing would have required a CITES certificate for every 8g nest. The cost of this certification would have threatened the viability of the trade. This was considered by parties involved in this trade as a non-trivial cost. The swiftlet nest trade had a retail value of about US$1 billion (Er et al, 1995). This cost would have additionally fallen largely on developing countries in Southeast Asia (Er et al, 1995). This is because regulatory costs cannot be passed in their entirety on to buyers. Both buyers and sellers end up sharing the burden, and in the case of sellers who are 'price takers', the prediction is they will have to absorb most of the costs. The potential costs were in fact highest for Indonesia, who at this stage was threatened with an export-ban in all CITES-listed species. An up-listing of swiftlets may have halted all their exports.

Further, as information about the species accumulated, it emerged that the distribution of swiftlets was actually increasing (Er et al, 1995). Part of the problem is that sampling methodology (movement counts out of caves) for swiftlets is neither precise nor reliable, so that many of the declines were not statistically significant. The reason for increase in swiftlet distribution appeared to lie in the investments being made in swiftlet habitat (nesting sites in particular). This encouraged their spread. Thus, the population status of these species would have conceivably declined under the trade restrictions.

## Precaution in the biodiversity context

This example illustrates the problem with applying the precautionary principle in a biodiversity context. This case involved conservation through sustainable use. In this instance wildlife use is not equivalent to the production of (potentially) hazardous substances. While wildlife use does carry some dangers, use may also support or enhance conservation measures. Banning or restricting use does not necessarily eliminate the threat of population decline. Indeed, it can precipitate environmental harm by shifting a species on to an alternative extinction path. If wildlife is seen as having no economic value, then habitat conversion and competition from commercially valuable species can result in extinction (Swanson, 1994). Conservation entails reciprocal threats under competing management strategies.

The second issue is that applying the precautionary principle in this instance would lead to costs being allocated inefficiently, and this may be inequitable. Wildlife use is often undertaken by low-income rural communities or by developing countries. Requiring these parties to absorb the costs of proof does not allocate costs according to the usual juridical and economic reasons, which require that they should be borne by parties most able to support them. These parties may have the least ability to carry the cost of providing proof. Adding this burden of proof may be seen to be highly inequitable from a poverty alleviation perspective.

The precautionary approach still mitigates the problem of irreversibility. Nonetheless, it can be shown that this is not an outcome that is unique to the precautionary principle. It can also be shown that application of the precautionary principle in biodiversity conservation can lead perversely to suboptimal conservation outcomes.

## Perverse outcomes

To illustrate these points, consider the following example. Suppose there is one species that is threatened with extinction. The species has a *minimum viable population* (MVP) of 500. There are only two feasible conservation strategies ($S_1$ or $S_2$). Each strategy has the same cost and the available budget restricts the manager to just one strategy. A conservation strategy has to be adopted before the outcome of the strategy is known.

Assume further there are two possible outcomes associated with each strategy. These outcomes are termed 'states of the world' and denoted as $\omega_1$ and $\omega_2$. These states are measured as a population level. Uncertainty is simulated by having no objective knowledge of the probability distribution of outcomes. The assumptions of two strategies and two states of the world are made purely as a simplifying device. This allows the decision-problem to be represented as a matrix.

In this problem, only one strategy involves the threat of an irreversible harm. If $\omega_2$ occurs *and* strategy $S_2$ has been selected, then the population will fall below its minimum viable level. The application of the precautionary principle will lead to $S_1$ being preferred to $S_2$ and the threat of irreversible harm will be avoided.

**Table 10.1** *Matrix 1*

|  | $S_1$ | $S_2$ |
|---|---|---|
| $\omega_1$ | 500 | 600 |
| $\omega_2$ | 500 | 400 |

Nonetheless, this conclusion is not unique to the precautionary principle. For instance, the absence of a known probability distribution may justify a Bayesian approach (Woodward and Bishop, 1997). With no prior information we might invoke the *principle of insufficient reason*. This would weight the states equally so that the prior probabilities would become 50 per cent for each state of the world. Here the potential gain from adopting $S_2$ is 100 in $\omega_1$ and the potential loss is 100 in $\omega_2$. The certainty of having 500 animals should be preferred by risk-averse managers. Given that risk-averse behaviour is normal, it then follows that $S_1$ would be preferred to $S_2$. This is because they have the same expected pay-off but $S_2$ is discounted more because of its inherent risks. In other words, the precautionary principle will tend to yield the same (reasonable) results as other risk-averse decision rules.

Another example would be the safe minimum standard (SMS) advocated by Ciriacy-Wantrup (1952) and Bishop (1978). This standard was devised explicitly to deal with conservation in circumstances of uncertainty. The rule here is to prevent a population ever falling below some predetermined safe level (equivalent to the MVP in this instance); unless the costs of doing so are prohibitively high. With no difference in costs, only $S_1$ is guaranteed to prevent the population falling below the SMS.

Now consider the following pay-off matrix:

**Table 10.2** *Matrix 2*

|  | $S_1$ | $S_2$ |
|---|---|---|
| $\omega_1$ | 500 | 1500 |
| $\omega_2$ | 500 | 499 |

In this case, $S_2$ again carries the threat of an irreversible harm ($\omega_2$). It also has the option of a large potential gain ($\omega_1$). In effect, by accepting the risk of the population falling by one individual, the manager obtains the option of a gain of 1000 individuals. In this situation, however, application of the precautionary principle would still favour $S_1$.

The reason the precautionary principle prefers $S_1$ is as follows. The precautionary principle is formulated to avoid irreversible costs. It is most frequently defined to exclude consideration of potential benefits. As such it is a rule that completely ignores the potential gains from a strategy if this carries any possibility of an irreversible harm. The idea of going for the big gains, as made possible from $S_2$, is *completely* discounted. The precautionary principle is about avoiding serious harms – potential gains are in effect irrelevant. This means that the precautionary principle will be suboptimal, as no decision rule that ignores potential gains can be efficient. While it is appropriate to discount the potential gains in the presence of irreversible outcomes, completely ignoring the gains is suboptimal. The matrices above show that this is most likely when differences in potential gains between different management options are high.

Other decision rules are not so timid in the face of uncertainty. For instance, the SMS rule might prefer $S_2$. This is because the costs of selecting $S_1$

are very high. Selecting $S_1$ in this case means foregoing a potential gain of 1000 individuals in order to avoid a loss of one individual. The opportunity cost (potential benefits foregone) may simply be too high.

To illustrate this point, consider the following case. In New Zealand the Chatham Island black robin had declined to a population of seven birds. This included a mere two females. The population had been transferred to a reserve on Mangere Island. At this time, the main management tool used to preserve rare bird species in New Zealand was the creation of island reserves. This reserve had 120,000 trees planted to provide habitat for the species.

Nonetheless, this was not considered to be enough. A decision was then made to attempt cross-fostering the black robin with the Chatham Island grey warbler. This involved removing egg clutches from the black robin and placing them in grey warbler nests. The black robin would lay a replacement clutch and the grey warbler would raise the first clutch. This in effect doubled the rate of increase in the species. This resulted in a large increase in the population to 250 birds.

This shift in management strategy was made in the face of considerable uncertainty. There was no prior evidence that the black robin would respond positively to a more active management approach. The passive reserve approach had been successful with other species. Hence, the shift in strategy may have elevated the risk of extinction of the robin. To avoid this threat, the precautionary principle would require that no switch in strategy occur until it could be proven that cross-fostering posed no threat to the species.

In reality, managers were unwilling to devote the time or resources to prove that the cross-fostering would work. Rather, the option of a large gain dominated the decision to proceed with cross-fostering. As events showed, this was the correct approach.

## Scenario Planning

The main merit of the precautionary principle is that it deals with irreversible environmental harms. Nonetheless, the exclusive focus on avoiding harm ignores potential environmental gains from different strategies. This makes the precautionary principle extremely timid. The fear of a loss dominates the choice of strategy. While some risk aversion is warranted – and this is especially the case in the presence of irreversibility – this timidity leads to foregone opportunities to improve conservation outcomes. Essentially any decision rule that copies the precautionary principle's avoidance of irreversible outcomes *but* also considers potential benefits as relevant, will dominate the precautionary principle. Dominate in this context means that any alternative decision rule will do just as well or better than the precautionary principle.

Hence, the issue is how to preserve the merit of the precautionary principle without becoming too timid or reckless with environmental threats. One solution is to simultaneously adopt other decision rules that incorporate the precautionary principle. These rules can be made more elaborate to avoid the problem of timidity.

This approach was employed in a scenario planning exercise undertaken for Great Mercury Island in New Zealand. This provided a tool for considering how to make conservation management decisions in circumstances of uncertainty. In this exercise, concern for environmental irreversible harms was allied with other rules for selecting strategies.

Great Mercury Island is a privately owned island in New Zealand, part of seven islands known collectively as the Mercury Islands. As the name suggests Great Mercury is the largest of these islands: larger than all the other islands put together. The task entrusted to Massey University was to devise an island management plan for its owners. There was a request for the management plan to place emphasis on invertebrates. This immediately brought the problem of uncertainty to the fore.

The fact that the island had been in private hands for so long meant that no scientific surveys of the island had been undertaken. Thus, unlike the adjacent islands, there was no prior information on the existence or distribution of rare or threatened species. In the face of this uncertainty a scenario planning experiment was carried out.

## Outline of scenario planning

Scenario planning is an approach used to select strategies in the face of uncertainty. Its theoretical foundations stem from the work by the economist Shackle (1973). These argue that using traditional expected pay-off rules to select strategies is inappropriate in a situation of uncertainty. The confusion between strategic choice in the face of risk and choice in the face of uncertainty led many firms to make costly investment mistakes in the 1970s (as alluded to above).

Shackle (1973) argued that the problems with using expected pay-offs were twofold. The first problem was that as managers imagined more potential outcomes, the likelihood of each outcome became rather elastic. As probabilities must add up to one, the effect of incorporating additional outcomes is to reduce the likelihood of unsurprising outcomes. In other words, unsurprising events become less likely and receive insufficient weight in the expected pay-off framework.

The second problem is that an expected pay-off approach selects a strategy that has the highest pay-off on average. Thus, if the same strategy is applied in repeated instances, it will on average give a higher value to the objective than any other strategy. In other words, it is about 'winning on average'. This is not appropriate where repeated trials are not possible. For instance, if a firm becomes bankrupt after one application of this strategy, it is of no use to attest that repeated applications of the same strategy will tend to generate the highest profits. Similarly, the optimal conservation strategy is of little use if a species becomes extinct in the first trial.

These points are exacerbated when managers are influenced by events that do not occur. If two possible states of the world are mutually exclusive, an expected pay-off approach still incorporates both into the decision. For instance, the desire to utilize sustainable use (trade) as part of the conservation strategy for the Australian saltwater crocodile was hindered by fears that this would increase poaching (Webb, 1997). Here there are two relevant states of the world. In $\omega_1$, trade leads to increased poaching and smuggling. In $\omega_2$ trade leads to a decrease (as poachers are crowded out by legitimate traders). Clearly both states cannot occur simultaneously. In this case, $\omega_2$ was the realized future state, but for a time the management decision was influenced by the unrealizable $\omega_1$.

Under the influence of Shackle, scenario planning was developed to correct the problems described above. Scenario planning is based on the notion of proposing several scenarios that describe how the future may unfold (Wack, 1985a, b; Schoemaker, 1997). Strategies are then selected on the basis of these scenarios. The decisions reached in this instance are based on considerations of robustness and adaptability. These rules incorporate the risk aversion of the precautionary principle but do not replicate its suboptimal timidity. This highlights a major point. Any decision rule that avoids irreversible environmental outcomes but *does* include potential benefits and costs will generate outcomes either as good as or better than the precautionary principle.

## Scenario planning: application

In the case of Great Mercury Island, the sources of uncertainty were ignorance about the true state of the island, as well as the likelihoods that different states would occur. To capture this uncertainty, four scenarios were proposed.

The rationale for using four scenarios was to avoid the problem of mid-point scenarios. If three scenarios are proposed, managers often select the central scenario as the most likely case on which to base their strategy choices. This defeats the purpose of scenario planning. The exercise is not intended to develop a forecast of the future. Rather, its value lies in highlighting the uncertainty the manager should be prepared for. Four scenarios have no natural mid-point and are usually the practical minimum.

The scenarios were labelled 'Scorched Earth', 'Life-Boat', 'Hidden Treasure 1' and 'Hidden Treasure 2'. This is the norm for scenario planning. Scenario titles function as a kind of shorthand. A good title is evocative of the key features of the scenario, aiding the manager's memory of the scenario (Schoemaker, 1997).

The scenarios in this case described the conservation status of the island. They were motivated by the time and resources required to undertake a comprehensive ecological survey. Such an effort is costly as it involves recruiting experts from a wide range of disciplines. This is assuming that such experts even exist. Some invertebrate taxa have no researchers currently working on them and, as a result, are classed as orphan taxa. In addition to this is the cost of time. Surveys can be lengthy exercises, especially where invertebrates are involved. The time needed to process them is considerable (the author of this report, for instance, in 1989 identified false scorpions that had been collected in 1914, as well as many that had been identified in surveys undertaken 20–30 years ago). This assumes that it will even be possible to collect samples from rare invertebrates using random sampling techniques.

There are two further conservation costs involved in surveying work. If populations are in decline, then delaying any interventions until surveys are complete implies populations will be smaller (or extinct) by the time conservation strategies are implemented. The second cost is that survey work on invertebrates is often fatal for the individuals caught. Hence, survey work could in fact raise the risk of extinction of (undiscovered) threatened species.

The scenarios were used as an initial substitute for survey work. The scenarios were selected using a surprise metric. This required that each scenario be plausible in the sense that if it was true, none of the experts would be surprised.

The 'Scorched Earth' scenario was a pessimistic one. The history of human settlement of Great Mercury had wrought many significant changes in the landscape, with both pastoral farming and exotic forestry having taken place. The key feature of this scenario was that there were no native species left of conservation value. The only species remaining were common in New Zealand and under no threat. Under this scenario the proposed strategies included eradication of mammalian pests in order to establish populations of other threatened species (for example kiwis).

The 'Life-Boat' scenario considered that there were some species of conservation interest left on the island. These species were not recognized as threatened nationally. Nonetheless they were representative of the Mercury Island ecological district. As such, their conservation would enhance the conservation value of the entire district. This was considered unsurprising given that Great Mercury had two landscapes not present on the other islands. Great Mercury was the only island to have a mainland forest (the others only had coastal forests) and the only island to have a permanent river.

The 'Hidden Treasure 1' scenario considered the case that there were some species of national importance for conservation. This was also plausible as the adjacent Middle Island (which had previously been cleared for farming activities) contained a new species of giant tusked weta. This species was restricted to an area of a quarter of a hectare. While Great Mercury had been extensively modified, there were several large patches of relatively undisturbed forests in the south. These sites were inaccessible and uneconomic to farm.

The 'Hidden Treasure 2' scenario considered the case that there were some species of international importance for conservation. This was also plausible as the Red Mercury Island had a population of tuataras and a tuatara skeleton had been discovered on an islet of Great Mercury.

Describing each scenario is the first stage of the planning process. This highlights for managers the uncertainties that are attached to each scenario. The next step is to propose conservation strategies that are appropriate for each individual scenario. This generates a menu of strategies.

The second stage of scenario planning is to select from the menu a number of strategies that will be implemented. This selection process is based on two criteria. In the above example, each strategy was assessed on the basis of robustness and adaptability.

The principle behind robustness is that it delivers a *satisfactory* result in a wide range of scenarios. For instance, all of the scenarios included a strategy to first develop the southern part of the island as a conservation area. Robustness ensures that whatever state of the world occurs, it is likely that a positive conservation outcome will be achieved.

The principle of adaptability is that a strategy can be easily adapted in the presence of new knowledge. The aim of this is to avoid commitment strategies. For instance, the strategy of leaving the Californian condor to breed *in situ* committed the US Fish and Wildlife Service to this for decades. This commitment contributed to the sustained decline of the species. In this case, the strategy was 'fenced in' by preventing any experiments with active management under an implicit precautionary approach.

To achieve adaptability, the conservation plan has to be open to discovering new knowledge. To generate new knowledge (to innovate), strategies have to incorporate an active learning process. The problem with uncertainty is partly caused by ignorance. If this ignorance is resolved then decision-making will not be so sensitive to surprises. Hence, all strategies or actions have to incorporate experimental learning. This is prioritized knowledge that could (potentially) change the management plan. In the above case, new data that could not motivate a switch in strategy were not demanded by managers. For instance, while the southern part of Great Mercury was favoured for conservation work there were still patches in the north that could contain species of high conservation value. Hence, there was little point in surveying a patch in the south to discover whether there were three or four species of wetas. This would not affect the management decision to preserve these patches. Surveying a patch to the north, however, could lead to the discovery of a species that could change the management plan.

## Scenario planning and the precautionary principle

Robustness and adaptability can be contrasted with precaution. Like precaution, robustness seeks to avoid irreversible harms. Suppose we have four possible strategies $\{S_a, S_b, S_c, S_d\}$ and four possible states of the world $\{\omega_1, \omega_2, \omega_3, \omega_4\}$. Each state has also been described as a scenario. Consider the following matrix.

**Table 10.3** *Matrix 3*

|  | $S_a$ | $S_b$ | $S_c$ | $S_d$ |
|---|---|---|---|---|
| $\omega_1$ | 1500 | 5000 | 50 | 1000 |
| $\omega_2$ | 750 | 100 | 100 | 500 |
| $\omega_3$ | 750 | 100 | 100 | 500 |
| $\omega_4$ | 50 | 50 | 5000 | 500 |

If we take 500 individuals to be the satisfactory minimum, then $S_d$ appears to be the most robust. Note that it is by definition not the optimal strategy because there is always at least one other strategy that does better than $S_d$ in whatever state of the world is actually realized. For instance, if $\omega_4$ occurred, then we could always have done better by adopting strategy $S_c$ instead. The problem with $S_c$ in this case is that it is not robust. It only delivers a satisfactory outcome in one case. In all other cases it delivers unsatisfactory outcomes. This implies that robustness incorporates precaution as one of its properties.

Adaptability is also a property that is risk averse. The key difference is that it is also concerned with improving gains. For instance, if we adopt $S_d$ we know that in three scenarios, our pay-off could be improved by switching to $S_a$. Adaptability gives us another means to distinguish strategies. For instance, if $S_a$ is very adaptable and $S_d$ is not, then this heuristic may mean we prefer $S_a$ to $S_d$. If we start with $S_a$ and can switch to $S_d$ and if we observe that $\omega_4$ is the realized state, then this 'switching' approach gives a higher pay-off than committing to one strategy. If we start with $S_d$ and through its lack of adaptability cannot switch to $S_a$, opportunities for gain in states $\omega_1$, $\omega_2$ and $\omega_3$ will be foregone. So even though $S_d$ appears to be more robust, 'adaptability' permits riskier options to be tried for big gains, if this strategy can be easily corrected.

Robustness and adaptability appear to be similar to precaution. Nonetheless, two important differences remain. The first is that robustness explicitly recognizes that there can be reciprocal threats of environmental harm in any strategy selected. It is not possible to presume (as with the precautionary principle) that there is a single safe bet that ought to be preferred. The second difference is that this process is willing to experiment with strategies that could yield high gains. Rather than waiting for proof of its safety to be demonstrated, this approach incorporates learning into the choice of strategy. This is also why scenarios try to identify early signals that indicate which state of the world is true, so management can adapt to this knowledge.

# CONCLUSIONS

The precautionary principle's chief merit is the drive to avoid irreversible environmental harms. The precautionary principle is, however, difficult to apply in conservation work because of its extremely timid nature. Uncertainty in the biodiversity context differs from the original industrial context of the precautionary principle, as environmental harms are associated with *many* of the management options facing decision-makers. The focus on avoiding harm implies that the opportunities for conservation gains are lost if they are associated with any potential harms. This gives rise to the very timid nature of the precautionary principle in a biodiversity context. This means that opportunities to improve conservation outcomes will tend to be foregone. This generates the perverse likelihood that conservation outcomes will be worse if the precautionary principle is applied. The requirement for the party carrying out the potentially harmful action to provide proof can give rise to improved intergenerational equity. Nonetheless, in the biodiversity context this may involve a loss in equity by shifting costs of proof to developing countries and impoverished rural communities.

In order to make the precautionary principle work in the area of biodiversity conservation, it needs to be embedded into other rules reached as a result of certain decisions. The twin rules of robustness and adaptability, for instance, retain the precautionary principle's desire to avoid irreversible outcomes. Hence, it can be argued that the precautionary principle is embedded in these rules. Nonetheless, it is inefficient to wait for proof of a strategy's safety before embarking upon it. For this reason, adaptability is a better method to seek out and discover which strategies are 'safe' and where conservation gains may be had. In order to employ these rules, a scenario planning approach may be employed.

# REFERENCES

Ciriacy-Wantrup, S. V. (1952) *Resource Conservation: Economics and Policies*, University of California Press, Berkeley, CA

Bishop, R. C. (1978) 'Endangered species and uncertainty: the economics of a safe minimum standard', *American Journal of Agricultural Economics*, vol 60, no 1, pp10–18

Er, K. B. H., Vardon, M. J., Tanton, M. T., Tidemann, C. R. and Webb, G. J. W. (1995) *Edible Birds' Nest Swiftlets and CITES: A Review of the Evidence of Population Decline and Nest Harvesting Effects*, CRES Working Paper 1995/3, ANU, Canberra

Haigh, N. (1993) 'The precautionary principle in British environmental policy', mimeo, Institute of Environmental Policy, London

Henry, C. (1974) 'Investment decisions under uncertainty: the "irreversibility effect"', *American Economic Review*, vol 64, no 6, pp1006–12

Knight, F. H. (1921) *Risk, Uncertainty and Profit*, Houghton Mifflin, Boston, MA. Frequently reprinted, most recently in 2002 by Beard Books, Washington, DC

Shackle, G. L. S. (1973) *Epistemics and Economics: A Critique of Economic Doctrines.* Cambridge University Press, Cambridge, UK

Schoemaker, P. J. H. (1997) 'Disciplined imagination: from scenarios to strategic options', *International Studies of Management and Organisation*, vol 27, no 2, pp43–70

Swanson, T. M. (1994) 'The economics of extinction revisited and revised: a generalised framework for the analysis of the problems of endangered species and biodiversity losses', *Oxford Economic Papers*, vol 46, pp800–21

Troëng, S. and Drews, C. (2004) *Money Talks: Economic Aspects of Marine Turtle Use and Conservation*, WWF International, Gland, Switzerland

Wack, P. (1985a) 'Scenarios: uncharted waters ahead', *Harvard Business Review*, Sep/Oct, pp73–89

Wack, P. (1985b) 'Scenarios: shooting the rapids', *Harvard Business Review*, Nov, pp139–150

Webb, G. (1997) 'Crocodiles', *Australian Biologist*, vol 10, no 1, pp31–39

Woodward, R. T. and Bishop, R. C. (1997) 'How to decide when experts disagree: uncertainty-based choice rules in environmental policy', *Land Economics*, vol 73, no 4, pp492–507

# 11

# Parrots, Precaution and Project Elé: Management in the Face of Multiple Uncertainties

*Jorge Rabinovich*

## INTRODUCTION

The concepts of sustainability of resource use, burden of proof, the limitations of science, uncertainty and risk are at the core of the application of the precautionary principle in the management of living resources. This chapter will describe a particular example of a wildlife resource management programme that represents a clear case of the application of a precautionary approach in the way it addresses a range of uncertainties, sustainability, adaptive management and the burden of proof. In particular, the following discussion aims to demonstrate that, even with fragmentary knowledge, optimal, sustainable and conservative management can be achieved, and that this provides a much better management option than a total ban on the use of resources.

## THE PROJECT ELÉ PROGRAMME

Project Elé is a programme of the Government of Argentina, the objective of which is to conserve and manage the blue-fronted parrot (or blue-fronted amazon) *Amazona aestiva* and its habitat. This programme has involved over a decade of planning and field work. The author would like to acknowledge the work over this period of Victoria Lichtschein, Ricardo Banchs and Flavio Moschione, which made this study possible, and express his sincere gratitude for their cooperation, access to data and inputs into this chapter. A fairly complete description of Project Elé can be found on the Internet in Spanish (SAyDS, 2005a) and in English (Rabinovich, 2004). This section will briefly

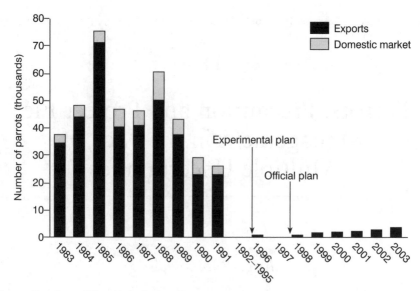

*Source:* Banchs and Moschione (in press)

**Figure 11.1** *Provincial official permits granted for the trade, export and domestic trade of the blue-fronted parrot*

describe the blue-fronted parrot and its environment, and will then present a summary of the more relevant features of Project Elé as a background to understanding the precautionary approach that has been adopted for its management.

The blue-fronted parrot has a high learning capacity and is in demand for its fine competence as a speaker. This species inhabits the xerophilic forests of the subtropical warm climate region. The region is home to a great diversity of environments, but the arid and semi-arid Chaco (where the blue-fronted parrot programme is being implemented) is dominated by xerophilic forests (identified commonly by the Spanish term *Impenetrable*), and by savannas and grasslands. The remaining area of the Chaco Forest covers some 230,000km².

Between 1983 and 1991 over 360,000 live blue-fronted parrots were authorized for export as part of the pet trade by Argentinian provinces. When *A. aestiva* was included in Appendix II of the Convention on International Trade in Endangered Species (CITES) in 1981, this level of extraction was considered excessive and between 1992 and 1995 a moratorium was declared on its export (see Figure 11.1).

In addition to being excessive, this extraction was carried out within a context that made the extraction of blue-fronted parrots not only biologically but also socially unsustainable. Some of the most notorious problems associated with their extraction between 1983 and 1991 included:

- quotas based upon trade criteria and not harvest criteria;
- an extremely unequal distribution of the wealth derived from the trade, with local people receiving an insignificant fraction of the value of the parrots in trade;

- no uniform policy for granting permits among the provinces responsible;
- a low level of control with low confidence about the real origin of specimens;
- extraction carried out with the systematic destruction of nest trees;
- killing of the blue-fronted parrot in high numbers in citrus plantations, where they are considered to be a pest; and
- a high level of mortality during stockpiling and transport.

In 1996, a two-year experimental management plan was initiated. This led to the gathering of experience and biological knowledge that was then used to devise a sustainable management plan. This plan was implemented in 1998 and is still in place today. The programme was designed in such a way as to avoid the pitfalls described above. Its main objective is habitat conservation and the sustainable management of the blue-fronted parrot in Argentina, for commercial use as a pet bird. The project is being carried out by the Secretariat of Environment and Sustainable Development of Argentina (SAyDS), in partnership with five provinces (Formosa, Chaco, Salta, Santiago del Estero and Jujuy), and in association with four other provinces (Córdoba, Corrientes, Santa Fe, and Tucumán). Parrots are collected as chicks and fledglings in the Dry Chaco area in the summer, and as flyers in the piedmont forests of Salta and Jujuy in the winter.

Some of the key features of Project Elé in the Dry Chaco area can be summarized as follows:

- Local collectors have to be landowners (or show proof that they have initiated the purchase or acquisition of the land they use).
- After the harvest, every nest has to be left with at least one fledgling.
- Nest trees are not felled but a hole is made to extract the chicks, which is later covered, so that the same nest tree may be reused in the next reproductive season.
- A special numbered ring identifies each individual parrot collected.
- A team of around 40–50 people works in the field for five to six months per year.
- All costs are covered by the programme itself, with resources collected from middlemen and exporters and administered by a trusteeship fund managed by a non-governmental organization (NGO), in other words Project Elé is a financially self-sustaining operation.
- Local collectors receive an increased share of the final export price, and the price per collector is established by Project Elé.
- Harvest quotas are based on a computer simulation model developed to establish the optimal sustainable levels of extraction, and based upon a 'fixed escapement' rule of management.
- The total extraction of fledglings has been increasing slightly since 1998 by extending the area under harvest (that is, including more local people receiving harvest quotas), but with quotas in each harvested unit remaining relatively constant.

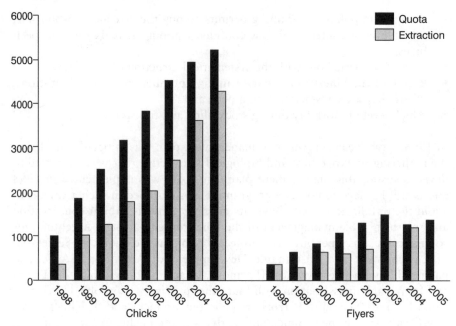

*Note:* no data available for the actual extraction of flyers in 2005.

*Source:* SAyDS (2005b); updated with data for 2005 from Project Elé Director Ricardo Banchs (personal communication)

**Figure 11.2** *Quotas and extraction levels of the blue-fronted parrot from 1998 to 2005 under the present management scheme for fledglings and flyer parrots*

- Around 21,600 parrots have been harvested over the eight years between 1998–2005, only around 8 per cent of those harvested under export permits (about 270,000 parrots) delivered in the eight years between 1983–90.
- The main area under management in the Chaco Province (about 20,000km²) represents only about 12 per cent of the total region of the distribution of the blue-fronted parrot.
- Using the resources of Project Elé's trusteeship fund, three blue-fronted parrot reserves have been created: the 235km² Loro Hablador Natural Reserve in Chaco, the 100km² Las Lancitas Reserve in Jujuy, and the 130km² Laguna Pintascayoc Reserve in Salta. These reserves are used to carry out biological and ecological research and serve as a possible popula-tion 'source' for replenishing harvested areas.

Extraction levels under the management scheme that has been in operation over the last eight years are set out in Figure 11.2, which shows that extrac-tion remains below the permitted quota.

# UNCERTAINTIES SURROUNDING THE USE AND MANAGEMENT OF THE BLUE-FRONTED PARROT

The precautionary principle addresses the problems of uncertainty and ignorance. Identified below are some of the uncertainties associated with the use of the blue-fronted parrot, along with a description of their characteristics and of the way they are addressed by and incorporated in Project Elé.

Uncertainty can be distinguished from risk and from ignorance. Risk is associated with an event with a known probability, while true uncertainty is associated with an event with unknown probability. In both instances the various possible events/outcomes are known. However, when the possible events or outcomes are not known, then we are faced with ignorance (Faber et al, 1992). Over the last decades there has been a shift from trying to reduce uncertainty to trying to incorporate uncertainty and ignorance in the modelling and decision-making processes of natural resource management (Policansky, 1993; Taylor et al, 2000).

Variability is an intrinsic property of biological systems, and process complexity is typical of ecological systems. In resource management these emerge as uncertainty and surprise: unexpected behaviour of ecosystems, unforeseen response of populations, and unpredicted results of human interventions. There are additional uncertainties derived from the dynamics of the legal, economic, political, social and cultural context of resource management. In natural resource management, unlike some areas, these uncertainties have major impacts on sustainability, so that a precautionary management framework must necessarily take them into account.

The blue-fronted parrot project is an example (presented in a very simplified fashion) of the use of a resource that is extracted by local people, taken to distribution centres by middlemen, kept and cared for by stockpilers, sent abroad by exporters, received by importers, distributed by retailers and bought by final consumers. This is similar to most other living natural resource management programmes for export markets. In this long chain of utilization there are not only different economic interests, but also other actors involved, such as governments (interested either in protecting the resource or in tax collection from the trade, and sometimes both) and NGOs looking at the conservation of the species and their habitats.

Despite this complexity and the many vested interests involved, this chapter will seek to present a simplified treatment of uncertainties by considering three types: first, biological/ecological uncertainties; second, legal, policy and management uncertainties; and third, socio-economic uncertainties. All three are related, although there is a stronger relationship between the last two.

## Biological/ecological uncertainties and complexity

The main biological and ecological uncertainties can be referred to as demographic stochasticity and environmental stochasticity. Demographic stochasticity involves chance events of individual mortality and reproduction, usually considered to operate independently among individuals, so that it tends to average out in large populations and has a greater impact on small populations. Environmental stochasticity involves temporal fluctuations in the probability of mortality and the reproductive rate of all individuals in a population in the same or similar fashion – this is similar for small and large populations, and an important risk of population decline in all populations regardless of their abundance at a given location (Lande et al, 2003).

In the blue-fronted parrot project, only the environmental stochasticity has been incorporated into the simulation model of sustainable management for the purpose of determining quotas. It has been defined in terms of the variability of K, the carrying capacity of the environment. The uncertainty of this parameter was expressed as possible annual variations of 20 per cent and 40 per cent in the carrying capacity. The higher the variability in the carrying capacity, the lower the extraction should be, as expected on theoretical grounds, in order to maintain the sustainable extraction of blue-fronted parrot fledglings. Demographic stochasticity will be incorporated in the near future, in the form of variability in survivorship and fecundity.

Biological/ecological complexity also plays a role because the more complex the system, the more difficult it is to know about its real behaviour and dynamics, and the risks of unexpected events are higher. These aspects are dealt with below, in the section on adaptive management.

## Legal, policy and management uncertainties

Argentina has a federal political organization. This has a strong impact on the management of natural resources because, under the National Constitution, each province has primary authority over its fauna, flora, water and fossil fuels, both over and underground. The blue-fronted parrot is found over a range of many provinces, with the result that laws and policies are susceptible to being modified over parts of its range, thereby constituting a source of uncertainty. Management is particularly sensitive to these uncertainties, for it depends basically upon provincial regulations, that is, norms that can be changed at lower levels of the administration without changing the law. For example, taxes, duties and levies can be modified easily at the provincial level, dramatically changing the rules of the game and impinging on the sustainability of the use of a given resource.

The blue-fronted parrot project has responded to these sources of uncertainty (legal, policy and management) in three ways:

1   The national government has established agreements with five provincial governments (see below), thereby stabilizing regional policy.
2   As the issue of CITES export permits is a responsibility of the national government, there is a concurrent competence over natural resources, providing the national government with some degree of enforcement over compliance with the agreement by the provincial governments.

3   At the management level, the uncertainties derived from the prevailing relatively corrupt conditions in Argentina have been minimized. This has been achieved by enforcing the use of a special numbered ring that identifies each individual parrot collected. Additionally, SAyDS has provided adequate personnel and conditions of honesty. While petty bribery may still be present to some degree, collectors, dealers and exporters are finding the legal trade more attractive than the illegal one.

## Socio-economic uncertainties

Several socio-economic uncertainties have been identified in relation to Project Elé. Exchange rates and inflation rates, two intimately related factors, are known to have an impact upon the sustainable use of renewable natural resources. The higher the inflation rate, the higher the pressure on the harvest (Clark, 1973). As export is the primary fate of the blue-fronted parrot, changes in the exchange rate are reflected in pressure on extraction (more pesos for every dollar or euro, more pressure on the resource).

Project Elé experienced and responded to this 'surprise' during the Argentinian devaluation in 2002. Thus during the 1 peso/US$ decade, collectors were receiving 30 pesos per fledgling, and after December 2001, with an exchange rate of 3 pesos/US$, collectors received 70 pesos per fledgling; and in the last season (2004–05) they received 80 pesos per fledgling.

Market prices are another source of uncertainty. A drop in the market price in Europe (the main destination of blue-fronted parrots) is reflected in a reduction of exporters' profits, which are normally 'passed' down to middlemen and collectors. To 'cushion' this effect, Project Elé not only establishes the price paid per parrot per collector, but also defines the annual quota in order to keep a certain balance between supply and demand. By cutting down the quota per collector (and not extending the area under extraction) the total number collected diminishes, and so does the total number of parrots ready for export each year. However, blue-fronted parrots also enter European markets from aviaries within Europe. As these facilities are not under strict control in the European Union, the mechanism used by the Project Elé provides only a relative degree of buffering for this source of uncertainty.

Another socio-economic uncertainty has its source in possible protectionist measures, resulting either from business imperatives (for example, pressure from the European aviary trade) or from partial or complete import bans as a result of lobbying against animal cruelty by conservation groups. The former does not seem to be an immediate potential 'surprise', but conservation groups have already mounted a strong campaign at high levels of the EU for a complete ban on the trade of wild birds in EU countries (World Parrot Trust, 2005), and could result in the closure of Project Elé. In relation to this possibility, please see the discussion of the relationship between trade bans and poaching later on in this chapter.

Lack of management coordination between neighbouring countries that share the range of the blue-fronted parrot with Argentina (for example Bolivia and Paraguay), or an increase in the supply to markets of parrots from those neighbouring countries, are also potential sources of surprise for the sustainability of Argentina's blue-fronted parrot project.

In summary, there are many uncertainties associated with the sustainable use of the blue-fronted parrot. Some of them have been straightforwardly addressed and minimized by Project Elé, but others, mainly the biological/ecological ones, require a particular approach: adaptive management.

## ADAPTIVE MANAGEMENT AS A WAY TO ADDRESS UNCERTAINTIES

Adaptive management (Holling, 1978; Glantz and Thompson, 1981; Hilborn et al, 1999) is able to cope with uncertainties from many sources, particularly those of a biological/ecological origin. It can also incorporate some of the socio-economic, legal, policy and management uncertainties, although not equally efficiently. Adaptive management can be a highly complex approach, involving some degree of experimentation within natural systems, such as applying variable levels of harvest and analysing the response of the harvested populations. This section describes the use of a much simpler form of adaptive management: the use of feedback harvest rules.

Feedback harvest rules (Walters, 1986; Lande et al, 2001) are regimes in which management actions are not fixed, but depend upon the 'state' of the system. One of them is the fixed escapement rule (also known as threshold harvesting), which involves establishing a threshold population level or density, and harvesting only the population in excess of this threshold. This is the rule evaluated in Project Elé. Computer models are used to evaluate the effects of the different sources of uncertainty on the sustainability of the population under management, and to assess the optimal parameters under the fixed escapement rule. However, this rule requires some experience of long-term management as well as basic 'hard' scientific information, which is rarely available in these cases; so the uncertainty derived from the absence of reliable field information has also to be evaluated (see below).

### Adaptive management and the precautionary principle

Some supporters of the application of the precautionary principle in its most strict sense propose that no action (in this case harvesting) should be taken until all the significant evidence (biological parameters in this case) are known (Holm and Harris, 1999; Tickner, 2002). In the particular case of the parrot trade Beissinger and Bucher (1992) consider that 'there is still much methodology to be perfected, parrot biology to be learned, and sociological research to be conducted before a generic recipe for sustained harvesting of parrots can be developed'. This position rules out any kind of management until 'adequate' scientific information has been collected, precluding the acquisition of key biological and ecological data.

Project Elé has taken an alternative stance: rather than postponing management until everything important is known, the best available estimates of some parameters are used (when unavailable, 'best-guesses' are resorted to, or extrapolation from similar species or environments is applied), and adaptive management is designed so that it responds conservatively to any unexpected population or environmental change, whether caused by harvesting or other reasons. Frequently this approach, by measuring the response of the population to management, allows the manager to obtain empirical knowledge about most of the processes necessary for sustainable management. Thus adaptive management minimizes risks and addresses uncertainties, while at the same time filling in the gaps in critical management information, consistent with the precautionary principle. No partial or complete ban demonstrates these characteristics.

## Adaptive management and the fixed escapement rule

Management of any biological population depends upon a theoretical model being able to predict population change as a result of human intervention. The population model used for the blue-fronted parrot was the logistic model of population growth, while human intervention was based on the 'fixed escapement' rule of population management. The latter can be expressed in the following verbal manner: if population density $(D)$ is equal or less than a certain value, called the escapement or threshold density $(E)$, then the harvest $(H)$ is fixed to zero; if population density $(D)$ is larger than the escapement density $(E)$, then the harvest $(H)$ is set to the density of individuals in 'excess' of the escapement density $(D)$:

$$H = D - E$$

If there is an unanticipated event (for example an abnormally dry period or a disease epidemic) that results in an unusually low blue-fronted parrot population (in relation to the one expected under normal circumstances), then the fixed escapement rule will recommend a reduced (and eventually nil) extraction. This mechanism is a sort of sustainability assurance that there is no danger of overexploitation. Another advantage of this rule is that it also takes into account the effects of poaching. As a result of poaching, future blue-fronted parrot populations will be smaller than expected, and the extraction would then be reduced accordingly. There is a well-developed body of literature showing that the fixed escapement rule is an excellent tool for incorporating uncertainty (Ludwig and Walters, 1981; Walters, 1981, 1986; Hilborn and Walters, 1992; Lande et al, 2001).

## Application of modelling and management to the blue-fronted parrot population in the absence of reliable field information

The logistic model of population growth requires the estimation of two parameters: the intrinsic rate of natural increase ($r$), and the carrying capacity of the environment for the blue-fronted parrot population ($K$) (expressed as fledglings/km$^2$). Assigning numerical values to these parameters (they can rarely be measured directly in the field) entails the estimation of additional biological information: maximum lifespan, age-specific survivorships and age-specific fecundities. In the absence of this information for the blue-fronted parrot from the wild or from captivity, eight different age-specific survivorship curves, as well as several age-specific reproductive curves, were used. Demographic traits such as the age of first reproduction and the 'skipping rates' (intermittence of reproduction) were also considered. Additionally six methods were used to estimate the intrinsic rate of natural increase, and five methods of density estimation were used as indicators of carrying capacity (Rabinovich, 2004). From these many combinations some coherent (robust) estimates could be obtained for these two parameters. Thus, even in the absence of reliable field and laboratory information, a relatively narrow range of parameter values was obtained to run the sustainable management model.

## Requirements of the fixed escapement rule and difficulties of implementation

The fixed escapement rule requires that population density be estimated every year before harvest to determine the number of parrots to be extracted, creating some methodological and administrative difficulties. An easy, reliable and cheap sampling method still has to be devised, which is no simple task. Sampling should wait until parrot pairs have selected their nests, but counting nest trees at this time is dangerous for the successful establishment of a nest. Administrative problems occur if the sampling is too close to the start of the harvest period: there may be little time for processing the sampling results, establishing the size of the population to be harvested, producing the formal ministerial resolutions signed by the corresponding authorities, and transmitting the results to the people in the field. These problems are being addressed by replacing sampling by a calibration of road transect surveys of flying parrots as a means to estimate the population size, as required by the fixed escapement rule.

## POSITIVE AND NEGATIVE IMPACTS OF THE BLUE-FRONTED PARROT PROJECT

The precautionary principle is often used to argue against wildlife management (sustainable or not) and trade unless almost total knowledge is available.

Additionally, in general only the dangers are presented, and rarely the positive aspects of wildlife use. However, assessing what decisions and management are likely to be sustainable requires examination of a range of threats and benefits, not just the threat of overexploitation. This section adopts the reverse of the typical approach: it mentions some potential negative consequences of Project Elé but illustrates in some detail the positive effects of the project.

## Negative impacts of Project Elé

The current extraction programme of Project Elé appears to pose little conservation threat to species or habitat. Unlike the destructive practices in use before 1998, it involves conservation of individual nest trees and of the Quebracho forest in general. The area under management has grown slowly, but still comprises less than 8 per cent of the *A. aestiva* range (the area under management in the Dry Chaco region, computed as the sum of all properties assigned a quota, is of the order of 1500km², while the *Impenetrable* in that region has a surface area of about 20,000km²).

Some of the problems that can be anticipated are relatively normal problems that characterize the use of many renewable natural resources. For example, Project Elé has generated a permanent dependence on the process of supervision of all the actors involved (collectors, middlemen, stockpilers and exporters); this makes Project Elé relatively sensitive to possible political interference and opens the door to some degree of corruption. On the other hand, Project Elé is also very sensitive to external factors such as prices (for example in export markets) or the state and tendencies of the national economy (for example inflation or possible increases in taxes on exports). Finally, adaptive management implies taking flexible and fast decisions, possibly exceeding the administrative capacity of existing state provincial and national structures. However, these are wide-ranging difficulties that occur even in developed countries and in contexts where there is a strict prohibition on use.

## Positive effects of Project Elé

### Improvement in local livelihoods and income distribution (equity)

Project Elé has delivered significant livelihood benefits to the local and indigenous people involved in the project. The income produced from the blue-fronted parrot represents an important source of income for the peasant economy in the Dry Chaco region. Table 11.1 shows that the blue-fronted parrot activity ranks second as a source of income after cattle-raising and represents almost one fifth of the total annual cash income. In absolute terms, in a subsistence economy such as that of the Dry Chaco peasants, an average of almost 500 pesos/year per household derived from the blue-fronted parrot activity allows many peasant families to cover medical emergencies, pay the cost of sending a son or daughter to school, or replace dead or injured cattle. The prices received by collectors have compensated for inflation and kept pace with the devaluation of the peso by increasing the price paid per chick

**Table 11.1** *Ranking of the weighted average income per household per economic/subsistence activity* * in the Argentinian Dry Chaco region*

| Economic/ subsistence activity | Proportion of households carrying out each activity | Total income per year in pesos (in US$)*** | Weighted income per year in pesos (in US$)*** | Average percentage of total income per household per activity |
|---|---|---|---|---|
| Cattle-raising | 1 | 1463 (499) | 1463 (499) | 55.2 |
| Blue-fronted parrot extraction | 0.76 | 651 (222) | 495 (169) | 18.7 |
| Fence posts | 0.47 | 487 (166) | 229 (78) | 8.6 |
| Cheese production | 0.24 | 882 (301) | 212 (72) | 8.0 |
| Odd jobs (outside the ranch) | 0.43 | 330 (103) | 142 (48) | 5.4 |
| Other wildlife species** | 0.9 | 117 (40) | 105 (36) | 4.0 |

*Notes:* * The economic activity of charcoal production could not be quantified.
** Mainly the lizard locally called iguana (*Tupinambis rufescens*).
*** Conversion from pesos to US$ was made using an exchange rate of 2.93 pesos/US$ (all monetary figures rounded to integer values).

*Source:* data obtained from Grilli and Natale (2002)

collected. This has allowed, even with a fixed chick quota per peasant family and per indigenous group, an increase in their total cash income over the period of Project Elé.

In addition, there has been a change in the equity of the distribution of income along the trade chain from collectors to exporters. Under Project Elé an increased and still increasing proportional share has remained in the collectors' pockets (see Table 11.2).

The importance to conservation of these livelihood benefits is that they provide tangible economic incentives for the sustainable management of the parrots and their habitat by peasants, and counter pressures for conversion of land to intensive agriculture.

### Changing attitudes of the local population toward sustainability

Project Elé is designed to increase local people's perceptions of the value of the forest habitat. For this reason the project requires local collectors to be landowners (or show proof that they have set in motion the administrative steps to become owners). The philosophy behind this requirement is to shift people's feelings towards sustainable management and forest conservation, based on the belief that people value and care about what belongs to them or what may result in future benefits to them. Informal surveys have confirmed this premise (Ricardo Banchs, personal communication). The peasant activities of cattle raising and tree felling for fence posts (including the *Quebracho*

**Table 11.2** *Distribution of the net income produced from the blue-fronted parrot trade among the different links of the commercial chain*

| Link in the blue-fronted parrot commercial chain* | Value (in pesos) received per blue-fronted parrot chick | | | | Value (percentage) received per blue-fronted parrot chick | | | |
|---|---|---|---|---|---|---|---|---|
| | Pre 1992 | 1996–2001 | 2002–2004 | 2005 | Pre 1992 | 1996–2001 | 2002–2004 | 2005 |
| Collector | 5 | 30 | 70 | 80 | 2.5 | 12.9 | 25.0 | 25.5 |
| Middleman | 18 | 18 | 20 | 24 | 8.9 | 7.7 | 7.1 | 7.6 |
| Exporter | 180 | 185 | 190 | 210 | 88.7 | 79.4 | 67.9 | 66.9 |

*Note:* * Middlemen's and exporters' net profits were estimated by informal interviews and are not documented.

*Source:* Ricardo Banchs in correspondence with J. Rabinovich

*colorado* trees used for nesting by the blue-fronted parrot), result in a very slow degradation of the Dry Chaco forest, and do not appear to impinge dramatically on the conservation of the blue-fronted parrot. Additional projects to promote sustainable resource management are being planned, such as collecting honey from wild bees.

## Resisting pressures for conversion of habitat

A major threat to blue-fronted parrots, unrelated to extraction, is the conversion of land by large corporations to soybean plantations, involving massive deforestation and complete destruction of the blue-fronted parrot habitat. If peasants value their land more highly they are more likely to resist selling their land to large corporations. Recent assessments indicate that the process of conversion is worrying, although it does not show an alarming pace. Montenegro et al (2003) have shown that in four years (from 1998 to 2002) the province of Chaco has lost 167,948ha out of the 4,531,077ha in existence in 1998, which represents about 3.7 per cent, or 0.093 per cent annually. Although the *Impenetrable* forest proper may have suffered a different rate of loss, this is an indication that the blue-fronted parrot habitat is still subject to a relatively minor threat. Of course, even at this pace, a few more decades of this land-use conversion will inevitably seriously threaten the *A. aestiva* habitat.

Project Elé is directly supporting three strictly protected reserves for blue-fronted parrots. These are financed from resources collected from middlemen and exporters in the parrot trade and now add up to some 465km$^2$. While these constitute a relatively small percentage of the blue-fronted parrot habitat, they represent not only a population source to replenish harvested areas but also may stall the loss of habitat to a certain degree.

# To Ban or not to Ban: What is the Precautionary Decision in the Face of Risky Options?

In the face of the widespread, unsustainable exploitation of wild birds, the basic alternatives for importing countries seeking to promote conservation are: first, a total ban on wild bird importation, and second, selective importation, based upon the identification of sustainable harvest practices. The former option would protect all wild bird species, satisfying the interests of conservation groups and individuals, while participants in the sustainable trade would be penalized. The latter option would filter out only the unsustainable use of birds in their wild habitat, while allowing the distribution of benefits to all stakeholders associated with the sustainable use of birds. This is a highly topical issue. In 1992 the US effectively banned the import of all wild birds under the Wild Bird Conservation Act (WBCA), and recently a consortium of NGOs has called on the EU to ban the import of all wild birds into Europe (World Parrot Trust, 2005). The latter has a list of signatories that includes over 200 organizations. While the precautionary principle is invoked to justify a complete ban, it can be argued that this approach leads to the risk of generating a potential increase in poaching and illegal trade.

The relationship between legal markets and trade is complex. A study by Wright et al (2001) is frequently used to demonstrate that there is a strong positive correlation between the existence of legal markets for parrots and levels of illegal trade (World Parrot Trust, 2005). This rests on a single simple correlation: a decrease in the poaching rate of ten species of parrots after the passing of the US WBCA, compared to before. However, as the authors point out, no such relationship held when data for all species was examined, and the relationship could be confounded by other factors such as increased protection efforts over this period. Experience in Argentina shows that when the international blue-fronted parrot trade was banned between 1992 and 1995 the parrot trade continued to be active, essentially because of an increase in domestic trade (mostly underground) (Barbarán and Saravia Toledo, 1997).

Total bans are not necessary, except in cases where a species is in a serious threat category (for example endangered or critically endangered), or when it plays an important role in a complex ecological situation, and when the degree of uncertainty is very high and ecological relationships are poorly understood. If these conditions do not apply, in general, adaptive management, if effectively implemented, can provide the necessary answers to a safe sustainable use of wildlife. However, it is worth noting that the potential for trade to be banned through an EU import restriction, or through inclusion in CITES Appendix I, exerts important pressure, particularly at the provincial government level, to ensure the regulatory environmental mechanisms for a sustainable programme remain in place. The ban is an effective 'big stick', but without the 'carrot' of trade, it loses all impact.

Total bans also constitute a relatively negative decision for solving the problems generated by the uncertainties in the management of renewable natural resources: they always carry with them the chance of impeding a change that would reduce risks. In this sense they share the same drawbacks as the regulation of other common risks: health and safety hazards, pollution from electric power generation, or the transport of hazardous wastes. Total bans may be a major obstacle to new solutions and innovation, and they may also aggravate the hazard they are supposed to avert – such as increasing levels of poaching. Conservation and resource decision-makers should make decisions in accordance with the view that the effects of a ban on a risky process depend entirely on what is being left behind after a risk is removed (Huber, 1983). Regulation must involve benefit/risk balancing, given the fact that new natural resource management programmes are usually more sustainable than the old ones they replace, as in the case of Project Elé.

# REFERENCES

Banchs, R. A. and Moschione, F. N. (in press) 'Proyecto Elé: Para la conservación y el aprovechamiento sustentable del loro hablador (*Amazona aestiva*) en la Argentina', in M. L. Bolkovic and D. E. Ramadori (eds) *Manejo de Fauna Silvestre en Argentina: Programas de Uso Sustentable*, Dirección de Fauna Silvestre, SAyDS, Buenos Aires

Barbarán, F. R. and Saravia Toledo, C. J. (1997) 'Monitoring an export moratorium of the blue-fronted amazon parrot (*Amazona aestiva*) in Salta Province, Argentina (1992–1996)', *Vida Silvestre Neotropical*, vol 6, nos 1–2, pp3–7

Beissinger, S. R. and Bucher, E. H. (1992) 'Can parrots be conserved through sustainable harvesting?', *Bioscience*, vol 42, no 3, pp164–74

Clark, C. W. (1973) 'The economics of overexploitation', *Science*, no 181, pp630–34

Faber, M., Manstetten, R. and Proops, J. L. R. (1992) 'Humankind and the environment: an anatomy of surprise and ignorance', *Environmental Values*, vol 1, no 3, pp217–42

Glantz, M. H. and Thompson, J. D. (eds) (1981) *Resource Management and Environmental Uncertainty: Lessons from Coastal Upwelling Fisheries Vol 11*, John Wiley & Sons, Chichester

Grilli, P. and Natale, G. (2002) *Segunda Encuesta sobre los Recursos Naturales del Gran Chaco Argentino y la Economía de Subsistencia de sus Pobladores Rurales*, preliminary report presented to SAyDS, Buenos Aires

Hilborn, R. and Walters, C. J. (1992) *Quantitative Fisheries Stock Assessment. Choice, Dynamics and Uncertainty*, Chapman and Hall, London

Hilborn, R., Walters, C. J. and Ludwig, D. (1999) 'Sustainable exploitation of renewable resources', *Annual Review of Ecology and Systematics*, vol 30, pp45–67

Holling, C. S. (ed) (1978) *Adaptive Environmental Assessment and Management*, John Wiley & Sons, Chichester

Holm, S. and Harris, J. (1999) 'Precautionary principle stifles discovery', letter published in *Nature*, no 400, p398

Huber, P. (1983) 'Exorcists vs. gatekeepers in risk regulation', *Regulation*, vol 7, no 6, pp23–32

Lande, R., Saether, B. E. and Engen, S. (2001) 'Sustainable exploitation of fluctuating populations', in J. D. Reynolds, G. M. Mace, K. H. Redford and J. G. Robinson (eds) *Conservation of Exploited Species*, Cambridge University Press, Cambridge, UK, pp3–15

Lande, R., Engen, S. and Saether, B. E. (2003) 'Demographic and environmental stochasticity' in *Stochastic Population Models in Ecology and Conservation: An Introduction*, Oxford Series in Ecology and Evolution, Oxford University Press

Ludwig, D. and Walters, C. J. (1981) 'Measurement errors and uncertainty in parameter estimates for stock and recruitment', *Canadian Journal of Fisheries and Aquatic Sciences*, vol 38, pp711–720

Montenegro, C., Strada, M., Parmuchi, M. G., Gasparri, I. and Bono, J. (2003) *Mapa Forestal Provincia del Chaco. Actualización Año 2002*, Dirección de Bosques, SAyDS, Buenos Aires

Policansky, D. (1993) 'Uncertainty, knowledge, and resource management', *Ecological Applications*, vol 3, no 4, pp583–84

Rabinovich, J. E. (2004) *Modelling the Sustainable Use of the Blue-Fronted Parrot (Amazona aestiva) in the Dry Chaco Region of Argentina*, available at www.ecopaedia.com.ar/publico/Blue_fronted_parrot_Model.pdf

SAyDS (2005a) *Proyecto Elé*, available at www.medioambiente.gov.ar/?idseccion=53/

SAyDS (2005b) *Proyecto Elé: Estado de avance del Plan de Aprovechiamento*, available at www.medioambiente.gov.ar/default.asp?IdArticulo=1083

Taylor, B. L., Wade, P. R., de Master, D. P. and Barlow, J. (2000) 'Incorporating uncertainty into management models for marine mammals', *Conservation Biology*, vol 14, no 5, pp1243–1252

Tickner, J. A. (2002) 'Developing scientific and policy methods that support precautionary action in the face of uncertainty – The Institute of Medicine Committee on Agent Orange', *Public Health Reports*, vol 117, pp534–545

Walters, C. (1981) 'Effects of measurement errors on the assessment of stock–recruitment relationships', *Canadian Journal of Fisheries and Aquatic Sciences*, vol 38, pp704–711

Walters, C. (1986) *Adaptive Management of Renewable Resources*, Macmillan, New York

World Parrot Trust (2005) *Wild Bird Imports Threaten Species Survival*, havailable at www.worldparrottrust.org/trade/declaration3.htm

Wright, T. F., Toft, C. A., Enkerlin-Hoeflich, E., Gonzalez-Elizondo, J., Albornoz, M., Rodriguez-Ferraro, A., Rojas-Suárez, F., Sanz, V., Trujillo, A., Beissinger, S. R., Berovides A., V., Gálvez A., X., Brice, A. T., Joyner, K., Eberhard, J., Gilardi, J., Koenig, S. E., Stoleson, S., Martuscelli, P., Meyers, J. M., Renton, K., Rodríguez, A. M., Sosa-Asanza, A.C., Vilella, F. J. and Wiley, J. W. (2001) 'Nest poaching in neotropical parrots', *Conservation Biology*, vol 15, pp710–720

# 12

# Precaution in the American Endangered Species Act as a Precursor to Environmental Decline: The Case of the Northwest Forest Plan

*Stephen P. Mealey, Jack Ward Thomas, Harold J. Salwasser, Ronald E. Stewart, Peter J. Balint and Paul W. Adams*

*A paradox is a statement that appears contradictory or unsupported by common sense but is nevertheless true. The common sense underlying most current management actions related to the American Endangered Species Act is (1) that preserving habitat for listed species is critical, and (2) that the best or only way to preserve habitat is to preserve the ecosystem(s) on which the species depend. It may seem contradictory to say that altering the habitat is essential to its long term maintenance. However, it seems that alteration may be exactly what is indicated by at least some assessments of relative risks. In such cases, managers must be prepared to accept the paradox and act. (Mealey and Thomas, 2002)*

## INTRODUCTION

The paradox referred to by Mealey and Thomas (2002) is that the alteration of ecosystems, seemingly contradictory to ecosystem and species preservation, may nevertheless be necessary if some protected species are to be preserved. The US Endangered Species Act of 1973 (ESA) and the federal agencies administering it can and have blocked both acceptance of this paradox and of the management it requires. This obstruction finds its justification in laws, regulations and federal court decisions and in agency policies and culture that are narrowly precautionary. In its current application, this highly restrictive form of precaution demands no action that would change the environment unless there is certainty that no immediate harm will result. This principle has manifested itself in the short-term, risk-averse policies adopted by the implementing federal agencies. Practitioners often ignore, without inquiry, the potential long-term harm from inaction in the short term and fail to take management actions needed for long-term ecosystem maintenance. Ironically, this excessively precautionary approach has contributed to the long-term decline of the very resources the law is intended to protect: hence our chapter title. We write to document this irony and offer options for a broader, less restrictive concept of precaution that honours the paradox and defeats the irony.

Much of America's environmental policy has been established in the past 40 years through federal laws that protect wilderness, rivers, water, air, wildlife and fish, and other resources, and also provide for human health and safety. The Endangered Species Act is often referred to as one of the 'crown jewels' of this policy. One of the main purposes of the ESA is 'to provide a means whereby the ecosystems upon which endangered species and threatened species depend may be conserved' (ESA, s2(b)). A fundamental intent is to recover native plant and animal species in peril. The Act relies on a process founded on an 'absolutist no harm rule ... for precautionary reasons' (Bodansky, 1994). Once listed as threatened or endangered, a species is given virtually complete protection, at least in the immediate future, as will be seen. At the time of its adoption the ESA was unprecedented in the world as a nation's commitment to a land ethic and stewardship. In the 30 years since its implementation there have been notable successes, including the recovery of the American alligator, the American peregrine falcon and the brown pelican, and significant population increases for the bald eagle, grizzly bear and grey wolf.

However, less well known or understood are the significant environmental declines or potential declines in the west of the US. In this chapter we highlight some of these declines by focusing on a primary federal forest plan in the western United States: the Northwest Forest Plan (US Department of Agriculture and US Department of Interior, 1994). The Northwest Forest Plan features extensive networks of designated federal forest reserves in the states of Washington, Oregon and California, intended primarily for species protection, including the protection of the northern spotted owl *Strix occidentalis caurina*. In this chapter we argue that increasing risks of uncharacteristic, lethal, stand-replacing fire in some forests (Schmidt et al, 2002), and loss of northern spotted owl habitat (US Fish and Wildlife Service, 2004) are some of the outcomes of the ESA's narrowly restrictive precautionary approach and precaution-driven administration. We shed light on the declines in a manner that demonstrates that they can be seen as avoidable and preventable, and that their causes in the overly restrictive ESA and its administration can be repaired, thereby strengthening America's environmental legacy.

After establishing the setting for this case study, we examine precaution in relevant US law and policy and in the Northwest Forest Plan. We then go on to examine the effects of precaution on conservation and on decision-making, and examine the relationship between precaution and science. Finally we draw lessons from this case study and forward our conclusions.

## SETTING

The Northwest Forest Plan covers 24 million acres of federally managed, mostly national forest land in Oregon, Washington and northern California. It was initiated in 1994 to guide all land management decisions within the range of the northern spotted owl, a threatened species listed under the ESA in 1990. The management strategy consists of extensive standards and guidelines applicable to seven different categories of land allocated and classified by the plan. Six of the categories, or about 84 per cent of the area, are essentially reserves where active management of timber harvesting is an exception. No timber harvest is pre-programmed in reserves.

An example is Late Succession Reserves, which cover 30 per cent of the area and are designed primarily to provide habitat for the northern spotted owl and other late-forest succession and old growth related species. Active management is limited in Late Succession Reserves which contained most of the remaining high quality late-succession forest habitat at the time of their establishment. In Late Succession Reserves in the drier forests east of the Cascades and in southern Oregon and north western California, reduction of the risk of stand-replacing fire by prescribed fire and mechanical thinning is permitted. In forest reserves west of the Cascades, thinning of stands younger than 80–110 years to accelerate development of old forest conditions is also permitted. These limited management activities, however, have been conditional on the completion of inter-agency consultations required by the ESA, management assessments including watershed analysis, and until 2004, 'survey and manage' procedures designed to conserve nearly 300 rare and little known species not covered by the ESA. In addition, other more specific assessments related to fire and associated treatments are required.

Another example is Riparian Reserves that contain more than 11 per cent of the area established to protect the aquatic system and its dependent species. These were to be included in watershed analyses resulting in refinement of stream buffer widths and management activities needed to retain their resilience. Active management proposed here is also subject to inter-agency consultations under ESA.

## PRECAUTION IN LAW AND POLICY

### Law

The ESA calls for the conservation of endangered species and threatened species and of the ecosystems 'on which' they depend. Under Section 4 of the law, species may be listed as either 'endangered' or 'threatened'. Federal agencies must conserve listed species and not jeopardize their survival. They do so by following the Section 7 consultation process, which requires that federal land management agencies, commonly the US Forest Service and the Bureau of Land Management, consult with the US Fish and Wildlife Service and the National Oceanic and Atmospheric Administration–Fisheries (regulating agencies) that administer the ESA. This process is intended to ensure that actions proposed by managers do not jeopardize listed species. Section 9 of the ESA extends to private individuals and property by making it unlawful for a person to 'take' a listed species.

The ESA takes a strong but narrowly defined precautionary approach in the face of uncertainty about risk to species. It focuses on and seeks to prevent mainly near-term potential and/or uncertain harms or risks. In consultations, proponents (the managing agencies) of actions must demonstrate (to the regulating agencies) that proposals would not be harmful regardless of time frame. The ESA and its application do not commonly recognize the time dimension of risk, that is, that some short-term risks to species can result in longer term benefits to those same species. Rather than mainly documenting actual or probable risks, or comparing and balancing the short- and long-term risks and benefits of proposals and then regulating, the law takes a narrower precautionary approach. In summary, the ESA compels regulating where *any* risks are believed to be likely. This seems a stronger application of precaution than Article 15 of the 1992 Rio Declaration on the precautionary principle, which states: 'Where there are threats of serious or irreversible damage, lack of full scientific certainty shall not be used as a reason for postponing cost-effective measures'.

Raustiala (2002) notes that precaution is obvious in the ESA listing process: full certainty about a species status is not required prior to listing, but rather a species must only be shown to be 'in danger of extinction' and 'likely to become endangered' before being listed. Precaution is more strongly reflected in the consultation process where harm to a species need not be affirmatively shown – instead agencies must ensure that proposals will 'not likely jeopardize' a listed species. 'Likelihood' as opposed to certainty is the trigger, which adds to the precautionary nature of the provision.

Wirth (2002) has observed that the most precautionary policies are those that tolerate absolutely no risk. In that light, the ESA is seen to embody a virtual 'zero risk', highly restrictive precautionary philosophy because federal agencies must assure that each of their actions 'is not likely to jeopardize the continued existence' of listed species. Courts have interpreted this language as a broad prohibition on federal actions that may cause any harm to listed species.

Ruhl (2004), while arguing that the ESA does not *require* using precautionary principle methods, does acknowledge that many substantive programmes of the ESA, such as the prohibition of jeopardy and the restriction against take, are precautionary in orientation.

ESA case law resulting from Northwest Forest Plan litigation coming mostly from the Ninth Circuit Court of Appeals has consistently reinforced the precautionary features of the ESA and the requirement that regulators implementing the Act be risk averse in their decision-making.[1]

## Policy

In 1999, the White House, addressing environment and trade, issued a policy statement on precaution and implementing federal law: 'Precaution is an essential element of the US regulatory system given that regulators often have to act on the frontiers of knowledge and in the absence of full scientific certainty' (Wirth, 2002). This Executive Branch policy is reflected in ESA implementing philosophy. The *Consultation Handbook* (US Fish and Wildlife Service and National Marine Fisheries Service, 1998) prepared by the regulating agencies states that 'The Services are then expected to provide the benefit of the doubt to the species concerned' when there are gaps in the information for consultations.

A narrow, highly restrictive precautionary philosophy is apparent in the definitions in the *Consultation Handbook*. The phrase 'is likely to adversely affect' is defined as 'the appropriate finding ... if *any* adverse effect to listed species may occur ... and the effect is not discountable (is measurable), insignificant (harm is possible) or beneficial'. In other words, *any* immediate non-beneficial, measurable effect with any possibility of harm, regardless of magnitude and regardless of potential offsetting longer term benefits is 'likely to adversely affect' the species. Such a finding would trigger a formal and usually expensive and time-consuming process to determine jeopardy or how to avoid it by making modifications to the project. To avoid the process, proponents must propose projects with no immediate risk.

# PRECAUTION IN THE NORTHWEST FOREST PLAN

A recent review of the application of the Northwest Forest Plan on national forests in California (Thomas, 2003) reported that:

- There was little or no active management carried out to reduce fire danger in Late Succession Reserves in the fire-influenced landscapes identified.
- There was little or no thinning in younger stands within Late Succession Reserves.
- Very few watershed assessments were completed and default riparian buffers remained in place and unmanaged. That produced greater fire risks, especially in Late Succession Reserves in fire-influenced landscapes. What had been intended as a temporary application of the precautionary principle became permanent.
- Adaptive Management Areas were managed no differently from the rest of the area so no new information was available for adaptive management, and wood products expected from the plan were reduced.

- The 'survey and manage' strategy precluded most harvest of older forests in the 'matrix' lands outside of Late Succession Reserves. It was also a barrier to fuel reduction treatments in Late Succession Reserves. Significant costs were added to timber management making planned harvests uneconomic.

Thomas (2003) noted that while the Forest Ecosystem Management Assessment Team had originally designed a dynamic, long-term plan, in its implementation the Northwest Forest Plan became a 'static', preservationist strategy. The 'survey and manage' procedure was a large factor because it was demanding and difficult to complete (US Department of Agriculture and US Department of Interior, 2003). The process required that any proposed activity in Late Succession Reserves be preceded by a survey for rare or little known species and if discovered they would be protected until it was proven unnecessary. Thomas (2003) sees such measures as actually more conservative than those required by the ESA and the process as more precautionary than any required by law.

Frequent litigation in federal courts related to the ESA and other procedural 'hooks' in the regulations or the plan itself was also found to delay the implementation of the plan. Judicial decisions together with their required procedures have dramatically changed the execution of the plan and reinforced its restrictive precautionary nature. In general, these findings for the national forests in California hold for the entire Northwest Forest Plan Area (Irwin and Thomas, 2002).

The US Department of Agriculture Forest Service (2003) identified the ESA requirement for consultation with regulatory agencies as one of several major reasons for Thomas's (2003) findings. Consultation was found to be complex and expensive. Regulators were noted to have a 'strong tendency to focus on short term adverse environmental effects of a project rather than recognize longer run environmental benefits that would justify such short term effects'. It was also admitted that the US Forest Service, 'for various reasons' designs projects to align with this short-term, risk-averse philosophy of regulators in order to reach a 'not likely to adversely affect' conclusion and avoid formal consultation. This often eliminated projects in Late Succession Reserves or in riparian areas that had long-term benefits for northern spotted owls as a result of reduced fire risk, but also had some near-term adverse effects.

However, there has been recognition that an alternative approach that balances risks from these different sources is required. US Forest Service Chief Dale Bosworth acknowledges this issue in a report to Congress:

> *Problems (implementing fire risk reduction projects) arise when the regulatory agencies require the Forest Service to focus on the short term consequences of a proposed plan or project instead of the long term health of the landscape in question.* (Bosworth, 2002)

In response to federal agency uncertainty about handling risk in ESA consultation, President Bush has placed high priority in the Healthy Forest Initiative (Bush, 2002) on 'developing guidance for weighing the short term risks against the long term benefits of fuels treatment and restoration projects'. Regulating agencies issued a policy that ESA Section 7 consultations should balance the 'long term benefits of fuel treatment projects ... against any short or long term adverse effects' (Williams and Hogarth, 2002). However, this policy has not been incorporated into the *Consultation Handbook*, which as national policy for consultation is binding.

The Healthy Forest Restoration Act of 2003 has gone even further in addressing the issue of short-term versus long-term risks and benefits of fuel reduction projects including, with conditions, those covered by the ESA. In Section 106 of the Act, it requires what amounts to a 'comparative ecological risk assessment'. Courts are to:

> *balance the impact to the ecosystem likely affected by the (hazardous fuel reduction) project of the short and long term effects of undertaking the agency action against the short and long term effects of not undertaking the agency action.*

In preparing this case study on the implementation of the Northwest Forest Plan, however, we found no sign that (as part of the Section 7 consultation process to demonstrate that proposals would not be harmful) either the Forest Service or the Bureau of Land Management had routinely completed comparative ecological risk assessments examining the effects on northern spotted owls of proposed management actions compared with short- and long-term effects of the absence of such actions. Without such analysis, regulating agencies appear to have 'defaulted' to the narrow precautionary conclusion that *any* short-term adverse effects are harmful and should be avoided. In summary, the precautionary principle is being narrowly applied in the Northwest Forest Plan, deriving from ESA provisions and their interpretation: no action is allowed unless there is certainty that at least no immediate harm will result, ignoring without inquiry the potential harm from inaction.

# CONSERVATION EFFECTS OF PRECAUTION

## Uncharacteristic fire risk in the Northwest Forest Plan Area

In general, in the warmer, drier, lower elevation forests covered by the plan, habitat has changed dramatically in the past few decades (Agee, 2002; Irwin and Thomas, 2002). In the past, frequent low-intensity ground fires maintained many stands and habitat whereas now, high-intensity crown fires *replace* stands and habitat more frequently than before. Today's stand-replacing fires tend to be uncharacteristic: larger, more severe, more intense and more frequent than in previous decades (Franklin, 2003). Recent fires of this type have burned forests beyond the natural range of variability with perceived long-lasting ecosystem changes.

Fire suppression in landscapes where fire was relatively frequent is seen as a major factor in this change. Generally, fire is changing from low severity to high severity because of fuel build up. Agee (2002) notes that the more forests have been protected from fire, the worse the fire risks have become. Recent fire statistics show a dramatic increase in the trend for fire severity and in the area burned in western forests. Given this predicament, he observes: 'a realistic management goal in reserved and unreserved forests is to reduce potential wildfire intensities and to lower crown fire potential'. Franklin observes:

> *Active management of these forests is required to maintain and restore these ecosystems... The negative consequences of allowing wildfire to return to these forests without prior treatment ... will often be large and unacceptable.* (Franklin, 2003)

Much of the area reserved for the protection of northern spotted owls is at high risk of uncharacteristic fire and loss of major ecosystem components (Irwin and Thomas, 2002). In 2002, coarse-scale assessment tools were developed to project fire hazards and related ecosystem risks in terms of Condition Classes (Schmidt et al, 2002). Condition Class 3 identifies an area at high risk of losing one or more components that define and make up an ecosystem. Around 2 million acres of the area covered by the Northwest Forest Plan (27 per cent of all Late Succession Reserve acreage) are in Condition Class 3.

## EFFECTS OF PRECAUTION ON NORTHERN SPOTTED OWLS

The US Fish and Wildlife Service completed its status review of the northern spotted owl in November 2004 (US Fish and Wildlife Service, 2004). They found that between 1994 and 2003, habitat loss mostly from wildfire in southwest Oregon in 2002 totalled 224,041 acres, leading to a 3.03 per cent decline in available habitat range wide. Local losses of habitat were often much more dramatic. Uncharacteristic wildfire was the greatest cause of habitat loss that occurred during the nine-year period. For this and other important reasons, the agency decided that the northern spotted owl would remain listed as a threatened species. Thomas (2003) found that the narrow and restrictive application of the precautionary principle in the Northwest Forest Plan had increased the risk of fire and consequently the risk to owls by discouraging management to mitigate fire risks and risks associated with drought that could harm owls, owl habitat and related resources. These results are similar to those reported by Stewart et al (2004) for the Sierra Nevada Forest Plan Amendment (US Department of Agriculture Forest Service, 2001), where a precautionary plan did little to protect California spotted owls (*Strix occidentalis occidentalis*) and reduce fire risks on 11.5 million acres of 11 national forests in the

Sierra Nevada Mountains of northeast and east central California.

In both cases, highly restrictive precaution embedded in standards and guidelines has been a barrier to restoration management to reduce fire risk and an obstacle to the achievement of intended conservation goals. This calls into question the evolved conservation practice evident in the western United States of attempting to maintain essentially 'static' unmanaged conservation reserves in dynamic, fire-prone forests. Recent assessments of risks of uncharacteristic fire indicate that the *absence* of active management to mitigate fire risks in such areas may be the greater threat to vulnerable species (Mealey and Thomas, 2002; Agee, 2002, 2003; Franklin, 2003). Ironically, continuation of highly restrictive precautionary principle driven, short-term, risk-averse protection measures could lead to the deterioration of the very resources the ESA is intended to protect.

## DECISION-MAKING EFFECTS OF PRECAUTION

The precautionary principle, as a keystone of the ESA, supported by related court decisions and the absence of comparative ecological risk assessments, has made understandable the practice of restrictive, risk-averse decision-making as a default strategy, if not supportable. It has limited the 'decision space' in the Northwest Forest Plan. The evolved processes of implementation are taking far longer and are more expensive and cumbersome than originally envisaged. As a result, the plan has failed to fulfil many of its longer term environmental promises, and 'the results and actions underway no longer even resemble what was anticipated at the time of adoption' (Thomas, 2003). Adaptive management and Adaptive Management Areas intended to develop and test new management approaches to integrate and achieve ecological, economic and social and community objectives have been sacrificed, apparent victims of highly restrictive precaution.

As pointed out earlier, comparative ecological risk assessments are required in federal law and in a regulatory agency policy directive, and they are of demonstrated feasibility (Roloff et al, 2004; O'Laughlin, in press; Roloff et al, in press). The US General Accounting Office (GAO) in 2004 noted the need for better information and a coordinated approach for conducting such comparative risk assessments: it recommended that the Secretaries of Agriculture and Interior should direct the Forest Service and the Bureau of Land Management to 'clarify existing guidance ... on the assessment and documentation of the risks of environmental effects associated with not conducting fuel reduction projects' (US GAO, 2004). However, the combined response to this recommendation from the Departments of Agriculture and Interior was that:

> *emergence of models or a methodology ... that meaningfully assesses the risks associated with treating fuels or not treating fuels across time and at multiple spatial scales seems unlikely...*

> *We do not agree that such a calculus can be developed.* (Rey and Scarlett, 2004)

Ruhl (2004) offers a feasible framework for resolving differences about ESA decision-making methods. He sees 'professional judgement' (encompassing 'best available scientific evidence' including comparative risk assessments) providing the main rationale for most ESA decisions. The precautionary principle (in its restrictive form) would be a discretionary tool used only on a limited basis in cases where evidence is limited and the consequences of decision error for species survival are severe. Such exceptional cases would be the subject of independent scientific peer review to determine the degree of variance of decisions with the best available scientific evidence. To be credible, such an approach would likely require formalization in at least regulation and policy.

## RELATIONSHIP BETWEEN PRECAUTION AND SCIENCE

Science and scientists played a prominent role in establishing the foundations of the Northwest Forest Plan. In the 1970s and 1980s, research and monitoring raised serious concerns about populations and the habitat of owls and other species. The ESA and other challenges prompted political and agency leaders to appoint scientists to evaluate these problems and recommend management options for federal lands. Scientists had to shift from traditional research to synthesis and interpretation of scientific information to develop previously unused, and hence untested, broad-scale management strategies.

The most notable groups in this role were the Interagency Scientific Committee (Thomas et al, 1990) that developed a conservation plan for the northern spotted owl that laid the groundwork for the Forest Ecosystem Management Assessment Team and the strategies that underlay the options from which the Northwest Forest Plan was derived. The main risk to the northern spotted owl identified by these science-based teams was rapid depletion and fragmentation of late-succession forests through aggressive harvesting of forests by clear-cutting. Analyses also acknowledged the dynamic nature of ecosystems with disturbances such as fire in dry forests that could sometimes adversely affect important species. They recognized the need for active, 'hands on' management to maintain and restore the conditions required by vulnerable species and ecosystems.

The final form of the Northwest Forest Plan was generally consistent with the work of the scientists. However, the Northwest Forest Plan includes standards and procedures that were added after the selection of the Forest Ecosystem Management Assessment Team's 'Option 9', and which are substantially more restrictive and precautionary. Much of the shift was intended to fend off legal challenges. Changing political and agency cultures favouring restrictive precaution magnified this impact. During the 'Clinton era' in the 1990s, the time when the Northwest Forest Plan was finalized, politically appointed administrators in the Departments of Agriculture and Interior and the Council on Environmental Quality apparently had narrow, short-term risk-averse precautionary views that influenced the final form of the plan and its implementation.

Implementation of the Northwest Forest Plan often strayed from a science-based approach with choices of 'no action' options over those emphasizing 'action'. Justification for such choices has often been the lack of scientific certainty about the effects of action and the inability of science to assure that negative consequences would not result from proposals for action. This ignores the fact that science cannot prove a negative; it cannot prove that an undesired effect or event will not occur. Other implicit assumptions of such precaution are that no action is safer and morally preferable to action in the presence of scientific uncertainty. However, contrary to a science-based process, no attempt has been made to evaluate these assumptions.

## CASE STUDY LESSONS

We have documented that the highly restrictive precautionary features of the ESA and its administration and adjudication have generally not been positive for northern spotted owls and their habitat in dry fire-prone forests covered by the Northwest Forest Plan. Lacking comparative ecological risk assessments from management agencies, regulating agencies have defaulted to narrow, restrictive actions aimed at the elimination of risks of immediate harm in forest restoration proposals, without simultaneously considering the long-term effects of not doing so. The practical effect has been to allow the declining quality of dry-forest owl habitat to worsen and to continue to expose owls and other resources to unnecessary and preventable risks of uncharacteristic fire. The precautionary principle in this narrow, restrictive form has not, and most likely will not, prove either effective or useful in advancing natural resources conservation and sustainability.

None of this is consistent with a conclusion of the National Research Council (NRC), which in 1995 explored the relationship between science and the ESA:

> *The concept of risk is central to the implementation of the ESA...*
> *The main risks are risks of extinction and risks associated with*
> *unnecessary expenditures or curtailment of land use in the face of*
> *substantial uncertainties about the accuracy of estimated risks of*
> *extinction and about future events...* Some crises involving imper-
> illed species may call for short time horizons on the order of tens
> of years, but ordinarily it will be necessary to view extinction over
> longer periods, on the order of hundreds of years, so that short
> term considerations do not create long term problems. (NRC,
> 1995, emphasis added)

# CONCLUSION

In the introduction to this study we stated: 'We write to ... offer options for a broader, less restrictive concept of precaution that honours the paradox and defeats the irony'. In November 2004, World Conservation Union (IUCN) member organizations put forward a draft motion entitled 'The Precautionary Principle in Environmental Governance' to IUCN's World Conservation Congress in Bangkok. We suggest that four components of this text (which was not approved in this form) offer a less restrictive and more responsive precautionary context for effective ESA legal, regulatory and implementation strategies:

1   Precaution should be part of an adaptive management strategy.
2   Precaution should emphasize collaboration in decision-making.
3   Precaution should include careful assessment of likely benefits and risks of alternative courses of action and inaction.
4   Precaution should include socio-economic understanding as well as environmental science.

Of particular relevance is point 3, calling for assessment of the benefits and risks of action and inaction referred. This obviously encompasses comparative ecological risk assessments. Cooney (2004) also presents the need for assessment of relative conservation risks and benefits of alternative strategies (action and inaction) in applying precaution as a management tool.

We suggest that in the context of the ESA, this broader precautionary approach could be integrated by requiring that in ESA Section 7 consultations, management agencies complete comparative ecological risk assessments – balancing, as in Section 106 of the Healthy Forest Restoration Act, the 'impact to the ecosystem likely affected by the project of the short and long term effects of undertaking the agency action; against the short and long term effects of not undertaking the agency action' and requiring that regulatory agencies consider them in related decision-making. With this mandate there would be no need to 'default' to a narrow and restrictive application of the precautionary principle, as in this case. Not only would the standard for precaution be broadened, but the ecological context of the ESA would be expanded and updated as well. A requirement in the ESA for an adaptive management approach to species recovery would also be an important complement.

We offer a second option that applies the broader concept of precaution to the case where the ESA does not directly apply, for instance in the case of the Sierra Nevada Forest Plan Amendment and the California spotted owl. Here we suggest that the four components of the precautionary approach considered by IUCN offer a responsive precautionary context for implementing the 1969 National Environmental Policy Act (NEPA). In appropriate NEPA applications we recommend that management agencies require comparative ecological risk assessments, as for the ESA and the Healthy Forest Restoration

Act, to facilitate effective decision-making. This appears consistent with the requirements of the NEPA and its implementing regulations at 40 CFR 1502.16, which call for discussion of 'the relationship between short term uses of man's environment and the maintenance and enhancement of long term productivity'.

The consequences of not removing more of the growing biomass from the dry, fire- and drought-prone forests in the west because of restrictive, precautionary, short-term risk-averse ESA-based decisions, could be grave. Salwasser (2003) noted that conditions in dry western forests with high fire risks will likely worsen because of the effects of the current Pacific Decadal Oscillation (PDO) with its unusually hot dry summers that intensify fires. For example, in the Sierra Nevada national forests of California, where growth exceeds harvest by 1.35 billion board feet each year, potential fuels accumulation in the absence of intervening fire or management could approximate 220 billion board feet in 40 years. When combined with another predictable PDO, this fuel build-up will, without treatment, inevitably result in widespread and large-scale stand-replacing fires. This is highly undesirable for threatened or endangered species associated with late-succession forests, such as the spotted owl, and will have significant adverse social and economic consequences.

Clearly, the current high-risk conditions of fire-prone western federal forests were not envisaged when the ESA was written in 1973. Equally clearly, new knowledge and insights require a broader concept of precaution in management and governance that facilitates the risk balancing demanded by current and foreseeable forest conditions. Conserving 'the ecosystems upon which endangered species and threatened species depend' demands no less.

## ACKNOWLEDGEMENTS

We thank James K. Agee, Professor of Forestry, University of Washington, and Jay O'Laughlin, Professor, Department of Forest Resources, University of Idaho for their valuable assistance in completing the manuscript. We also thank Boise Cascade LLC for its financial support. Most of all we thank Jack Blackwell, Regional Forester for the US Forest Service California Region, for his critical review of the Northwest Forest Plan and the Sierra Nevada Forest Plan Amendment, which made this study possible.

## NOTES

1    Examples of particularly compelling decisions are Case Nos 03–35279, Gifford Pinchot Task Force v. US Fish and Wildlife Service, 6 August 2004; 99–36027 and 99–36195, Pacific Coast Federation of Fishermen's Associations v. National Marine Fisheries Service, 31 May 2001; and Pacific Rivers Council v. Thomas, 1994.

# REFERENCES

Agee, J. K. (2002) 'The fallacy of passive management: managing for firesafe forest reserves', *Conservation Biology in Practice*, vol 3, no 1, pp18–25

Agee, J. K. (2003) 'Burning issues in fire: will we let the coarse filter operate?', in K. E. M. Galley, R. C. Klinger and N. G. Sugihara (eds) *Proceedings of Fire Conference 2000: The First National Conference on Fire Ecology, Prevention and Management*, Miscellaneous Publication No 13, Tall Timbers Research Station, Tallahassee, FL, pp7–13

Bodansky, D. (1994) 'The precautionary principle in US environmental law', in T. O'Riordan and J. Cameron (eds) *Interpreting the Precautionary Principle*, Earthscan, London, pp203–28

Bosworth, D. (2002) *The Process Predicament: How Statutory, Regulatory, and Administrative Factors Affect National Forest Management*, USDA Forest Service, Washington, DC

Bush, G. W. (2002) *Healthy Forests: An Initiative for Wildfire Prevention and Stronger Communities*, The White House, Washington, DC

Cooney, R. (2004) *The Precautionary Principle in Biodiversity Conservation and Natural Resource Management: An Issues Paper for Policy-makers, Researchers and Practitioners*, IUCN Policy and Global Change Series, no 2, IUCN, Gland, Switzerland and Cambridge, UK

Franklin, J. F. (2003) 'Challenges to temperate forest stewardship – focusing on the future', in D. B. Lindenmayer and J. F. Franklin (eds) *Towards Forest Sustainability*, CSIRO Publishing, Collingwood, Australia, pp1–9

Irwin, L. L. and Thomas, J. W. (2002) 'Policy conflicts relative to managing fire-adapted forests on federal land: the case of the northern spotted owl', in S. A. Fitzgerald (ed) *Fire in Oregon's Forests: Risks, Effects, and Treatment Options*, Oregon Forest Resources Institute, Portland, OR, pp96–107

Mealey, S. P. and Thomas, J. W. (2002) 'Uncharacteristic wildfire risk and fish conservation in Oregon', in S. A. Fitzgerald (ed) *Fire in Oregon's Forests: Risks, Effects, and Treatment Options*, Oregon Forest Resources Institute, Portland, OR, pp85–95

National Research Council (NRC) (1995) *Science and the Endangered Species Act*, National Academy Press, Washington, DC

O'Laughlin, J. (in press) *Conceptual Model for Comparative Ecological Risk Assessment of Wildlife Effects on Fish, With and Without Fuel Treatment*, Forest Ecology and Management (accepted November 2004)

Raustiala, K. (2002) 'Precaution in the federal legislation of the NAFTA parties', in *Report No. 10*, North American Environmental Law and Policy, Commission for Environmental Cooperation of North America, Montreal, pp195–218

Rey, M. and Scarlett, P. L. (2004) *June 9, 2004 Letter to Barry T. Hill, Director, Natural Resources and Environment, General Accounting Office*, United States General Accounting Office Report GAO-04-705, Washington, DC, pp82–85

Roloff, G. J., Mealey, S. P., Clay, C. L. and Barry, J. (2004) 'Evaluating risks associated with forest management scenarios in areas dominated by mixed severity fire regimes in southwest Oregon', in *Proceedings of the Conference. Mixed Severity Fire Regimes: Ecology and Management*, 17–19 November, Spokane WA, Washington State University, Pullman, WA

Roloff, G. J., Mealey, S. P., Clay, C., Barry, J., Yanish, C. and Neuenschwander, L. (in press) *A Process for Modelling Short- and Long-term Risk in the Southern Oregon Cascades*, Forest Ecology and Management (accepted November 2004)

Ruhl, J. B. (2004) 'The battle over Endangered Species Act methodology', *Environmental Law*, vol 34, no 2, pp555–603

Salwasser, H. J. (2003) 'Closing comments', in *Proceedings of the Conference: Risk Assessment for Decision-making Related to Uncharacteristic Wildfire*, Portland, OR, 17–19 November, Oregon State University, Corvallis, OR

Schmidt, K. M., Menakis, J. P., Hardy, C. C., Hann, W. J. and Bunnell, D. L. (2002) 'Development of coarse-scale spatial data for wildland fire and fuel management', *Gen. Tech. Rep. RMRS-87*, Fort Collins, CO, USDA Forest Service, Rocky Mountain Research Station

Stewart, R. E., Walters, L. C., Balint, P. J. and Desai, A. (2004) *Managing Wicked Environmental Problems*, 30 March, unpublished report to Jack Blackwell, Regional Forester USDA Forest Service, Pacific Southwest Region, George Mason University, Fairfax, VA

Thomas, J. W. (2003) *Northwest Forest Plan Review. Plans and Reports: Application of the Northwest Forest Plan in National Forests in California*, 25 July, unpublished report to Jack Blackwell, Regional Forester USDA Forest Service, Pacific Southwest Region, University of Montana, Missoula, MT

Thomas, J. W., Forsman, E. D., Lint, J. B., Meslow, E. C., Noon, B. R. and Verner, J. (1990) *A Conservation Strategy for the Northern Spotted Owl: A Report of the Interagency Scientific Committee to Address the Conservation of the Northern Spotted Owl*, USDA Forest Service and USDI Bureau of Land Management, Fish and Wildlife Service, National Park Service, Portland, OR

US Department of Agriculture Forest Service (2001) *Record of Decision: Sierra Nevada Forest Plan Amendment Environmental Impact Statement*, January, USDA Forest Service, Pacific Southwest Region, Vallejo, CA

US Department of Agriculture Forest Service (2003) *Northwest Forest Plan Review: Plans and Reports*, June 23–27, Northwest Forest Plan Review, Pacific Southwest Region Findings, USDA Forest Service, Pacific Southwest Region, Vallejo, CA

US Department of Agriculture and US Department of Interior (1994) *Record of Decision for Amendments to Forest Service and Bureau of Land Management Planning Documents Within the Range of the Northern Spotted Owl (Northwest Forest Plan)*, USDA and USDI, Portland, OR

US Department of Agriculture and US Department of Interior (2003) *Draft Supplemental Environmental Impact Statement. To Remove or Modify the Survey and Manage Mitigation Measure Standards and Guidelines*, USDA and USDI, Portland, OR

US Fish and Wildlife Service (2004) 'Northern spotted owl five year review: Summary and evaluation', 15 November, unpublished report, Region 1, US Fish and Wildlife Service, Portland, OR

US Fish and Wildlife Service and National Marine Fisheries Service (1998) *Endangered Species Act Consultation Handbook: Procedures for Conducting Activities under Section 7 of the Endangered Species Act Consultation and Conference*, Final ESA Section 7 Consultation Handbook, March 1998, Washington, DC. See www.fws.gov/endangered/consultations/s7hndbk/toc-glos.pdf

US General Accounting Office (GAO) (2004) *Forest Service and BLM Need Better Information and Systematic Approach for Assessing the Risk of Environmental Effects*, United States General Accounting Office GAO-04-705, Washington, DC

Williams, S. and Hogarth, W. T. (2002) *Evaluating the Net Benefits of Hazardous Fuels Treatment Projects. Memorandum to Regional Directors, Regions 1–7; Manager,*

*California and Nevada Operations; and Regional Administrators, NOAA Fisheries,* US Department of Interior and US Department of Commerce, Washington, DC

Wirth, D. A. (2002) 'Precaution in international environmental policy and United States law and practice', in *Report No. 10*, North American Environmental Law and Policy, Commission for Environmental Cooperation of North America, Montreal, pp221–68

Section Four

# The Precautionary Principle
# and Local Livelihoods

# 13

# People, Parks and Precaution: The Evolution of the Precautionary Principle in Wildlife Conservation in India

*Nanki Kaur, C. S. Silori, Nupur Chowdhury and M. A. Khalid*

## INTRODUCTION

Precaution has emerged as a response to growing appreciation of the scientific uncertainties surrounding threats of irreversible or serious environmental degradation or biodiversity loss (Perrez, 2002). When discussing threats to conservation in this chapter, we use the term threat to encompass: *direct threats*, which directly stress the biological components of natural ecosystems; *indirect threats*, which drive the direct threats; and *underlying causes* (following CBD, UNEP/CBD/SBSTTA/9/INF/3). To take a concrete example: illegal hunting of wildlife poses a direct threat to wildlife conservation; an indirect threat driving it may be illegal markets for wildlife products; and underlying causes may include poverty and policy failures. Determining the impact or potential impact of threats on wildlife conservation is often difficult. Scientific uncertainty frequently surrounds the qualitative description of threats and assessment of their magnitude and likelihood, stemming from the ecological system itself, from the assessment mechanism or process, and/or from socio-economic and political factors related to use of biodiversity/natural resources. This chapter takes an interdisciplinary approach to scientific uncertainty, which includes social and political science.

The traditional 'formal' (state-initiated and led) means of implementing precaution in conservation and natural resource management has heavily relied on restrictive, protectionist conservation approaches. Such approaches have relied on top-down state control and, in order to minimize complexities, have often relied on automatic links between biological indicators of threat (such as species status) and specific management responses (such as prohibitions on use) (Cooney, 2004). An example of such an approach is a protected area, defined by the CBD as a 'geographically defined area, which is designated or regulated to achieve specific conservation objectives' (CBD, Article 2). Protected areas are viewed as fundamental elements in precautionary approaches to conservation, acting as benchmarks for and buffers to the impacts of human use of natural resources (CBD, UNEP/CBD/SBSTTA/9/INF/3). Within the framework of protected areas, national parks are seen as the cornerstone of the world's conservation efforts (Child, 2004), and are typically perceived and managed as 'wilderness areas' where there is no significant human impact and where the place of humans is restricted to visitors. This chapter focuses on protected areas as a means to implement a precautionary approach to conservation threats.

The implementation of these restrictive approaches has, however, raised a number of problems for people and conservation. Implementation of top-down approaches based on restricting access to natural resources has led to significant adverse impacts on local communities. In particular, they have impacted on communities that value and rely on wild resources within protected areas for their contribution to livelihoods in terms of fuel wood, fodder, dietary supplements and income (Kothari et al, 1989; Badola, 1998; Sharma, 1998; Baviskar, 1999; Singh and Rawat, 1999; Badola and Hussain, 2003). These adverse livelihood impacts have in turn raised major and unforeseen threats to conservation in the form of park–people conflicts (Saberwal et al, 1994; Saberwal and Kothari, 1996; Sekhar, 1998; Maikhuri et al, 2000), the loss of local incentive to conserve resources and support conservation initiatives (Kothari et al, 1995), and the loss of traditional ecological knowledge[1] (TEK) practices and institutions aimed at conservation (Machlis, 1992; Gadgil et al, 1993).

TEK practices may include the monitoring of the status of the resource, affording protection through the preservation of keystone species, protection of habitats through sacred groves, or seasonal and periodic restrictions on the gathering of forest resources (Berkes et al, 2000). In consequence, protectionist measures aimed at addressing and buffering uncertainty surrounding risks to wildlife conservation have been undermined by increased incidences of poaching, illicit felling of trees, grazing, electrocution of wildlife in national parks, unsustainable use of resources, and enforcement failures (Saberwal et al, 2001; Kothari et al, 1989).

In order to address these unexpected problems resulting from wider social dimensions of conservation threats, 'alternative' and adaptive management approaches are increasingly being applied to implement the precautionary principle. Alternative management reorients environmental protection discussions from problems to solutions and seeks to identify, assess and implement alternatives to high-risk activities (Tickner and Geiser, 2004). An alternative approach to high-risk local resource-use activities is designed to promote coexistence between people and wildlife on the basis that local subsistence may be safeguarded without necessarily involving the extractive use of natural resources (Mishra et al, 2003). A conservation example of alternative management is programmes that aim at providing an alternative to resource-dependent livelihoods through alternative income-generating activities, fuel sources and so forth. This approach does not 'waste time' in determining beyond doubt that local resource use is a risk – if there is some evidence of a threat it emphasizes a search for alternatives to reduce the risk. So if grazing poses a potential threat to wildlife in a protected area, fodder is provided from buffer areas or through markets at a subsidized rate.

Adaptive management relies on careful monitoring to provide continuous feedback to inform and guide management strategies that deal with uncertainty in high-risk activities (Lee, 1999). Because ecologically adaptive TEK practices help monitor, interpret and respond to dynamic changes in ecosystems and the resources and services that they generate, adaptive management incorporating TEK also reduces the uncertainty around conservation threats. A fundamental characteristic of these approaches is participation, ensuring a means of eliciting the 'values' and the perspectives of the community involved so that the multiple dimensions of risk can be taken into account early on in the assessment of threats (Amendola, 2001) or in the management of threats.

The chapter focuses on precautionary approaches to wildlife conservation in India, examining the extent to which these address the broader, socially mediated dimensions of threats to conservation. It focuses specifically on the threat of local resource use within protected areas, and examines uncertainties related to this threat, and the extent to which India has implemented adaptive and/or alternative management based on participation to mitigate such uncertainty and manage the threat. The analysis is based on a review of literature, legal and policy documents and case law, as well as a case study in one protected area.

## THE PRECAUTIONARY PRINCIPLE AND WILDLIFE CONSERVATION IN INDIA: A PROGRESSION IN THINKING

This section assesses the application of the precautionary principle in wildlife conservation in India. It begins by focusing on implicit guidance provided by the policy and management framework regarding the management of scientific uncertainty surrounding the threat to wildlife posed by local resource use. This guidance in India can broadly be divided into two phases: guidance implementing a protectionist approach and guidance implementing an alternatives-based approach. The section then examines a case study illustrating these dynamics in practice in Pench National Park, Madhya Pradesh, focusing on the Totladoh fishing case.

## Protectionist application of the precautionary principle

An implicit application of the precautionary approach to manage scientific uncertainty in the threat posed by local resource use on the status of wildlife may be found in the pre-colonial, colonial (1858–1947) and post-colonial (1970–90) period in India.

During the pre-colonial and the colonial period, wildlife was valued by the state primarily for its utilitarian value. The impact of local resource use on the status of wildlife was perceived as a threat and was mitigated through protectionist measures. For instance, during the Mauryan period (250 BC) the elephant was valued by the state for its utility in war and as a status symbol. Based on these values, all competing resource-use practices impacting elephants and their habitats, like local resource use and poaching, were defined as threats. The *Arthashastra*, containing maxims of ancient statecraft, guided the management of such threats through the establishment of protected forests, the subjugation of forest tribes, and the imposition of fines and capital punishment for poaching and slaying elephants (Rangarajan, 2001).

Similarly, during the colonial period, wildlife was valued by the administration and the princely states primarily for its game value. Hunting, local resource use and management practices were identified as the main threats to wildlife, leading to rarity of valued game species. In order to manage such threats the state implemented protectionist management policies and frameworks that attempted to suppress local rights to natural resource use by bringing those resources under the ownership and control of the state. One of the earliest examples of such a consolidated act is the Indian Forest Act of 1927, which brought forests under state control.

In the post-colonial period, beginning in the 1970s, a landmark decade for wildlife conservation, the attitudes of the scientific and urban political communities placed an increased value on wildlife per se (Rangarajan, 1996). During this period, hunting, trade, habitat conversion and overexploitation of natural resources were identified as the major threats to wildlife conservation. Local resource-use practices, lack of effective regulatory policies and agendas driven by development priorities were in turn identified as the main driving forces behind those threats. The scientific uncertainty surrounding the threats related mainly to the difficulty in determining their impact and probability of their occurrence. In order to mitigate this scientific uncertainty, a range of legal, policy and management measures, implicitly precautionary in nature, were developed.

In 1972, India adopted a comprehensive national law, the Wildlife (Protection) Act (WLPA), intended solely to protect wildlife. In the 'Statement of objects and reasons', the Act states:

> *the rapid decline of India's wild animals and birds, one of the richest in the world, has been a cause of great concern. Some wild animals and birds have already become extinct in this country and others are in danger of being so.*

It then goes on to state that there is therefore 'an urgent need to ... provide for the protection of wild animals and birds'. Although there is no explicit mention of the precautionary principle in the Act, it does identify as the status quo a rapid decline in wildlife and the resultant threat of extinction, and focuses on protection as a mechanism to deal with threat. In dealing with the scientific uncertainty surrounding the impact of threats to wildlife conservation, the Act mandates the implementation of a host of precautionary measures including a ban on hunting, strict regulation of trade in wildlife, and the establishment of a protected area network. For instance, Article 36(6) reverses the burden of proof: it does not allow any person to 'destroy, exploit or remove any wildlife from a national park or destroy or damage the habitat of any wild animal', unless the Chief Wildlife Warden is convinced that the removal of wildlife is necessary for the better management and improvement of wildlife.

It is important to note that the Act appears to allow room for issues of local equity to guide decisions under the Act. For instance, Article 36(6) goes on to say that in such cases a permit can be issued for the removal of wildlife in order to meet the personal, bona fide needs of the people living in and around the sanctuary, but not for commercial purposes. If TEK was accepted as a basis to demonstrate that removal would lead to better management of wildlife, this could allow for local participation in the identification and management of resource-use threats and facilitate adaptive management. However, in its current application, implementation of Article 36(6) does not appear to have facilitated local participation in decision-making on these threats.

The protected area (PA) network is the central component of India's wildlife conservation programme. It is comprised of national parks and sanctuaries (and has recently been expanded to include community and conservation reserves). The PA network includes 578 wildlife protected areas covering 4.7 per cent of the country's geographical area (Rodgers et al, 2002). Of this, national parks constitute 1.17 per cent of the country's geographical area (National Wildlife Database, 2004) and are based on the concept of 'core zone management', excluding all human activity within core areas. Within national parks, which are established to afford protection to an area that has significant conservation value (Article 35(1)), the level of precaution implemented through a protectionist approach is significant. The guidance under this approach mandates that all land rights must be vested with the state (Article 35(4)(b)), and that all extractive measures are to be prohibited, including the collection of minor forest produce (MFP) and livestock grazing.

Complementing the WLPA, which affords protection to ecosystems or habitats protecting a number of species automatically, protection is also imparted to specific species under programmes like Project Tiger, which keep the habitat of protected species free of biotic pressures that have the potential to lead to species loss (Upadhyay and Upadhyay, 2002; see also MEF, undated).

Thus, apart from managing the impact of a host of other identified conservation threats, these measures also aim at managing the potential adverse impact of local resource use in driving wildlife loss. These measures implement a protectionist approach restricting local resource-use practices of livestock grazing and/or the collection of MFP.

## Participatory and alternatives-based precautionary approaches

Following the emergence of unforeseen threats raised by protectionist strategies in terms of park–people conflicts, India has recently changed its approach and attempted to implement participatory alternatives-based strategies for the conservation of wildlife. Though these strategies do not explicitly incorporate the precautionary principle, they aim at responding to the social dimensions of uncertainty surrounding threats to conservation and are implemented through use of alternatives-based policy and management tools often associated with the precautionary principle (Tickner and Geiser, 2004). Such an approach may be defined as an implicit means to implement a proactive precautionary strategy that aims at avoiding future dependency and conflict.

This shift towards a more participatory approach to wildlife conservation began in the 1990s (Panwar, 1990, 1992; Kothari et al, 1995), incorporating the values of diverse stakeholder groups. Such values include the conservation of wildlife per se (as identified by the state and some of the scientific community), but also the livelihood needs of local communities (as identified by the increasingly empowered local communities, some of the scientific and donor community, politicians representing diverse political parties, and mass tribal organizations). This has been motivated primarily by widespread conflict generated by protectionist approaches at the local level (Greenough, 2004), which has undermined the objective of conservation in most national parks. It responds also to recent socio-political trends in the country, which include the decline of the ruling single majority, a strengthened multi-party system (Pantham, 2003) and vibrant social movements (Fuchs and Linkenbach, 2003), which have brought local and tribal agendas related to resource use to the forefront of decision-making.

In consequence, there is now a growing recognition of the role played by social factors underlying and driving these threats. Socio-political and economic systems remain in a constant state of flux and have a major influence on the acceptance of biologically informed regulatory and governance systems. It has become increasingly difficult to assume a cause-and-effect relationship between biological indicators of threats (such as species status) and specific management responses (such as protected areas or prohibitions on use). Given the underlying scientific uncertainties and the various and competing values connected to conservation, decision-making on conservation threats has become a political process exposed to vigorous lobbying from groups with varied political agendas.

Despite recognition by formal management mechanisms of this complexity in values and drivers of threats, the identified threats to wildlife conservation remain more or less the same as those identified by the WLPA. However, the diverse values attached to wildlife are addressed through participation in alternatives-based approaches to dealing with conservation threats. The shift toward participatory alternative approaches is reflected through the policy and management framework, comprised of national policies and action plans. It is important here to note that national policies are critical in this context. Since the WLPA (1972) leaves significant room for the exercise of administrative discretion, any policy-guiding tool on this issue is important. National policy initiatives on wildlife include the Wild Life (Protection) Amendment Act [of 2002], the Ministry of Environment and Forests' National Wildlife Action Plan (2002–16), Wildlife Conservation Strategy (2002), and the newly released National Environmental Policy (NEP) (draft).

The WLPA Amendment established Conservation Reserves (Article 36A) and Community Reserves (Article 36C) on government and community land respectively. Such reserves are established in consultation with local communities, whose representatives also participate in the management committees.

One of the identified priority projects under the National Wildlife Action Plan is the 'preparation of time bound programs to assist voluntary relocation and rehabilitation of people living in national parks and sanctuaries'. This statement draws a causal connection between wildlife conservation and encroachment of habitat. People living within national parks and sanctuaries are therefore identified as threats leading to a loss of wildlife. The Action Plan guides the mitigation of this threat by providing a possible solution, that of rehabilitating such people.

The Wildlife Conservation Strategy makes two important comments. First, it states that, while strengthening protective measures against threats to wildlife, adequate attention should also be paid to newer threats, such as toxic chemicals and pesticides. This statement is a clear reflection of the need felt by the government to give equal weight to the significance of non-human threats. Second, it states that the interest of the poor and tribal people living around protected areas should be handled with sensitivity and maximum participation of the affected people. This is an important policy directive since it calls for a participatory approach to threat management (if not identification of threats).

The NEP explicitly recognizes the precautionary principle as a guide to the activities of the different sectors specified in it, including the sections on 'forest and wildlife' and on 'biodiversity, traditional knowledge and national heritage'. The NEP reaffirms the threats that lead to forest loss as set out under the WLPA. These include: conversion of forested land to agriculture settlements; infrastructure and industry; commercial extraction of fuel wood; illegal felling; and grazing of livestock. The NEP also reaffirms the previous approach to mitigate such activities through increased protection, aiming to:

> strengthen the protection of areas of high endemism of genetic resources (biodiversity hotspots), while providing alternative livelihoods and access to resources to local communities who may be affected thereby.[2]

The NEP therefore does provide for stakeholder participation in threat management – however, it denies participation in threat construction and assessment. This translates into local resource use still being perceived necessarily as a threat to wildlife conservation. However, local communities are involved in the identification of alternative strategies to their existing resource-use practices, so that the threat to wildlife is mitigated and future local dependency is either reduced or met through other resources – thus leading to the reduction in conflict.

At a management level, India has implemented a strategy of alternative development or management to address local values attached to wildlife and wild habitats in national parks. This aims at reducing the impact of local dependence on natural resources. An example is the India Ecodevelopment programme that emerged in the 1980s. The concept of ecodevelopment aimed at complementing the existing protectionist strategy, which was under threat due to conflict created as a result of inequitable social impacts. Ecodevelopment aims to provide alternatives to resource-use practices and alternative income-generating avenues through the participation of various stakeholder groups to overcome unsustainable and incompatible resource-use practices in and around PAs (Badola et al, 2002). Such management strategies thus aim at addressing the indirect threats of poverty and traditional dependency that drive direct threats of resource use within the core area. They also aim at building a local support base for conservation activities – an attempt to mitigate conflict and undermine the factors that threaten conservation outcomes through eroding political support.

The courts have also, to some extent, reflected this shift of approach. The Supreme Court of India has played an important role in the environmental protection of the country and has strengthened the constitutional mandate that explicitly states the national commitment to protect and improve the environment. The Supreme Court has explicitly incorporated the precautionary principle as the law of the land in respect of the so-called 'brown judgements'[3] (referring to judgements on environmental pollution control), requiring the government authorities to anticipate, prevent and attack the causes of environmental pollution. In this context the principle has supported reversal of the burden of proof to the developer or industrialist to show that his or her actions are environmentally benign.[4]

In the context of the potential threats of local resource use within protected areas, the Supreme Court has adopted an alternative development approach that is to an extent participatory in nature (primarily in the process of threat management). In Pradeep Krishen versus Union of India,[5] the petitioner challenged the commercial exploitation of minor produce (a right granted by the state government), especially tendu (*Diospyros melanoxylon*) leaves from sanctuaries and national parks, claiming it would disturb flora and fauna and affect the ecosystems of the sanctuaries. The Court held that:

> the total forest cover is far less than the ideal minimum of one
> third of the total land – and if one of the reasons for the shrink-

*age is the entry of villagers and tribals living in and around the sanctuaries and national parks – there can be no doubt that urgent steps must be taken to prevent ... damage to the environment.*

These steps amount to the final notification of the area as a national park and government acquisition of all rights to land, resource use, public way or common pasture. These rights are acquired by awarding compensation in land, money or alternative public way or common pasture. The underlying logic for awarding compensation is therefore to make available adequate funds for the awardees to engage in alternative livelihoods, thus relieving the pressure on the national parks. It is therefore an example of the alternative development approach.

Similarly, in the Totladoh fishing case (discussed below) the Court stated that any attempts to preserve the fragile ecology of the forest area must be reconciled with the right of the tribals to earn a livelihood. It drew an uneasy balance between tribal rights and an exclusionist environmental protection policy with recourse to the provision of alternative livelihoods. The Court therefore also chose an alternative development approach by firstly recognizing the claims of the tribals in terms of fishing rights and then directing the forest department to settle the claims by way of compensating the claimants before declaring it a national park.

The progression of thinking, policy and management set out above is summarized in Table 13.1. This table depicts the progression in the application of the precautionary principle in wildlife conservation in India, highlighting the values attached to wildlife by diverse stakeholders, threats identified, the scientific uncertainty involved, and the management strategies adopted.

# PENCH NATIONAL PARK: A CASE STUDY

## The area

Pench National Park (in the state of Madhya Pradesh) has an area of 292.85km$^2$ (see Figure 13.1). In 1983 it was first carved out of the Pench Sanctuary (created in 1977): the initial step in its declaration as a National Park. In 1992 the National Park was notified as the 19th Reserve in the Project Tiger network (Jain, 2001).

## Conservation and livelihood values

Both conservation and local livelihood values are attached to the park. Located in Madhya Pradesh, which harbours 19 per cent of India's tiger (*Panthera tigris*) population, the area covered by Pench represents much of the Central Indian Highlands' diversity of flora and fauna, making it of significant conservation value (Pench Management Plan, 2001). The forests of the park include moist deciduous teak forest and moist deciduous teak-dominated miscella-

**Table 13.1** *Application of the precautionary principle to wildlife conservation in India*

| Time period | Values attached to wildlife | Threat | Scientific uncertainty | Policy/management strategy | Stakeholder |
|---|---|---|---|---|---|
| Pre-colonial | Utilitarian | Competing resource use | Threat assessment (impact of threat) | Protectionism | State |
| Colonial | Game | Hunting and local pressure | Threat assessment (impact of threats) | Protectionism | British administration and Princely States |
| Post-colonial (1970–90) | Conservation of biodiversity | Hunting, conversion of land, local pressure | Threat assessment (underlying biological state, impact of threats) | Protectionism | State and scientific community |
| Post-colonial (1990–current) | Conservation and livelihoods | Illegal hunting, habitat loss, trade, local resource use and the impact of social systems | Threat assessment (biological state, impact of social systems, magnitude and likelihood of threat) and qualitative description of threats (emergence of diverse values) | Protectionism and alternative management | State, scientific community, Supreme Court, local and political actors |

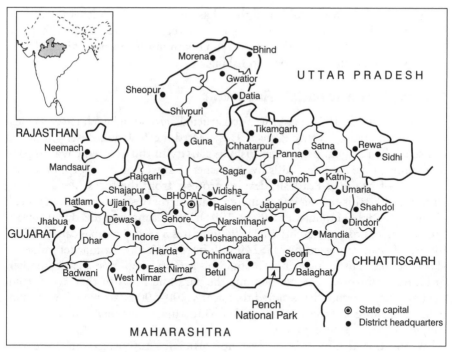

*Source:* adapted from www.mapsofindia.com

**Figure 13.1** *State of Madya Pradesh, India, showing location of Pench National Park*

neous forest. The area also supports a sufficient prey base for flagship species, like the tiger, and is the habitat for many other species protected under national law, such as the Indian bison (*Bos gauras*), leopard cat (*Felis bengalensis*), Indian wild dog (*Coun alpinus*), sloth bear (*Melursus ursinus*) and the freshwater crocodile (*Crocodilus palustris*) (Schedule I, WLPA, 1972). The area also harboured elephant (*Elephas maximus*), black buck (*Antelope cervicapra*) and cheetah (*Acinonyx jubatus*) populations, which are now locally extinct (the cheetah is extinct in India).

The park supports local livelihoods and is thus valued for its resources. Ninety-nine villages surround the park, consisting mainly of Gond tribal communities. These communities have been traditionally dependent on the forests. Under the colonial administration such dependence included local resource-use practices and resource-use rights (*nistaar*), like shifting cultivation, unrestricted grazing and timber harvesting. Current local resource-use patterns include grazing and the collection of non-timber forest products (NTFPs) and medicinal plants. Tendu, grass, gum and aonla (*Emblica officinalis*) are collected for commercial and large-scale harvest, and fruits, fibres, mahua (*Madhuca indica*) flowers, honey, wax and medicinal plants are collected for subsistence use and for sale in the local market. In addition, fishing in the park has been an important economic activity.

Since the park was established there has been an ongoing level of conflict between park authorities and local people regarding access to the park resources (Chief Wildlife Warden, personal communication). This is elaborated in more detail with respect to fishing.

## Fishing in the Totladoh Reservoir

Between 1974 and 1987 a dam was constructed across the Pench River as part of the Pench Hydro Electric Project. This created the Totladoh Reservoir in the centre of the national park area. Fishing activity in this reservoir was apparently initiated in the late 1980s by the Fisheries Development Corporation of the State of Madhya Pradesh, despite protests from the forest department. Until recently, this fishing constituted a major activity supporting many local villagers (Pench Management Plan, 2001). An estimate made during peak (unauthorized) fishing activities in 1994 indicates a record annual catch of 700 tonnes of fish, representing US$240,000 in royalties and a market value of US$1 million. Our findings indicate that this activity supported a large number of locals both from areas surrounding the park and areas further away from the park. Local respondents stated that nearly 300–500 boats were involved in fishing, earning a daily income of 300–350 rupees per day, which in turn supported 3000–3500 families.

While this fishing was at first not officially authorized, in 1996 the Collector of Chindwara District (Madhya Pradesh) wrote to the Secretary of State, stating that the persons displaced by the dam had traditional fishing rights within the park area and had no other alternative livelihoods. Consequently, under instruction from the State of Madhya Pradesh, in 1996 the Chief Wildlife Warden issued 305 fishing permits to tribal fishermen to fish in the Totladoh Reservoir in lieu of traditional fishing rights, providing a legal sanction to the ongoing activity. This would not have been lawful if the national park had been finally declared. However, while initial establishment of the park had taken place, final notification of a national park requires a process of settling of pre-existing claims over the land and resources, which had not taken place at this stage.

## The Totladoh fishing case

The order of the Chief Wildlife Warden granting 305 fishing permits to tribal communities sparked legal conflict. The order was challenged by an urban-based association of lawyers and other persons concerned with the protection of the environment, leading to the case of Animal and Environmental Legal Defence Fund versus Union of India (Totladoh fishing case)(1997)[6]. The petitioners argued that the issue of 305 permits for fishing was a violation of the WLPA. They argued that fishing at the heart of the park would seriously affect the biodiversity and ecology of the area; that it could also lead to illegal felling of trees or poaching; that effective monitoring would be impossible; and that fishermen could light fires for cooking and other purposes and deposit garbage and polythene bags. As the petitioners' claims relied on potential damage rather than on any clear evidence of imminent or actual harm, they were clearly relying on the precautionary principle to support their case.

However, the Supreme Court recognized that while endeavouring to maintain the ecology of the forest area, the right to livelihood of the tribals formerly living in that area also had to be considered. Their judgement upheld fishing by those affected by the dam as an activity to meet their livelihood requirements. However, in recognition of the need to ensure conservation of the area it also set out a series of detailed conditions for the proper implementation of licence conditions, including the issuance of photo identity cards for permit holders, restrictions on the route travelled while entering and leaving the park, a prohibition on lighting fires and strict monitoring by the state government to ensure that there was no poaching. Finally, it called on the state government to expedite issuance of the final notification of Pench National Park, which would necessarily involve the ending of fishing in the core area.

## Notification of the park and the ban on resource use

Pursuant to the Supreme Court judgement, the process of settlement of claims over resources was initiated and carried out. These tribal claims, including those of the 305 fishing licence holders, were settled by compensation payments. The Pench Management Plan of 2001, developed after this process was completed, imposes strict protection within the core area, including relocation of two villages and a ban on all local resource-use practices and traditional passage within the core area of the park. In particular, all fishing activity within the park, including that of the previous permit holders, was banned. The plan incorporates the provision of alternative livelihood options by incorporating the Ecodevelopment programme as a means to meet local livelihood needs through alternative avenues of income generation and alternatives to resource use.

However, the conflict between park managers and local resource users continues because of ongoing illegal fishing, poaching and logging. In part, this is due to the provision of alternative livelihoods not being a great success. Many of those who previously held fishing rights want them back. We turn now to examine what this case tells us about management responses to uncertain threats to conservation and livelihoods, informed by our interviews and field work in the area.

## Uncertainty, threats and management responses

Examination of this case illustrates that perceptions of threats to conservation vary between groups. The Pench Management Plan and the petition filed in the Totladoh fishing case focus on poaching, livestock grazing, felling, collection of NTFPs, traditional passage through the national park and fishing in Totladoh Reservoir. Local resource uses are viewed as the major threats to conservation. However, our own research in the park found that local residents, by contrast, identified the main threats to wildlife in the areas as poverty and lack of alternative income-generating avenues, leading to illegal logging and unsustainable resource-use practices. This raises the fundamental question of 'who decides?'. Whose viewpoint should be reflected in management responses to the problem?

A high level of scientific uncertainty surrounds the actual or potential impact of local resource-use practices on wildlife. Further, these uncertainties are not simply reducible to biological/ecological factors. For instance, in the case of fishing, the petitioners in the Totladoh case argued that fishing by local people in the heart of the national park would seriously affect the biodiversity and ecology of the area. However, our examination suggests that the impact of fishing, in terms of the amount of fish caught and the extent or frequency of the movement of fishermen within the park, is affected by a complex set of factors. The market demand for fish in the neighbouring city and the increased commercialization of the activity had a large role to play in determining the extent and probability of fishing within the park. Furthermore, the level and impact of fishing is also affected by effectiveness of regulatory/enforcement mechanisms, which is partly dependent on local political support for the regulatory regime in place.

Finally, the case illustrates the different strategies employed in India to manage threats to conservation. Strict protection within the core area imposed by the Pench Management Plan reflects the adoption of a protectionist strategy to protect wildlife. In particular, the Management Plan bans all fishing in order to mitigate its potential impact on wildlife. However, management responses have also incorporated alternatives to resource use to address local livelihood needs based on the Ecodevelopment programme and compensation for lost fishing permits. However, both approaches, each of which could be considered as reflecting a degree of precautionary thinking, still exclude the perspectives of the local resources users themselves in their basic identification and framing of the conservation problem.

## Conservation and livelihood impacts of adoption of a precautionary approach

Precautionary management of threats through the Supreme Court judgement and the Pench Management Plan has resulted in excluding local use and access to natural resources within the national park. It has also resulted in financial losses to local people due to crop and property damage by large herbivores, the impact of which is borne mostly by the poor and marginal landowners (JPS Associates, 2004). These factors have affected local livelihood opportunities and local people's traditional role in the management of natural resources. For instance, in our interviews, village respondents stated that the restrictions placed on local passage through the park imposed by the park authorities adversely impacted the transport of farm products, often leading to their decay and eventually to changed cropping patterns and unemployment in some cases. In terms of management practices, respondents stated that restricted access to natural resources has led to a loss of TEK among the younger generation.

The conservation impacts are ambiguous. Local respondents stated that the blanket ban on fishing has resulted in increased poaching and illegal collection of timber within the core area in order for people to meet basic livelihood needs. Cases of illegal felling and fishing have also been reported during the most recent phase of the India Ecodevelopment programme (JPS Associates, 2004). There has been large-scale opposition to a ban by fishermen, culminating in conflict between park management and locals. Thus the unforeseen threats attached to precautionary protectionist strategies in this case are significant.

## CONCLUSIONS

The study indicates that the application of the precautionary principle in wildlife conservation in India is widespread, although largely implicit. In the context of managing scientific uncertainty related to local use of wild resources, initial implementation of the precautionary principle has taken the form of top-down protectionist strategies guided by the policy and management framework, that is, the WLPA and the Project Tiger programme. It is apparent that these strategies have not had a participatory base, and have reflected the values of only one stakeholder group, the conservationist lobby, in the identification and management of threats.

Due to the adverse impacts of this protectionist approach on local livelihoods, wildlife conservation in India is faced with new and unforeseen threats. These take the form of park–people conflicts, in which potential threats are largely determined by socio-economic factors. In order to address these uncertain threats, the second phase of precautionary application (implicit in nature) has involved alternative management strategies. This approach aims at addressing local priorities by providing alternative resource-use options and income-generating avenues in consultation with local communities

However, implementation of alternative management strategies also, like the protectionist model, presupposes that local resource use necessarily poses a threat to wildlife. It thus does not address or incorporate the diverse values attached to resources and wildlife in its identification of threats. Threats to conservation may be viewed differently according to value judgements and prevailing power structures. By not involving and reflecting these diverse values and perspectives there is a danger that conservation strategies motivated and guided by precautionary tendencies may provoke further unforeseen conservation threats. It is thus suggested that precautionary wildlife conservation strategies should involve participatory adaptive management, incorporating traditional ecological knowledge, in order to ensure local participation in the identification and management of threats and effective monitoring of management interventions.

# ACKNOWLEDGEMENTS

We would like to thank Mr N. S. Dungriyal (Field Director, Pench Tiger Reserve), Mr Subharanjan Sen (Deputy Field Director) and their staff, for the help and guidance provided during the field survey. Our sincere gratitude to Vasant Saberwal, Sunita Dubey and Rosie Cooney for reviewing and commenting on an earlier version of this chapter. We would also like to thank S. K. Pandey, Rajiv Kher, Anirban Ganguly, Pia Sethi and Vikram Dayal for insightful discussions and comments on the paper.

# NOTES

1  Traditional ecological knowledge is defined as a cumulative body of knowledge, practice and belief, evolving by adaptive processes and handed down through generations by cultural transmissions, about the relationship of living beings (including humans) with one another and with their environment (Berkes et al, 2000).
2  The NEP has drawn criticism from several stakeholders on its failure to provide for stakeholder participation and its ignorance on issues of equity considerations that are inherent in the application of the precautionary principle, especially in the case of management of forests and wildlife (see Kothari, 2004).
3  Vellore Citizens Welfare Forum v. Union of India (AIR 1996 SC 2715) and A P Pollution Control Board v. Prof M. V. Nayudu (Retd.) (AIR 1999 SC 812)
4  Tarun Bharat Sangh, Alwar v. Union of India (AIR 1992 SC 514)
5  AIR 1996 SC 2040
6  AIR 1997 SC 1071

# REFERENCES

Amendola, A. (2001) 'Recent paradigms for risk informed decision-making', *Safety Science*, vol 40, pp17–30
Badola, R. (1998) 'Attitudes of local people towards conservation and alternatives to forest resources: a case study from the Lower Himalayas', *Biodiversity and Conservation*, vol 7, no 10, pp1245–59
Badola, R. and Hussain, S. A. (2003) 'Conflict in paradise – women and protected areas in the Indian Himalayas', *Mountain Research and Development*, vol 23, no 3, pp234–37
Badola, R., Bhardwaj, A. K., Mishra, B. K. and Rathmore, B. M. S. (2002) *Ecodevelopment Planning for Biodiversity Conservation: A Guideline*, Wildlife Institute of India
Baviskar, A. (1999) *Assessment of Socio-economic Conditions of People Using Great Himalayan National Park and Wildlife Sanctuary, Final Report*, submitted to the Wildlife Institute of India, Dehradun
Berkes, F., Colding, J. and Folke, C. (2000) 'Rediscovery of traditional ecological knowledge as adaptive management', *Ecological Applications*, vol 10, no 5, pp1251–62

Child, B. (2004) *Parks in Transition: Biodiversity, Rural Development and the Bottom Line*, Earthscan, London

Cooney, R. (2004) *The Precautionary Principle in Biodiversity Conservation and Natural Resource Management: An Issues Paper for Policy-makers, Researchers and Practitioners*, IUCN Policy and Global Change Series, no 2, IUCN, Gland, Switzerland and Cambridge, UK

Fuchs, M. and Linkenbach, A. (2003) 'Social movements', in V. Das (ed) *The Oxford India Companion to Sociology and Social Anthropology, Volume II*, Oxford University Press, Oxford

Gadgil, M., Berkes, F. and Folke, C (1993) 'Indigenous knowledge for biodiversity conservation', *Ambio*, vol 22, no 2–3

Greenough, P. (2004) 'Pathogens, pugmarks, and political "emergency": The 1970s South Asian debate on nature', in P. Greenough and L. Tsing (eds) *Nature in the Global South: Environmental Projects in South and South East Asia*, New Perspectives in South Asian History 7, Orient Longman, Delhi

Jain, P. (2001) *Project Tiger Status Report*, Project Tiger, Ministry of Environment and Forests, Government of India, New Delhi

JPS Associates (2004) *Consolidated Final Report for 7 Protected Areas and Project Tiger Office*, Intensive Project Performance Review, India Eco-Development Project (Phase III), Office of Director (Project Tiger), Ministry of Environment and Forests, Government of India, New Delhi

Kothari, A (2004) 'Draft National Environmental Policy: A critique', *Economic & Political Weekly*, vol 39, no 43, 23 October, pp4723–4727

Kothari, A., Pande, P., Singh, S. and Variava, D. (1989) *Management of National Parks and Sanctuaries in India: A Status Report*, Indian Institute of Public Administration, New Delhi

Kothari, A., Suri, S. and Singh, N. (1995) 'Conservation in India: a new direction', *Economic & Political Weekly*, vol 30, pp2755–2766

Lee, K. N. (1999) 'Appraising adaptive management', *Conservation Ecology*, vol 3, no 2, p3. Available at www.consecol.org/vol3/iss2/art3/

Machlis, G. E. (1992) 'The contribution of sociology to biodiversity research and management', *Biological Conservation*, vol 62, pp161–170

Maikhuri, R. K., Nautiyal, S., Rao, K. S., Chandrasekhar, K., Gavali, R. and Saxena, K. G. (2000) 'Analysis and resolution of protected area–people conflicts in Nanda Devi Biosphere Reserve, India', *Environmental Conservation*, vol 27, no 1, pp43-53

MEF (undated) *Project Tiger*, Ministry of Environment and Forests, Delhi. Available at www.projecttiger.nic.in

Mishra, C., Allen, P., McCarthy, T., Madhusudan, M. D., Bayarjargal, A. and Prins, H. H. T. (2003) *The Role of Incentive Programs in Conserving the Snow Leopard*, Conservation Biology, vol 17, no 6, December

National Wildlife Database (2004) *National Parks*, National Wildlife Database. Available at www.wii.gov.in/nwdc/nparks.htm

Pantham, T. (2003) 'The Indian nation-state from pre-colonial beginnings to post-colonial reconstructions', in V. Das (ed) *The Oxford India Companion to Sociology and Social Anthropology, Volume II*, Oxford University Press, Oxford

Panwar, H. S. (1990) *Status of Management of Protected Areas in India: Problems and Prospects*, paper presented at the Regional Expert Consultation on the Management of Protected Areas in the Asia Pacific Region, organized by FAO Regional Office for Asia and the Pacific, Bangkok

Panwar, H. S. (1992) *Ecodevelopment: An Integrated Approach to Sustainable Development for People and Protected Areas in India*, paper presented in the IVth World Congress on National Parks and Protected Areas, Caracas, Venezuela

Pench Management Plan (2001) *Pench Tiger Reserve Management Plan. Period 1999–2004*, Government of Madhya Pradesh

Perrez, F. (2002) 'Precaution from Rio to Johannesburg: an introduction', in UNEP, *Precaution: From Rio to Johannesburg. Proceedings of a Geneva Environment Network Roundtable*, United Nations Environment Programme, Geneva

Rangarajan, M. (1996) 'The politics of ecology: the debate on wildlife and people in India, 1970–95', *Economic and Political Weekly*, vol 31, pp35–43

Rangarajan, M. (2001) *India's Wildlife History*, Permanent Black, Delhi

Rodgers, W. A., Panwar, H. S. and Mathur, V. B. (2002) *Wildlife Protected Area Network in India: A Review (Executive Summary)*, Wildlife Institute of India, Dehradun

Saberwal, V. K., Gibbs, J. P., Chellam, R. and Johnsingh, A. J. T. (1994) 'Lion–human conflict in the Gir Forest, India', *Conservation Biology*, vol 8, no 2, pp501–507

Saberwal, V. K. and Kothari, A. (1996) 'The human dimension in conservation biology curricula in developing countries', *Conservation Biology* vol 10, no 5, pp1328–31

Saberwal, V. K., Rangarajan, M. and Kothari, A. (2001) *People, Parks and Wildlife: Towards Coexistence*, Orient Longman, Delhi

Sekhar, N. U. (1998) 'Crop and livestock depredation caused by wild animals in protected areas: the case of Sariska Tiger Reserve, Rajasthan, India', *Environmental Conservation*, vol 25, no 2, pp160–71

Sharma, V. (1998) *Dependence of Human Population on Non-Timber Forest Produce, Final Report*, submitted to Wildlife Institute of India, Dehradun

Singh, S. and Rawat, G. S. (1999) *Floral Diversity and Vegetation Structure in Great Himalayan National Park, Western Himalaya, Final Report*, submitted to Wildlife Institute India, Dehradun

Tickner, J. A. and Geiser, K. (2004) 'The precautionary principle stimulus for solutions- and alternatives-based environmental policy', *Environmental Impact Assessment Review*, vol 24, pp801–24

Upadhyay, S. and Upadhyay, V. (2002) *Handbook on Environmental Law: Forest Laws, Wildlife Laws and the Environment, Volume I*, LexisNexis, New Delhi

# 14

# Managing Uganda's Forests in the Face of Uncertainty and Competing Demands: What is the Precautionary Approach?

*Abwoli Y. Banana*

## INTRODUCTION

The sustainable management of forests in Uganda, and elsewhere in the developing world, presents a great challenge not only for forest managers but also for policy-makers. This is because forest ecosystems are complex, and yet the population is heavily dependent upon them as a source of energy, employment, livelihoods, government revenues, business opportunities, environmental functions and services (Republic of Uganda, 2001). Uganda is confronted with the problem of balancing forest conservation and forest exploitation. A major question being asked globally is: how can rural communities use their natural resources (community assets) to enhance community vitality, support sustainable livelihoods and improve their economic and food security, without overexploiting and degrading their resources?

Major causes of unsustainable forest management in Uganda, and in many other developing countries, include:

- inadequate data about the condition of forestry resources;
- limited information about how the management of forestry resources responds to socio-economic and institutional reforms; and
- limited scientific understanding of the complex links between community-level forest resource use, access, management strategies and the condition of forests (for example forest/tree cover dynamics) through space and time.

In addition, complex ecosystems like Uganda's tropical rainforests do not lend themselves easily to long-term predictions of their dynamics. This is because of their great complexity and the non-linear nature of the relationships between their many interacting components (Wilson, 2002).

The precautionary principle is a principle to guide decision-making and management on environmental threats, when the scientific and evidence basis regarding those threats is uncertain or incomplete. It highlights uncertainty and emphasizes that this uncertainty should not be ignored in decision-making, but that action should be taken to avert unknown or poorly understood environmental harms without waiting for adequate scientific data to be made available (Precautionary Principle Project, 2003).

What is the relevance of the precautionary principle to the management of Ugandan forests? There have been calls at international level to apply the precautionary principle to the conservation and management of forests (Brunée and Nollkaemper, 1996; Cotter et al, 2000). At national level, Uganda seeks to implement the 1992 Convention on Biological Diversity (CBD), which includes in its Preamble an exhortation to apply the precautionary approach, and it is also a signatory to the African Convention on Conservation of Nature and Natural Resources (signed in Maputo in 2003, but not yet in force), which strongly emphasizes the obligation of parties to apply the precautionary principle. Decision-makers and managers clearly face a high level of uncertainty, therefore the precautionary principle appears a highly relevant principle for Uganda to consider in forest management. However, the forest sector in Uganda appears not to have explicitly contemplated the precautionary principle: it is not mentioned in the Uganda Forest Act of 1964, the Uganda Forest Policy of 2001 or in the recent Uganda Forest Act of 2003.

How might the precautionary principle translate in practical operational terms in this sector? It has been pointed out that the precautionary principle, to be effective in delivering conservation outcomes, will generally need to be translated into more specific policy frameworks, guidelines, regulations and management guidance (Cooney, 2004). In the forest context, the most obvious and perhaps the most typical way to interpret the precautionary principle is through establishment of strict forest reserves and restrictions on harvesting, in order to ensure that there are large areas of undisturbed forest in a close-to-natural state to maintain species, ecological relationships and ecosystem resilience. While this appears intuitively sensible, in considering and assessing the meaning of a precautionary approach we must examine the real impacts of conservation approaches in the face of both great uncertainty and competing demands for forest use and conservation.

The chapter explores this interpretation of the precautionary approach by providing a selective review of different approaches to forest management in Uganda. In particular the complex impact of different policy and legislative approaches are assessed, including a strict protective approach, in terms of conservation and impact on local people; these policies and approaches are also examined in the light of the precautionary principle.

# POLICIES USED TO MANAGE THE FOREST SECTOR IN UGANDA

Despite the lack of adequate scientific data about forestry resources in the country, the objective of the 2001 Forestry Policy (Republic of Uganda, 2001), was to achieve the sustainable management of forests, woodlands and trees in Uganda, in order to provide ecological and social services, produce economic goods for current and future generations of Ugandans, while at the same time, contributing to the well-being of the global community (Republic of Uganda, 2002). This vision correlates with the objectives of the World Commission on Environment, which defined sustainable development as 'development that meets the needs of the present generation without compromising the ability of future generations to meet their own needs'.

How can this vision be achieved when there is inadequate data about forest resources and limited scientific understanding of the complex linkages between community-level forest resource use and the condition of forests? The government has taken a range of approaches over time to the conservation of forest resources. These policies and legislation include the following:

- colonial-era forest policies that emphasize strict conservation;
- restrictive/prohibition-based forest management practices and legislation;
- policy for the creation of a national permanent forest estate; and
- policy aimed at the decentralization of the management of the forest sector.

These different approached are now addressed in turn.

# COLONIAL-ERA FOREST POLICIES THAT EMPHASIZE CONSERVATION

The British colonial government initiated the scientific management of forest resources in Uganda at the beginning of the 20th century (Uganda Forest Department, 1951). At that time, there was considerable scientific uncertainty surrounding several issues relating to the management of tropical forests. Consequently, early forest policies and legislation on conservation and management of forestry resources included elements that are reflected in the concept of the precautionary principle as it stands today.

The first national Forest Policy of 1929 stressed the environmental role of forests, both directly as a source of economic benefits, and indirectly by their role in modifying the climate, protecting water supplies and preventing excessive soil erosion. This policy downplayed timber production, harvesting and utilization (Kamugisha, 1993). In order to minimize harm to the tropical forest, only salvage harvesting and selective logging, on an 80-year rotation period, were permitted in the tropical high forests.

The subsequent policies of 1939 and 1948 also placed greater emphasis on the conservation of tropical high forests. These policies stressed the need for the establishment of softwood plantations as an alternative source of timber in order to conserve the tropical high forests (Uganda Forest Department, 1951). The colonial government, together with local governments, initiated major afforestation schemes. However, the post-independence Forest Policy of 1970 downplayed the role of forests in the protection of the environment. Instead, it promoted the production, harvesting and utilization of timber.

The outcome of the colonial-era forest policies that emphasized conservation was ecologically positive. The colonial government established a network of central forest reserves and local forest reserves that were well managed using elaborate management plans. Forest rules were monitored and strictly enforced by the forest service. In addition, the colonial government established and built capacity for assessing and systematically collecting scientific data on forests and forestry activities. The information gathered was used to revise forest management plans and to develop a code of forest management practices.

However, such top-down conservationist policies failed to achieve social justice. Local communities felt alienated from forest resources. They neither participated in decision-making nor received direct benefits. Forests therefore contributed little to the welfare and livelihoods of local communities at that time.

# RESTRICTIVE/PROHIBITION-BASED FOREST MANAGEMENT PRACTICES AND LEGISLATION

This section provides a range of examples and illustrations of forest management practices and approaches based on restrictions and prohibitions.

## The policy of 'reserved tree species'

In the 1960s, there were several tree species of commercial importance whose ecology and silvicultural management practices were not well understood. The 1964 Forests Act empowered the minister in charge of forests, through the chief conservator of forests, to protect these species. Such species were classified as 'reserved tree species' and included the mvule or the iroko tree (*Milicia excelsa*) and various species of African mahogany (*Khaya anthotheca* and *Entandrophragma* species).

The objective of this policy was to regulate and restrict harvesting of these tree species to levels that would enhance their population. These species could only be harvested after permission had been obtained from the chief conservator of forests, even if the tree was growing on private land. At the same time, the research section of the Forest Department (FD) put its energy into gathering more information on the ecology and management of these tree species.

On the whole, the outcome of the 'reserved tree species' policy was negative. Over time, the policy of 'reserved tree species' was misused by the

FD staff. Because of suspected corruption and government bureaucracy, obtaining a licence to harvest these species was not only cumbersome, but also very expensive. In addition, the population understood it solely as a negative law that restricted people's access to and use of tree species with a high timber value. It acted as a disincentive for farmers to plant and manage trees on their land because it created considerable uncertainties over tree ownership and tree tenure in the minds of people. Seedlings and saplings of these tree species were cut by farmers and cleared from their landholdings. The law against harvesting these species was repealed in 2003 when the new Forest Act was enacted by the Ugandan parliament.

## Policy restricting the harvesting of hardwood trees from Echuya Forest Reserve

The Echuya Forest Reserve, located in southwestern Uganda, presents a special case of specific restrictions. It is an Afromontane forest. It was first designated as a forest reserve in 1939. At that time, not only was the reserve dominated by bamboo *Arundinaria alpina* (Eggling, 1934), but there was also limited information on the regeneration and establishment of hardwood tree species in this high altitude forest. Under legislation enacted, the harvesting of hardwood trees was prohibited in 1968 (Kingston, 1968; Former District Forest Officer, personal communication).

Today, the bamboo vegetation is being replaced by hardwood tree species (Banana et al, 1993; Davenport et al, 1996; Banana and Tweheyo, 2001). Comparisons of aerial photographs taken in 1954 and 1990, coupled with a recent study by Banana and Tweheyo (2001) show that the area occupied by pure bamboo has decreased from 21 per cent to 13 per cent. In addition, the area covered by a bamboo–hardwood mixture has decreased from 48 per cent to 26 per cent. Correspondlingly, the area under pure hardwood trees has increased drastically from 16 per cent to 51 per cent in the last 50 years. The major species reported to be colonizing the area are moist tropical species such as *Macaranga kilimandscharica*, *Maesa lanceolata* Forssk, *Neoboutania macrocalyx* Pax, *Dombeya rotundifolia* Hoschst, *Nuxia congesta* and *Xymolos monospora*.

From a conservation perspective, the ban on the harvesting of hardwoods was a success because it led to an increase in the area occupied by hardwood trees and an increase in the numbers of these trees. This was the desired outcome of the management policies for the Echuya forest at that time. In addition, the livelihoods of local communities were not negatively affected since they continued to harvest bamboo stems for building poles, firewood and handicrafts. However, today, the rapid displacement of bamboo clumps by hardwood trees is causing concern among ecologists and policy-makers: the restrictions should have been eased in the early 1990s but this was never done (Banana et al, 1993; Davenport et al, 1996; Banana and Tweheyo, 2001).

## The recent ban on harvesting timber from tropical high forests

In order to minimize harm to the forest resource during the early 1990s, when there was a high demand for forest products, the FD banned the harvesting of timber from the central government tropical forest reserves. At the time, there was limited quantitative timber inventory data from forest reserves in Uganda. Timber concessions in tropical high forests were suspended. The population was encouraged to use softwood timber harvested from softwood plantations established by the colonial government in the late 1950s and early 1960s.

In order to determine whether the ban was effective in conserving timber and biodiversity, between 1994/1995 and 1999/2000, forest data was collected from the Mpigi District forest estate (located 25km from Kampala). The data revealed that the ban on harvesting timber from tropical high forests in the 1990s had not been effective since the harvest of timber and fuel wood actually increased between 1994 and 2000 (Banana et al, 2004).

Interviews with local communities and village councils revealed that district forest staff enforced the timber ban selectively. District forest officials fraudulently allowed powerful individuals from within and outside the community to harvest timber illegally. This bred resentment among the poor members of the community. Thus, lack of transparency and corruption by forest officials significantly affected the implementation of the timber ban policy. Since harvesting of timber and charcoal were allowed to continue on private and customary land outside government forest reserves, the local communities continued to access forest products for subsistence.

## The ban on the use of chainsaws in processing hardwood logs into timber

In order to promote efficient processing of saw logs and to reduce the rate of forest clearance by local people, a ban on the use of chainsaws in the felling and sawing of logs in Uganda was put in place in the 1990s and continues to the present day. Individuals are allowed to produce timber using a manual sawing method popularly known as pit sawing. This method uses thin saw blades that produce less waste in the form of sawdust. This method of converting logs is also slow and reduces the rate of forest clearance thereby minimizing harm to the national forest estate.

The enforcement of the ban on the use of chainsaws in processing hardwood logs into timber has, however, not been very successful. The failure to enforce environmentally sound harvesting and processing techniques, including the ban on the use of chainsaws, may be attributed to corruption within the forest service. Unfortunately, until today, Uganda's wood industry sector is characterized by unsustainable harvesting and inefficient conversion by the wood-processing industries (Republic of Uganda, 2001).

# POLICY FOR THE CREATION OF A NATIONAL PERMANENT FOREST ESTATE

There is uncertainty about the rate of loss of forest cover in Uganda. During the formulation of the new Forest Policy of 2001, it was decided that a permanent forest estate should be created as a precautionary measure against loss of forest cover. Mechanisms are being put in place to give incentives to private landowners or communities to 'reserve' land for forestry and keep it under forest cover in perpetuity. This will then form part of the permanent forest estate.

If successful, there will be great conservation advantages to maintaining a permanent forest estate. A well-managed permanent forest estate would ensure continued provision of ecological goods and services and biodiversity conservation. However, the owners of private forested land are the guardians of 70 per cent of Uganda's forests and woodlands. Given the high value of alternative land uses such as grazing and agriculture, much of the private forests are being converted to agriculture or grazing land, with charcoal as a major by-product. Private forests are being acquired as land banks for cash and agriculture or grazing as it is more profitable to deforest than to keep the land permanently under forest cover (Namaalwa et al, 2001). There are very few incentives for individuals to set aside forestland and maintain it as a forest in perpetuity.

# POLICY AIMED AT THE DECENTRALIZATION OF THE MANAGEMENT OF THE FOREST SECTOR

National government forest departments in many developed and developing countries have been notably unsuccessful in their efforts to regulate forestry resource use (Ostrom, 1999, 2001). It is often argued, however, that decentralization of the forest resource is an effective conservation strategy and delivers good conservation outcomes, by avoiding the risks associated with centralized government control of forest resources (Lind and Cappon, 2001).

As part of public sector reform, the Government of Uganda decided to devolve power to lower levels of government following the enactment of the Decentralization Statute of 1994 and the Local Government Act of 1997. The decentralization process involved substantial transfers of political, financial and planning responsibilities from the central government to local governments and their districts and sub-counties. This empowered the local governments to take increasing responsibility for the delivery of services, including forest management.

However, it appears that decentralization of forest resources raises other risks and uncertainties. As mentioned earlier, following decentralization there was a decline in forest conditions in the Mpigi District and elsewhere in Uganda. The decline in forest conditions was caused by a reduction in funding for the forest sector following decentralization, lack of financial and human capacity and corruption by local government officials (Banana et al, 2004). Consequently, enforcement, which is a key to maintaining forests in good condition (Banana and Gombya-Ssembajjwe, 2000; Gibson et al, 2005), declined following decentralization.

Pushed by financial constraints, local governments focused on the provision of traditional social services such as health, education and roads and gave low priority to the forest sector. Therefore, the argument that decentralization of the forest resource is an effective conservation strategy and delivers good conservation outcomes by avoiding the risks associated with centralized government control of forest resources may not always be correct. This conclusion is also backed up by the findings of Ribot (1999), Lind and Cappon (2001) and Ribot and Larson (2004) who point out that the assumption that the decentralization of the management of forestry resources to local communities will result in better environmental practices is not clearly demonstrated.

## How Do these Policies and Legislation Relate to the Precautionary Principle?

Past forest policies in Uganda have alternated between strict conservation policies implemented during the colonial period, the liberal policies of the 1970s that promoted economic use of forest resources, and recent restrictive/prohibition-based forest conservation policies. The overall objectives of the policies and legislation described in this case study are to minimize harm to the forest resource against a background of great uncertainty surrounding most aspects of the forest resource and the impact of its degradation on people. They can all be seen as broadly in line with the functions of the precautionary principle. However, it can be seen that they have been far from universally successful in averting environmental damage. All approaches have an element of exclusion of local communities and consequently bring about complex social costs and benefits.

Analysis of these forest policies and legislation reveals that neither the top-down protectionist approach nor the decentralized co-management approaches have been uniformly effective in averting threats to forests. There are conservation threats and benefits associated with each, and there seems little basis to link conceptions of a precautionary approach to forest management with approaches based on strict protection and exclusion of use. This is because finding ways to restrain or prevent human activity in forest ecosystems without hurting the society, especially its poor, is very difficult, and yet without the support of local communities conservation is unlikely to be successful over the long term. It is clear that the development of a precautionary approach to forest policy and management should take into account the on-the-ground realities of the complex socio-economic pressures on forests. It is also clear that a precautionary policy is not always translated into precautionary practice

– in this regard poor governance and lack of enforcement are major barriers to any precautionary approach.

## CONCLUSIONS AND RECOMMENDATIONS

As a signatory to the Convention on Biological Diversity, the Ugandan Government is committed to the conservation and sustainable use of natural biological diversity. The Government of Uganda has, over the decades, formulated a range of policies and approaches for managing Uganda's forests in the face of the major challenges of uncertainty and the competing burdens of conservation and demand for resources.

Availability of high quality information about the forest sector is essential for the sustainable management of forestry resources. Priority must be given to building capacity for assessing and systematically collecting data on forests and forestry activities so that informed decisions and strategies can be made. New information gathered and lessons learned must be fed back into the decision-making process.

Given that the reality is that poor or incomplete information is the norm, it would be desirable for the precautionary principle to be explicitly incorporated into national forest policy in Uganda. This would enhance awareness of the principle among policy-makers, forestry professionals and private sector entrepreneurs. Parliament would have to make appropriate laws under the Forest Act to implement the principle. This would encourage and enable a range of strategies for increasing available scientific information and reducing threats, including monitoring programmes, the use of performance bonds for large-scale timber concessions, and the development and use of indicators of best practice in the forest sector.

While precaution is important in principle, its impact in practice in the forest sector will be limited without a forest governance system that is transparent and strong enough to monitor regulations that are based upon it, and without a level of support for precautionary conservation measures across a broad range of stakeholders. Corruption in government will seriously undermine the effectiveness of the principle. Furthermore, to be widely implemented and accepted, precautionary measures may need to be based on a process of sensitization and awareness raising among stakeholders such as local communities, policy-makers and forestry professionals.

However, implementation of the precautionary principle should not hurt society, especially the poor. Where restrictive prohibitive approaches are adopted, programmes that mediate their effects on the livelihoods of the local community must be put in place. For example, trade-offs should be made to allow local people to access resources that are vital for their livelihood, while at the same time recognizing the necessity for sustainable forest management. Conservation initiatives cannot be successful as long as the people living adjacent to conservation areas are very poor (Chetri et al, 2004).

# REFERENCES

Banana, A. Y., Kizito, P., Bahati, J. and Nakawesi, A. (1993) *Echuya Forest Reserve and its Users*, Uganda Forest Resources and Institutions Research Centre, Research Paper no 3, Department of Forestry, Makerere University, Kampala

Banana, A. Y. and Gombya-Ssembajjwe, W. (2000) 'Successful forest management: the importance of security of tenure and rule enforcement in Ugandan forests', in C. C. Gibson, M. A. McKean and E. Ostrom (eds) *People and Forests: Communities, Institutions, and Governance*, MIT Press, Cambridge, MA, pp87–98

Banana, A.Y. and Tweheyo, M. (2001) 'The ecological changes of Echuya afromontane bamboo forest, Uganda', *African Journal of Ecology*, vol 39, pp1–8

Banana, A. Y., Vogt, N., Gombya-Ssembajwe, W. and Bahati, J. (2004) *Decentralization, Local Governance, and Forest Conditions: The Case of Forests in Mpigi District of Uganda*, CIPEC Working Paper CWP-05-03, Center for the Study of Institutions, Population, and Environmental Change (CIPEC), Indiana University, Bloomington

Brunnée, J. and Nollkaemper, A. (1996) 'Between the forests and the trees – an emerging international forest law', *Environmental Conservation*, vol 23, no 4, pp307–14

Chetri, P. B., Aboneka, M. and Kyamuhangire, D. (2004) 'Planning income generating activities in conservation: KSCDP Experience', in P. B. Chetri, E. G. Barrow and A. Muhwezi (eds) *Securing Protected Area Integrity and Rural People's Livelihoods: Lessons from Twelve Years of the Kibale and Semuliki Conservation and Development Project*, International Union for Conservation of Nature and Natural Resources, pp98–109

Cooney, R. (2004) *The Precautionary Principle in Biodiversity Conservation and Natural Resource Management: An Issues Paper for Policy-makers, Researchers and Practitioners*, IUCN Policy and Global Change Series, no 2, IUCN, Gland, Switzerland and Cambridge, UK

Cotter, H. J., Johnston, P. and Santillo, D. (2000) *The Precautionary Principle and Forest Exploitation: Implications for the Implementation of the FSC Principle 9*, Greenpeace Research Laboratories Technical Note 08/00, University of Exeter, UK

Davenport, T., Howard, P. and Mathews, R. (1996) *Echuya and Mafuga Forest Reserves*, Forest Biodiversity Report, no 22, Uganda Forest Department, Kampala

Eggling, W. J. (1934) 'Note on the flora and fauna of Uganda', *Uganda Journal*, vol 1, pp51–65

Gibson, C. C., Williams, J. T. and Ostrom, E. (2005) 'Local enforcement and better forests', *World Development*, vol 33, no 2, pp273–284

Kamugisha, J. R. (1993) *Management of Natural Resources and Environment in Uganda. Policy and Legislation Landmarks, 1890–1990*, Regional Soil Conservation Unit/SIDA, Nairobi

Kingston, B. (1968) *Working Plan for Echuya Central Forest Reserve*, Uganda Forest Department, Entebbe

Lind, J. and Cappon, J. (2001) *Realities or Rhetoric? Revisiting the Decentralization of Natural Resources Management in Uganda and Zambia*, African Centre for Technological studies, Nairobi, Kenya

Namaalwa, J. R., Gombya-Ssembajjwe, W. S. and Hofstad, O. (2001) 'The profitability of deforestation of private forests in Uganda', *International Forestry Review*, vol 3, no 4, pp299–306

Ostrom, E. (1999) 'Coping with the tragedies of the commons', *Annual Review of Political Science*, vol 2, pp493–535

Ostrom, E. (2001). 'Commons, institutional diversity of', *Encyclopedia of Biodiversity*, vol 1, pp777–91

Precautionary Principle Project (2003) *What is the Precautionary principle?* Precautionary Principle Project, a partnership of IUCN, TRAFFIC, FFI and ResourceAfrica. Available at www.pprinciple.net/the_precautionary_principle.html

Republic of Uganda (2001) *The Uganda Forestry Policy*, Ministry of Water, Lands and Environment, Kampala

Republic of Uganda (2002) *The National Forestry Plan*, Ministry of Water, Lands and Environment, Kampala

Ribot, J. C. (1999) 'Accountable representation and power in participatory and decentralized environmental management', *Unasylva*, vol 50, pp18–22

Ribot, J. C. and Larson, A. M. (2004) 'Democratic decentralization through a natural resources lens: experiences from Africa, Asia and Latin America', *The European Journal of Development Research*, vol 16, no 1

Uganda Forest Department (1951) *A History of the Uganda Forest Department, 1898–1929*, Uganda Forest Department, Entebbe

Wilson, J. (2002) 'Scientific uncertainty, complex systems, common pool institutions', in E. Ostrom, T. Dietz, N. Dolsak, P. C. Stern and E. U. Weber (eds) *The Drama of the Commons*, National Academy Press, Washington, DC, pp327–59

# 15

# The Precautionary Approach and Local Livelihoods: A Study of a Protected Landscape and Seascape in the Philippines

*Tonie O. Balangue*

## INTRODUCTION

This chapter examines the significance and impacts of the precautionary principle with respect to a protected area in the Philippines, the Peñablanca Protected Landscape and Seascape (PPLS), with particular focus on its implications for local livelihoods. Specifically, the chapter examines the policy and management approach adopted for the protection of the PPLS, particularly the National Integrated Protected Areas System (NIPAS) Act. It assesses whether and how measures for the conservation of the PPLS equate to a precautionary approach, and it examines the implications of this approach for local livelihoods and poverty.

The chapter is based on a review of literature and on a series of discussions that took place among focus groups, as well as on personal interviews held by the Resources, Environment and Economics Center for Studies, Inc. (REECS) with village leaders, members of the PPLS Protected Area Management Board, the local People's Cooperative in Aggugadan Village, Peñablanca, and other key informants, held in August 2004 and February 2005.

# The Peñablanca Protected Landscape and Seascape, Cagayan Province, the Philippines[1]

The PPLS covers 118,108ha in the Municipality of Peñablanca, Province of Cagayan in Region 2, northeast of Luzon Island about 508km north of Metropolitan Manila. It connects with the Sierra Madre Biodiversity Corridor in the south, which is a part of the Northern Sierra Madre Protected Area System that stretches from the Province of Isabela in the north and down to the Province of Quezon in the south. It was established in its current form in 2003, thereby extending the previously established but much smaller protected areas.

The topography of the PPLS is varied, and includes rolling hills and a steeply sloping complex of mountain peaks and ridges in the centre. Land use/cover patterns in the PPLS include agricultural (2310ha), much of it involving irrigation, grassland (2395ha), brush land (15,106ha) and woodland (82,239ha). Woodlands are extensive along the southern and northern boundaries of the park, where approximately half of the area is old growth forest and the other half is secondary forest.

The combined population of the 15 villages found within the protected area was approximately 25,700 in 2000 and is growing at an annual rate of 2.7 per cent (the national growth rate is 2.3 per cent). The dominant ethnic

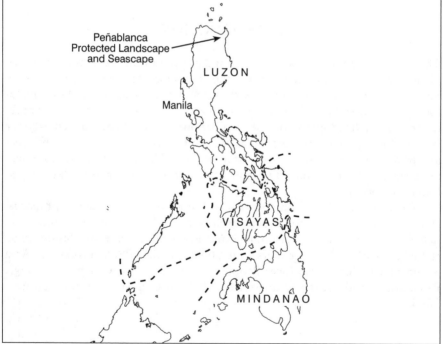

Source: Acay (undated)

**Figure 15.1** *Peñablanca Protected Landscape and Seascape (PPLS)*

groups are the Itawes and Ilocanos. Roman Catholicism is the dominant religion and 85 per cent of the population is literate.

## EXPLOITATION OF PEÑABLANCA NATURAL RESOURCES PRIOR TO NIPAS

Prior to the enactment of the National Integrated Protected Areas System (1992), the forestlands of Peñablanca were open to all forms of natural resource extraction including logging, mining, grazing and slash and burn farming. While slash and burn farming was illegal, law enforcement was not strict. Agriculture, fuel wood collection and charcoal making were not illegal as long as they were carried out by local people and confined to their private lands.

Because of the availability of necessary operational capital, large commercial interests were given priority over local people in access to and the extraction of natural resources. Because of its rich timber stock, two Timber License Agreements (TLA) were issued by the then Bureau of Forestry, to local logging companies that covered 64 per cent (63,000ha) of the total forestland stretching from the forested areas on the western side to the eastern coastal villages of Peñablanca. In about two decades, some 60 per cent of the total TLA area was logged, approximately 40 per cent of the total forestland. In principle, harvesting involved the selective logging of only mature, over-mature and defective trees. In reality, even immature timber was harvested using mechanized and cable logging, this resulted in clear-cutting in most areas. Logging, therefore, was generally destructive especially to soil, wildlife and other elements of the forest. The tenure of TLAs is 25 years, renewable for a further 25 years subject to forestry laws and regulations. No measures such as environmental impact assessment (EIA), which requires the issue of Environmental Compliance Certificates, or monitoring and evaluation of the impact of logging on the forest ecosystem, were mandatory during this period.

This management regime led to extensive destruction of timber stands, soil erosion and damage to wildlife and biodiversity, both as a result of logging operations and road construction. It is widely believed that logging operations caused a substantial reduction in the old growth natural forest from its original area of 98,244ha to 41,968ha. TLA holders abused harvest limits such as annual permissible volumes, limits on the diameter of the cut and the extent of the operable logging area. Permanent deforestation of over-logged areas was accelerated when abandoned logging workers turned to slash and burn farming, involving periodic cutting and burning of regenerating forest species. In any one location, after three to five years only brush and grass species survived and productivity declined, forcing occupants to move to another residual forest to practice the same farming methods. Because of population growth and uncontrolled land-use practices, a substantial area of Peñablanca's forest was converted into grasslands and brush in this way.

Mining is a more economically valuable activity than logging in those areas where valuable mineral stock, such as gold, is located. Any individuals, groups or corporations that were financially capable of mining were granted mining permits in Peñablanca, even in thickly forested areas. Permits were granted by the then Department of Agriculture and Natural Resources (DANR; later Department of Natural Resources, DNR; and later still given its current title, Department of Environment and Natural Resources, DENR) without consultation with the members of the communities, local government units, regional DANR and DNR offices, and other direct stakeholders. The techniques used included open pit and tunnel mining. The former was highly destructive, involving the complete destruction of the vegetation and wildlife habitat and causing extreme soil erosion, but the latter also had a substantial impact on timber because of the need for mine props.

A further threat posed by uncontrolled resource exploitation was river flooding. This was a particularly important consideration for downstream communities who needed to safeguard their houses and corn lands. For them river flooding caused landslides, the scouring of fertile soil and deposition of silt and stones on agricultural land, thereby seriously threatening the food security of some villages.

This policy and management regime was clearly non-precautionary. There were no policy or management measures to assess, control or avert the potentially detrimental impacts of resource extraction. High priority was placed on developing rural areas through resource extraction, providing short-term employment to local people and delivering major gains to business. Little value was placed on flood control, soil fertility and biodiversity. Decision-making was highly centralized, so local concerns and impacts carried little weight. Because of the virtually complete lack of environmental education, awareness or available information and interest, there was in any case practically no local recognition of the environmental and human impacts of uncontrolled resource extraction.

## CHANGES IN ENVIRONMENTAL POLICY IN THE PHILIPPINES: THE NEW CONTEXT FROM THE EARLY 1990S ONWARDS

This policy and management context changed dramatically in the 1990s, with the enactment of major laws and policies both for environmental protection and to support the poor in rural areas. In the environmental context, this happened because of several catastrophes that occurred in the late 1980s and early 1990s in various parts of the country. These were a direct consequence of logging, mining, slash and burn farming and other deforestation activities. The most tragic of these events was the Ormoc tragedy in 1990, in which thousands of people in Ormoc, Leyte Province in the Visayas Islands died in a flash flood. This incident spurred the environmental protection movement into action and helped it to gain ground by advancing new ideas. Specifically, the movement was able to influence policies on the environment and natural resources by arguing in favour of significant reductions in the extraction of natural resources. During this period protected areas, biodiversity conservation, wildlife protection and reforestation were given added emphasis in resource management policies and in grassroots projects. Protected areas were expanded to include the remaining old growth forests, watershed reserves and mangrove reserves.

These areas were proclaimed part of the National Integrated Protected Areas System under the NIPAS Act of 1992. This Act limits the use of protected areas to non-extractive uses that are compatible with the primary use of these areas. NIPAS requires the establishment of buffer zones. These zones are designed both for multiple use by the residents within NIPAS areas and concurrently to protect the area. At the same time, the zoning system identifies areas wherein no development activities of any kind are allowed. To make implementation of this law more effective at the grassroots level, it contains provisions for the creation of a Protected Area Management Board (PAMB), a policy-making, planning body and a clearing house for all kinds of activities to be undertaken within the protected area. The membership of this body is composed of individuals representing different stakeholder interests. The PAMB is also responsible for regularly monitoring and evaluating the activities carried out in all protected areas.

Additionally, the Wildlife Resources Conservation and Protection Act of 2001 provides for the conservation and protection of wildlife resources and their habitats to promote ecological balance and enhance biodiversity, regulate collection and trade of wildlife, and initiate or support scientific studies on biodiversity conservation.

At the same time, the Philippines enacted a series of pro-poor laws aimed at enhancing livelihood opportunities for rural people by providing more secure tenancy rights over the land they occupied and/or the resources on which they were dependent. Previously, access to natural resources utilization was limited to rich individuals and corporations. People from the uplands and coastal people were merely subsistence workers in logging and mining operations. After these operations, most workers were left behind, forced to live there and establish highly destructive slash and burn farms in logged areas.

The pro-poor laws include the 1996 Community-based Forest Management Programme (CBFMP) and the 1997 Indigenous People's Rights Act (IPRA).[2] The CBFMP provides tenure and incentives to develop, utilize and manage specific portions of forestlands. The implementation of this programme has opened up access for people living in the uplands, especially those engaged in slash and burn farming, illegal logging, illegal gathering of fuel wood and charcoal making and other illegal activities, to the development, utilization and management of forest resources. The IPRA allows indigenous peoples access to biological and genetic resources found within their ancestral lands subject to their customary laws on access and management.

Access to NIPAS areas by the local and/or indigenous people under the CBFMP requires a Community-based Protected Area Management Agreement especially in the most strictly protected zones where use is limited to resource rehabilitation, protection and management. Resource utilization is allowed only in the buffer zone. In terms of IPRA and NIPAS, as yet there are no guidelines on how conflicts in resource access can be reconciled. In both cases, use rights provide these people with alternative livelihood opportunities to illegal and destructive forest-based activities like slash and burn farming, timber poaching, fuel wood gathering and charcoal making, and collection of non-timber plant products. Livelihood opportunities include craft making, sales of seedlings and other planting materials and non-timber forest products, as well as animal husbandry.

## DO THESE BROADER LAW AND POLICY DEVELOPMENTS REFLECT OR INCORPORATE THE PRECAUTIONARY PRINCIPLE?

The precautionary principle, or precautionary approach, is not explicitly referred to or incorporated into any of these laws. However, many legal, policy and management measures may be implicitly precautionary – they may operationalize a precautionary approach without referring explicitly to the precautionary principle. A very wide range of specific policy measures may be considered precautionary (see Cooney, 2004), depending on the nature of the threat involved, the level of knowledge surrounding it, where the burden of proof is placed, and the protective action taken.

Relevant Philippines laws on biodiversity and natural resource management include a wide range of protective measures against uncertain threats to biodiversity and resources, which often assume that an action poses a threat unless it meets certain conditions or undergoes an approval process. For example, the NIPAS prohibits hunting, destroying, disturbing and mere possession of any plants or animals or any products derived from them without a permit from the PAMB. Logging, mining, slash and burn farming, gathering of fuel wood and charcoal making are strictly prohibited in protected areas. The Wildlife Resources Conservation and Protection Act prohibits the hunting, collecting or possession of wildlife species, except under narrow specified conditions. The 1978 Environmental Impact Assessment/Statement (EIA/EIS) law means that an EIA is required for all projects that have a high potential for significant negative impact or projects that are to be undertaken in environmentally sensitive areas. Even DENR natural resources rehabilitation projects in watersheds, mangroves and other areas are required to undergo EIA.

However, there also appear to be important gaps with respect to certain potentially serious and irreversible harms. For instance, the CBFMP is silent regarding measures to deal with potential threats to biodiversity, soil and water resources, caused by resource utilization allowed under the programme. The extent to which these laws and policies operationalize a precautionary approach is likely to vary according to context. To understand their impact in the context of the PPLS it is necessary to examine the specifics of this case more closely.

## CURRENT POLICY AND MANAGEMENT OF PPLS: PRECAUTION IN PRACTICE?

The declaration of the PPLS was a direct result of the initiative of national and local government agencies headed by the Department of Environment and Natural Resources (DENR) in Cagayan Province, Region 2 together with leaders of the provincial and municipal governments, the village leaders and the people of Peñablanca, non-governmental organizations (NGOs) and other concerned stakeholders. This effort finally materialized as a result of an information and education campaign conducted by DENR about the negative effects of resource extraction on the environment. This served as an eye-opener to the local people who began to understand the negative impact of the environmental of damage caused by commercial resources extraction. It motivated them to conserve the remaining natural resources and biodiversity for sustainability and environmental stability.

The declaration of the PPLS as part of NIPAS terminated all forms of commercial natural resources extraction. Under NIPAS, all activities undertaken must henceforth be consistent with its primary use as a protected area. Commercial natural resources extraction activities, including logging, mining, fuel wood gathering, charcoal making and other natural resources extraction activities are strictly prohibited. Fuel wood collection and charcoal making for household use are limited only to a buffer or multiple use zone that is located in the immediate vicinity of the residential area in the villages. Grasslands that are rehabilitated or reforested through community-based initiatives under the CBFMP in protected areas, are subject to the issue of a Community-based Park Management Agreement. This is issued to community organizations whose members live within the villages in the PPLS to provide them with livelihoods and enable them to participate in the different rehabilitation and reforestation activities, by performing different tasks that ensure the productivity and sustainability of managed plantations.

In common with other parks in the Philippines, the PPLS is managed by a multi-sectoral board created under the NIPAS, called the Protected Area Management Board. This board includes a wide range of stakeholders, including government and village representatives.[3] All plans and projects have to be reviewed and approved by the PAMB. At the field level, the PPLS is managed by a protected area superintendent and is under the direct supervision of the DNR. Regular meetings of PAMB are conducted and are open to the community.

On the face of it, it appears that these regulations involve the implementation of a strong precautionary approach to natural resource management and biodiversity conservation. All commercial resource extraction is assumed to pose a threat and prohibited, and collection of resources for household use is strictly limited to a buffer zone immediately adjoining villages. Even rehabilitative activities cannot proceed without an assessment of their environmental impact.

## WHAT ARE THE IMPLICATIONS FOR LOCAL LIVELIHOODS AND POVERTY?

The implications of the adoption of these strong protective measures for local livelihoods and poverty are complex and difficult to measure precisely. However, from interviews and focus-group discussions with village leaders and PAMB members,[4] it is possible to draw some broad inferences regarding which resources were most valued by local people, and the benefits and costs to their livelihoods of the protective measures instituted for the PPLS.

In all the communities, the natural resources that were most directly related to food security and life support were perceived as the most valuable. In particular, land/soil, water and fish were very highly valued. Forest cover was highly valued as a mechanism to minimize soil erosion and control water flow. Biodiversity and wildlife, and indeed trees and lumber in themselves, were valued only minimally. This could be explained by the perceived lack of importance and direct benefits of biodiversity and wildlife to their lives. In the case of trees and lumber, they were only perceived as useful for house repair and construction.

Prior to the establishment of the PPLS in 1992, the forest was subject to largely unregulated mining, logging, slash and burn farming, and uncontrolled charcoal and fuel wood extraction. The main benefits to local people under this management were derived from employment (albeit it minimal) in logging and mining operations, although this was often transitory and unskilled. Access to and exploitation of resources, while widespread, were largely reserved for capitalist activities that were mostly non-resident, commercial operations. Major livelihood costs were incurred as a result of destructive flooding, accelerated soil erosion, silting and deviation of riverbeds, and lowered agricultural productivity due to deposition of stones and pebbles from flooding.

Strict protection of the PPLS has had a range of benefits and costs for local livelihoods. On the benefit side, there has been a significant reduction in river flooding, increased water supply for domestic use, reduced soil erosion, reduced deposition of stones and pebbles in fields leading to improved agricultural harvests, and improved water quality (beneficial for fish stocks). These benefits are, however, primarily realized by downstream communities. Furthermore, protected and regenerating habitats and wildlife are starting to increase nature-based tourism to the area, and this is yielding some livelihood benefits for those close to tourist destinations (primarily the Callao Caves). The benefits in upland communities differ from those of the lowland communities in terms of nature and magnitude. Significant reductions in soil erosion, cooler temperatures, cleaner air, increased wildlife populations and pleasant scenic values, have been observed by a majority of the village leaders. The effect of tourism in upland communities is not perceived by most of the village leaders because of the absence of unique tourist spots in their respective villages and because of inferior roads.

Costs include loss of employment in extraction activities, loss of livelihood for the (few) hunters and orchid collectors, and loss of access by charcoal makers and fuel wood gatherers in areas beyond the buffer zone, which have already exhausted their fuel wood stock according to some key informants interviewed. These are particularly important for the people of the upland villages, where few alternative employment opportunities exist.

## PRECAUTION, LIVELIHOODS AND ENVIRONMENTAL PROTECTION: THE COMPLEXITIES AT MANAGEMENT LEVEL

To further explore the dynamics of implementing a precautionary approach and its conservation and livelihood impacts, this section looks beyond macro-level policy and examines on-the-ground management and impacts.

It is clear that there are still some forms of natural resources extraction being undertaken by local people in the PPLS.[5] These include guano extraction (from the Callao Caves), which is being revived by the Cooperative after a three-year moratorium, and illegal extraction of timber and fuel wood and charcoal making in upland villages such as Bugatay, Lapi, Quibal, San Roque, Malibabag and Sisim.

### Guano extraction in the Callao Caves

Until three years ago, permits for guano extraction in the Callao Caves were issued by the Provincial Government Office of Cagayan to the Aggugadan Cooperative only, under a memorandum of agreement between the provincial government and the Department of Environment and Natural Resources, which limited provincial government jurisdiction to ecotourism management of the Callao Caves. This agreement was silent on mining permits inside the Callao Caves (interview with the Protected Area Management Specialist Officer of DENR, Region 2). Under the law, mining permits are issued through the DENR unless they are covered by an agreement that devolves authority to issue the permit. Permits were issued to generate revenue for the provincial government with little apparent technical rationale, and no investigation of potential impacts. Recently, the PAMB decided to stop issuing extraction permits because of administrative inconsistencies and uncertainty regarding potential impacts on bat breeding. During extraction, it was observed that the bat habitat and breeding pattern were affected, thereby driving the bats away. This was the reason why DENR intervened and cancelled the Cooperative's permit to mine the guano in Callao Caves. Furthermore, the benefits from the guano that went to the Cooperative were not high because it was being sold as raw material for fertilizer to buyers in other municipalities, thereby losing internal employment benefits. This had a major impact on the Aggugadan Cooperative, which relied on guano extraction as one of its sources of revenue. Since then, members have continued to seek approval for guano extraction.

At the time of writing, a final decision had not been made by the PAMB. Such extraction appears inconsistent with the nature of a strictly protected area. However, extraction was also viewed by PAMB members as involving a range of interlinked conservation and livelihood benefits. If guano is processed within Peñablanca for organic fertilizer for rice and corn production, as compared to synthetic, more expensive, inorganic fertilizers, a higher net benefit could be realized. Reduction of the quantity of guano in the Callao Caves also reduced unpleasant odours thought to discourage tourists from visiting the area, and prevented unwanted seepage of guano into the river, which affects water quality.

The NGO members of PAMB have recommended that there is a need for a further study of the trade-off of guano mining versus ecotourism to determine which would provide the highest net benefit, before issuing permits for guano mining in the Callao Caves. Conservation International Philippines (an NGO member of the PAMB) has proposed that before the PAMB acts on the request, studies should be carried out on the biology of the bats (including carrying capacity and effects of extraction methods on the bats' population and breeding).

This situation raises a series of important questions and issues related to the adoption and implementation of the precautionary principle, and management in the face of uncertainty. Precaution appears to argue in favour of restricting the issue of extraction until adequate research has been carried out to establish whether this would be harmful, before allowing extraction. However, the costs and benefits of different courses of action are complex. Restricting extraction clearly minimizes the potential direct negative impacts on the bat population. However, not issuing permits may potentially be associated with some negative conservation and livelihood impacts, including loss of a source of affordable fertilizer and loss of income for a group with few alternative livelihood options. Examining these various costs and benefits in order to arrive at a decision involves an examination not only of the scientific uncertainties related to the bat population, but also of uncertainties surrounding economic factors such as the dynamics of the guano market. Different stakeholders (such as the NGOs and the village representatives of the PAMB) may weigh and value these consequences differently, emphasizing the need for a broad participatory approach in such a situation.

## Timber poaching, fuel wood gathering and charcoal making

Despite the strict prohibition of these activities in the PPLS, the majority of the villagers interviewed reported that timber poaching, fuel wood gathering and charcoal making for sale in Tuguegarao city market continue (Tuguegarao City is adjacent to Peñablanca). It appears that these illegal activities are being carried out for subsistence because there are no alternative livelihood opportunities, the economic conditions of the poor are worsening, and there are high demands for lumber due to growing scarcity of wood for housing, fuel and charcoal, brought about partly by continuous increases in the price of petroleum products.

Enforcement of the prohibition faces major practical obstacles. The majority of the village leaders reported that those involved in timber poaching, commercial fuel wood gathering and charcoal making and illegal transport of such products, use modern communication, protection and transport facilities. By contrast, the DENR Forest Guards are outnumbered, ill-equipped and immobile due to a lack of much needed resources, making detection of illegal activities very difficult. In the view of PAMB members, effective action against such activities would require substantially intensified patrols, surveillance, prosecutions, enforcement capacity and information and education activities. It would also require the establishment of alternative, legal sources of fuel wood and charcoal to satisfy demand.

This situation leads to several insights for the implementation of the precautionary principle. It is clear that the legal/policy commitment to an implicitly precautionary approach for PPLS is not sufficient to ensure its precautionary management. In the absence of adequate capacity and resources for enforcement, such laws or policies may not translate into on-the-ground protection. Furthermore, people in this situation have few other livelihood options. For precautionary regulations to be effective, and not to worsen current poverty, alternative livelihoods will have to be provided. These complexities are likely not unique to the Philippines (see Box 15.1).

## CONCLUSIONS

A number of conclusions can be drawn from this case study on the application of precautionary principle in the Philippines. First, non-precautionary management of natural resources for short-term commercial gain can have very serious negative consequences on the sustainability and productivity of the environment and natural resources as well as on the livelihoods and poverty of the local people. In most cases, non-precautionary natural resources management ends in resource depletion.

Second, the forest as an ecosystem is a complex one and the interrelationships of its elements are not yet fully and accurately measurable by science and technology. Thus, there are a lot of immeasurable dependencies where potential responses are most likely uncertain. In cases of uncertainties, it is always a wiser decision to take precautionary measures before committing mistakes, to prevent permanent disastrous effects.

Third, specific precautionary measures to be implemented must undergo a thorough evaluation and analysis of their benefits and costs in terms of conservation and local livelihoods.

Fourth, adoption of a precautionary management regime can yield both costs and benefits for local livelihoods and poverty. In this case study, benefits

---

## Box 15.1 Managing living natural resources under uncertainty in Vietnam

Vietnam is a country where biodiversity is under threat, there are considerable ecological uncertainties, poverty reduction and livelihood development are major issues for communities dependent on forest resources, and the capacity to implement effective management strategies is limited. Implementation of the precautionary principle through adaptive management approaches could play an important role in this situation. Such an approach would need to engage all stakeholders in active dialogue and use all sources of relevant information including scientific, local and cultural knowledge. However, for this to happen, certain conditions are necessary. These include:

- acknowledgement among relevant agencies that science does not have immediate answers to management questions, and that state agencies themselves do not have the capacity to manage and monitor all sites effectively;
- acceptance that precaution in management of sites requires effective monitoring and active iterative management planning regardless of what management regime has been selected, for example no use of specific species/areas, sustainable use of specific species/areas or a combination of both;
- active engagement of local communities in forestland management, with secure and unambiguous land tenure, and benefit streams in place and monitored for their impact on biodiversity and on livelihood development;
- attention to institutional issues including lack of capacity (technical, financial and managerial), a range of perverse incentives for managing agencies, and corruption within a plethora of law enforcement agencies; and
- inclusion of the principle of precaution in the state's socio-economic development planning processes. Possibilities include incorporation in the EIA process; or a more fundamental inclusion, for example in the proposed Law on Environmental Protection and/or Biodiversity Conservation.

*Source:* Sheelagh O'Reilly in communication with R. Cooney 2005.

---

include the forest's protective values, watershed protection, flood control and agricultural productivity, whereas costs include loss of short-term employment and access to resources such as guano, timber, fuel wood and charcoal.

Fifth, protectionist approaches to conservation, which rely on strict prohibitions on resource access and use, may not effectively conserve the resources in question unless accompanied by careful consideration of the economic, social, political, cultural and management context. Reducing one impact may worsen another. Strong laws may not be translated into effective action on the ground due to lack of enforcement and resources. If people have no other livelihood options, they are unlikely to stop illegal extraction.

Finally, the precautionary principle can be a very important policy principle and management tool for sustainable natural resource management and biodiversity conservation and for supporting local livelihoods. However, its application should be based on careful assessment of the wide variety of factors that will affect its impact.

## NOTES

1 This section draws principally from DENR Region 2 (2002).
2 Others include adopting Selected Integrated Social Forestry (ISF) and other community-based projects such as the Centre for People's Empowerment in the Uplands (CPEU) (DAO 93–05), the People's Small Mining Act of 1991 (RA 7176).
3 The PAMB includes representatives from the Department of Environment and Natural Resources (Region 2), Provincial Government of Cagayan, Department of Tourism (Region 2), Municipal Government of Peñablanca, (Cagayan), Philippine Tourism Authority of the Municipal Government of Peñablanca, Conservation International, Women's Association of Peñablanca, Committee on Environment and Natural Resources of the Municipality of Peñablanca (law-making body of the Municipal Government of Peñablanca), Aggugadan Farmer's Cooperative, and Local Government Units of the following villages: Aggugadan, Bugatay, Buyun, Cabasan, Callao, Lapi, Malibabag, Mangga, Minanga, Nabbabalan, Nanguilitan, Nannarian, Quibal, San Roque and Sisim.
4 The following is based on focus-group discussions with the Aggugadan Farmers' Cooperative in Aggugadan village, a downstream community, and 12 upland village and three downstream village leaders, and members of the PPLS PAMB.
5 This is based on a review of the Callao Caves PAMB meeting minutes and resolutions enacted by the PAMB, and interviews with its members.

## ACKNOWLEDGEMENTS

The author is grateful for the input of Ms Anabeth Indab of the Resources, Environment, and Economics Center for Studies, Inc., The Philippines.

## REFERENCES

Acay, J. (undated) *Towards Updating the Initial Management Plan of Peñablanca Protected Landscape and Seascape and Harmonizing All Sectoral Development Plans with the Park*, Conservation International, Tuguegarao City
Cooney, R. (2004) *The Precautionary Principle in Biodiversity Conservation and Natural Resource Management: An Issues Paper for Policy-makers, Researchers and Practitioners*, IUCN Policy and Global Change Series, no 2, IUCN, Gland, Switzerland and Cambridge, UK
DENR Region 2 (2002) *Protected Area Suitability Assessment (PASA) on Site Observation*, Department of Environment and Natural Resources, Manila, The Philippines

# Section Five

# Analytical Perspectives on Precaution

# 16

# Economics, the Precautionary Principle and Natural Resource Management: Key Issues, Tools and Practices

*Lucy Emerton, Maryanne Grieg-Gran, Mikkel Kallesoe and James MacGregor*

## INTRODUCTION

The precautionary principle is concerned with reducing the risk of serious or irreversible harm to the environment. It recognizes that making informed decisions in natural resource management (NRM) and biodiversity conservation is often compromised by a lack of knowledge about the environmental and human implications of such decisions. If precautionary approaches are to succeed and be sustainable in practice, they have to be economically and financially viable for those concerned. Furthermore, both the goals and success of precautionary principle approaches have to be judged at least partly in terms of economic impacts. Economic criteria are therefore important factors in weighing up natural resource decisions and in justifying the application of the precautionary principle.

This chapter aims to provide an economic framework for understanding and implementing the precautionary principle. Starting from an analysis of its basic economic rationale and justification, the chapter identifies key economic issues and assumptions associated with implementing the precautionary principle in practice. Case studies and real-world examples are used to highlight best practice in the implementation of the precautionary principle, and to illustrate how economic decision-making tools can strengthen practice. The chapter concludes by outlining a set of steps that can be used to assess the economic costs, benefits and impacts of applying approaches to NRM based on the precautionary principle.

## THE ECONOMIC RATIONALE FOR THE PRECAUTIONARY PRINCIPLE

This section describes the economic justification and rationale for applying the precautionary principle, and examines the economic interpretation of different definitions. It also links the different interpretations to management approaches.

### Interpreting and defining the precautionary principle

Action based on the precautionary principle is always related to situations where the risk of serious or irreversible harm is coupled with scientific uncertainty about harmful impacts. The principle implies that precautionary action should be taken before scientific certainty of cause and effect is established, which in turn implies shifting the burden of proof – that is, requiring some evidence that actions are harmless instead of waiting to change a course of action once it is proven harmful. Precautionary action also often implies that alternatives to the potentially harmful action are identified and evaluated, and that goals are defined and set for preventive measures.

The usefulness of economic analysis as a tool depends on the interpretation and definition of the precautionary principle that is adopted by decision-makers – this ranges from strong to weak interpretations (see Box 16.1). As with defining sustainability, the stronger the interpretation, the more restrictive and clear-cut a definition. Also the stronger the interpretation, the less economics has to offer in terms of justifying the principle.

Advocates of a strong interpretation are not prepared to bear any environmental risk and are basically arguing that the value of environmental goods is infinite and should be protected at all cost (Productivity Commission, 2004). Weaker interpretations require that precautionary measures be cost effective relative to alternative management options, and assuming the same outcome, that an option with lower costs should be chosen.

Decision-makers should consider the trade-offs that society is willing or wishes to make – applying the precautionary principle is not costless. However, while considering the costs is important, equally important is the assessment of environmental benefits obtained through precautionary actions. Their estimation is difficult and often neglected in the decision-making process, as shown below.

### Justifying a precautionary approach to natural resource management

In broad terms the main justification for applying the precautionary principle

---

## BOX 16.1 VERSIONS OF THE PRECAUTIONARY PRINCIPLE AND SHIFTING THE BURDEN OF PROOF

There are various definitions of the precautionary principle. These range from 'strong' versions such as the Greenpeace definition: 'do not admit a substance until you have proof that it will do no harm to the environment', to 'weaker' versions such as that adopted in the Rio Declaration:

> *In order to protect the environment, the precautionary approach shall be widely applied by States according to their capacities. Where there are threats of serious or irreversible damage, lack of scientific certainty shall not be used as a reason for postponing cost-effective measures to prevent environmental degradation.*

A key defining characteristic of strong versions of the precautionary principle is that they require shifting the burden and raising the standard of proof – by requiring proponents of activities to prove that they will not cause harm. This implies that the public is not prepared to bear any environmental risk. In economic terms, the public is unwilling to consider the possibility of trade-offs.

*Sources:* Morris (2000); Lofstedt (2002); Productivity Commission (2004)

---

in natural resource management is to reduce the risk of serious or irreversible harm to the environment under scientific uncertainty. In economic terms, the core justification comes from the assumption that it could be rational to undertake restrictive measures now (thereby incurring present costs, often at the expense of foregone benefits) in order to avoid possibly greater future costs and/or secure possible greater future benefits. An example would be the justification of the current cost of undertaking measures to avert a threat of unsustainable extraction of timber and non-timber forest products (NTFPs) (and to also forego a portion of the present income they yield for forest users) in exchange for the possible higher future benefits that would be secured through maintaining the flow of forest goods and services.

Other important economic justifications for the precautionary principle include: securing future flexibility in allowing for new and as yet unknown benefits to be captured; capturing the societal perception that the environment holds an intrinsic value; and incorporating the nature of attitudes towards risk, such as risk aversion. The crucial challenge posed by the precautionary principle is to compare these costs and benefits given the associated uncertainty. Economic theory distinguishes between risk and uncertainty (see Box 16.2).

Economic analysis and tools provide guidance on balancing risks to biodiversity against risks to people's livelihoods, income, trade and food security. (As mentioned, this does not apply to the strong interpretations of the precautionary principle where the possibility of trade-offs is not accepted.) In order to determine whether future benefits flowing from a decision actually do outweigh present costs, a more detailed analysis is required that addresses

## BOX 16.2 HOW ECONOMIC THEORY SEES RISK AND UNCERTAINTY

### Risk

In an economic context risk is defined as the statistical probability of a specific event occurring. The estimated economic impacts of this event can be weighted by this probability. A statistical probability distribution can be constructed – showing the possible outcomes of a decision-maker's choice of action – and the decision that maximizes social welfare chosen. Economic analysis contributes to determining whether projects are worthwhile in economic terms.

### Uncertainty

Uncertainty denotes a situation where we have limited or no experimental or scientific evidence that can be used to calculate objective probabilities. The inability to assign probabilities to the outcomes of different courses of action complicates the use of economic analysis. In cases of uncertainty, subjective probabilities determined by scientific experts may be relied on to guide the decision-making process (Azar, 1998).

Opponents of the precautionary principle might argue that scientific uncertainty is not a problem, but is something that would be taken care of as time passes under the assumption of continuing scientific and technical progress – that the answer to questions lies in our future. From this perspective, the precautionary principle could be seen to hinder progress by reversing the burden of proof. It simply becomes too risky and expensive to develop new technology.

*Sources:* Morris and Shin (2000); Lofstedt (2002); Productivity Commission (2004)

distributional and time issues, as well as tackling problems of meaningfully valuing these uncertain future benefits. These difficulties are dealt with later in this chapter, along with the economic and policy measures that might prove necessary to ensure an effective outcome when applying the precautionary principle.

## Linking management strategies, economic costs and benefits to different interpretations of the precautionary principle

Common to all interpretations of the precautionary principle is an underlying insistence that the overall capacity of environmental systems to act as buffers for human well-being must be adequately protected. Within this general framework, however, the different interpretations of the precautionary principle set out above can be linked to different strategies for managing biodiversity. Protectionist conservation approaches would fall within a strong interpretation whereby resource use would be only permitted if it were proven that no harm would come to the environment. To this end, current costs would have to be incurred to protect biodiversity regardless of the perceived current and future benefits. Sustainable use approaches, ecosystem approaches and adaptive management strategies are covered by weaker interpretations.

Economic costs and benefits are involved under all interpretations, and in each pose difficulties for assessment. For instance, ecosystems are diverse and extremely complex; making predictions about likely impacts on biodiversity and the goods and services provided by the environment is very difficult. Costs and benefits also change over time making their precise valuation doubly difficult. Irreversibility introduces further difficulties: we simply do not know enough about the behaviour of natural systems to be able to identify critical thresholds – points beyond which irreversible damage may occur – although a good understanding might exist of the broad parameters. There remains much debate on incorporating the uncertain aspects of ecosystem functioning, structure and dynamics into economic analysis (Holling et al, 1994; Perrings, 1995; Moran and Pearce, 2000).

Assessing potential environmental impacts in economic terms requires examining the causes and effects of human–environment interaction. Human influence on natural resources is easily misunderstood or omitted in deliberations on the precautionary principle. Changes in policy, price and market conditions can affect people's actions and motivations to conserve natural resources. Our understanding of science with respect to environmental issues should include not only assessing biodiversity in economic terms, but also the incentives governing the human environment. In other words, scientific considerations should cover natural *and* social sciences. To this end, weaker interpretations can encompass such thinking.

# ECONOMIC ISSUES IN APPLYING THE PRECAUTIONARY PRINCIPLE

This section examines the main economic issues and assumptions associated with implementing the precautionary principle in natural resource management. As described above, assessing the impacts of the precautionary principle in terms of costs and benefits is not an easy task. The different costs are presented and the concept of total economic value is used to illustrate which environmental benefits could be lost as a consequence of inflicting harm on the environment. Finally some of the assumptions and elements of economic analysis are discussed.

## Identifying the economic costs of conservation

Applying the precautionary principle inevitably involves incurring costs now in order to secure benefits later. From an economics standpoint, these costs must be defined and assessed in order to gauge the justification, and likely impacts, of different natural resource management options. Generally speaking, the direct costs of limiting and changing natural resource utilization can

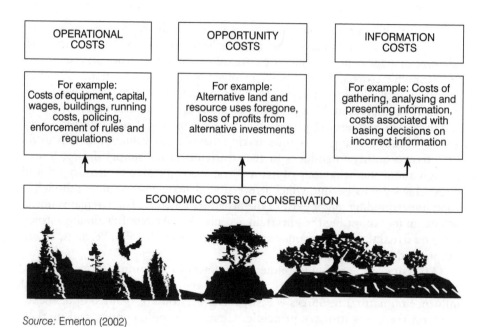

*Source:* Emerton (2002)

**Figure 16.1** *Economic costs of conservation*

be defined as operational costs, opportunity costs and information costs (see Figure 16.1). These costs are discussed in more detail below.

### Operational costs

The most tangible costs of applying the precautionary principle are the physical expenditures associated with applying management regimes and the costs of enforcing actions resulting from precautionary measures, as well as transaction costs. These costs include such elements as equipment, infrastructure, staff, running costs and maintenance.

### Opportunity costs

Curtailing or restricting the use of natural resources may reduce or preclude other economic opportunities. Opportunity cost can be interpreted as foregone income for, for example, a commercial timber harvesting company. While the cost incurred by the timber company is in the form of a financial loss there may very well be other less privileged groups that experience the restriction as severe impacts on their livelihoods. An example would be local communities living around national parks and depending on forest resources for subsistence. It is worth emphasizing that often opportunity costs form the major component of the economic costs associated with applying the precautionary principle, and the ability to balance or offset these costs is a major deciding factor in whether such an approach can be sustained (see Box 16.3).

---

## Box 16.3 The importance of considering the opportunity costs of conservation

In many cases the indirect and opportunity costs of natural resource conservation are far higher than the direct management expenditures, which have traditionally been the focus of conservation budgeting and cost estimation. Dixon and Sherman (1990), for example, estimate the total economic costs incurred by Khao Yai National Park in Thailand and find that opportunity costs in terms of local resource use foregone are almost nine times higher than direct management costs. Howard (1995) likewise shows that the US$110 million annual opportunity costs of protected area (PA) conservation to the Ugandan economy far exceed management costs and outstrip revenues generated by PA agencies.

Choosing to apply some level of protection to natural resources can imply significant losses to other economic activities in neighbouring areas. Dixon and Sherman (1990) estimate the indirect costs of Kangaroo Island PA in Australia in terms of losses caused to adjacent landowners owing to the movement of park animals onto agricultural land. Indirect costs arise from competition over grazing, fencing costs, ammunition and time required to conduct culling, restrictions on private land development and fire hazards arising from activities in the PA, and are estimated at AUS$100,000 per year – almost as large as the operating cost of the neighbouring national park. Emerton (2001) presents several estimates of PA wildlife-related agricultural losses in rural Kenya, calculating annual crop losses at more than US$1 million around Mount Kenya Forest Reserve, disease transmission to domestic animals in Laikipia District at US$27 per $km^2$, livestock kills and injuries around the Maasai Mara National Reserve at US$100 per $km^2$ and farm damage of more than US$250 per household around Shimba Hills National Reserve.

---

### Information costs

Applying precautionary measures should be based on information on the likely impacts and implications of different management options. Gathering information is costly. It is, however, important to gather as much information as possible, since increased understanding and knowledge raises the likelihood of making decisions that minimize potential economic loss. Information can provide an acceptable level of proof of harm or of no harm, and of the direct and indirect consequences of actions prescribed by the precautionary principle. Note that in the context of natural resource management, the risks and uncertainties are not only about the implications of the loss of a habitat or loss of a local species, but also related to the impacts of certain human activities on a species or habitat as well as the impacts of measures taken with the aim of conservation or sustainable management. The notion expressed before that science should include natural and social considerations is key here, and information relating to both needs to be collected.

Often decisions based on the precautionary principle are supported by questionable information about what drives the demand. As economic and market information on natural resources is often privately held and confiden-

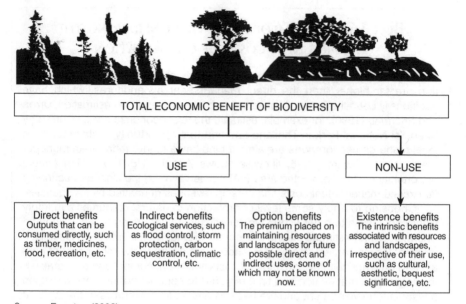

*Source:* Emerton (2002)

**Figure 16.2** *Economic benefits of biodiversity*

tial, it can be difficult to obtain. However, there exist critical industry characteristics that can guide decision-making. Wild species often have 'peculiar' demand profiles – with higher prices even stimulating demand for final sale luxury goods (MacGregor, 2002; MacGregor et al, 2004). Equally, misguided causal assumptions are often made about human–environment interactions owing to both poor available economic information and/or limited interaction with industry participants. Economic information and analysis here can relatively simply support or refute an argument pursuant to a decision based on the precautionary principle.

## Identifying the economic benefits of conservation

Except under the strong interpretation of the precautionary principle where risking environmental harm should be avoided at all cost, the decision to incur the above costs is driven by an expectation either that larger costs can be avoided later or that substantial benefits can be secured for the future. Being able to understand, articulate and express costs and benefits is usually a critical consideration in choosing between different natural resource management options. In an effort to conceptualize environmental values, the framework of total economic value was introduced a decade or so ago, and has now become one of the most widely used frameworks for identifying and categorizing environmental benefits. Instead of focusing only on direct commercial or extractive uses, total economic value also encompasses subsistence and non-market benefits, ecosystem services and non-use values (see Figure 16.2).

## Defining sustainability

The concept of economic sustainability is closely linked both to the distribution of costs and benefits and to the relative weight that future costs and benefits are perceived to have as compared to current values (see below). Securing sustainability rests on an ethical assumption that the present generation has an obligation towards future generations. Ideally, resources should be managed in a way that will allow all future generations to achieve the same level of welfare over time.

The extent to which there is an overlap between interpretations of the precautionary principle and sustainable development depends on the assumptions made regarding the rate of substitution between different kinds of capital. A strong interpretation dictates that natural resources and environmental services (natural capital) cannot be replaced/substituted entirely by produced goods and human capacity (man-made capital and human capital), contrary to a weak interpretation where there is no limit to substitution. Economic sustainability is constrained by the necessity for ecosystem sustainability, which necessitates that a certain minimum of key species and ecological processes are required to be maintained and conserved to secure the stability and self-regenerating capacity of ecosystems. Thus the concept of critical natural capital dictates that the conventional economic optimization principle allowing for full substitution, has to give way to a precautionary principle in the form of safe minimum standards of conservation.

## Discounting: coping with time

Since the precautionary principle involves weighing up current and future costs and benefits, another important element of dealing with economic aspects is how we deal with time. Costs and benefits occurring at different times need to be brought to one comparable value, which requires the use of the concept of discounting.

People generally prefer to enjoy benefits now and costs later. Discounting reflects this and a given future benefit (or cost) is given less weight than a present benefit (or cost), giving values relatively less weight the further into the future they accrue. It thus follows that a high discount rate reflects a strong preference for present consumption, and a low discount rate reflects longer term considerations and preferences. In most cases, the discount rate is based on the opportunity cost of capital – the prevailing rate of return on investments elsewhere in the economy.

## Enabling economic conditions

Many of the goods and services associated with natural resources are undervalued by the market, or ignored in macroeconomic and sectoral policies. For example, low forest royalty rates in Africa and Asia fail to reflect the full value of forest resources, to maximize income or to encourage sustainable forest management (Gray, 1997). There is also ample evidence that various 'perverse' subsidies act to make biodiversity-depleting or environmentally damaging activities and sectors more profitable or financially attractive than those that are compatible with conservation. In doing so, this increases the opportunity costs of biodiversity conservation in terms of alternative land and resource uses foregone. For example, in the Brazilian Amazon, official development strategy and economic policies directed almost exclusively at the expansion of corporate forestry, ranching and agriculture and mining interests are thought to have accounted for at least 35 per cent of all forest altered by 1980 (Barbier, 1989).

The precautionary principle is unlikely to be viable in practice if there are insufficient financial resources to implement it or if it has a demonstrably negative economic impact – overall or for particular natural resource users or managers. Certain economic and financial measures will most likely also have to be established to provide enabling conditions for implementation. These might, for example, involve raising funds, setting up compensation schemes or reforming the policies, markets and prices that currently make it unprofitable to conserve biodiversity or that may pose threats to natural resources in the future.

## APPLYING ECONOMIC TOOLS TO THE PRECAUTIONARY PRINCIPLE

This section considers how economic tools can be used to strengthen the decision-making processes associated with the application of the precautionary principle.

### Valuing economic costs and benefits

Having identified and measured economic costs, benefits and trade-offs, a challenge in the context of the precautionary principle is to place a value on these benefits and costs when they are inherently uncertain.

Economic valuation has become an increasingly important step in biodiversity assessment and planning. In connection with the precautionary principle, demonstrating the total economic value of biodiversity will illustrate the benefits associated with its conservation and sustainable use, but also can outline the large and wide-ranging economic costs associated with the loss or degradation of biodiversity and its components. Calculating economic values is thus often an important argument in justifying the use of the precautionary principle (especially for policy-makers, planners and decision-makers in non-environmental sectors). It underlines the fact that biological resources and their diversity constitute far more than a static biological reserve. Biodiversity forms a stock of natural capital, which if managed sustainably, can yield in perpetuity a wide range of direct and indirect economic benefits to human populations, which in developing countries would often mean the poorer groups.

Parallel to the advances that have been made in the definition and conceptualization of total economic value, techniques for quantifying environmental benefits and expressing those in monetary terms have also moved forward over the last decade (see Winpenny, 1991; Pearce and Moran, 1994; Phillips, 1998). A wide range of market and non-market methods are now available with which to value species and ecosystems; however, this is beyond the scope of this chapter.

## Economic decision-support tools

Economic decision-making relies on a range of tools to judge the relative desirability of different actions. Such tools present useful frameworks for incorporating economic aspects into the application of the precautionary principle and into natural resource decision-making.

### Conventional tools

Cost–benefit analysis (CBA) remains the most commonly used tool for appraising and evaluating programmes, projects and policies and one that is a required part of many government and donor decision-making procedures. CBA assesses profitability or desirability according to net present benefits – the total annual benefits minus total annual costs for each year of analysis or project lifetime, discounted in order to be expressed as a single measure of value in today's terms (Gittinger, 1982; Dixon et al, 1994).

Cost-effectiveness analysis (CEA) judges the minimum cost way of attaining a particular objective (for example conserving a particular species or ecosystem, or maintaining a particular level of water quality). It is useful where a course of action has no measurable benefits, or where a particular goal has already been set – as is often the case when the precautionary principle is being applied (Gittinger, 1982; Dixon et al, 1994).

### Tools to address distributional impact

When assessing the economics of the precautionary principle we need to know both the overall costs, benefits and impacts of implementing the precautionary principle, and also which groups are affected and when. This is important not just for assessing the likely economic impacts of a particular natural resource management approach, but also for identifying the additional measures, which may have to be employed to ensure that it is economically and financially sustainable (see Box 16.4).

The impacts of applying the precautionary principle to natural resource management could be perceived as either positive or negative depending on the specific precautionary action that is implemented, as well as who is affected. In a case where local communities were to be restricted in their access to and use of adjacent natural resources, for example a forest, these people would experience a cost in terms of foregone NTFP collection. If on the other hand, restrictions were imposed on a commercial timber company, they would bear the cost of the precautionary action, whereas the local community could experience benefits associated with securing livelihoods.

BOX 16.4 THE DISTRIBUTION OF CONSERVATION COSTS AND
BENEFITS IN LAKE MBURO NATIONAL PARK, UGANDA

Lake Mburo National Park (LMNP) in Uganda, covers 260km$^2$ of savanna and
wetlands. Although there is a long history of conservation in the area, Lake
Mburo was formally gazetted as a National Park in 1983. The area that is LMNP
forms an important component of local livelihoods and production systems for
the 50,000 *Bairu* cultivators and *Bahima* pastoralists who live around the PA, and
pressure on the park's land and resources remains high.

In 1997 the park had access to an annual operating budget of some
US$400,000, of which three-quarters was contributed by foreign donors and just
under a quarter came from tourism revenues and resource user charges. Of this
total income, approximately US$370,000 was used to cover staff salaries and PA
operating costs, while US$30,000 was invested in local community development
activities such as educational, water and health projects. In addition to these
revenue sharing arrangements, local communities were also permitted to
harvest certain park resources at a subsistence level, worth an estimated
US$200,000 per year.

Meanwhile, the costs of LMNP to local communities totalled more than
US$700,000 in 1998. These costs included crop and livestock damage by wildlife
(50 per cent), restrictions on resource utilization (30 per cent), loss of grazing
land (20 per cent) and cash and in-kind contributions to community development activities (>1 per cent). These costs are significant and tangible at the local
level. More than 90 per cent of households living next to the park suffer regular
crop destruction, livestock kills and transmission of disease from wild animals to
domestic stock. The establishment of LMNP took out of production an area of
pasture sufficient to support more than 10,000 cattle and small stock, including
critical dry season grazing land. The total value of local resource use in LMNP
was roughly halved by park rules and regulations.

Given the problems, and gaps, in both the quality and form of LMNP's
benefits and costs at the local level it is perhaps hardly surprising that
human–park conflicts continue. Park authorities, already over stretched in both
budgetary and human resource terms, continue to find it difficult to control
unsustainable and illegal use of LMNP's land and resources.

*Source:* Emerton (1998)

Conventional economic methodology is normally not concerned about the
distributional aspects of any action as long as the overall result is positive. It is
then merely a case of redistributing the benefits so that everyone becomes
better off. However, modifications can be made to cost–benefit analysis to take
account of the fact that changes represent different marginal costs and benefits
to different income groups. One way of doing this is to assign impact weights
– that is to value negative impacts towards rich people lower than if the impact
were to affect poorer groups (Squire and van der Tak, 1975).

# COMBINING ECONOMIC AND NON-ECONOMIC MEASURES: MULTI-CRITERIA ANALYSIS

Although they are important and influential decision-making tools, economic and financial measures are not the only criteria by which decisions are made as to whether or not to apply precautionary principle approaches. There will always be certain values that cannot be expressed in monetary terms, and there are many non-economic considerations in weighing up alternative projects, policies and programmes, and in deciding which is the most desirable.

Multi-criteria analysis provides one of the most useful and increasingly common tools for integrating different types of monetary and non-monetary decision criteria. It has been developed to deal with situations where decisions must be made taking into account multiple objectives, which cannot be reduced to a single dimension. Multi-criteria analysis is usually clustered into three dimensions: the ecological, the economic and the social. Within each of these dimensions certain criteria are set, so that decision-makers can weigh the importance of one element in association with the others. Here, monetary values and CBA measures can be incorporated as one of the criteria to be considered, and weighed against the others in decision-making.

## Tools to address risk and uncertainty

Cost–benefit analysis often incorporates sensitivity analysis to examine how the results change if different assumptions are made about trends in key variables. Risk–benefit analysis (RBA) focuses on measures to prevent events carrying serious risks (for example investing in flood prevention). It compares the expected cost of inaction with the cost of preventive measures. The expected cost is given by the estimated economic damage from the event weighted by the probability of its occurrence. The benefit of inaction is the saving in the cost of preventive measures (Dixon et al, 1994). This tool is useful where risk is a major consideration in projects – as is the case in many applications of the precautionary principle, and can be assessed in monetary terms.

Decision analysis (DA) examines the implications of different attitudes to risk. It weights the expected values of a given course of action by attitudes to risk, to give expected utilities. It draws up and assesses decision-makers' preferences, judgements and trade-offs in order to obtain weights that are attached to outcomes carrying different levels of risk (Keeney and Raiffa, 1976). In conditions of uncertainty, where there is insufficient objective information available, a range of expert opinions can be drawn on to derive probability distributions. Due to its comprehensive consideration of risk, decision analysis is a useful tool for supporting the application of the precautionary principle approach.

# IMPLEMENTATION OF THE PRECAUTIONARY PRINCIPLE: ECONOMIC BEST PRACTICES

So far, this document has looked at the economic rationale, issues and tools that apply to the precautionary principle. They present a useful, but perhaps bewildering, array of concerns and options. What, then, are the essential elements and best practices when we apply an economic approach to the precautionary principle? How do we maximize its positive impacts, minimize or offset its negative impacts, increase the likelihood of success and work within the confines of risk and uncertainty?

Some of the elements that constitute best practice, from an economics perspective, in the implementation of the precautionary principle include: comprehensive examination and evaluation of options and trade-offs; transparent treatment of uncertainty; attention to distributional impacts and compensation mechanisms; and monitoring and adaptation. Each of these elements is examined in detail below.

## Comprehensive examination and evaluation of options and trade-offs

One critical element of best practice is ensuring that there is a comprehensive examination and evaluation of the different options and trade-offs associated with following a particular course of action. Both the precautionary principle, and most economic decision support tools, can be criticized for over-emphasizing one alternative and focusing on specific impacts. They pay less attention to the causal links between actions and threats, and sometimes fail to take account of other factors that affect the threat in question (see Box 16.5). In reality, there typically exist a complex series of factors that underlie and drive how different actors will respond to alternative courses of action, and it is always necessary to understand and analyse the biophysical linkages and knock-on effects that will arise from following particular courses of action.

In turn, a comprehensive examination and evaluation of options and trade-offs involves examining the causal chain and comparing various options and scenarios, including taking no action.

### Examining the causal chain

Many different factors link a particular course of action with a particular outcome. These include biophysical processes (such as the links between forest cover and downstream water supply and quality, or the impacts of losing one species in terms of the overall food chain), as well as policy, legal, institutional and market influences and causes (for example the knock-on effects of agricultural subsidies on land use, the indirect effects of removing food price support on bush meat consumption, or of structural adjustment measures on natural resource utilization levels and patterns).

---

## BOX 16.5 PRECAUTION AND THE CITES LISTING OF THE TANIMBAR CORELLA

The Tanimbar corella (*Cacatua goffini*), a parrot species, is endemic to the Tanimbar Islands, Indonesia, and has been traded internationally for at least several decades, with trade during the 1980s averaging over 5000 birds per year. Yet the sustainability of this trade was unclear until recently. This and virtually all other parrot species were included in Appendix II of the Convention on International Trade in Endangered Species of Wild Fauna and Flora (CITES) in 1981. Responding to concerns regarding its limited geographical range and the level of international trade in the species, but on the basis of little information on biological status, in 1992 the species was up-listed to CITES Appendix I – an action interpretable as precautionary.

However, population information provided by the Indonesian authorities did not support this up-listing; rather indicating that the parrot was abundant and raided maize crops. Nevertheless, the proposal was accepted. Following the up-listing, new population surveys were completed that incorporated both the distribution of human economic activity and the supply chains for the traded parrots. These concluded the parrot was widely distributed at high densities, that catching was limited to agricultural areas and certain times of the year as birds raided crops, and harvests for international trade appeared sustainable and likely to be a considerable boost to local incomes. Further, trade did not appear to be the primary driver of the harvest, but rather was a by-product of agricultural activity on the Islands – birds were caught when the species raided maize crops.

However, these findings failed to provoke sufficient support for a down-listing of the parrot at the subsequent CITES meeting in 1994. This was due to a range of factors. Sceptical CITES members and non-governmental organizations (NGOs) argued that the evidence conflicted with earlier evidence and that trend data over five years were needed. Commentators suspected that the delay in the down-listing owed more to political considerations over Indonesia's perceived lax enforcement of other duties under the Convention and a face-saving exercise by some of the NGO experts who had originally backed an up-listing in 1992.

Analysis of the management context and supply chain for this species prior to up-listing may have avoided some of the problems associated with this decision and the negative ramifications for the integrity of both CITES and conservationists.

*Source:* Jepson (2003)

---

It is necessary to identify these different factors, and wherever possible to establish their causal links and likely effects on each other and on the resource or conservation management issue in question. These should be informed by factual evidence – for example where precaution is recommended as a hedge against apparent market-led depletion, it is crucial to observe and record the industry's various drivers. Making these links and hypotheses explicit, and taking steps to investigate and test them, is one way of reducing uncertainty about the likely future outcomes of following a particular course of action.

### Comparing various options and scenarios, including taking no action

Taking action to avert a threat may in turn lead to other threats or negative impacts. Establishing protective regimes or curtailing certain natural resource utilization activities may, for example, impact negatively on local livelihoods (which may, in turn, actually lead to resource overexploitation or unsustainable harvesting for other species or locations). A wide range of costs and benefits need to be considered and analysed, not just the ones that have clear commercial or market values. It is also important to identify and model the range of factors that can have an impact on the threat so that the 'no action' scenario can be fully understood. This will make trade-offs transparent.

For example, we might consider the costs and benefits associated with a range of options available to maintain wildlife populations on settled lands outside protected areas. One option would be to take no action – in which case it would be important to consider, and to factor into analysis, both the costs associated with the likely decline in wildlife populations (and their associated earnings) as well as the costs to local agricultural populations of wildlife-related crop and livestock damage. A second option, invoking the strong interpretation of the precautionary principle, could be to enforce strict protection of this wildlife and a ban on natural resource-based activities that jeopardize ecosystem integrity. This option would incur both direct operational management costs to the wildlife managing agency, as well as local wildlife-related costs and opportunity costs of land and resource utilization activities foregone. A third option, perhaps based on wildlife tourism and sustainable use, might still entail a similar level of direct and indirect costs, but also provide the means to generate significant revenues and economic benefits to offset them.

We cannot limit these options and scenarios to the short term. Consideration must be given to the future management of the resource and its protection. For example a situation of no action to conserve the areas in and around a national park may lead to a situation where predator populations (such as lions or leopards) decline at the same time as the protected area becomes progressively 'fenced in' by surrounding farms and settlements. The consequent rise, and concentration, of populations of certain large herbivores (for example, antelopes) might have devastating impacts on both the ecology of the national park, as well as increasing competition for grazing resources with other herbivores. Here it may become necessary not just to instigate conservation measures, but also to take action to redress the change in species balance.

## Transparent treatment of uncertainty

A decision to act based on the precautionary principle implies that the benefits of taking the action to avert the threat are considered to outweigh the costs, even though some of these costs and benefits are highly uncertain. A high value has been assigned, implicitly or explicitly, to the costs of the uncertain threat, regardless of the lack of knowledge about the probability of its occurrence, the extent into the future when it is likely to occur and the groups that it will affect. Moreover, it implies that this value is considered to be higher than the costs associated with taking action to avert the threat, even where there is less uncertainty associated with the magnitude of these costs.

Ultimately, taking a decision on this basis is somewhat subjective. The important issue is the reasoning process that leads to high values being placed on uncertain costs and benefits and the extent to which it is informed by stakeholder perspectives and held up to scrutiny. This requires transparency in the setting out of the assumptions and value judgements involved. Economic tools can play a role here by clarifying the trade-offs involved between different courses of action.

Where probabilities can be assigned to these uncertain costs and benefits, economic decision tools can help in this, by estimating expected values and examining the risk preferences of different groups. Where no probabilities can be assigned other than on a subjective basis, economic tools also face challenges but can still contribute. Poor practice in cost–benefit and cost-effectiveness analysis has involved the exclusion of uncertain costs or benefits from the analysis altogether, in effect assigning zero value or zero probability to both. Better practice has involved the discussion of uncertain costs and benefits in qualitative terms as something to weigh up against the monetary terms, or has included the employment of additional decision-support tools such as risk–benefit, decision or multi-criteria analysis. These tools have the capacity to deal with risk and uncertainty in detail, including both quantitative and qualitative or perceptional aspects.

Another alternative is to adopt a scenario approach in which the uncertain outcome is assumed to occur (in other words the worst case scenario happens) and the cost–benefit implications are explored. Other scenarios involving different actions to avert the threat can also be explored in this way. The conclusions drawn from this approach will also depend on other assumptions made in the scenarios about discount rates, risk aversion, marginal utility of wealth. These scenarios can form a basis for discussion with stakeholders about the probability and seriousness of the uncertain threats. This could lead to participatory development of a set of weights.

To return to the example of the wildlife populations on settled lands outside protected areas, the options are no action, strict protection or a sustainable use approach. All three involve some uncertainty over the consequences for wildlife populations. Discussion with relevant stakeholders on the different options could result in a weighting for the probability and seriousness of declines in wildlife populations, which could aid decision-making.

## Attention to distributional impacts and compensation mechanisms

Understanding the economic and financial impact of the precautionary principle decision on resource users and other relevant stakeholders is important for reasons of effectiveness, equity and sustainability. Actions taken as a result of invoking the precautionary principle will affect different groups in different ways and there will almost inevitably be losers and winners. At the same time, any natural resource management option incurs monetary costs to implement and maintain, and sufficient financial resources must be secured to cover these.

If a particular course of conservation action does not appear desirable in economic terms (or cannot be financially sustained) to the people who are responsible for managing a resource, or if other courses of action remain more economically desirable to those who have the potential to degrade natural resources, it is unlikely to succeed in practice. This is not only a case of people's preferences and willingness, it may also be an economic necessity – especially in cases where people are in a weak economic position and thus unable to tolerate the costs that a particular conservation approach incurs to their livelihoods or economic survival (see Box 16.6).

Best practice will therefore be to identify both losers and winners and understand their key characteristics (for example income levels, livelihood strategies and attitudes to risk). It is also necessary to assess the continued threat the losers pose to the resource targeted by decisions based on the precautionary principle, and highlight the kinds of measures that may be needed to compensate or reward these people. These could include alternative livelihood activities, generation of income or revenues, for example through payments for environmental services or provision of other monetary and non-monetary benefits. However, the definition of those who require compensation could include a large group of industry participants. For instance, stopping crocodilian harvests in a particular area will affect not only some relatively poor hunters but some relatively wealthy traders. Where should compensation end? If the primary motive is to promote equity then compensation should be targeted at the poorest users of the resource. But what are the likely ramifications if we do not reward the wealthier trader for not dealing in the skins? If the trader is the de facto employer of the hunters, local compensation only is unlikely to have the desired outcome of promoting compliance.

---

### BOX 16.6 THE LIVELIHOOD IMPACT OF THE PRECAUTIONARY PRINCIPLE: CHARCOAL BURNING IN KENYA

A complete ban on charcoal burning in natural forests was imposed in Kenya in order to avoid potential serious harm to the forest resource. While sustainable management of the forest resource is crucial in the long term to support the livelihoods of the rural poor, charcoal burning provides an income for households in arid and semi-arid lands in times of crisis. When there is rainfall failure and consequent food insecurity, charcoal production is an important coping strategy for these poor households. There is also a substantial demand for charcoal in Kenya, with 82 per cent of the urban population depending on it for their prime source of energy. The ban on charcoal burning therefore proved to be not only inequitable but unenforceable because it was widely ignored.

*Source:* Muyanga (2004)

Equally, we should not forget the winners. Where particular groups or sectors gain high net benefits from a particular course of action, there may well be opportunities to capture or redistribute some of these benefits – for example as revenues or finance – to support conservation.

Care needs to be taken to incorporate the *relative* values involved and address the ethical questions this raises, particularly since local residents in biodiversity-rich countries, who often bear conservation costs, tend to be considerably poorer than those non-residents holding existence values over a species or ecosystem.

## Monitoring and adaptation

As new information becomes available and as data on the responses to and impacts of the action taken in the name of the precautionary principle are collected, the grounds for the original decision need to be reviewed and adjustments made. As such, flexibility is necessary to mould the precautionary principle framework around the reality of natural resource management.

The context and conditions under which a precautionary principle approach is applied are also dynamic. Policy, legal and institutional changes all alter the conditions and motivations under which natural resources are managed and used. For instance, exchange rate devaluation can change overnight the incentives facing harvesters. External factors can lead to new or changed threats affecting natural resources. For example, terror threats can halt tourism to local or community ventures.

One key aspect of monitoring and adaptation is to monitor changes in economic values and conditions over the period following a precautionary principle decision. It is possible to begin to check if reasoning was correct in the initial decision, and also to further pursue genuine efficiency savings as the practicality of the decision produces incentives and actual outcomes. Best practice means carrying out such monitoring, and also acting on its findings and on changing needs and circumstances to modify the precautionary approach accordingly (see Box 16.7).

# CONCLUSIONS

Finally, a caution and a reality check on economics, the precautionary principle and natural resource management. Economic approaches and tools are not by themselves a panacea, stand-alone activity or undertaking. Decisions about natural resources are made on the basis of multiple criteria, in which economic factors – although important – are just one consideration. The value of economic tools and approaches lies in their use as one component of an integrated approach that takes into account scientific, institutional, policy, social and other factors.

The use of economic approaches and tools also involves inherent limitations and risks. For example estimates of value, however useful, can rarely be

---

**BOX 16.7 THE IMPORTANCE OF MONITORING FOR UPDATING FISHERY MANAGEMENT PLANS**

Reef and fishery management and conservation are key requirements of the Marine Aquarium Council standard for ecosystem and fishery management. Concerned parties in harvest areas are required to develop a Collection Area Management Plan (CAMP) through a multi-stakeholder consultation process in order to apply for Marine Aquarium Council certification. These plans involve no-take areas and thresholds for resource status and catch levels. Since there is lack of information on target species' abundance and distribution and previous harvest levels, development of the management plans involves a precautionary approach. The Marine Aquarium Council in partnership with the Global Coral Reef Monitoring Network has developed a monitoring protocol for assessment of coral reefs and populations of organisms harvested for the aquarium trade. A baseline assessment is required for certification, and management plans are required to be adapted as improved information becomes available.

*Source:* Kusumaatmadja (2004)

---

seen as exact or definitive figures. Rather they present the best information available that can be used to inform management planning and practice. Given the uncertainty about the likelihood and impacts of a threat, valuation of the costs and benefits of precautionary measures is heavily dependent on assumptions made about probability of occurrence and attitudes to risk. Increased monitoring of wildlife populations, as many people advocate, can help to reduce this uncertainty but this comes at a cost. Economic approaches and information are also heavily influenced by a particular person's or group's conception at a specific point in time. They are not necessarily universally valid or applicable to different groups, areas and species, or over time. In some cases it is not appropriate to use economic tools at all, even when, in theory, they are applicable. Ethical and moral issues, as well as the local context in which a precautionary approach is being applied, must always be considered. It is also important to remember that there is no guarantee that economic approaches will in every case point to decisions that support the application of the precautionary principle to natural resource management.

However, taking these cautions into account, as we have seen in this chapter, economic tools and approaches form an essential, and practical, part of planning and implementing precautionary approaches to natural resource management. In the past, economic aspects have often been ignored, by both conservation and development planners, when decisions are made about natural resources. In turn, economic information can present convincing arguments and support for the precautionary principle, and economic measures can increase significantly the likelihood that such approaches will be successful in practice.

# REFERENCES

Azar, C. (1998) 'Are optimal emissions really optimal: four critical issues for economists in the greenhouse', *Environmental and Resource Economics*, vol 11, pp301–15

Barbier, E. (1989) *Economics, Natural-Resource Scarcity and Development*, Earthscan, London

Dixon, J. A. and Sherman, P. B. (1990) *Economics of Protected Areas: A New Look at Benefits and Costs*, Earthscan, London

Dixon, J. A., Fallon Scura, L., Carpenter, R. A. and Sherman, P. B. (1994) *Economic Analysis of Environmental Impacts*, Earthscan, London

Emerton, L. (1998) *Balancing the Opportunity Costs of Wildlife Conservation for the Communities Around Lake Mburo National Park, Uganda,* Evaluating Eden, Discussion Paper EE DP 05, International Institute for Environment and Development, London

Emerton, L. (2001) 'The nature of benefits and the benefits of nature: why wildlife conservation has not economically benefited communities in Africa', in D. Hulme and M. Murphree (eds) *African Wildlife and Livelihoods: The Promise and Performance of Community Conservation*, James Currey Press, Oxford

Emerton, L. (2002) *The Use of Economics in National Biodiversity Strategies and Action Plans: A Review of Experiences, Lessons Learned and Ways Forward,* Regional Environmental Economics Programme for Asia, Karachi

Gittinger, J. P. (1982) *Economic Analysis of Agricultural Projects*, EDI Series in Economic Development, John Hopkins University Press, Baltimore

Gray, J. A. (1997) 'Underpricing and overexploitation of tropical forests: forest pricing in the management, conservation, and preservation of tropical forests', *Journal of Sustainable Forestry*, vol 4, pp1–2

Holling, C., Schindler. D., Walker, D. and Roughgarden, J. (1994) 'Biodiversity in the functioning of ecosystems', in C. Perrings, C. Folke, C. Holling, B. Jansen and K. G. Mäler (eds) *Biological Diversity: Economic and Ecological issues*, Cambridge University Press, Cambridge, UK

Howard, P. (1995) *The Economics of Protected Areas in Uganda: Costs, Benefits and Policy Issues*, MSc thesis submitted to the University of Edinburgh, Edinburgh

Jepson, P. (2003) 'The need for a better understanding of context when applying CITES regulations: the case of the Indonesian parrot – Tanimbar corella', in S. Oldfield (ed) *The Trade in Wildlife*, Earthscan, London

Keeney, R. L, and Raiffa, H. (1976) *Decisions with Multiple Objectives: Performances and Value Trade-Offs*, Wiley, New York.

Kusumaatmadja, R. (2004) 'Applying the precautionary principle for coral reef conservation and a responsible marine aquarium trade through MAC Certification', in *Workshop Final Report, The Precautionary Principle in Natural Resource Management and Biodiversity Conservation*, Manila, 20–23 June. Available at www.pprinciple.net

Lofstedt, R. (2002) *The Precautionary Principle: Risk, Regulation and Politics*, Merton College, Oxford Press, Oxford

MacGregor, J. (2002) *International trade in crocodilian skins*, unpublished report commissioned by Crocodile Specialist Group, IUCN, Gland, Switzerland

MacGregor, J., Karousakis, K. and Groom, B. (2004) *Using Economic Incentives to Conserve CITES-listed Species – ITQs for Sturgeon in the Caspian Sea*, Environmental Economics Programme Discussion Paper 04-02, International Institute of Environment and Development, London

Moran, D. and Pearce, D. (2000) *Handbook on the Applied Valuation of Biological Diversity*, prepared for Environment Directorate of OECD, Paris

Morris, J. (2000) *Rethinking Risk and the Precautionary Principle*, Butterworth Heinemann, Oxford

Morris, S. and Shin, H. S. (2000) *Market Risk with Interdependent Choice*, Oxford University Press, Oxford

Muyanga, M. (2004) 'Impacts of precautionary charcoal burning and conservation policy: integrating households food security with natural forests in Kenya', in *Workshop Final Report, Managing Uncertainty: Risk and the Precautionary Principle in Biodiversity Conservation and Sustainable Use*, Dar es Salaam, 9–11 June. Available at www.pprinciple.net

Pearce, D. and Moran, D. (1994) *The Economic Value of Biodiversity*, Earthscan, London

Perrings, C. (1995) 'Biodiversity as insurance', in T. Swanson (ed) *The Economics and Ecology of Biodiversity Decline*, Cambridge University Press, Cambridge, UK

Phillips, A. (ed) (1998) *Economic Values of Protected Areas: Guidelines for Protected Area Managers*, IUCN, Gland, Switzerland and Cambridge, UK

Productivity Commission (2004) *Impacts of Native Vegetation and Biodiversity Regulations*, Report no 29, Melbourne. Available at www.pc.gov.au/inquiry/nativevegetation/finalreport/index.html

Squire, L. and van der Tak, H. G. (1975) *Economic Analysis of Projects*, John Hopkins University Press for the World Bank, Baltimore, MD

Winpenny, J. T. (1991) *Values for the Environment: A Guide to Economic Appraisal*, HMSO Press, London

# 17

# Fairness and the Costs and Benefits of Precautionary Action

*Barney Dickson*

## INTRODUCTION

The precautionary principle urges that action should be taken against threats to the environment even when there is some uncertainty about those threats. Its application has the potential to affect what individuals, organizations and even countries can and cannot do in connection with the environment. It can affect their ability to use the environment in certain ways, whether as a sink for pollutants, or as a source of resources or services. Its application can also safeguard other individuals, organizations and countries from the risks of harm to the environment. Thus the application of the precautionary principle can alter the distribution of costs and benefits that are faced by a range of actors. At its simplest, those who are engaged in an activity that is identified as possibly harmful (and therefore the object of precautionary action) may face costs or a loss of benefits, after precautionary action has been undertaken, if their freedom to engage in that activity has been circumscribed. Conversely, if precautionary action prevents harm occurring, then those who would have suffered as a result of that harm will be better off as a result of that precautionary action.

The costs and benefits, whose distribution is affected by the application of the precautionary principle, may or may not be of a monetary sort. They could include better or worse health, a world richer or poorer in biodiversity, or a more or less aesthetically attractive environment. Economists may contend that all of these benefits can be expressed in monetary terms, but the discussion here does not rest on the truth of that contention.

Since the application of the precautionary principle alters the distribution of costs and benefits, the results of that application may be considered more or less fair. It is argued here that there is, therefore, a need to take fairness into account when applying the precautionary principle. It is suggested that distributional issues may arise with particular force when the principle is applied to the conservation of wild species.

## THE DISTRIBUTIONAL CONSEQUENCES OF APPLYING THE PRECAUTIONARY PRINCIPLE

When the precautionary principle first emerged in Europe it was originally conceived as a tool for addressing issues of pollution and public health. One type of case to which it might have been applied was where a by-product of a manufacturing process was being released into the environment and there was some evidence that this by-product was damaging the environment or public health, but an absence of certainty. Being precautionary in this type of case would have involved taking action to restrict or ban the release of the by-product in order to safeguard the environment. The likely beneficiaries of the precautionary action would have been, in the first instance, the ordinary citizens who were most likely to be affected by the by-product. Their environment or health would have been protected by the action. The costs, in the first instance, would have been borne by the manufacturer, who would no longer be able to release the by-product into the environment as before.

The distributional consequences in this type of case would appear to be mildly progressive, in that it would be ordinary people who would benefit from the precautionary action and more powerful private sector interests who would pay the costs. This view of the distributional impact might be challenged on the grounds that the costs of precautionary action can spread beyond the individual companies subject to regulation to their workers and customers and ultimately to society at large (Sunstein, 2002). Nevertheless, the fact that a specific analysis of the distribution of costs and benefits might be disputed does nothing to support the view that the application of the principle is distributionally neutral. Moreover, the fact that in many of the early cases the distributional impact appeared to be progressive can help to explain why environmentalists – who were often situated on the socially progressive wing of politics – did not pay much attention to the distributional consequences of applying the precautionary principle.

Subsequently the precautionary principle came to be applied to other issues, including biodiversity conservation. At the international level it was incorporated into the Convention on Biological Diversity in 1992, while the Convention on International Trade in Endangered Species endorsed a version of the principle in 1994 (Dickson, 1999). Much of the biodiversity that is currently threatened is in developing countries, and many of those who are most directly dependent on using biodiversity are poor rural people in those countries. Thus, to the extent that precautionary action to conserve biodiversity will involve taking action to restrict use, one might expect that applying the precautionary principle will impose costs on developing countries and poor people. Examining some of the examples described elsewhere in this book suggests that this expectation is met, although these cases also indicate that the consequences are quite complex and depend on the specific features of the individual case.

Castro (Chapter 7) describes a case where the precautionary principle was used to justify action to halt the harvesting of green sea turtles (*Chelonia mydas*) on Costa Rica's Caribbean coast. He notes that this action 'has had winners and losers'. The beneficiaries include all those in Costa Rica and beyond who valued the continued existence of the species. Other beneficiaries are those who benefit from the turtle-watching tourism industry. This latter group includes former turtle fishermen who now work as licensed tour guides. The losers have included those fishermen who did not have the opportunity to make the transition to tour guides, and the local people for whom turtle meat was a source of protein. Castro does not describe the impact on the fishermen, nor the numbers involved, but it seems possible that they lost one of the most important sources of their livelihoods.

There was also a mixed outcome in the Philippines case described by Balangue (Chapter 15). He analyses the impact of regulatory changes in Peñablanca, Cagayan Province, including the creation of the Peñablanca Protected Landscape and Seascape. He suggests that these changes were introduced, in part, on implicitly precautionary grounds. The changes resulted in much stricter protection of the forests and other biodiversity. The landscape in this area is mountainous and in outlining the livelihood impacts of the protectionist measures, Balangue notes the differential impacts on downstream and upstream communities. For the former, the benefits included 'a significant reduction in river flooding, abundant water supply for domestic use, reduced soil erosion, reduced deposition of stones and pebbles on fields leading to improved agricultural harvests and improved water quality (beneficial for fish stocks)'. But the upland communities faced costs, including the loss of employment in extraction activities, the loss of opportunities for hunting and orchid collecting and a loss of access to their resource for charcoal makers and fuel wood gatherers. These losses were particularly important since there were few other employment opportunities in these communities.

These are only two examples, but in both of them we see that the application of regulatory measures – explicitly or implicitly justified on precautionary grounds – resulted in some winners and some losers. Local people fell into both categories. These differential impacts reflect the many and different ways in which people may depend on and use biodiversity resources. An examination of other cases would reveal further complexities, including the distinction between short-term and long-term outcomes. In some cases local resource users might suffer from restrictions on use in the short term, but benefit if these made continued use possible in the longer term. But in the context of this chapter the significant lesson from the two cases mentioned here is that the losers appeared to include some of the poorest and most vulnerable people. In the next section we consider whether this fact should be of any significance for those responsible for applying the precautionary principle.

# THE APPLICATION OF THE PRECAUTIONARY PRINCIPLE SHOULD TAKE DISTRIBUTIONAL IMPACTS INTO ACCOUNT

The view that those applying the precautionary principle should take the distributional impacts into account is not one that is much expressed in existing formulations, guidelines and discussions of the precautionary principle. This can be seen by looking briefly at Principle 15 of the Rio Declaration (1992), the European Commission's guidelines on applying the principle (European Commission, 2000), and the 'Wingspread Statement on the Precautionary Principle' that was developed by a group of North American NGOs, academics and others (Raffensperger and Tickner, 1999).

Principle 15 of the Rio Declaration on Environment and Development includes the statement that 'in order to protect the environment, the Precautionary Approach shall be widely applied by States according to their capabilities'. The assumption lying behind this clause seems to be that adopting the precautionary approach can be quite onerous and therefore states with less capacity cannot, in fairness, be expected to apply the principle as extensively as those with more capacity. In that sense the clause has been motivated by considerations of fairness. However, the principle of fairness is being applied not in relation to the distributional impact of applying the principle, but in relation to the degree to which countries apply the principle at all.

The communication prepared by the European Commission on the precautionary principle includes guidelines for applying the principle. Several of these are said to be part of the 'general principles of risk management' that are held to apply also to the use of the precautionary principle. Among them is the guideline that there should be 'examination of the benefits and costs of action and lack of action'. In explicating this, the Commission document states:

> *The measures adopted presuppose examination of the benefits and costs of action and lack of action. This examination should include an economic cost/benefit analysis when this is appropriate and feasible. However, other analysis methods, such as those concerning efficacy and the socioeconomic impact of the various options, may also be relevant. Besides the decision-maker may, in certain circumstances, be guided by non-economic considerations such as the protection of health.*

While this piece of guidance emphasizes taking account of the costs and benefits of precautionary action, it is concerned with the overall balance of costs and benefits, rather than their distribution. There is no reference to the issue of who bears these costs and benefits and no reference to the relevance of fairness in determining that distribution.

The Wingspread Statement on the Precautionary Principle contains a paragraph on the application of the principle:

> *The process of applying the principle must be open, informed and democratic, and must include potentially affected parties. It must also involve an examination of the full range of alternatives, including no action.*

While this paragraph does include evaluative judgements about the application of the principle and urges that potentially affected parties are involved in that application, there is no explicit reference to the need to take account of the distributional impacts of the principle.

The reason why these statements and formulations do not make reference to the distributional impacts of applying the precautionary principle may be the one alluded to earlier – that, for the issues to which the principle was originally applied, the distributional impacts often appeared to be progressive and so did not constitute a problem for the application of the principle. However, where the benefits of precautionary action are shared by wealthier groups or by society at large and at least some of the costs are borne by the poorest there is a strong case for taking this into account. More specifically, considerations of fairness suggest that there is little justification for imposing those costs on the most vulnerable and that the principle should be applied in such a way as to not impose such costs or, if that is impossible, that measures should be taken to mitigate those costs.

While the assumption that the precautionary principle can be applied in a distributively neutral way may have been quite common in discussions in the North, it has been less so in the South. In Chapter 14, for example, Banana expresses the view that:

> *implementation of the precautionary principle should not hurt society, especially the poor. Where restrictive prohibitive approaches are adopted, programmes that mediate their effects on the livelihoods of the local community must be put in place. For example, trade-offs should be made to allow local people to access resources that are vital to their livelihood, while at the same time recognizing the necessity for sustainable forest management.*

In the case of the Costa Rican example referred to in the previous section, acceptance that the costs and benefits of precautionary action should be distributed fairly implies that the principle should have been applied in a way that did not impose costs on the fishermen or, failing that, that other measures should be taken to compensate them. Castro notes that such measures were, in fact, attempted, indicating that the relevance of considerations of fairness was accepted in this case. Of course in this case, as in others, it is important not just that considerations of fairness are accepted in principle, but also that they are acted on in practice. In the case of the Philippines example, fairness would seem to require action to address the costs borne by the upland communities who were most affected by the regulatory measures.

In addition to the importance of fairness there is also the pragmatic point that a failure to avoid imposing costs on the poorest may actually undermine the conservation goals of the precautionary measures. For where the poor are living closest to biodiversity and where enforcement capacity is weak, they will often have reason and the opportunity to subvert those measures. The corollary of this point, that providing local people with incentives to support precautionary conservation measures often makes sound sense, is made by Rabinovich in Chapter 11. After describing the benefits to local harvesters of the parrot project in Argentina he notes that:

> *The importance to conservation of these livelihood benefits is that they provide tangible economic incentives for the sustainable management of the parrots and habitat by peasants, and counter pressures for conversion of land to intensive agriculture.*

Similarly, in the case described in Box 17.1, applying the precautionary principle in a way that took account of the needs of local resource users in the Muzi Swamp, South Africa, was not only important from the point of view of their livelihoods, but also probably instrumental in achieving a better conservation outcome.

To hold that the consideration of fairness is relevant to the distribution of the costs and benefits of applying the precautionary principle does not entail that the formulation of the principle itself should be changed to incorporate this. Rather, the requirement bears on the way in which the principle is applied. The appropriate place to incorporate such a requirement is in guidelines for the application of the principle. This point is consistent with the view that emphasizes that the precautionary principle should be treated as a principle rather than a rule (Dickson, 1999). That is, it 'states a reason that argues in one direction, but does not necessitate a particular decision' (Dworkin, 1977). Viewing the precautionary principle in this way has the advantage of recognizing that there may be other principles and values that bear on the decision of what to do in a particular case. What has been argued here is that fairness in the distribution of the costs and benefits of precautionary action is one such value that should be taken into account.

The focus in this chapter has been on the distributional consequences of applying the precautionary principle. Distributional questions also arise in connection with the costs of providing the evidence that determines if and how the precautionary principle is to be applied. It is commonly said that the precautionary principle 'reverses the burden of proof'. By this it is meant that whereas prior to the introduction of the principle, opponents of a potentially harmful activity had to show it would indeed be harmful before it would be stopped, under a precautionary regime it is the proponents of such an activity who have to show that it is safe before it is allowed to proceed. To the extent that the principle does indeed 'reverse the burden of proof' in this sense, it also causes a consequent change in who has to bear the cost of providing the relevant evidence. However, in the case of activities that possibly threaten

## Box 17.1 Uncertainty, communities and conservation: managing use of *Phragmites australis* in the Muzi Swamp, South Africa

The Tembe Elephant Park in northern KwaZulu-Natal, South Africa, includes a large proportion of the Muzi Swamp, an emergent palustrine wetland of great importance both for biodiversity and for the local livelihoods of the Sibonisweni community bordering the park. This community was relocated when the park was established on condition they would retain limited access to some resources. The most important resources are the reed beds of *Phragmites australis* that dominate the swamp, and access is granted to permit holders to harvest reeds in a limited area. The reed harvest is economically important, with an estimated annual value of 100,000 South African rand. Research on reed harvesting in Europe suggested such harvesting could have negative impacts, and research in the swamp confirmed that the harvesting regime was producing measurable degradation of reed quality. However, the seriousness of this harm and its impact on broader swamp biodiversity is very unclear. *P. australis* is the dominant species of the Muzi Swamp, and overharvest of the reed could jeopardize this valuable wetland with potentially serious biodiversity impacts. However, management of the swamp must deal with a large set of unknown variables: many aspects of biology, ecology and species' interaction and interdependence in the swamp have been little studied to date.

A strong precautionary approach might suggest entirely stopping harvesting in the park to ensure biodiversity values are conserved. However, this would have major negative livelihood impacts on local people. In addition, prior experience in the park suggests that denying communities harvest would be highly controversial and cause an immediate uproar from the community and tribal authorities. At the extreme this could result in the closure of the park by the tribal authorities, which gave curatorship to the conservation authorities. A more sensitive application of the precautionary principle is called for in this scenario, one in which the needs of resource users and conservationists are both taken into account. A management regime has therefore been proposed that is designed to improve the quality of the reedbeds, while allowing the communities to continue to harvest the same level of reeds. It involves extending the entire area under harvest, but harvesting in winter rather than summer (which is less detrimental to the reeds), and harvesting on a rotational basis to avoid heavy impacts on one area. The rotation of the harvesting areas will also allow adequate recovery time for the reeds after being harvested. Further, it involves instituting as an integral feature a monitoring scheme to allow feedback and adaptation of management if necessary. Finally, community participation in monitoring and adaptive decision-making would be involved. Inclusion of resource users in precautionary management should ensure not only that their priorities and perspectives are taken into account, but that management measures are also accepted and effectively implemented.

*Source:* Jason Alec Tarr, in communication with R. Cooney, 2005

biodiversity, it may be that reversing the burden of proof shifts that burden onto the poorest and most vulnerable. For, as has already been argued, it is sometimes the use of biodiversity by the poor that can threaten that biodiversity. Thus, in considering who bears the evidential burden, the question of fairness may be just as relevant as it is when considering the distribution of the costs and benefits of precautionary action. In this chapter we continue by focusing on the distribution of cost and benefits, but the conclusions are readily transferable to the issue of the evidential burden.

## FOUR OBJECTIONS

As was implied earlier, there has been little published discussion of the distributive impacts of the precautionary principle. Hence there has been little consideration of the merits and demerits of the view advanced here. It is therefore worth considering four possible objections to this view. None of these objections hold that distributional impacts are of no consequence; however, they all challenge the view that considerations of fairness should actually shape the application of the precautionary principle in the way suggested here.

The first objection is that the precautionary principle is a principle of environmental regulation and in dealing with environmental issues there is no obligation to also address distributional issues. These are separate questions and should be dealt with separately. However, what this objection overlooks is that addressing environmental problems (and taking precautionary action is one way of doing this) does impose real costs and benefits on people and those responsible for such regulation cannot evade questions about the distribution of those costs and benefits by labelling the issue an 'environmental' one. One person's environmental issue is another person's livelihood. It is not an additional responsibility that is being suggested, but rather that responsibility is accepted for the impact of measures undertaken on environmental grounds.

Another thought that may be behind this objection is that environmental agencies who are responsible for applying the precautionary principle are not best placed to also deal with distributional issues, especially those relating to poverty. There may be considerable truth in this. However, this is an argument for why other agencies may need to be involved when problems are addressed through precautionary action, rather than for ignoring the distributional impacts of precautionary action.

A second objection is that if someone, as a result of precautionary action, is not able to continue activities that threaten the environment, this is not a loss that brings any obligation to avoid or compensate. Such a person has not been deprived of any legitimate benefits. But while there may be some truth to this in some cases, there is little reason to think that it is true of all cases. Whether someone's losses can be discounted in this way will depend on the specific facts of the case, including the explanation of how they came to be engaged in the potentially damaging activity and their state of need. Poor people may take up damaging activities for a complex set of reasons, many of which are beyond their control, and their needs may be such that they cannot be ignored.

A third objection is that the requirement to take account of the distributional consequences of applying the precautionary principle will undermine the principle. In the real world there are many pressures on the environment and we should not be giving opponents of environmentalism another tool to weaken the precautionary principle. They will appeal to the alleged negative distributional impacts of the principle to query its legitimacy. However, the appropriate response to such opponents is not to hold that distributional concerns should be ignored, but to argue that only legitimate ones will be addressed. One does not undermine the principle by holding that there should be some fairness in the distribution of the costs and benefits of precautionary action. Indeed, in many circumstances this will actually strengthen support for the principle. It is also important to recognize that it will rarely be the case that there is a stark choice between respecting the value of fairness and undertaking precautionary action. Rather, the value of fairness will manifest itself primarily in the *way* in which the principle is applied, rather than in determining whether it will be applied at all.

The fourth objection is of a rather different sort. It accepts that we should be taking account of the impact of precautionary action on people, but it queries whether this is best done in terms of the fairness in the distribution of costs and benefits. Rather, a human rights framework is preferred. On this view the crucial requirement is that the application of the precautionary principle should respect human rights. Nothing that has been said here is intended to suggest that human rights can be ignored in the application of the precautionary principle. They should be respected. Nevertheless, it has been suggested that considerations of fairness in the distribution of costs and benefits are also important. These will not always be captured by a human rights framework, unless that framework is stretched very wide.

## SUMMARY

The application of the precautionary principle changes the costs and benefits for a range of actors. Considerations of fairness are therefore relevant in determining how the principle is to be applied. There is nothing special about the precautionary principle in this respect. The same is true of any other environmental principle that alters the distribution of costs and benefits. Nevertheless, distributional issues may be of particular relevance when precautionary action is proposed to safeguard biodiversity in developing countries, since the potential losers may include the very poor. To make this point is not to argue that the principle should not be applied in such situations. Rather, it is to recognize that it will be important to ensure that the costs of precautionary action are not borne unfairly by the poorest and most vulnerable.

# Conclusion

# 18

# Precautionary Principle, Precautionary Practice: Lessons and Insights

*Rosie Cooney and Barney Dickson*

The studies in this volume reflect a rich array of experiences and perspectives on precaution in principle and practice in the area of biodiversity conservation and sustainable use. Some authors (Low; Castro) describe successful applications of the precautionary principle, with few problems. Many (Sant; Tucker and Treweek; Di Paola and Machain; Banana; Rabinovich) are positive about the potential of the principle, but highlight a range of problems and barriers for successful implementation; and several examine the complexities of its translation into practice (Sant; Newton and Oldfield). Some authors focus largely on how the precautionary principle *should* be applied (Dickson; Emerton et al; Moyle). Some contrast what they view as good examples of precautionary action with poor applications of the precautionary principle (Rabinovich; Kaur et al). Some, while not critical of the principle itself, are critical of the way in which it has been invoked or applied in particular cases (Rosser et al; Andresen et al), and one describes examples of a precautionary approach with largely beneficial impacts, but highlighting problems or issues that need further attention (Balangue). Some are critical of the way in which it can be applied, and question whether it necessarily leads to optimal conservation outcomes (Moyle; Mealey et al; Newton and Oldfield).

This set of experiences provides the first extended examination of the role of the precautionary principle in conservation and management of biodiversity and living natural resources. It also, importantly, includes many perspectives from developing countries on the precautionary principle – perspectives that have often been absent from discussions to date on the precautionary principle in this area. This set of experiences cannot, of course, be considered comprehensive or necessarily representative. However, it provides useful lessons and insights for considering the importance of the precautionary principle; the circumstances in which it can be successfully applied; some of the factors that affect its impact and that need to be taken account of in its application; and recognition of the limitations of some conceptualizations of the precautionary principle.

Above all, however, these case studies take the debate forward. Discussion in this area remains frequently bedevilled by simplistic conceptions of polarized positions 'for' or 'against' the precautionary principle. We hope that these experiences and insights provide a rich seam of empirical and theoretical material to inform more sophisticated discussion, elaboration and implementation of the principle in a wide range of sectors, contexts and regions of the world. Here we set out our view of the major insights and lessons learned from these studies.

# UNCERTAINTY

Across the wide range of sectors covered by authors in this volume, the need to make decisions in the face of persistent uncertainty is fundamental. Whether the issue is forest management, marine turtle conservation, environmental impact assessment (EIA), wildlife trade, control of invasive species or commercial fisheries, it is clear that uncertainty is a basic and largely unavoidable aspect of biodiversity conservation and management. While there will always be an imperative for increased and better science and information on which to base decisions, it appears clear that a precondition for effective biodiversity conservation and management is that regulation and management is responsive to threats that cannot be unambiguously demonstrated by available information and science. This is true not just of the biodiversity conservation and sustainable use sector itself but of the production-oriented areas that have great impact on biodiversity – including agriculture, urban and infrastructure development, forestry and trade. Currently there remain major gaps in how uncertainty is dealt with. Tucker and Treweek, for instance, highlight that while EIA routinely deals with uncertain information, there is no guidance or standard practice for dealing with it in a consistent or precautionary manner. Low points out that most countries have no mechanisms to deal with alien species for which potential invasiveness is unknown.

Many of these studies strongly support the importance of the precautionary principle in providing a policy basis for action against uncertain threats. Castro illustrates the explicit role played by the precautionary principle in supporting a judicial decision against uncontrolled harvest of endangered marine turtles, when faced with the argument that information regarding detrimental impact was lacking. Di Paola and Machain highlight the difference made by the precautionary principle across a range of cases in Argentina. They suggest also that judicial application is particularly powerful, as administrative decisions are not necessarily coherent or proactive, and can be more responsive to political/economic pressures. Low emphasizes the necessity of a precautionary approach for weeds and the vital role it plays in supporting strong measures to prevent their entry – an area where there is no clear science to predict in advance damage that may be serious and irreversible, both environmentally and economically.

## CHALLENGES IN IMPLEMENTATION

There is growing awareness and consensus among many constituencies and countries of a need for a precautionary approach, and in some cases a legislative or policy basis exists for its application. However, these studies make clear that effective implementation of the precautionary principle faces some serious hurdles.

One major hurdle is that adoption of a precautionary approach may be opposed by powerful political/economic interests. Andresen et al point out in their analysis of several international environmental regimes that even when the science surrounding an environmental threat is clear and well established, decisions are made on multiple bases, among which science is rarely the most important. Unsurprisingly, there are even greater barriers to environmentally favourable decisions being made when evidence of impending damage is contested or uncertain, or when there is ignorance about possible outcomes. These authors find little evidence that the precautionary principle is invoked where it is opposed by powerful political interests.

Opposition by powerful economic forces is no doubt also the driver of a wide divergence in attitudes toward precaution between the conservation arena, where precautionary thinking is strongly entrenched, and the range of productive sectors that in practice have major impacts on biodiversity (such as trade, fisheries, forestry and agriculture). At a national level, Di Paola and Machain find that government officials in Argentina in economically important sectors were not likely to be supportive of the precautionary principle and more wary of its impacts on economic activities. At the international level, an analogous phenomenon can be seen by comparing the Convention on International Trade in Endangered Species of Wild Fauna and Flora (CITES), in which Rosser et al indicate the concept of precaution is well-established and indeed may be interpreted in *too* strict a manner, with the forest sector in general, which Newton and Oldfield show to be geared primarily toward production and where the concept of precaution is virtually absent, except in specific contexts or frameworks designed with biodiversity conservation in mind.

Implementation is further hampered by confusion and lack of clarity about what the precautionary principle means in practice. As set out by Cooney, there are many different formulations and understandings of the principle. Tucker and Treweek highlight how different conceptions of the principle can lead different parties to a decision to reach different conclusions about the acceptability of particular development proposals. Sant highlights the lack of shared understanding of the operational impact of precaution, and how it relates to uncertainty and information gaps in the Australian fisheries context, even among the fisheries agencies responsible for implementing the principle. He further points out that this lack of shared understanding is one reason that longstanding precautionary obligations do not appear to have had much impact on practice. These considerations suggest that consistent and effective implementation will require a shared understanding of the principle's meaning and implementation, including guidance for management measures in specific contexts, which might involve, for instance, specific placements of the burden of proof, and/or non-discretionary precautionary measures to be taken where there is a specified level of uncertainty about threats.

The characteristics of the biodiversity and living natural resource management sector may also pose their own challenges for wide adoption of a precautionary approach. Andresen et al point out that while the characteristics of the problem of biodiversity loss – particularly the prevailing high uncertainty about status, drivers of loss, strategies for conservation and impacts of loss – are those that signal the need for a precautionary approach, other characteristics of biodiversity make it perhaps particularly unlikely that a precautionary approach will be taken. There are no technological quick fixes that can be pursued at reasonable cost, there is limited scope for market-driven mechanisms, no consensus over the best strategy, and commercially important sectors such as agriculture, biotechnology, fisheries and forestry are implicated in the threats. Further, the slow incremental decline of biodiversity, its 'death by a thousand cuts', is rarely dramatic enough to win headlines, grab media attention or trigger strong precautionary action.

There is some suggestion in a number of chapters that a strong precautionary approach is most likely to be adopted only after a catastrophe has been experienced. While this may be true of conservation in general it will be true with added force for interventions that cannot be unambiguously justified by scientific evidence. Balangue's paper points out that in the Philippines strong habitat protection measures, which can be viewed as precautionary, were triggered by the devastating impacts of forest overexploitation, including catastrophic landslides killing many people. Likewise, Andresen et al point to the North Sea regime, a rare example of an early adoption of a precautionary approach, as triggered by well-reported and dramatic incidents of actual or threatened marine pollution by oil and chlorinated waste. Low's examination of weed risk assessment (WRA) in Australia appears to provide a good example of relative consensus around a strong precautionary approach – prompted perhaps by the devastating and irrefutable environmental and economic toll that invasive species have taken in Australia.

Major barriers highlighted in these chapters include limited technical and financial capacity, poor governance, corruption, lack of awareness and lack of coordination among different government players. Di Paola and Machain highlight the lack of a coherent, shared approach to biodiversity and natural resource threats across different government agencies. Banana points to governance failures in the forest sector in Uganda as a major reason for the failure of policy to translate into effective precautionary management in practice.

## GOVERNANCE AND PARTICIPATION

Many studies presented here have implications for decision-making and management processes that (implicitly or explicitly) involve the precautionary principle. Emerton et al propose that precautionary measures are more likely to be accepted when the process of identifying, evaluating and responding to uncertain conservation threats is a sound one – informed by various stakeholder perspectives, taking available information into account, and being explicit about uncertainties, assumptions, trade-offs and how these have been resolved. Low's examination of WRA in Australia, and the support it has won even from those restricted by it, suggests that precautionary restrictions are more likely to be accepted when they are supported by a clear, transparent, science-based process. Tucker and Treweek conclude that applying the precautionary principle requires clear communication and development of a shared understanding of the basis for decisions.

A clear and transparent process is particularly important as values, personal experiences and perspectives, and subjective opinions all come into play in decision-making where information is uncertain or limited. Andresen et al and Newton and Oldfield point out that in the context of biodiversity and natural resources, there is often a lack of consensus regarding values, which, added to the underlying scientific uncertainty, leads to the 'malign' or 'wicked' nature of these problems. This is supported by the study of Rosser et al, which details the different strategies that have been viewed as precautionary with respect to trophy hunting under CITES by groups with different attitudes and values.

In the context of biodiversity, especially in developing countries, several studies emphasize the importance of involving local people who live with and near wild biodiversity resources in the identification, characterization and management of threats. As Kaur et al discuss, identification and characterization of threats to biodiversity and resources by local people may present a very different picture to that of authorities. While authorities and urban groups may view local people as the threat, local people may view other factors such as poverty and lack of alternative livelihoods as the major threats to resources. Where those who bear the costs of precautionary measures are already poor and marginalized, there is a particularly strong case that they should be involved in decision-making in order to ensure their views and priorities are taken account of, and that decisions taken are feasible and likely to be implemented and complied with.

## THE IMPORTANCE OF LIVELIHOOD AND EQUITY ISSUES

A major emphasis through many of these chapters is the close relationship between biodiversity and livelihoods in many developing countries, and how being precautionary (or non-precautionary) with respect to use of biodiversity resources impacts on the livelihoods of those who rely on that use. As Dickson points out, these impacts can be positive or negative. For instance, taking a precautionary approach to commercial exploitation of living resources can clearly benefit local people who rely on subsistence use of these resources. For instance, Balangue highlights the detrimental consequences for local people of a clearly non-precautionary regime of logging and mining concessions over a forest area in the Philippines, where little attention was paid to potential impacts and no EIA or monitoring was carried out. Conversely, as Emerton et al point out – and illustrated also by the Philippines case – precautionary restrictions on forest resource use by local communities can severely restrict their livelihood options. Castro highlights the benefits, for those involved in ecotourism use of marine turtles, of relying on the precautionary principle to end poorly controlled harvest of these animals, while also mentioning the costs for others.

Much depends on how a precautionary approach is implemented. Rabinovich, for example, highlights the potential for a management scheme for wildlife use, motivated by precautionary considerations and involving local people, to offer significant livelihood benefits. However, Kaur et al highlight the costs for local communities of a precautionary approach to possible negative impacts of fishing in a reservoir within a national park in India. In this case there was a compensation scheme in place to reimburse communities for loss of access to resources. While this did not appear entirely effective in this case, it highlights one way to offset the costs of adopting a precautionary approach falling on already poor and marginal groups.

While there is a clear ethical imperative to address any negative equity impacts of precautionary measures, there is also a clear pragmatic or strategic argument. As Emerton et al point out, in scenarios of biodiversity conservation and management the 'losers' from precautionary measures can represent a continued threat to the resource. This is clearly illustrated by Kaur et al and Balangue. In each of these cases authors argue that precautionary interventions that do not consider the livelihood needs of local people are destined to be unsuccessful, and may indeed exacerbate illegal or unmanaged extraction of resources where no other livelihood options are available.

## NORTH–SOUTH ISSUES

Consideration of broader 'North–South' issues is crucial when considering global biodiversity conservation, given that most biodiversity is located in the South, most resources in the North, and that (without remedial measures) the costs of biodiversity conservation will be primarily borne by the South. These issues are particularly acute in the context of the precautionary principle, as in effect poorer countries may be asked to bear the costs of conservation when the threat to be averted is uncertain and may never happen, and this may involve diversion of resources or attention from other urgent priorities such as poverty alleviation. There is also a question of whose values and voices shape the characterization of and response to the perceived threat. In a number of contexts decisions can be made by Northern constituencies, reflecting Northern perspectives or priorities, with consequences and costs borne in Southern countries or communities. Rabinovich discusses the potential for wildlife trade decisions by consumer states, motivated by precaution but reflecting their own values, perspectives and available information, to derail a conservation programme believed to be effective in delivering conservation and livelihood benefits in Argentina. Rosser et al, in their analysis of decision-making within CITES, highlight the very different views among different countries and non-governmental organizations (NGOs) of whether a trophy-hunting programme could be viewed as a precautionary conservation response, but where the (developing) country concerned would have borne the conservation and economic costs involved.

## AN INTEGRATED APPROACH TO UNCERTAINTY: INCORPORATING NATURAL AND SOCIAL SCIENCES

In biodiversity conservation and natural resource management, threats typically involve complex causal chains involving people and the socio-economic and political factors that influence their behaviour. A narrow biological conception of what sources of uncertainty are relevant is unlikely to yield effective precautionary responses – rather, information relating to both the natural and social aspects of a conservation issue need to be taken into account. Rabinovich examines the wide range of sources of uncertainty that he considers a programme for management of wild species and habitats must take into account in order to be considered precautionary, including those deriving from biological/ecological sources, from potential shifts and changes in the legal, policy and management regime, and from the socio-economic environment, such as shifts in markets and prices. All these are sources of potential 'surprise' that could derail or jeopardize a programme of natural resource management and conservation. Kaur et al, in their examination of the shift in thinking that has taken place in the Indian protected areas system, highlight the way in which lack of attention to uncertainties deriving from local responses to conservation measures has undermined the success of approaches based on strict protection.

## CAN PRECAUTION BE ABUSED?

Unlike some other policy areas, where 'abuse' of the precautionary principle to pursue economic or political objectives is perhaps the primary issue of discussion related to the precautionary principle, this subject has received little attention in the biodiversity context. However, debate around the principle is shaped by considerations of abuse in the context of biodiversity-related trade measures, such as those applied to prevent entry and spread of invasive species. Cooney and Low both point out that concerns about being judged to be abusing the principle for trade-protectionist ends may discourage countries from taking strong precautionary measures to prevent such threats. This may also be relevant in some highly politicized contexts of biodiversity conservation and use. Andresen et al argue that within the International Whaling Commission, political and ideological objections to harvest of whales are pursued through precautionary arguments, that is, that there is inadequate information available to ensure sustainability. In contrast to cases where conservation measures are not followed even though they are scientifically justified, they contend that the case of whaling may represent a situation where protective measures are taken even where science suggests they are not necessary.

## THE COMPLEXITY OF COMPETING RISKS IN BIODIVERSITY CONSERVATION AND SUSTAINABLE USE

A major lesson emerging from the studies in this volume is that many scenarios of biodiversity conservation and natural resource management do not adhere to a model of decision-making in which there is one clearly risky strategy and one clearly 'precautious' one. Often decisions are between risk and risk, from different sources and over different timescales. There may be no single 'safe bet'. This is most obviously the case in consideration of wildlife use. The chapter by Rosser et al on markhor details the competing risks CITES parties had to consider when deciding whether to allow a quota for trade in trophy-hunted markhor. On one side were the risks of overexploitation and deleterious genetic impacts; on the other were the risks of limiting a conservation programme that appeared to be encouraging population recovery. Likewise in the case of the blue-fronted parrot programme explored by Rabinovich, neither a strategy for sustainable harvest nor a ban on harvest would be free of risks: one strategy raises threats of overexploitation, while the other raises threats of illegal trade and of diminishing incentives for habitat conservation. There are further conservation benefits to be considered: Rabinovich points out that the harvesting programme provides revenue for the management of three strictly protected areas of parrot habitat. Similar considerations are raised in the context of protected area conservation. While strictly excluding access to and use of resources is generally viewed as the more precautionary strategy, Kaur et al examine the unforeseen negative conservation consequences that have flowed from reliance on these approaches in India, including ongoing park–people conflicts, encroachment and illegal resource exploitation.

Some decisions that pose conservation threats may also offer conservation benefits. Moyle argues that in this respect use of wildlife is therefore not analogous to an action such as releasing a pollutant or introducing an alien species, because banning or restricting it does not necessarily reduce the conservation threat. Moyle points out that versions of the precautionary principle that focus only on avoiding irreversible risks, and that do not also consider benefits that may be gained from potentially risky strategies, can, perversely, deliver sub-optimal conservation outcomes through 'excessive timidity'. A focus on avoiding harm can lead to the loss of opportunities for conservation gains if they are associated with any potential harms. Mealey et al highlight this problem in the context of forest management for endangered species protection, pointing out that management of forests in a way that is highly precautionary against a specific short-term risk (affecting owl habitat) appears to be raising serious long-term risks of catastrophic fire, which may involve more serious risks for owls and in some areas has already led to diminution of available habitat.

In practice conservation risks are not independent but interconnected. Acting against one may exacerbate another: as Moyle points out, acting against the threat of overexploitation may shift species to an alternative extinction path through habitat loss. Newton and Oldfield highlight the potential for contradictory results if the precautionary principle is applied to the various options available, all of which (including the status quo) carry potential risks.

In thinking about the precautionary principle in biodiversity conservation there is sometimes an assumption that the 'no action' or 'no intervention' state is the precautionary one, and that this should be favoured where it cannot be clearly demonstrated that intervention does not pose any risks. For instance, Mealey et al highlight the assumption (guiding forest management) that non-intervention is the strategy that will protect spotted owls by averting risks of habitat loss and disturbance. However, attention to the risks and benefits that accompany competing strategies may often reveal that there is no 'default' state that can necessarily be considered risk-averse. In this case Mealey et al point out that the non-intervention strategy itself carries the risk of increasing habitat loss through uncharacteristic intense fire.

These considerations have led some authors, including Moyle, Newton and Oldfield and Mealey et al to question whether the precautionary principle offers useful guidance when competing strategies each involve potential conservation threats and benefits. One lesson that is clear is that effective application of the precautionary principle requires consideration of the different strategies available (including the status quo, non-intervention or no action), and examination of the conservation threats and benefits that they may involve. These may be complex, and, as Rosser et al point out, may not be unchangingly associated with particular strategies but may change with time and circumstance. Rosser et al argue, for instance, that prohibiting trade in trophies should be viewed as precautionary under some circumstances (for example where hunting is uncontrolled at local level) and non-precautionary under others (for example where trophy hunting is yielding conservation benefits that would thereby be curtailed).

# DELAYING DECISIONS TO WAIT FOR MORE INFORMATION

Where there are low or no costs associated with delaying a decision owing to uncertain information, there is a case for refusing or delaying a decision on a potentially threatening activity or substance until information increases. Low provides an example where decisions to import alien species can effectively be delayed until information regarding the potential threat is increased (through carrying out a WRA). Di Paola and Machain describe a number of Argentine judicial cases where judges have relied on the precautionary principle to delay consents for development until more information is forthcoming through further studies or monitoring. However, where delay itself carries conservation costs, waiting for more or better information before making a decision may yield poor conservation outcomes. For instance, in the context of trophy hunting under CITES examined by Rosser et al, it seems clear in retrospect that waiting for more information before allowing a trophy quota would have undermined the rise in population that has occurred since the decision was made.

# BETTER TOOLS AND MECHANISMS TO INFORM CHOICES BETWEEN COMPETING RISKS

The considerations set out above lead a number of authors, including Rosser et al, Newton and Oldfield, and Mealey et al, to highlight the need for better techniques to estimate the potential threats and benefits associated with different strategies. Several call for decision-making to be informed by some form of 'risk assessment', to help characterize and make explicit the consequences of different strategies. For instance, Mealey et al argue for the use of comparative ecological risk assessment to guide and inform the choice of options for forest decision-makers. While risk assessment as it is practised in industrial contexts is widely criticized by advocates of the precautionary principle, it is generally agreed that it has a role to play, and that its practice can be reformed in order to avoid assumptions and practices that inadequately address uncertain risks. Emerton et al suggest the use of scenarios, including examination of 'worst case' scenarios. Tucker and Treweek also suggest risk analysis could explicitly consider worst case scenarios, while Moyle highlights the use of scenario planning, with robustness and adaptability being the guiding criteria for choices, as an effective tool for making decisions in the face of uncertainty.

The decision as to which strategy is pursued, however, can never be determined by these tools. Indeed, as Newton and Oldfield point out, while the precautionary principle helps draw attention to uncertainties surrounding different threats, benefits and trade-offs, it does not necessarily offer any guidance for the trade-off. In making these decisions, as Moyle points out, irreversibility of impacts should be taken particularly seriously. Tucker and

Treweek highlight the need to safeguard ecosystem viability and the continued provision of ecosystem services. This is reflected in some policy statements concerning the precautionary principle. Sant, for instance, points out that the Australian Oceans Policy highlights that priority is to be given to maintaining ecosystem health and productivity. In any case, however, the rationale for decisions, the application of precaution, and any inherent trade-offs should each be stated explicitly and transparently.

One point that should be borne in mind is that systematic decision tools may be costly, in terms of money, technical expertise and time. It may be that in some circumstances, at least when there is a clear risk-averse strategy, adopting a precautionary approach may in practice be a low-cost measure when funds are not available for more rigorous treatments of uncertain threats.

## TOOLS FOR OPERATIONALIZATION

One clear message from the cases in this book is that the specific choice of strategies, methods, mechanisms or tools for implementation of a precautionary approach to biodiversity conservation and sustainable use is highly context specific. Tucker and Treweek, in the context of EIA, highlight the need for strategies such as the use of safety margins in project siting and design. Di Paola and Machain point out that judges in Argentina have used the precautionary principle to require a range of measures, from bans and prohibitions to further studies or specific mitigation measures. In the forest context, Newton and Oldfield argue that the practice of sustainable forest management is one tool currently implementing a precautionary approach to forest production, while Banana points out the potential of tools such as performance bonds, monitoring and indicators of best practice.

## FLEXIBLE AND ADAPTIVE MANAGEMENT IN THE FACE OF UNCERTAINTY

A major call from many authors in this volume, including Rabinovich, Rosser et al, Mealey et al, Moyle, and Emerton et al, is for decision-making and management under uncertainty, in most contexts of biodiversity conservation and management, to be adaptive and flexible. Effective decision-making must be able to incorporate and respond to changing circumstances and new and improved information over time. Many authors call explicitly for an adaptive management approach to be taken in response to uncertainty, a management approach that has been progressively defined and elaborated over recent decades.

The relationship between the precautionary principle and adaptive management, as elaborated in various chapters in this volume, is somewhat ambiguous. The relationship, and in particular whether an adaptive management approach should be viewed as a means of implementing the precautionary principle, may depend on the type of potential harm involved (including irreversibility and suddenness of impact) and whether the scenario involves multiple or single sources of risk. If a harm is likely to occur definitively, at a single point in time and irreversibly, an adaptive management approach is unlikely to be an appropriate means of responding to it in a precautionary manner. For instance, adaptive management would not be an appropriate means to achieve precautionary control of invasive alien species, as discussed by Low, which can quickly, and frequently irreversibly, lead to major environmental damage.

In scenarios of development planning and resource consents, as examined by Tucker and Treweek, objectors to a development may argue for withholding of consent on the basis of the precautionary principle, while developers may argue that any risks can be controlled through adaptive management. Tucker and Treweek suggest that adaptive management may be viewed as an effective way to manage risks in circumstances where there is some scientific uncertainty regarding environmental harm, but the threat is not so likely, great, uncertain or irreversible as to require a stricter precautionary approach and refusal of the proposal. Similarly, in the wildlife utilization and conservation context, Rabinovich suggests adaptive management is a necessary and effective approach to precautionary use and management of wild species, except in specific cases of very vulnerable species or ecosystems.

## CONCLUDING REMARKS

Those engaged in the conservation, sustainable use and management of biodiversity and living natural resources must tackle a wide range of threats, of varying kinds, from many sources and over timescales from the immediate to the historical. Uncertainty and ignorance characterize much of our understanding of these threats and their potential impact on biodiversity and the humans that rely on it. The history of decision-making and management in this area offers abundant testimony to the catastrophic consequences of failing to adopt a precautionary approach to uncertain threats. And yet the precautionary strategy is not always clear, choosing it may impose major costs or raise risks to other legitimate values, and the necessity for values, judgements and opinions to play a role offers fertile ground for conflict and controversy. Practical, effective and equitable solutions to these challenges will need to be worked out in detail in specific contexts. However, the insights drawn from these case studies, while not addressing all issues and not offering a complete set of solutions, make a substantive contribution to clarifying the role and operation of the precautionary principle in responding to uncertainty in biodiversity conservation and natural resource management.

# Appendix

# Guidelines for Applying the Precautionary Principle to Biodiversity Conservation and Natural Resource Management[1]

## INTRODUCTION

The uncertainty surrounding potential threats to the environment has frequently been used as a reason to avoid taking action to protect the environment. However, it is not always possible to have clear evidence of a threat to the environment before the damage occurs. Precaution – the 'Precautionary Principle' or 'Precautionary Approach' – is a response to this uncertainty.

The Precautionary Principle has been widely incorporated, in various forms, in international environmental agreements and declarations, and further developed in some national legislation. An element common to the various formulations of the Precautionary Principle is the recognition that lack of certainty regarding the threat of environmental harm should not be used as an excuse for not taking action to avert that threat (See Box A.1). The Precautionary Principle recognizes that delaying action until there is compelling evidence of harm will often mean that it is then too costly or impossible to avert the threat. Use of the Principle promotes action to avert risks of serious or irreversible harm to the environment in such cases. The Principle therefore provides an important policy basis to anticipate, prevent and mitigate threats to the environment.

There has been much debate about the nature of the concept of precaution, in particular whether it should be accepted as a legal principle in addition to being a sound policy approach. Some have argued against the recognition of precaution as a 'principle' of environmental law, which implies a broad obligation to apply precaution in decision-making, in favour of viewing precaution as merely one particular policy/management 'approach' to dealing with uncertain threats. While it is undisputed that in an increasing number of specific contexts there are clear legal requirements to apply precaution, there is an ongoing debate about whether precaution has become part of international customary law. The development of these Guidelines has not been

## BOX A.1 SOME EXAMPLES OF DIFFERENT FORMULATIONS OF THE PRECAUTIONARY PRINCIPLE

### Rio Declaration, 1992, Principle 15

In order to protect the environment the Precautionary Approach shall be widely applied by States according to their capabilities. Where there are threats of serious or irreversible damage, lack of full scientific certainty shall not be used as a reason for postponing cost-effective measures to prevent environmental degradation.

### Convention on Biological Diversity, 1992, Preamble

[W]here there is a threat of *significant reduction or loss* of biological diversity, lack of full scientific certainty should not be used as a reason for postponing measures to avoid or minimize such a threat.

### UK Biodiversity Action Plan, 1994, para 6.8

In line with the Precautionary Principle, where interactions are complex and where the available evidence suggests that there is a significant chance of damage to our biodiversity heritage occurring, conservation measures are appropriate, even in the absence of conclusive scientific evidence that the damage will occur.

### Convention on International Trade in Endangered Species of Wild Fauna and Flora, Resolution Conf. 9.24 (Rev. CoP13)

[T]he Parties shall, by virtue of the precautionary approach and in case of uncertainty either as regards the status of a species or the impact of trade on the conservation of a species, act in the best interest of the conservation of the species concerned and adopt measures that are proportionate to the anticipated risks to the species.

---

shaped by this distinction. The term 'Precautionary Principle' has been used throughout these Guidelines for consistency.

This document provides guidance on the application of the Precautionary Principle to the conservation of biodiversity and natural resource management. Throughout this document the term natural resource management (or NRM) refers only to the management of living natural resources. These Guidelines have been formulated through focusing on forestry, fisheries, protected areas, invasive alien species and the conservation, management, use and trade of wildlife. They may also be relevant to decision-making in other sectors that impact on biodiversity.

The primary target audience of these Guidelines is policy-makers, legislators and practitioners, but they also aim to create a culture of precaution in all sectors relevant to biodiversity conservation and NRM.

# THE GUIDELINES

To apply the Precautionary Principle effectively:

## Establish the framework

### Guideline 1: INCORPORATE

Incorporate the Precautionary Principle explicitly into appropriate legal, institutional and policy frameworks for biodiversity conservation and natural resource management.

*Elaboration:* Application of the Principle requires a clear legal and policy basis and an effective system of governance. It also requires the establishment and maintenance of adequately resourced institutions to carry out research into risk and uncertainty in environmental decision-making.

### Guideline 2: INTEGRATE

Integrate application of the Precautionary Principle with the application of, and support for, other relevant principles and rights.

*Elaboration:* Other principles and rights are also relevant to conservation and NRM, including prevention, liability for environmental damage, intergenerational and intragenerational equity, the right to development, the right to a healthy environment and human rights to food, water, health and shelter. These other rights and principles must be borne in mind when applying the Precautionary Principle. In some circumstances they may strengthen the case for precautionary action, while in others the Precautionary Principle may need to be weighed against these other rights and principles.

### Guideline 3: OPERATIONALIZE

Develop clear and context-specific obligations and operational measures for particular sectors and contexts, or with respect to specific conservation or management problems.

*Elaboration:* The Precautionary Principle is a general guide for action; it is not a 'rule' specifying that a particular decision should be made or outcome reached. To have conservation impact, it will typically require translation into concrete policy and management measures that are readily understood, that address the conservation problem and that identify actions to be taken in specific contexts. Without these, incorporation of the Principle in law or policy may have little influence on practice. However, there is also a need for flexibility: the specific decisions and management or policy measures that it supports may vary over time and with changing circumstances.

### Guideline 4: INCLUDE STAKEHOLDERS AND RIGHTHOLDERS

Include all relevant stakeholders and rightholders in a transparent process of assessment, decision-making and implementation.

*Elaboration:* Precautionary decision-making involves making decisions where there is uncertainty about the underlying threat. This means that judgements, values and cultural perceptions of risk, threat and required action must play a role. Therefore, it is important to include stakeholders and rightholders and to be transparent throughout the process of assessment, decision-making and implementation. Key stakeholders include those who bear the costs of the potential threat, such as those who will be impacted by degradation or loss of biodiversity or natural resources, and those who bear costs of precautionary action (if any), such as those whose legitimate use of natural resources will be restricted. Indigenous peoples and local communities often play a very important role in NRM or rely on biodiversity and natural resources, and should be included. They should have the opportunity and resources to represent themselves and their interests effectively, and this should not be precluded by logistical, technical or language barriers. The imperative of including key stakeholders should, however, be balanced against potential conservation costs of delaying a decision.

### Guideline 5: USE THE BEST INFORMATION AVAILABLE
Base precautionary decision-making on the best available information, including that relating to human drivers of threats, and traditional and indigenous knowledge.
*Elaboration:* All relevant information should be taken into account, including that relating to human drivers of threats to biodiversity, as well as biological and ecological information. The best available scientific information should be used. In addition, traditional and indigenous knowledge and practices may also be relevant and should therefore be taken into account in decision-making.

Efforts should be made to ensure evidence and information is independent, free of bias, and gathered in a transparent fashion. This can be facilitated by ensuring it is gathered by independent and publicly accountable institutions without conflict of interest. In addition, taking into account multiple sources of information can help minimize bias.

## Define the threats, options and consequences
### Guideline 6: CHARACTERIZE UNCERTAIN THREATS
Characterize the threat(s), and assess the uncertainties surrounding the ecological, social and economic drivers of changes in conservation status.
*Elaboration:* The threats addressed should include not only direct ones but also indirect, secondary and long-term threats, and the incremental impacts of multiple or repeated actions or decisions. Their underlying causes and potential severity should be assessed, and efforts made to determine what is known and not known, what knowledge can be easily improved and what cannot. There should be explicit recognition of ignorance, areas of uncertainty, gaps in information and limitations of the statistical power of available methods for detecting threats. Where threats may interact or be interrelated (for example, where action against one may exacerbate another) they should not be addressed in isolation. However, there is a need to balance the benefits of delaying a decision to gather more information against the potential threats raised by such a delay.

## Guideline 7: ASSESS OPTIONS

Identify the available actions to address threats and assess the likely consequences of these various courses of action and inaction.

*Elaboration:* The Principle should guide a constructive search for alternatives and practical solutions, and support positive measures to anticipate, prevent and mitigate threats. The potential benefits and threats raised by available courses of action and inaction should be assessed – these threats and benefits may be of various kinds, from various sources, and may be short or long term. There may be threats associated with all courses of action: often conservation and NRM decisions involve a choice between 'risk and risk' rather than between 'risk and caution'. In assessing the likely consequences of alternative courses of action and inaction the technical feasibility of different approaches should be taken into account.

## Guideline 8: ALLOCATE RESPONSIBILITIES FOR PROVIDING EVIDENCE

Allocate roles and responsibilities for providing information and evidence of threat and/or safety according to who is proposing a potentially harmful activity, who benefits from it, and who has access to information and resources.

*Elaboration:* In general, those who propose and/or derive benefits from an activity which raises threats of serious or irreversible harm should bear the responsibility and costs of providing evidence that those activities are, in fact, safe. The information itself should be the best available from a variety of sources (see Guideline 5). However, if this would involve requiring poorer, vulnerable or marginal groups to carry the responsibility and costs of showing that their activities (particularly traditional and/or livelihood activities) do not raise threats, either these responsibilities and costs should be placed on relatively more powerful groups, or financial/technical support should be provided. Moreover, in some circumstances, the different options available will *each* raise potentially significant conservation threats, in which case the guidance for assessing threats in Guideline 7 is relevant.

# Devise the appropriate precautionary measures

## Guideline 9: BE EXPLICIT

Specify that precautionary measures are being taken and be explicit about the uncertainty to which the precautionary measures are responding.

*Elaboration:* When decisions are made in situations of uncertainty, it is important to be explicit about the uncertainty that is being responded to and to be explicit that precautionary measures are being taken. This ensures transparency, and also provides a clear basis for monitoring and feedback to decision-making/management.

### Guideline 10: BE PROPORTIONATE

In applying the Precautionary Principle adopt measures that are proportionate to the potential threats.

*Elaboration:* A reasonable balance must be struck between the stringency of the precautionary measures, which may have associated costs (inter alia financial, livelihood and opportunity costs) and the seriousness and irreversibility of the potential threat. It should be borne in mind that countries, communities or other constituencies may have the right to establish their own chosen level of protection for their own biodiversity and natural resources.

### Guideline 11: BE EQUITABLE

Consider social and economic costs and benefits when applying the Precautionary Principle and, where decisions would have negative impacts on the poor or vulnerable, explore ways to avoid or mitigate these.

*Elaboration:* Attention should be directed to who benefits and who loses from any decisions, and particular attention should be paid to the consequences of decisions for groups that are already poor or vulnerable. Where the benefits of an existing or proposed threatening activity accrue to only a few, or only to the already powerful and economically advantaged, or are only short term, and potential costs are borne by the public and communities, by poorer or vulnerable groups, or over the long term, this argues strongly in favour of increased precaution. If the application of precautionary measures would impact negatively on poor or vulnerable groups, ways to avoid or mitigate impacts on these groups should be explored. Threats to biodiversity and living natural resources may need to be weighed against potential threats to livelihoods and food security, or resources may need to be invested in compensation or in support for alternative livelihoods.

## Implement effectively

### Guideline 12: BE ADAPTIVE

Use an adaptive management approach, including the following core elements:

- monitoring of impacts of management or decisions based on agreed indicators;
- promoting research, to reduce key uncertainties;
- ensuring periodic evaluation of the outcomes of implementation, drawing of lessons, and review and adjustment, as necessary, of the measures or decisions adopted; and
- establishing an efficient and effective compliance system.

*Elaboration:* An adaptive approach is particularly useful in the implementation of the Precautionary Principle as it does not necessarily require having a high level of certainty about the impact of management measures before taking action, but involves taking such measures in the face of uncertainty, as part of a rigorously planned and controlled trial, with careful monitoring and periodic review to provide feedback, and amendment of decisions in the light of new information.

Applying the Precautionary Principle may sometimes require strict prohibition of activities. This is particularly likely in situations where urgent measures are required to avert imminent threats, where the threatened damage is likely to be immediately irreversible (such as the spread of an invasive species), where particularly vulnerable species or ecosystems are concerned, and where other measures are likely to be ineffective. This situation is often the result of a failure to apply more moderate measures at an earlier stage.

As precautionary measures are taken in the face of uncertainty and inadequate evidence surrounding potential threats to the environment, their application should be accompanied by monitoring and regular review, both to examine whether knowledge and understanding of the threat has increased, and to examine the effectiveness of the precautionary measure in addressing the threat. Any new information gained through monitoring and further research or information-gathering can then be fed back to inform further management and decision-making. While in some cases this may lead to the precautionary measure no longer being needed, in others it may lead to the determination that the threat is more serious than expected and that more stringent measures are required.

If meaningful participation by stakeholders/rightholders is ensured throughout the process for implementing the Precautionary Principle, compliance is likely to be higher. The costs of compliance should be borne by the parties with the capacity to do it and at the least cost to society. Customary practices and social structures should be considered and, where appropriate, incorporated into the compliance scheme.

The management programme should be consistent with the available resource base (monetary and non-monetary). Governments, private organizations, communities and individuals can contribute to this base. In determining this base, managers should consider the relative benefits to the relevant parties. Resources must be employed efficiently and tasks should be supportive of the management programme.

# NOTE

1   These Guidelines have been developed by The Precautionary Principle Project – a joint initiative of Fauna & Flora International, IUCN (the World Conservation Union), ResourceAfrica and TRAFFIC. They are the product of an international consultative process carried out from 2002 to 2005, involving a wide range of experts and stakeholders from different regions, sectors, disciplines and perspectives. This process has included three regional workshops (for East/Southern Africa, Latin America, and South/Southeast Asia), a commissioned set of case studies, an open-access e-conference and a final international review workshop.

The Guidelines are also informed by meetings and discussions held at the World Summit for Sustainable Development, the IUCN World Parks Congress and the IUCN World Conservation Congress.

# Index